INTRODUCTION TO CURLING STRATEGY

Black & White Edition

Introduction to Curling Strategy
Black & White Edition

by Gabrielle Coleman

Copyright ©2014
First Edition (Black and White)
ISBN: 978-1-941164-02-0

Table of Contents

Chess on Ice	1
Part 1: Curling Basics	3
Curling Basics	5
What is Curling?	5
How to Score	6
Positions and Sweeping	6
Curl	8
The Hammer	9
Free Guard Zone	10
Curling Scoreboards	12
Timed Games	13
Basic Shots	14
Part 2: Strategy Basics	23
Intent	25
Three Types of Strategy	26
Game Plan	26
End Plan	27
Tactical Plan	32
"Simple End 1"	32
"Simple End 2"	39
"Simple End 3"	43
Aggressive vs. Conservative	45
Part 3: Tactics in Depth	47
Deuces	49
Intro to Deuces	49
Deuces—The Big Picture	50
"Deuce or Blank"	52
"Open Deuce"	56
"Tick Deuce"	59
"Center Pile Deuce"	62
"Open Wing Deuce"	65
"Conservative One-Corner Deuce"	69
"Aggressive One-Corner Deuce"	72
"Aggressive Two-Corner Deuce"	76
Tips for Using Corner Guards	80

Steals	**90**
Intro to Steals	90
Steals—The Big Picture	92
"Steal or Blank"	93
"Conservative Steal"	97
"Aggressive Steal"	103
Forces	**106**
Intro to Forces	106
Forces—The Big Picture	108
"Force or Blank"	109
"Aggressive Force"	113
Tips for Using Center Guards	**115**

Part 4: Strategy Scenarios   121

Beginner Strategy Scenarios (see detailed guide on the next pages)	123
Intermediate Strategy Scenarios (see detailed guide on the next pages)	203
Plan B and Pro-Side Error	285

Part 5: Putting It All Together and Playing in the Real World   295

Real-Life Game Sequence	297
New Curler Tactics	313
Arena Ice Tactics	317
Curling Folk Wisdom	328

Finally...   331

Appendix 1: Glossary   333

Beginner Strategy Scenarios

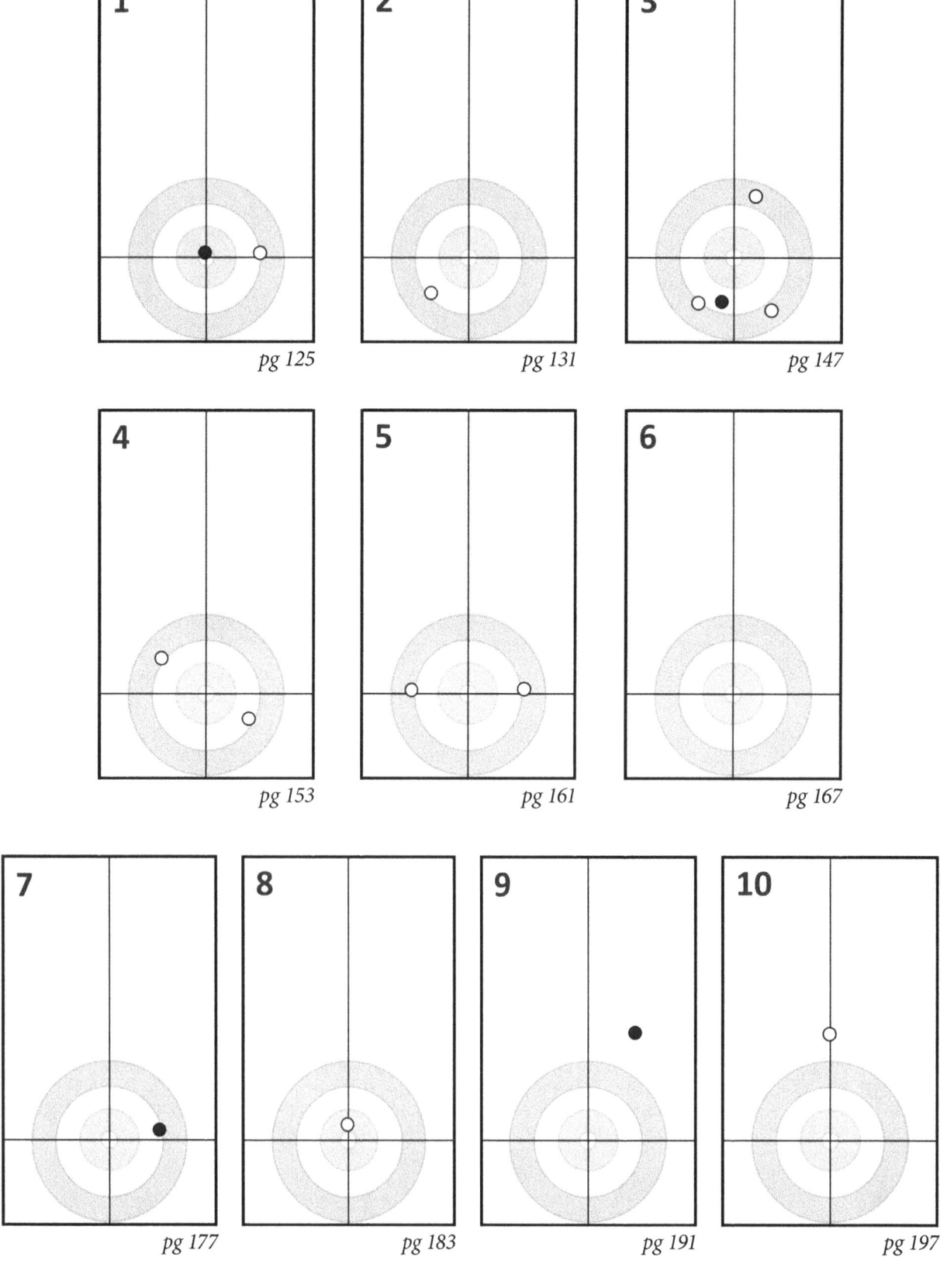

Intermediate Strategy Scenarios

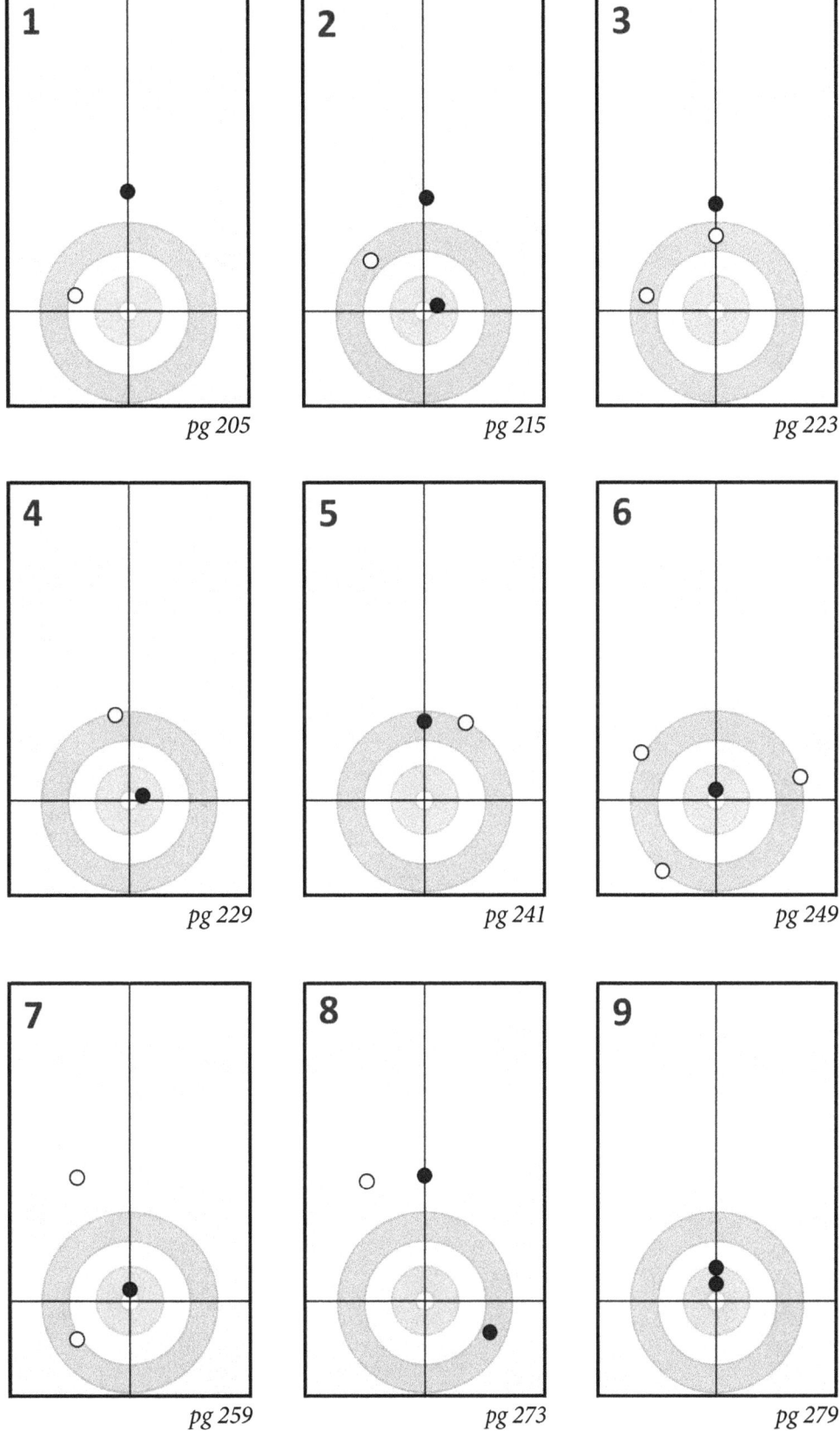

Acknowledgments

This book would not have been possible without the help of many people:

...my curling teachers and coaches, including, but certainly not limited to: Barry Ivy, Allan Barber, Lyle Sieg, Jerome Larson, Leslie Frosch, Yadranka Thompson, Greg McAulay, Bill Tschirhart, and Karen Watson. A special thanks goes to Barry Ivy, who taught me most of what I know about strategy and provided major editorial feedback on this book.

...my past and current teammates and coaches, who continue to help me though my development as a player and skip, which often includes learning strategy the hard way.

...my home club, the San Francisco Bay Area Curling Club, which continues to be a leader in curling development education.

...my other home clubs and ice providers: Jon Gustafson and the San Jose Sharks, the Wine Country Curling Club, Doug Bradley and the Richmond Curling Club, and Seattle's Granite Curling Club (which graciously allowed me to shoot the book's cover image on its ice).

...my host families on the road, including, but certainly not limited to: Cyndy Eng-Dinsel and Jeremy Dinsel; David and Linda Cornfield; and Yadranka Thompson and Greg McAulay.

...my work family at NBC, including the morning crew chess club, where I first learned how to structure strategy concepts.

...my many pre-readers who gave honest feedback and excellent suggestions, including: Allan Barber, Doug Bone, Karolynn Coleman, Norman Coleman, Tom Dias, Bernadette Forsburg, Barry Ivy, Davinna Ohlson Kong, Mason Kong, Michael Lynn, Stephen Marschall, Brian Patrick, Britt Rjanikov, Dave Sciacero, Wes Seeger, Thomas Vogelsang, and Ryan Winterbourne.

...the USCA, for supporting the new US Arena National Championships and for giving me permission to use examples of strategy from that event.

...Joe Calabrese and the 12th End Sports Network (TESN). Thank you for teaching and growing the sport of curling through your webcasts, and for allowing me to raid your archives.

...Team Garnet Eckstrand of Kalamazoo, MI, and Team Nick Myers of Dallas/Fort Worth, Texas, for giving me your blessing to use your US Arena Nationals Championship game as an example of strategy in action. It was many of my pre-readers' favorite section!

...Erin Panell, graphic designer extraordinaire, for the beautiful cover art!

...my parents, Norm and Karolynn Coleman, and my aunt Bernadette Forsburg, for supporting me through all of my curling challenges, from competing to writing.

And finally, to all the people who believe rocks and ice are just a small part of the game of curling...

Thank you—you are the Spirit of Curling.

This book is dedicated to the idea that by raising all boats, we can both win medals and make the world a better place.

Chess on Ice

Curling is often called "chess on ice," and in many ways, it is. The strategy is complex. Teams choose opening moves based on how they want each "end" to finish. And top strategists (or "skips") are always thinking several moves ahead.

But curling is different from chess in important ways, too. Curling strategy evolves as players improve—the better they get at shot making, the bigger their range of tactical choices. Curling novices who can only make simple draws are essentially starting with an all-pawn lineup. As they learn to reliably make hits, freezes, and doubles, they add more powerful game pieces, like bishops, knights, and rooks, to their arsenal. Mastering new shots allows curlers to increase the difficulty, complexity and variety of the game, so curling strategy stays fresh and challenging, no matter how good players get. This is why curling is so captivating—and enduring.

Another big difference between curling and chess is that in curling, the game pieces don't always end up where they're supposed to go. This means even if the skip makes a good shot choice, there's not guarantee of a good outcome.

Finally, although there is often one shot choice that is more likely to lead to success than others, most of the time, there are several shots that could help you reach your goal. Thus, the purpose of this book is not to give you "correct" answers to your strategy questions, but rather to give you a framework for thinking about curling strategy and to show you some basic patterns in the game.

I wrote this book for a wide range of readers—from Olympic fans who are watching for the first time, to experienced skips who have an intuitive sense for how to pick the right shot, but who have trouble explaining the "whys" of strategy to their teammates.

The book is organized into five parts:

Part 1	**Curling Basics**	A brief introduction to curling for people who are new to the sport, plus basic information you must know to understand the rest of the book
Part 2	**Strategy Basics**	Fundamental concepts that underlie all curling strategy
Part 3	**Tactics in Depth**	Opens and endings. Decide how you want an end to finish, then pick the right opening moves to get you there.
Part 4	**Strategy Scenarios**	Navigating the nebulous middle of an end. This section uses interactive puzzles to show you how to stay focused and steer play towards the ending you want.
Part 5	**Putting It All Together and Playing in the Real World**	Follow a real game, shot by shot, and see how skips make—and stick with—plans. This section also covers "real world" situations, like curling on arena ice, and playing with new curlers who are still learning to make basic shots.

I wrote the book as though it would be read in order, with each section building on concepts from the previous sections. That being said, some new curlers told me they found it helpful to read the basics in Parts 1 and 2, then skip forward to the real-life examples and folk wisdom in Part 5, before trying to tackle the detailed tactics in Parts 3 and 4. It's also perfectly okay to browse through the book and start with the parts that interest you!

A few more things you should know before beginning: I make two basic assumptions in the curling examples in this book. First, I assume that the ice conditions are good and the ice curls four feet inside and out on all parts of the sheet. (In real life, reading the unique surface characteristics of each sheet of ice and adapting your tactics to them are big parts of the game—especially at the elite level. I discuss ice reading a bit in the "Arena Ice Tactics" chapter.) Second, I assume all the players shoot equally well and can reliably make both hits and draws. (Alas, that's not always true in the real world. But never fear! I include tips for new and developing curlers in the "New Curler Tactics" chapter and throughout the book.)

Finally, in virtually every example, the team with the light-colored rocks has "the hammer" (last rock advantage). The only place that changes is in one of the real-life examples at the end of the book and it is clearly noted.

I have been very lucky to have had many experienced and patient curling teachers. I know most new curlers in the country are not so fortunate. I wrote this book because I want everyone to have an opportunity to experience the beauty of the game, and to reach their full potential in curling and life.

If you are looking for more information on curling technique and culture, please check out my first book, "Break Through Beginner Curling." It tells the story of my three-year journey from a learn-to-curl class to the Olympic Trials. It also explains a lot of curling cultural and technical topics, many of which aren't in any other books or web sources, including:

- Delivery and sweeping technical tips
- Rock timing and sweeping zone numbers
- How to set up an effective practice
- How to enter competitive events and select the one that's right for you
- What to expect when you get to Nationals
- Curling injuries

In the words of my coach, Barry Ivy, may you love the game first, and play the game second.

> Best wishes and good curling,
> Gabrielle

PART 1
CURLING BASICS

Curling Basics

What is Curling?

Curling is an ancient game of skill, strategy, and sportsmanship. The first recorded references to curling date back to the 1500s, but the sport itself may be much older.

Curling games are played by two teams of four people. Each team has eight rocks. The teams take turns sliding those rocks down a sheet of ice towards a bulls-eye target approximately 125 feet (40 meters) away called "the rings" or "the house."

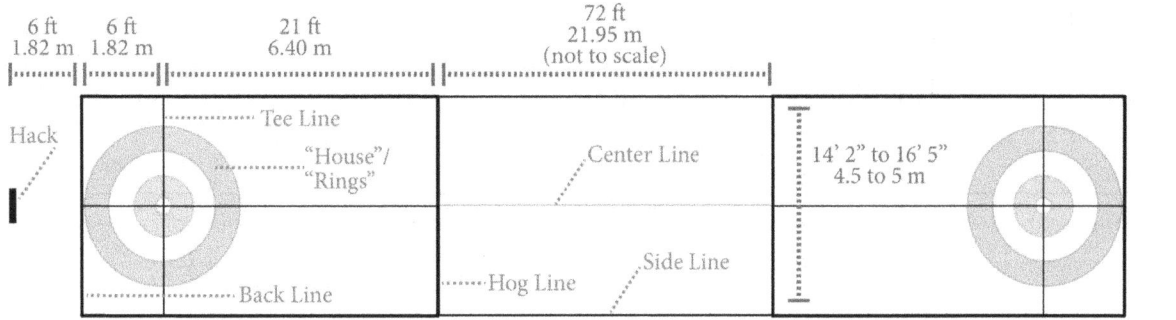

The width of a curling sheet can vary slightly to accommodate the available space in different clubs.

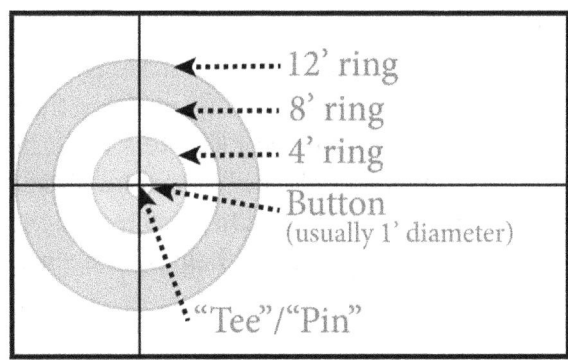

The technically-correct name for the dot in the center of the rings is the "tee," but most people call it the "pin." The size of the button can vary to accommodate advertising logos.

In order for a stone to be in play, the person throwing or "delivering" the rock must let go of it before the near hog line, and the rock must cross over the far hog line and stop on or before the back line. Rocks that touch the side lines are out. (The center line and tee line are helpful guide lines but aren't necessary for the game.)

Most games have eight or ten "ends," which are similar to baseball innings. Both teams throw all their rocks in one direction down the ice for the first end, then throw all their rocks back in the other direction for the next end, and so on.

How to Score

A team scores one point for each of its rocks closer to the center of the target than the closest opponent stone. Only rocks that touch some part of the house can count as points. There are no extra points for being on a particular ring or on the center of the target. (Those lines and marks are just there to make it easier to see which rocks are closest to the center.) Only one team can score per end.

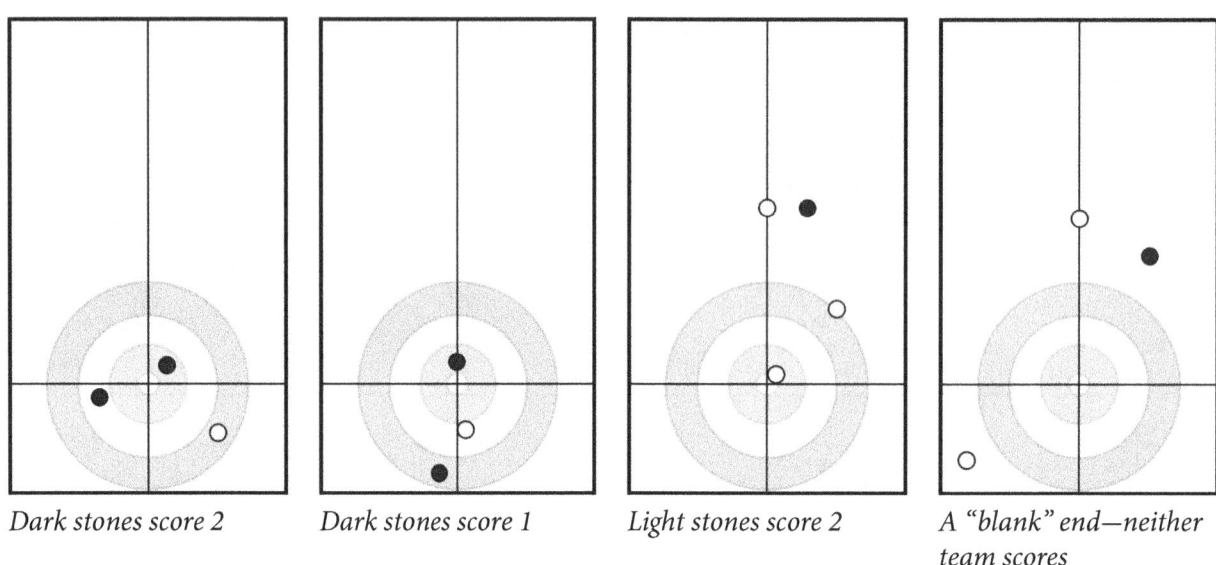

Dark stones score 2 *Dark stones score 1* *Light stones score 2* *A "blank" end—neither team scores*

Positions and Sweeping

The players take turns throwing stones and either sweeping or calling strategy. There are four positions on a team: lead, second, third, and fourth. The lead throws the team's first two stones, the second throws the second two stones, the third throws the third two stones, and the fourth throws the last two stones. The person who stands on the far end of the ice and directs the strategy is the "skip." On most teams, the skip also throws the last two rocks. However, some teams have their skip throw earlier in the lineup if the team's best strategist is not one of its best shooters, or if the skip prefers not to have the pressure of both key roles. The person who holds the broom and directs the strategy while the skip is shooting is the "vice-skip," or simply, the "vice." On most teams, the vice throws third. The players who are not directing the strategy for a given shot help by sweeping.

The team that isn't shooting waits quietly in designated places outside the field of play.

Curling is a true team sport and every player helps make every shot. The skip tells the person who is shooting what shot to make, then places his or her broom on the ice as an aiming point. The shooter pushes or "throws" the stone. (The stone doesn't travel through the air, but curlers call it "throwing the stone" anyways. It's also called "shooting" or "delivering" the stone.) The sweepers scrub the ice to get the rock to the best spot. Sweeping works by clearing debris and warming the ice, which allows rocks to glide farther. Sweeping can also be used to slightly increase or decrease the amount of "curl"—the curved motion of the rock. Strong sweepers can add more than ten feet of distance to a throw on high-quality ice.

Sweeping is not just for fixing mistakes, it's used deliberately to make precision shots. For example, imagine that a team needs to throw a stone to the center of the target (the "button") to score. If the rock is moving too quickly, there's nothing anyone can do to slow it down. However, if the rock would naturally stop a few feet short of the button, the sweepers can sweep to help it glide to the perfect spot. The best sweepers have good "sweep judgment," which means they know when to sweep and when to let a rock glide on its own.

Good sweeping is a combination of brush head speed and pressure. The sweeper should have her head over the brush head and her hands under her shoulders for maximum pressure. For more technical tips like these, check out my other book, "Break Through Beginner Curling."

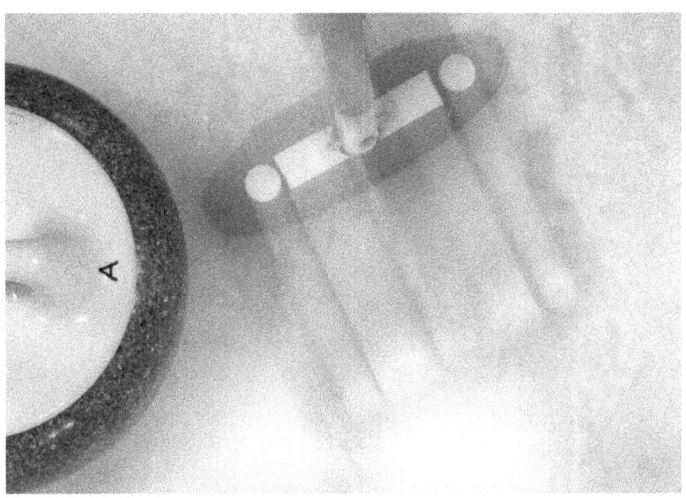

A good sweeping stroke is just long enough to cover the rock's path, but no longer, so the sweeper doesn't waste any effort.

Curl

The stone's rotation determines which direction it will "curl." A clockwise turn will cause the rock to curl to the shooter's right; a counter-clockwise turn will cause the rock to curl to the shooter's left.

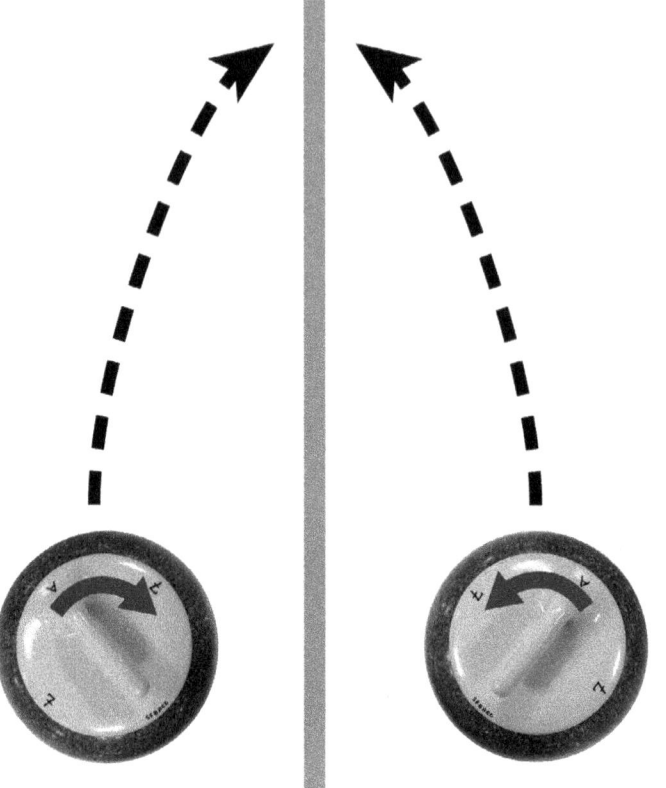

Curl is one of the elements of curling that make the sport so interesting. It allows teams to sneak rocks around guard stones and hit rocks that are hidden from a direct line of sight. Getting the right amount of rotation is a bit like "Goldilocks and the Three Bears." If the rock starts with no rotation, it will pick up a random rotation on its own and take an unpredictable path. If the rock starts with too much rotation, it will run straight. The "just right" amount of rotation for best control and curl is usually three full turns from the time the shooter releases the rock until it stops.

In order to make the rocks travel a long distance, the ice makers sprinkle droplets of water that freeze to the ice surface and are called "pebble." The rocks glide on top of these ice bumps, and so there's less friction than if the rock were on a smooth flat surface.

Light pebble over a fresh Zamboni scrape at an arena club

Heavy, layered "orange peel" pebble at a dedicated ice club

The bottoms of the rocks are carved to have a narrow, ring-shaped "running surface." This also reduces the amount of friction between the rocks and the ice, allowing the rocks to travel farther.

The amount of curl you will see in a game varies, depending on the ice conditions and the shape and roughness of the bottoms of the rocks. When conditions are ideal, rocks curl four feet. Warm ice (27 °F / -3 °C) curls more than cold ice (17 °F / -8 °C). Newly sharpened, rough rocks curl more and curl earlier than worn, smooth rocks. (A 2013 Swedish study published in the journal, "Wear," has shown that curl is caused by the rough surface of the bottom of a rock scraping microscopic grooves into the ice, then catching on those groves as it continues to rotate over them.)

The Hammer

The last rock thrown in an end is called "the hammer." There's nothing special or different about it other than the fact that it's the last rock, but that alone gives the team that throws it a major advantage. The "hammer team" can use that last rock to draw to the center of the target and bail itself out of trouble. It can also use "the hammer" to make a spectacular hit to clear out opponent rocks and score a big end. (So how big an advantage is the hammer? According to the "Curl with Math" blog by Kevin Palmer (http://curlwithmath.blogspot.com), data from elite competitions shows teams with the hammer in the last end of a tied game win approximately 75% of the time.)

Before each game, teams will either flip a coin or throw draws to the button to see who gets the hammer in the first end. The team that doesn't score in an end gets the hammer in the next end. (In other words, if Team A scores in the first end, then Team B gets the hammer in the second end.) If no one scores, the end is declared a "blank," and the team that had the hammer in that end gets to keep the hammer in the next end. (In other words, if Team B has the hammer in the second end and neither team scores, then Team B gets the hammer again in the third end.)

Having the hammer makes it easier to score, so controlling hammer possession is a big part of curling strategy. For example, if the game is tied with two ends remaining, the team with the hammer might deliberately try to blank the second-to-last end, so it can keep the hammer for the final end.

When teams have the hammer, they are usually happy if they score two points or blank. When teams don't have the hammer, they are usually happy if they "steal" one point ("steal" is slang for scoring without the hammer), or if they "force" the hammer team to score only one point. It may not sound impressive to force another team to score a point, but it is—and it can be very important to the outcome of the game. "Forcing 1" means the non-hammer team has successfully blocked the hammer team from getting either one of its usual two objectives (to "Score 2" or "Blank"), and it means the non-hammer team will get the hammer in the next end.

Free Guard Zone

The Free Guard Zone is the area outside the rings in front of the tee line, shown here in stripes.

In the old days, curlers played outdoors on frozen lakes with rocks they'd found lying around. This didn't exactly make for precision shot-making conditions. Once the game moved indoors and was played on specially-made ice with standard, manufactured stones, it got a lot easier to make shots. This was a good thing for players, but a bad thing for fans. The game got boring. The first team would put a rock in play and the opposing team would hit it, and so on and so forth. Twelve-end games would be won 2-1. Who wants to watch three hours of that?

In order to make the game more interesting, the World Curling Federation adopted the "Free Guard Zone" rule in the early 1990s. (Canadian greats Russ and Glenn Howard had a big role in this. You can read how the brothers' creative scrimmages inspired the Free Guard Zone rule in Russ Howard's autobiography "Hurry Hard: The Russ Howard Story.") The Free Guard Zone rule states that teams cannot remove an opponent's guard stone until the fifth rock of the end (the non-hammer team's third rock). If they accidentally do, they must put the guard rock back and remove the thrown rock from play. Teams can, however, remove their own guard stones from play, and tap opponent stones into the rings or the open area behind the tee line, where they can be removed from play on the next turn.

The Free Guard Zone rule transformed strategy because it helped hammer teams score multiple points in a single end, and because it made it easier for non-hammer teams to steal. In the past, once a team fell behind by a few points, it was virtually impossible to come back.

Here are some illustrations of how the Free Guard Zone works:

If a team accidentally takes out an opponent's guard during the Free Guard Zone time, the offending team's stone is removed and the guard is put back in position.

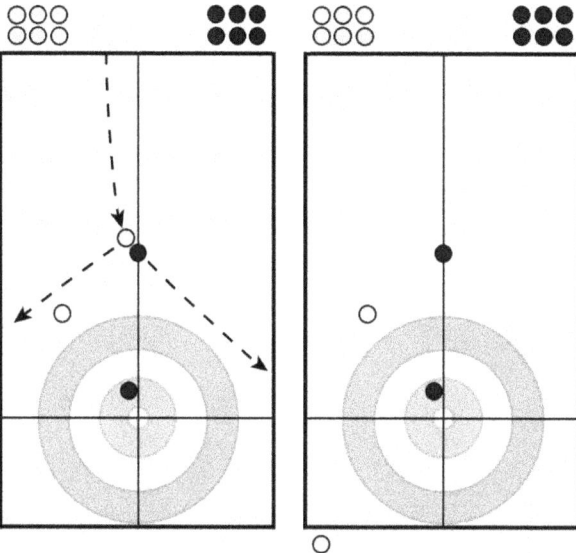

Teams can't remove opponent guards during the Free Guard Zone time. However, they can tap them back onto the rings, then hit them during a future turn.

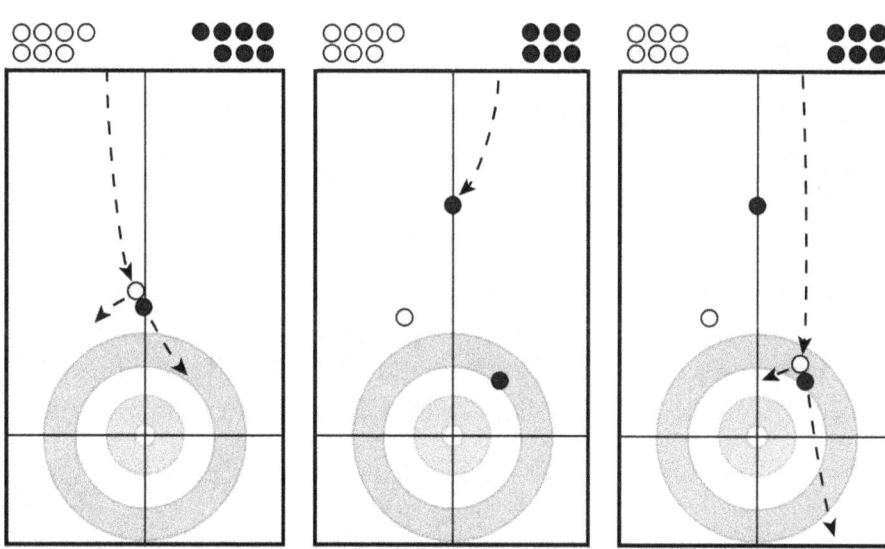

The Free Guard Zone rule only applies to opponent stones, so teams can take out their own guards. For example, if the non-hammer team meant to draw into the house with its first stone but accidentally put up a guard, it can take that out with its second stone.

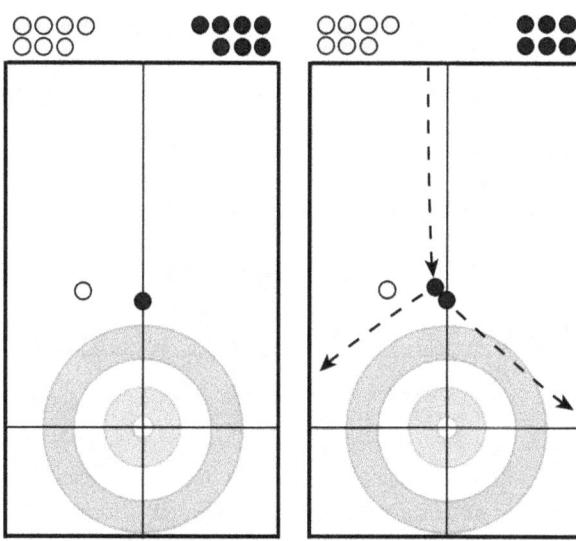

During the Free Guard Zone time it's bad to leave a "biter" (a rock half-on and half-off the rings) because the opposing team can take it out and roll to set up its own guard that can't be hit.

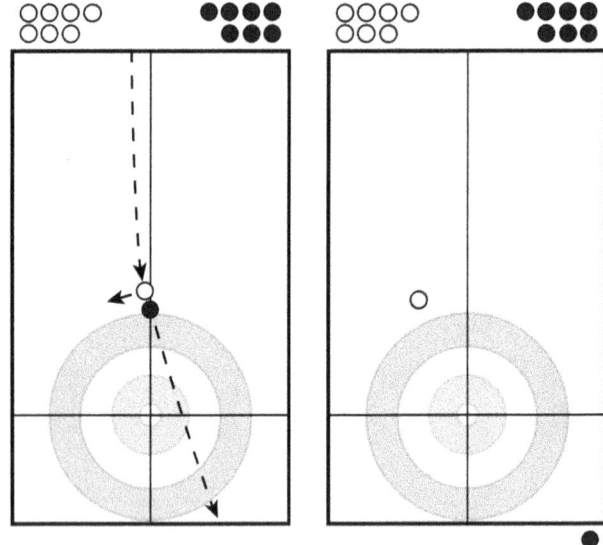

Curling Scoreboards

In baseball, the number of runs teams score in each inning is hung in a line, and the total is updated at the end of the row. World and Olympic curling events often use a similar scoring system because it's familiar to more viewers. A Swiss curling friend tells me this style of scoring is also widely used in Europe.

Traditional curling uses a different score marking system. The line of numbers across the middle of the board signifies the total number of points, and there are only 10 markers, one for each end. The team that scores in an end takes the marker for that end and hangs it on its side of the board by its new total score. If there's a blank, the team hangs that end marker on a special peg off to the side.

	1	2	3	4	5	6	7	8	9	10	Total
Team A	0	1	1	0	3	0	2	0	0	1	8
Team B	2	0	0	2	0	1	0	2	0	0	7

"Baseball-style" scoreboard. In this game, Team A won 8 to 7.

Team A		2	3			5		7	10			
	[9]	1	2	3	4	5	6	7	8	9	10	11	12
Team B			1		4	6		8					

This is the scoring for the same game as above, except that here, it's on a curling scoreboard instead of a baseball-style scoreboard. Again, Team A wins 8-7. Notice that the "9" is hanging in an out-of-the-way spot because it was a "blank" end in which no one scored.

Stacks of numbers piled behind a baseball-style scoreboard at a major event (along with a heap of competitors' clothing and snacks). One downside of the baseball-style system is that it requires a lot of score markers.

Timed Games

Polite curlers always play quickly to keep the game moving along. However, during elite competitions, curlers are required to play quickly because the games are timed. There are two systems for timing in curling—"total time" and "thinking time." Most competitions use total time. This works like timing in chess. Each team starts with the same amount of time on its clock (73 minutes for a 10-end game, which breaks down to approximately seven minutes per end). A team's clock starts running when its skip steps into the house to plan the shot, and stops running when the rock stops and the team yields the ice to its opponent. In a "total time" system, it can be an advantage to throw hits instead of draws, because hits take less time to travel down the sheet.

In a "thinking time" system, teams also start with the same amount of time on their clock (approximately 40 minutes for a 10-end game, or four minutes per end). As with total time, the clock starts when the skip enters the house to plan the shot, however, in thinking time, the clock stops when the shooter pushes out of the hack to throw the rock, not when the rock stops. This way, there is no penalty for throwing shots that need more travel time.

Basic Shots

There are two basic types of shots—draws and hits. Draws are light-weight shots that are used to get more rocks into play. Hits are big-weight shots that are used to remove rocks from play. The "weight" of a shot refers to the speed or amount of energy in a throw. Fast shots are said to have "big weight" and slow shots are said to have "light weight."

There are many variations of draws and hits, like the "guard," "freeze," and "hit-and-roll." Here's a guide to some common shot-type terms:

Guard

Guards are light-weight draw shots that are used to provide protection for scoring stones.

Sometimes teams put up guards early in an end (during the Free Guard Zone time) so they can draw behind them later. Sometimes teams put up guards late in the game to protect rocks that are already in play. Teams can tap guards back to score, or hit guards back onto rocks in the rings to score or remove opponent stones.

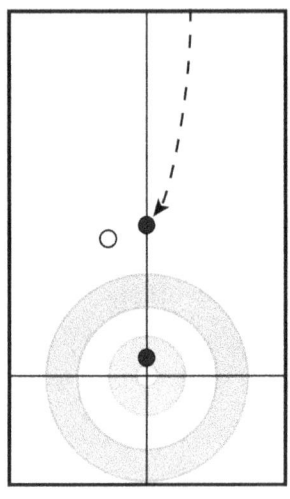

Using a guard to protect...

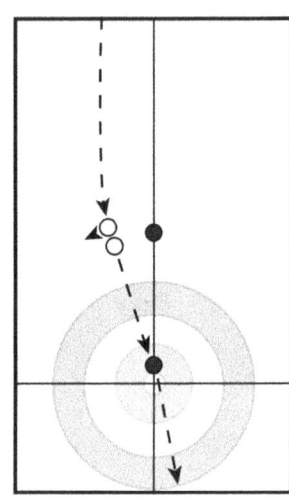

...and using a guard to attack

There are a few basic terms that are used to describe guards. For example, the terms "center guard" and "corner guard" describe a guard's lateral position. Center guards are positioned within one foot of the center line so they can protect rocks on the button. Corner guards are positioned at least one foot away from the center line.

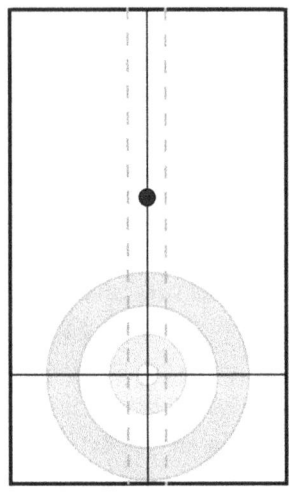

Center guard

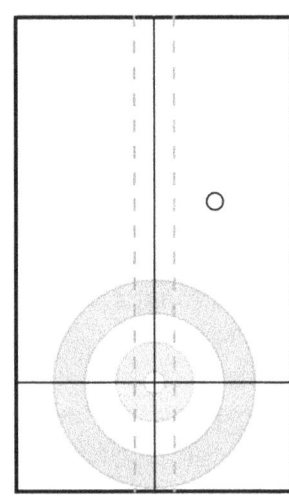

Corner guard

The terms "high guard," "mid guard," and "tight guard" describe a guard's distance from the house. The type of guards teams use depends on their strategic plan for the end and the ice conditions. For example, if the non-hammer team wants to steal and the ice is curling a lot, the team would use a very tight center guard. This way, the non-hammer team has room to draw around the guard to the button, but is protected from opponent hits that could curl around a high guard.

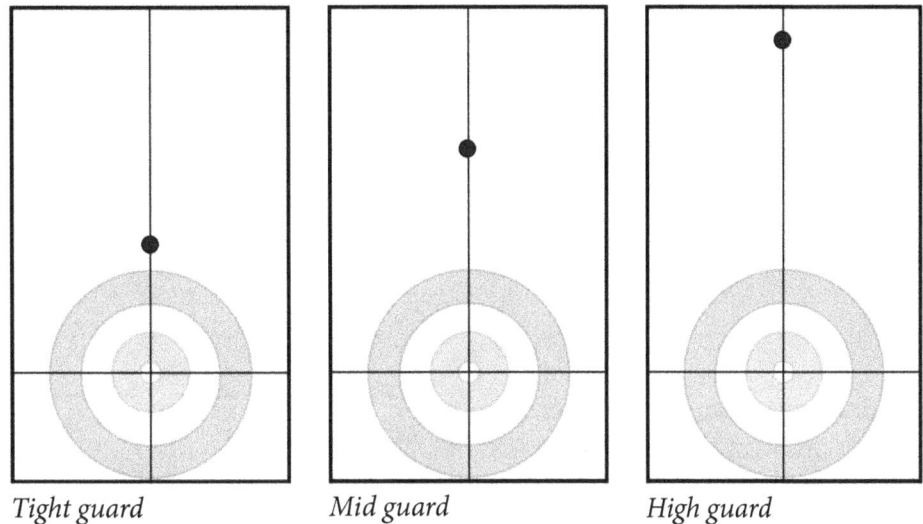

Tight guard *Mid guard* *High guard*

Draw

Even though all light-weight shots that stop in the field of play are technically "draw shots," during a game, most curlers use the term "draw" to mean shots that stop in the house.

The rock closest to the center of the target is called the "shot rock." The second-closest rock is called the "second shot," and the third-closest rock is the "third shot," and so on. (As a reminder, the only rocks that count as points are the ones closer to the center of the target than the nearest opponent stones.)

Teams use the "shot rock" terminology for faster communication. For example, if a few rocks are at approximately the same distance from the pin, the skip may take a close look, then tell his teammates, "Our opponents have first and third shot, but we're second." This tells them what their scoring risk and potential are.

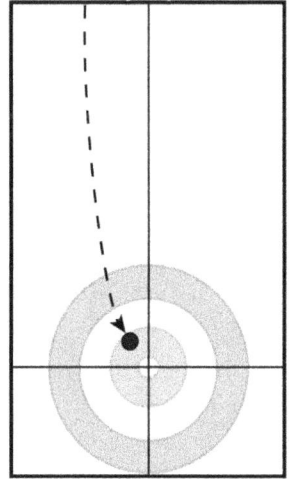

A draw

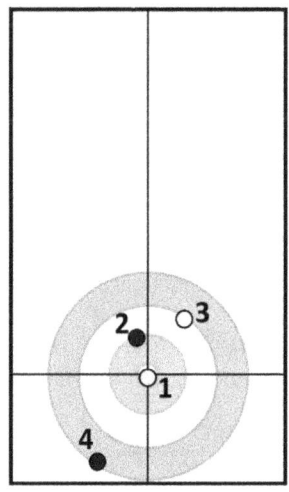

The light yellow rock (1) is first shot. The dark blue stone (2) is second shot, etc.

Most of the time, teams prefer their draws to be in front of the tee line so their opponents can't draw down to them and be shot.

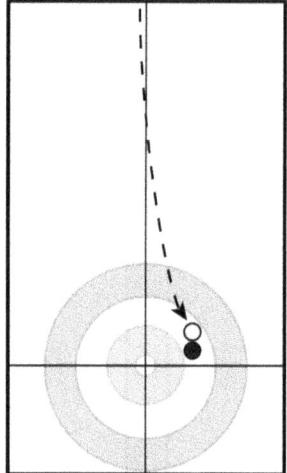 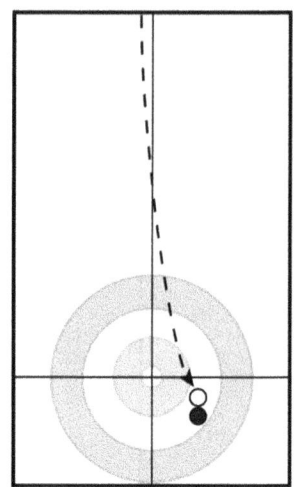

Freeze

A "freeze" is a draw shot that stops in contact with a rock already in play. A "nose" freeze sits directly in front of another stone. A "corner" freeze sits in front of another stone at an angle. If a team leaves a rock behind the tee line, its opponent can freeze to it and be shot.

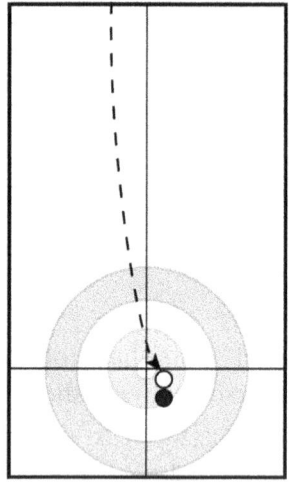 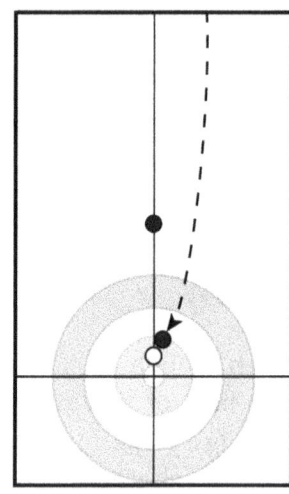

Nose freeze *Corner freeze*

Many people think freezes are the toughest shots in curling. A freeze needs to be the perfect combination of line, weight, rotation, and sweeping to stop at the correct spot. If a freeze is perfect, it can save an end, but if not, it can result in a major point loss.

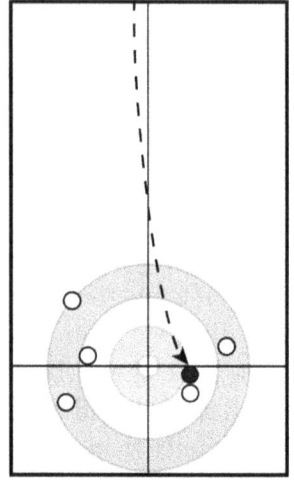 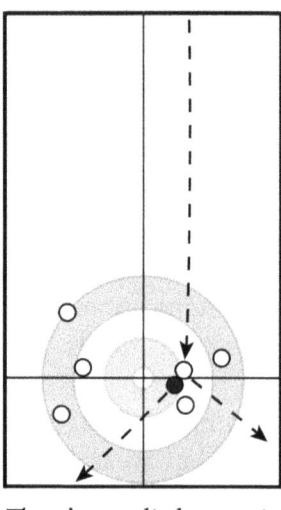

Perfect freeze *There's very little margin for error on freezes.*

Tap, Raise, and Bump

"Tap," "raise," and "bump" are terms for draw shots in which one stone pushes another back. The terms "tap" and "raise" usually refer to shots that move guards or rocks in the front half of the house. The term "bump" usually refers to shots that push rocks in the middle of the house to the back of the house.

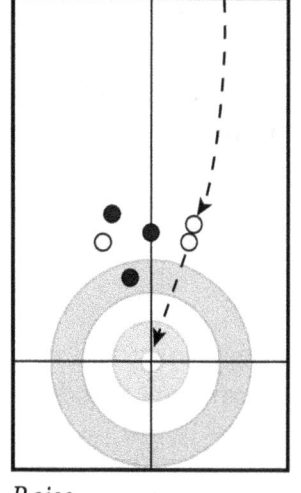
Raise

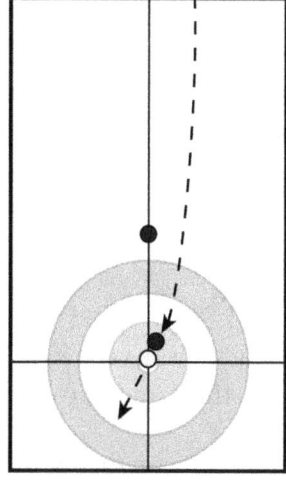
Bump

Split

A "split" is a draw shot that moves the team's own stationary rock to the side. For example, a team might split a guard onto the rings to get two counting stones. Or, a team might split a rock sitting in the middle of the rings to spread its stones out so they can't both be removed with one takeout.

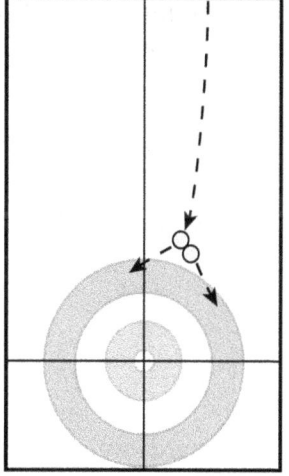

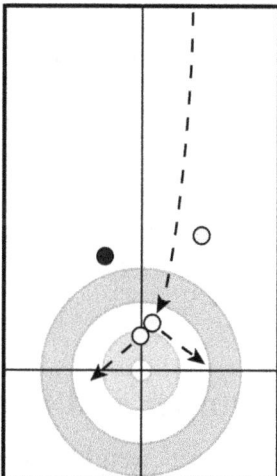

Tick

A "tick" shot is similar to a split, except the focus of the shot is usually on moving an opponent stone out of position. For example, let's say the non-hammer team is trying to steal and puts up a center guard with its first stone. The hammer team can't remove that rock because of the Free Guard Zone rule. However, the hammer team can "tick" the rock out of the way.

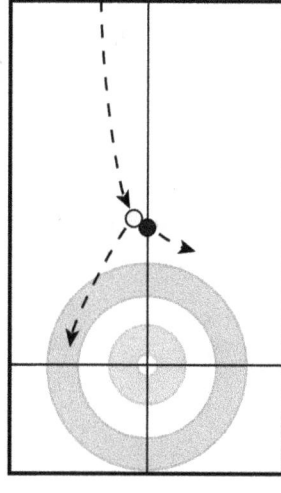

Takeouts and Takeout Weights

"Takeout" is the curling term for a hit. The biggest misconception about hits is that they aren't precision touch shots like draws and guards. Since weight has a major impact on curl, weight matters on hits, too. A light "hack-weight" hit might be able to curl behind a guard to pick out a shot stone, but a heavier "normal-weight" hit could run straight and miss completely.

Here are six common hit weights, listed here from lightest to heaviest:

Hack

"Hack" is a very light hit weight that will curl a lot—usually between one-third and two-thirds the amount that draw weight will curl.

If a hack-weight rock didn't hit anything, it would stop at the hack.

Hack weight is useful for:

- Curlers who have physical difficulty throwing more weight
- Curlers who have difficulty hitting the broom with more weight or who have difficulty changing between up-weight hits and draw weight
- Hitting rocks buried behind guards
- Hits in which it's very important to keep the shooter
- Ticking an opponent's center guard to the side while the Free Guard Zone rule is in effect

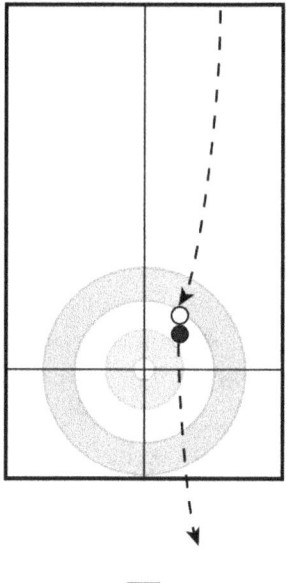

Bumper and Board

"Bumper" weight, also called "board" weight, is a very light hit weight that will curl a lot—usually between one-quarter and one-half the amount that draw weight will curl.

If a bumper/board-weight rock didn't hit anything, it would stop at the physical bumper or wooden boards that surround the ice at dedicated clubs. At an arena club, it would stop about three to four feet (one meter) past the hack.

Bumper/board weight is in between "hack" and "control" and can be used for the same general reasons as those weights, depending on the ice conditions.

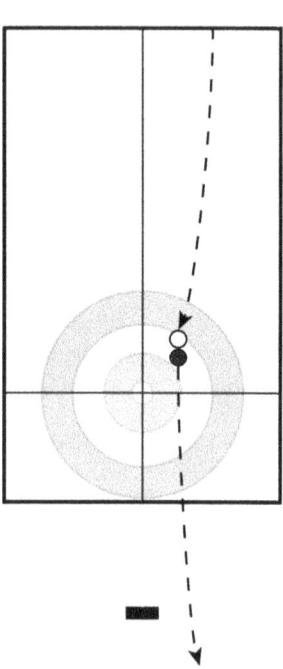

Control

"Control" is a light hit weight whose path can be easily "controlled" by sweeping and thus is forgiving if you miss the broom.

"Control" is enough weight to remove a rock from the house, but not necessarily enough to also remove the shooter.

If a control-weight rock didn't hit anything, it would stop about 5 to 10 feet (2 to 3 meters) past the hack.

Control-weight is useful for:

- Curlers who don't consistently hit the broom
- Hitting rocks buried behind guards
- Hits in which you need to keep the shooter
- Hits in which you need a short, but precise, roll

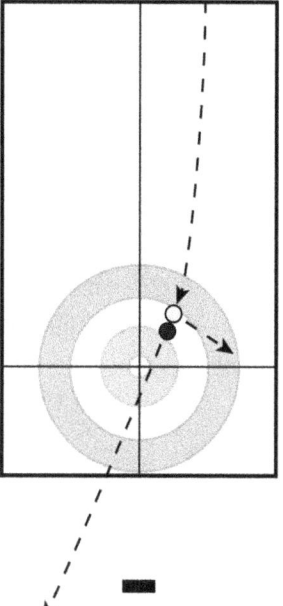

Normal

"Normal" is a medium hit weight whose path can be adjusted by sweeping and is somewhat forgiving if you miss the broom.

"Normal" is enough weight to remove one rock plus the shooter from the rings.

If a normal-weight rock didn't hit anything, it would stop about 10 to 15 feet (3 to 5 meters) past the hack.

Many top teams use normal weight for most of their hits because it can be controlled with sweeping but still produce long rolls.

Be aware—some skips also use "normal" to mean the weight the shooter normally throws, which could be a very light weight for some team members, and a heavy weight for others.

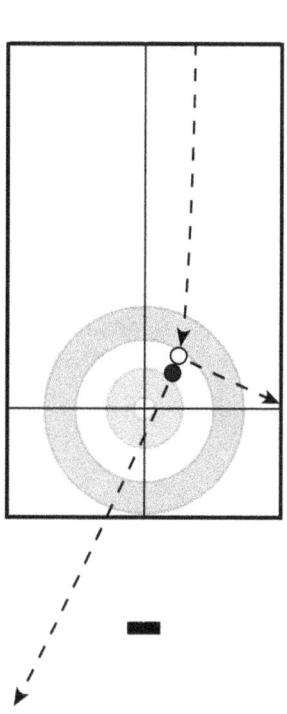

Firm

"Firm" is a hard hit weight that doesn't curl much.

"Firm" is enough weight to remove two rocks plus the shooter from the rings.

If a firm-weight rock didn't hit anything, it would stop 20 feet (6 meters) or more past the hack.

Firm weight is great for double takeouts. It's also useful for single hits when you're not sure how much the ice will curl and want to remove that variable from the equation.

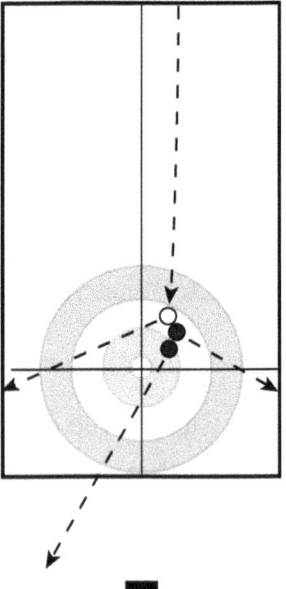

Peel

Peel is a very hard hit weight. Peel-weight rocks run virtually straight.

"Peel" is enough weight to remove three rocks plus the shooter from the rings.

If a peel-weight rock didn't hit anything, it would stop 30 feet (10 meters) or more past the hack.

Peel weight is useful for:

- Removing rocks when you absolutely do not want to keep the shooter (i.e., when you're removing guards to defend a lead)
- Removing lots of rocks
- Situations in which you don't want the rock to curl

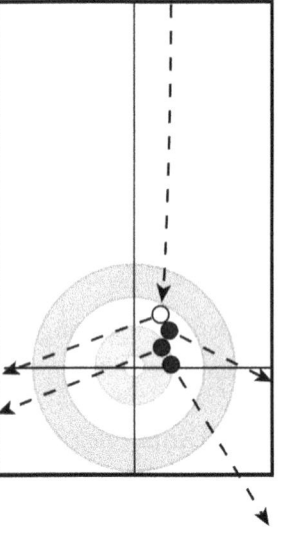

The exact speed of "normal" or "peel" can vary from team to team, depending on their skill level. Kevin Martin, for example, is quite strong and accurate, so he might be comfortable using my "firm" as his default or "normal" weight.

Some teams also define hits weights by times. For example, they might define "normal" weight as a shot that takes 10 seconds to go from hog line to hog line, and "peel" as an 8-second hog-to-hog shot. (For more on this and on timing in general, see my other book "Break Through Beginner Curling.")

Hit-and-Roll

A "hit-and-roll" is a hit in which the thrown rock rolls to a precise position, for example, behind a guard, or out to the wing.

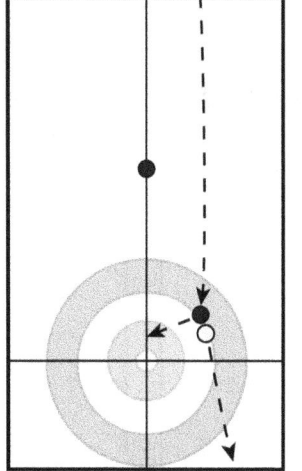
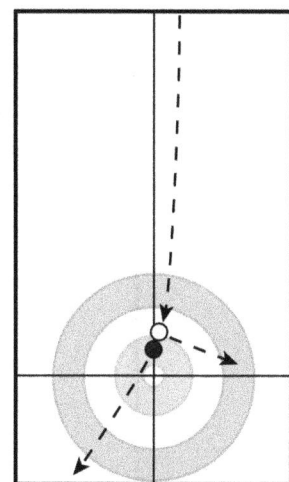

Double and Triple

"Doubles" and "triples" are shots that move two or three rocks. Those rocks could be removed entirely (e.g. a "double takeout"), or they could be nudged so they aren't counting (e.g. a "double tap").

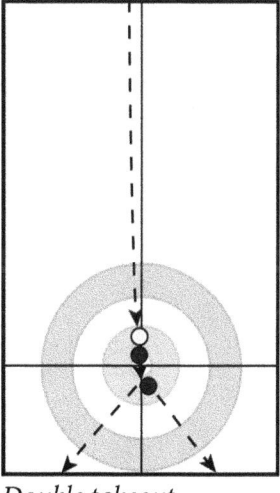
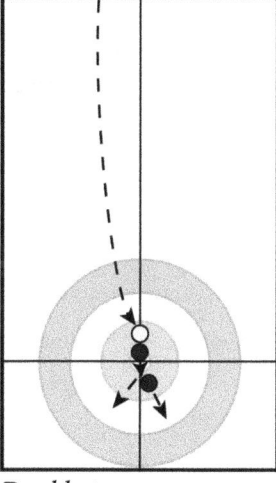

Double takeout *Double tap*

Runback

A "runback" is a hit in which the thrown stone hits one stationary stone and runs it back onto another stationary stone. The shot is usually called, simply, a "runback" if the first struck stone replaces the second stone. It is often called a "runback double" if it removes both struck stones.

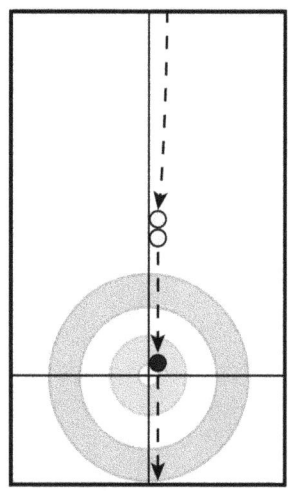
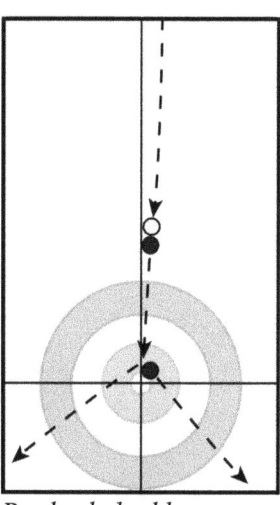

Runback *Runback double*

Angle Raise

An "angle raise" is a tap shot in which a stone near the front of the house is pushed back at an angle. An "angle raise takeout" is a hit in which a stone near the front of the house is hit into a rock on the rings at an angle. An "angle raise double" is a hit in which a stone near the front of the house is hit into a rock on the rings and both rocks are removed from play.

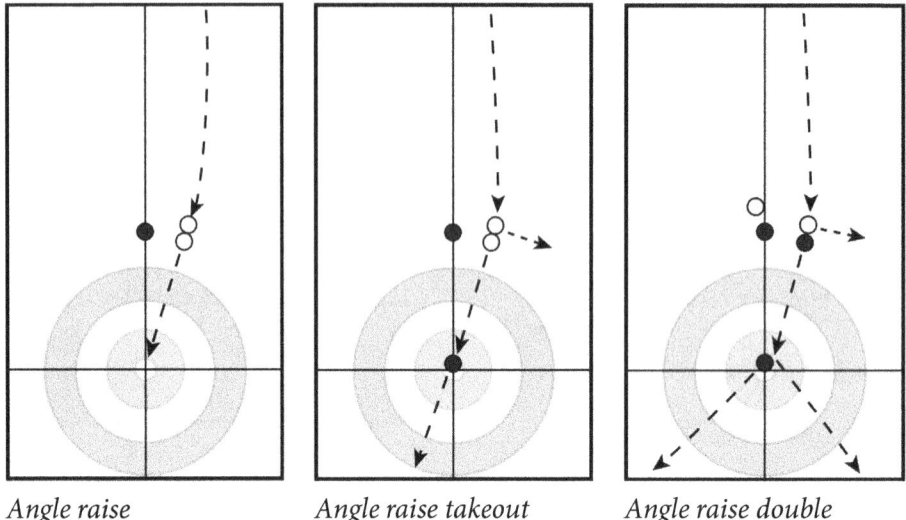

Angle raise *Angle raise takeout* *Angle raise double*

PART 2
STRATEGY BASICS

INTENT

Strategy is about intent. You and your team should know what you want to accomplish with every end and shot. If you do, the rest of your decisions become simpler. If you have a clear goal for the end, your skip can quickly narrow down his or her possible shot choices. If you have a clear goal for each shot, your shooter and sweepers will know the "pro-side" error for the shot and will be more likely to get the rock to an optimal position—even when it's a little off course.

Here's an example: Imagine it's the last end of the game. Your team is down by one point and doesn't have the hammer. You need to score to stay alive, so your plan is to "steal at all costs." (In other words, you're willing to risk giving up eight points in order to get a single point to tie and force an extra end.) Now that your team has a plan, the skip's decisions are easy. In order to steal one, your team will need a shot stone on or near the button, and at least one center guard to protect that stone. With your team's first stone, your skip will want to take advantage of the Free Guard Zone, and thus will call for a center guard.

The lead and the sweepers know how important it is to make sure the first rock is in the Free Guard Zone and not in the house where it can be hit. Therefore, the lead will throw the rock a little light and let the sweepers bring it to the perfect spot, rather than risk being heavy and in the house. The sweepers will also be conservative with their sweeping. Even if the skip asked for a guard one foot away from the rings, the sweepers know in this "steal at all costs" situation, it's better to be 10 feet short of the rings than one inch onto them.

When everyone understands how each shot is important to the team's strategy, then everyone can work together to get the best result possible from each rock.

> **BEGINNER TIP** Budgeting time for strategy discussions and explanations during a game can be challenging. Teams often use the one-minute gap between ends to meet for 15-30 seconds to pick an end plan, like "steal at all costs." After that, the skip will call the rest of the shots alone, unless the end has reached a turning point and the skip wants more input from the team. The skip may also indicate "pro-side errors" and "Plan Bs" when calling the shot, so the shooter and sweepers will know the best way to miss. (More on this in a later section!) It's great if new curlers have experienced teammates who can answer strategy questions while they play. However, new curlers often have so many questions, it can be tough to answer them all without slowing the game down. I like to carry a camera and notebook in my pocket to record situations I find interesting or puzzling, so I can discuss them later with the team or a coach. If you do this, remember to make a note of the end number, rock number, and score!

Three Types of Strategy

Good teams use three types of strategy all the time:

Game Plan The overall plan for the game (e.g., "We hit better than they do, so let's use a conservative, open style of play.")

End Plan The scoring goal for each individual end (e.g., "Steal 1" or "Score 2")

Tactical Plan The shot choices needed to execute the end plan (e.g., "We need to steal, so let's put up a center guard.")

Game Plan

The game plan is the "big picture" plan for the game. For example:

> *"We hit better than our opponents do, so let's set up an open style of play that favors hitting."*

> *"Our opponents prefer a clean, conservative style of play, so let's choose shots that will force a cluttered, aggressive game that will make them uncomfortable."*

> *"Our opponents' skip and third are very good shooters, so we'll put lots of rocks up front early in the end to keep them from having easy shots."*

If you don't know your opponents, you might make a game plan for the first two ends only, in which your goal is to find their strengths and weaknesses. Then, you would use your new knowledge to make a game plan for the remaining ends.

You might also have a plan that changes during different sections of the game. A ten-end game, for example, can be broken up into a beginning (ends 1–3), a middle (ends 4–7), and an end (ends 8–10). Your game plan might be: "In the beginning, we'll keep it simple as we learn the ice. In the middle, we'll play aggressively to build a lead. In the final part of the game, we'll either defend our lead by minimizing the other team's scoring opportunities or, if we're down, we'll play even more aggressively."

> ADVANCED TIP Top teams in big tournaments usually get a practice session before each game so they can learn the ice and break in the pebble to get the ice up to game speed. Because of this, they often start with very aggressive, complex play in the first end.

> ADVANCED TIP When you make your game plan, think about when, if ever, your team will want to play aggressively and take more gambles (i.e., When would you risk giving up a few points for a chance to get a few points?). Would you rather take big gambles early in the game when you have more time to come back from mistakes? Or, would you rather keep the score close for as long as possible and only make risky plays late in the game, if necessary?

End Plan

An end plan is your team's scoring goal for the end. Here are some examples:

Hammer Team End Goal Examples

Score 3 (or more) In high-level play, it's very difficult to score three or more. The tactics used to do that are different from those used to score two, and the hammer team usually needs a few misses from the non-hammer team to accomplish this.

Score 2 This goal, also known as a "deuce," is the most common end goal for hammer teams.

Score 1 Most of the time, the hammer team is disappointed if it only scores one point. The main exceptions to that are if the hammer team only needs one point to win, or if the hammer team nearly gave up a big steal and is simply grateful to have avoided a disaster.

Blank In a "blank" end, neither team scores, but the team with the hammer gets to keep it in the next end. Since having the hammer makes it easier to score, teams with the hammer will blank ends on purpose to carry that advantage into the next end. For example, if a game is tied with two ends left, the hammer team might blank the second-to-last end, so it can have the hammer in the final end.

Prevent the non-hammer team from stealing more than 1 (or 2, or more) Preventing an opponent from scoring is different than trying to blank or score one point. With a "prevent" goal, the hammer team is only focused on preventing its opponent from getting into a position to steal (e.g., by clearing center guards) and doesn't care whether it scores or blanks. A hammer team might choose this goal if it has a significant lead, or is tied or up in the final end.

Non-Hammer Team End Goal Examples

Steal 2 (or more)	"Steal" is curling slang for scoring without the hammer. In high-level play, it is very difficult to steal two or more points in one end.
Steal 1	This is a common end goal for non-hammer teams.
Force 1	The "force" is an under-appreciated, but very valuable end goal for non-hammer teams. A non-hammer team would choose to "force" when it wants to make sure the hammer team scores one and only one point. Here is an example of why it's so powerful: If your team can score two points every time you have the hammer, and force your opponents to take one and only one point every time they have the hammer, you will win handily. (There are sneakier reasons why teams force. For more on this, see the "Forces" chapter.)
Prevent the hammer team from scoring more than 1 (or 2, or more)	With a "prevent" goal, the non-hammer team doesn't care if it steals, forces, or blanks, as long as it keeps its opponent from scoring more than one (or two, etc.). (This is unusual, because most of the time, a non-hammer team would consider an end a failure if it allowed its opponent to blank, since it wouldn't get a point or the hammer in the next end.) A non-hammer team might choose a "prevent" goal if it has a significant lead, or is up by at least one in the final end.

So how do you know which plan to choose? You'll make that decision by thinking about your game plan, then considering:

- What end is it?
- What's the score?
- Who has the hammer?
- What are the ice conditions? (e.g., Will the curl in the ice make it easier or harder to hit? Does your team feel comfortable enough with the ice speed to draw consistently? Are the ice conditions changing?)
- What are your team's strengths and weaknesses?
- What are your opponent's strengths and weaknesses?

Here are two examples:

Example 1: It's the ninth end of a ten-end game. The score is tied and your team has the hammer. All things being equal, your odds of winning the game if you're tied with the hammer in the tenth end are good. (At the elite level, the hammer team would win approximately 75% of the time, according to Kevin Palmer's "Curl with Math" blog at http://curlwithmath.blogspot.com). Therefore, you choose "Blank" as your end plan for the ninth. ("Score 2" is also a good end plan. However, to get two points, you must put more rocks in play, and when you do that, you make it easier for the non-hammer team to steal—and you may not want to take that risk.)

Example 2: *It's the ninth end of a ten-end game. The score is tied, but this time, you don't have the hammer. This gets trickier. You definitely don't want your opponents to blank or score two, but is it better for you to steal or force your opponents to take one? The decision you make here depends on what you want the situation to be in the tenth end. For example, if you'd rather be up one without the hammer in the tenth, then you should steal the ninth. If you'd rather be down one with the hammer in the tenth, then you should force your opponent to score one point in the ninth. (Again, if you like stats, Kevin Palmer's "Curl with Math" blog says at the elite level, you have an approximately 60% chance of winning if you are up one without the hammer in the last end. For more stats like this, check out his entry from October 26, 2008 at http://curlwithmath.blogspot.com.)*

Every member of the team should know what the end plan is. Some teams hold mini-conferences between ends to pick a plan together. As you get more advanced, you should sit down as a team and decide which end plans you prefer in common situations, like those "tied in the ninth" scenarios.

"If Possible" versus "At All Costs" End Plans

It's also important to know how urgent it is to accomplish your end goal and how much risk you are willing to take to do it. Wanting to steal a point in the first end is very different from needing to steal a point in the tenth! It will be easier to make a tactical plan if your team can distinguish between a "steal, if possible" versus a "steal at all costs."

> ADVANCED TIP Instead of using the simple end goals listed earlier, like "Score 2" or "Steal 1," a high-level team might break those down into a more detailed list of goals like these:
>
> <u>"Score 2" End Goals</u>
>
> - Score 2 at All Costs
> - Score 2 Aggressively
> - Score 2 Moderately Aggressively
> - Score 2 Conservatively
> - Score 2 Very Conservatively or Blank
>
> <u>"Steal 1" End Goals</u>
>
> - Steal 1 at All Costs
> - Steal 1 Aggressively
> - Steal 1 Conservatively
> - Steal 1 Very Conservatively or Allow a Blank
>
> There's more on what terms like "aggressive" and "conservative" mean coming up in the "Tactical Plan" section.)

Playbook of End Plans

As I mentioned a moment ago, some teams sit down together and make standard plans for common situations. Some even develop elaborate playbooks of end plans for common scenarios.

Below is a playbook I used with a competitive women's team. It is much more complicated than what beginners need, but I've included it in the book as an example of how much advanced planning some teams do. Of course, your team may choose different end goals in these situations, depending on the strengths and weaknesses of your team and the playing style you prefer.

One key idea our playbook illustrates is that curling is a numbers game and it's important to "play the scoreboard." That means, the end plan you choose should reflect the score in the game and how many ends are left. Some teams try so hard to "win" every end, they lose the game. For example, it may feel like a bad thing to give up a steal, but if you have a four point lead with three ends to play, it's okay to let your opponent steal one in every end—you will still win the game!

(Again, there's more on what terms like "aggressively" and "conservatively" mean coming up in the "Tactical Plan" section.)

Example of team end goal playbook:

End	Score	End Goal with Hammer	End Goal without Hammer
1 to 3	-2	Score 2 conservatively or moderately aggressively	Steal 1 conservatively
	-1	Score 2 conservatively or moderately aggressively, or Blank	Steal 1 conservatively
	Even	Score 2 conservatively or moderately aggressively, or Blank	Force 1 conservatively, or Steal 1 conservatively
	+1	Score 2 conservatively or moderately aggressively	Force 1 conservatively, or Steal 1 conservatively
	+2	Score 2 conservatively or moderately aggressively	Force 1 conservatively
4 to 7	-3 or more	Score 2 moderately aggressively or aggressively	Steal 1 moderately aggressively
	-2	Score 2 moderately aggressively	Steal 1 conservatively, or Force 1
	-1	Score 2 conservatively or moderately aggressively	Steal 1 conservatively, or Force 1
	Even	Score 2 conservatively or moderately aggressively	Steal 1 conservatively, or Force 1
	+1	Score 2 conservatively or moderately aggressively	Steal 1 conservatively, or Force 1
	+2	Score 2 conservatively or moderately aggressively	Steal 1 conservatively, or Force 1 conservatively, or Prevent opponent from scoring more than 1
	+3 or more	Score 2 conservatively, Blank, or Prevent opponent from scoring	Prevent opponent from scoring more than 1

End	Score	End Goal with Hammer	End Goal without Hammer
8	-3 or more	Score 2 moderately aggressively or aggressively. Don't give up a steal.	Steal 1 at all costs
	-2	Score 2 moderately aggressively or aggressively. Don't give up a steal.	Steal 1 aggressively
	-1	Score 2 moderately aggressively, or Blank	Steal 1 conservatively or moderately aggressively
	Even	Score 2 conservatively or moderately aggressively, or Blank	Steal 1 conservatively to moderately aggressively, or Force 1
	+1	Score 2 conservatively, or Prevent opponent from scoring	Force 1, or Steal 1 conservatively
	+2 or more	Prevent opponent from scoring	Force 1 conservatively
9	-3 or more	Score 2 aggressively or at all costs	Steal 1 (or 2) at all costs
	-2	Score 2 aggressively. Don't allow a steal.	Steal 1 at all costs
	-1	Score 2 moderately aggressively to aggressively, or Blank	Steal 1 aggressively or at all costs
	Even	Blank, or Score 2 conservatively	Steal 1, or Force 1
	+1	Prevent opponent from scoring	Force 1
	+2 or more	Prevent opponent from scoring	Prevent opponent from scoring more than 1
10	-2	Score 2 at all costs, Score 3 if possible but not at rist of losing	Steal 2 at all costs
	-1	Score 2 aggressively, but get 1 at all costs	Stseal 1 at all costs, and 2 if possible but not at the risk of losing
	Even	Prevent opponent from scoring at all costs	Steal 1 at all costs
	+1	Prevent opponent from scoring 1, or 2 at most	Steal 1, or Prevent opponent from scoring more than 1
	+2 or more	Prevent opponent from scoring more than 1, or 2 at most	Prevent opponent from scoring more than 1, or 2 at most

Goal Charts: "Want," "Accept," and "Avoid"

Another tool teams use to discuss end plans is a goal chart. A goal chart lists the outcome the team "wants" to accomplish in the end, the outcome the team will "accept" as a reasonable result in that the end, and the outcome the team must "avoid" in that end. For example, in the first of end of the game, the hammer team's goal chart might look like this:

Hammer Team's Goal Chart (First End)
  Want: Score 2 or Blank
  Accept: Score 1
  Avoid: Steal

In some situations, a goal chart might have categories like "need" and "can't allow." For example, in the final end of a game when the hammer team is down by 1 point, the team's goal chart might look like this:

Hammer Team's Goal Chart (Final End, Down by 1)
  Want: Score 2
  Need: Score 1
  Can't allow: Blank or Steal

Tactical Plan

Once you pick an end plan, you need a tactical plan to accomplish it. Tactical plans are shot choices. Even though you must always respond to the situation you see in front of you during a game, you should at least start with an overall tactical plan, instead of simply playing the whole game shot-to-shot. Curling is called "chess on ice" because top skips plan their tactics several shots ahead. When they begin an end, they know how they want it to finish, and they know which shots they'll likely need to make in order for their plan to succeed. They also know what could go wrong and are able to recognize how and when to bail out.

The Most Basic Tactics

There are three basic questions in curling tactics:

Key Question 1 Should you put your first rocks in front of the house or in the house?

Key Question 2 Should you focus your play towards the center or the sides of the sheet?

Key Question 3 Should you throw mostly hits, or should you throw mostly draws and guards?

To begin to understand how teams make these choices, let's look at three simple curling ends.

Simple End 1: "Hit Everything!"

To start our "simple end" scenario, the non-hammer team draws its first rock to the button. If the hammer team doesn't move that rock, it will count as one point for the non-hammer team. So, the hammer team hits it and stays in its place. If the teams exchange hits like this (and roll a tiny bit here and there to stay in the rings), the hammer team will eventually score one point.

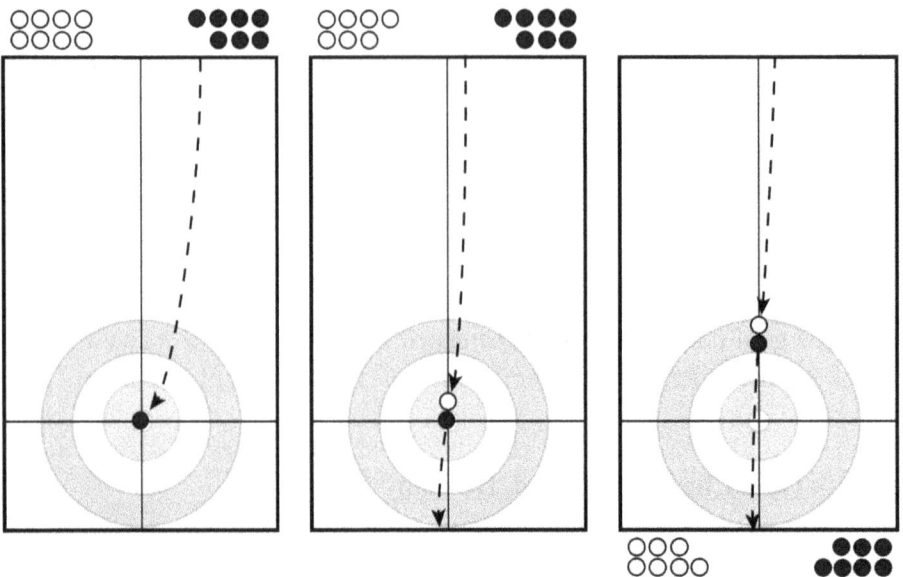

VARIATION 1 *The hammer team wants to score more than one point*

Most of the time, the hammer team isn't happy to score just one point—usually the hammer team doesn't consider an end successful unless it scores at least two points. So, this time, instead of hitting and sitting in the center where the opponent stone was, the hammer team hits and rolls its rock to the side of the sheet. This creates two advantages for the hammer team. First, because most curlers find it more difficult to hit rocks on the wings, there's a chance the non-hammer team might miss if it tries to hit that stone. Second, the reason having "the hammer" (last rock) is an advantage in curling, is because if things go badly, the hammer team can use that last rock to draw to the button and save the end. The hammer team wants to force the non-hammer team to play on the sides of the sheet, so the center will stay open for that last "bail out" shot, if necessary.

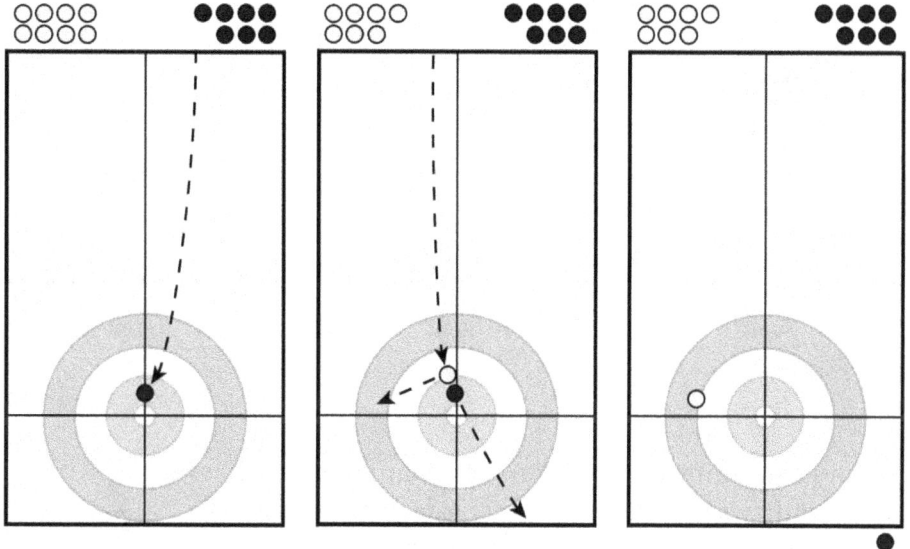

The non-hammer team responds by hitting and rolling back to the middle. Again, the hammer team will have to move the non-hammer team's rock if it wants to score.

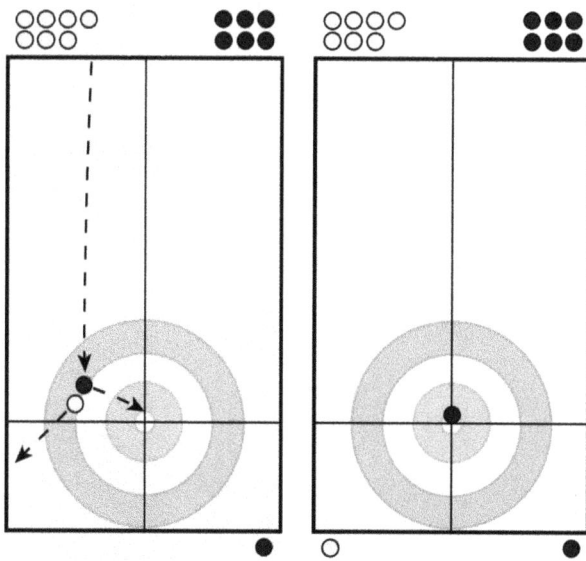

33

VARIATION 2 *What if the hammer team misses a hit?*

Let's take a step back. What if this time, instead of making the hit-and-roll back to the center, the non-hammer team misses the hit completely? Here's what this sequence might look like:

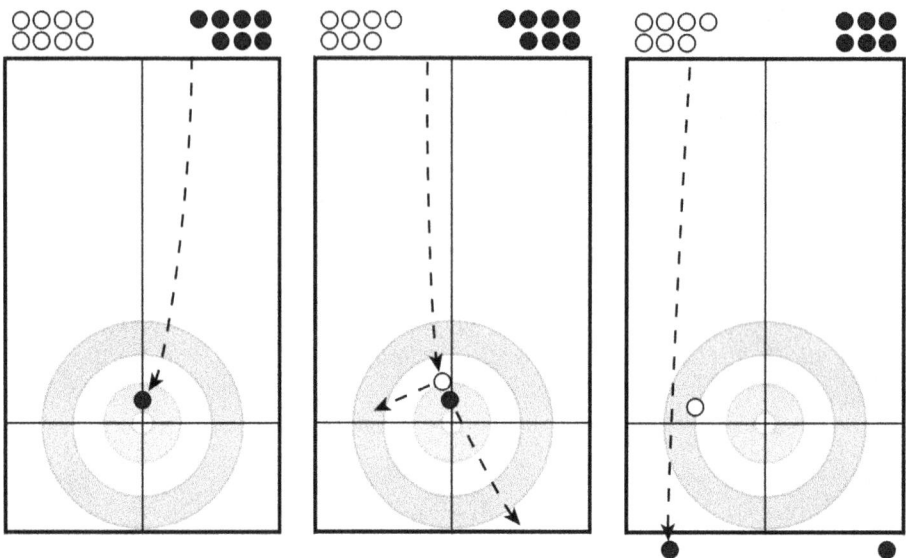

This plays right into the hammer team's plan. The hammer team seizes the opportunity, and draws a stone to the other side of the house. The stones are far apart and at the same "height" in the house, so the non-hammer team can't remove them both with a double takeout. This is called "splitting the house." Now the hammer team is set up to score two points.

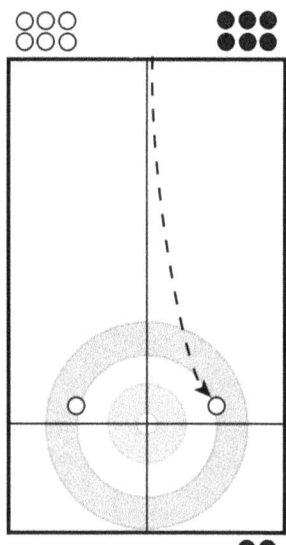

VARIATION 3 *What if the non-hammer team doesn't roll back to the middle?*

Let's take a step back again. This time, instead of missing completely, let's imagine the non-hammer team makes the hit but misses the roll, leaving its rock on the side of the rings. Here's what this sequence might look like:

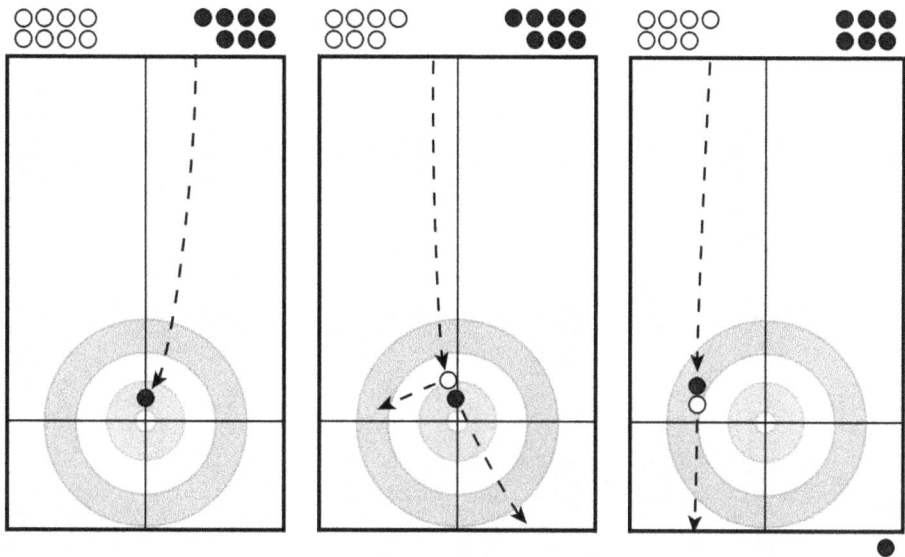

This is also a lucky break for the hammer team. The non-hammer team's rock is not a threat (because the hammer team's skip could easily out-draw it with the final stone), so the hammer team can use it to secure a rock in play. For example, the hammer team could corner freeze to the non-hammer team's stone and be shot. Or, if the non-hammer team's stone is high enough in the house, the hammer team could draw behind it and be shot.

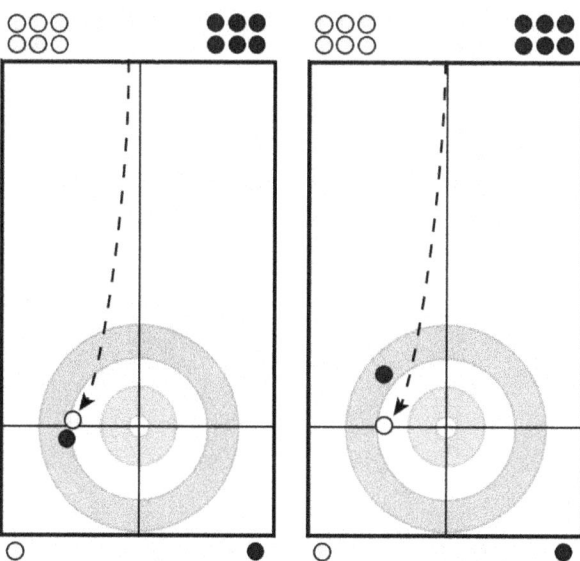

VARIATION 4 *What if the hammer team misses a hit?*

Let's start from the beginning again and look at what happens if the hammer team misses a hit:

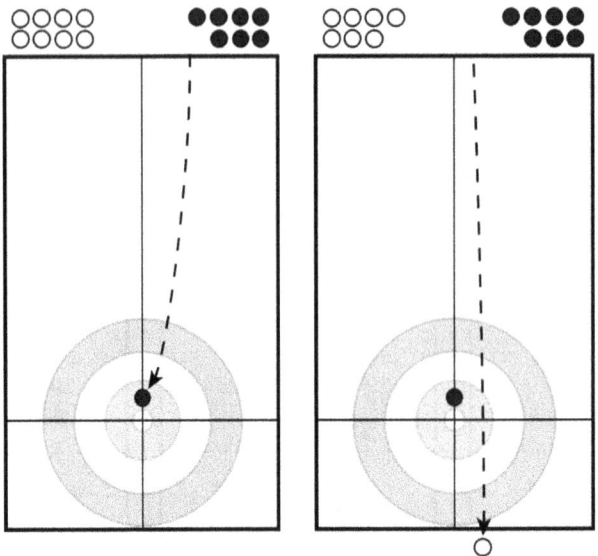

Now the non-hammer team can put up a guard to set up a steal.

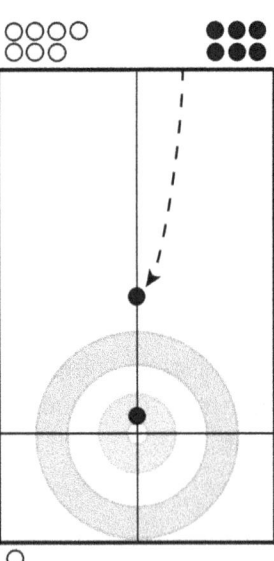

VARIATION 5 *What if a team rolls behind the tee line?*

If either team rolls a stone into the back half of the house, its opponent can freeze to that stone and be shot.

For example, if the non-hammer team hits and accidentally rolls behind the tee line, the hammer team can freeze to be shot. (In the "Deuces" chapter coming up, we'll talk about using tactics like this to score two.)

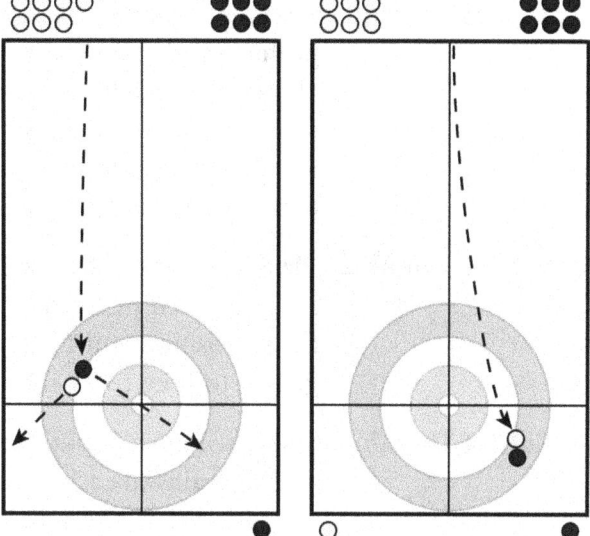

Or, if the hammer team hits and accidentally rolls behind the tee line, the non-hammer team can freeze and be shot. (We'll talk how to use tactics like this to force one in the "Forces" chapter.)

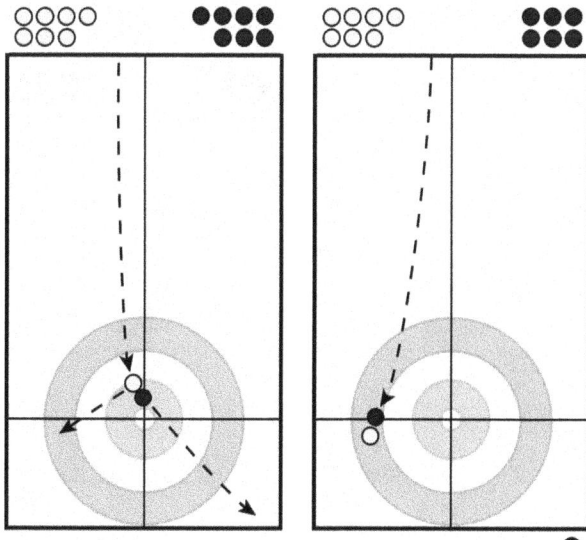

Rules of Thumb from Simple End 1

There are a few general rules of thumb and simple tactical ideas we can take away from this "Simple End 1":

Rule of Thumb 1   **The non-hammer team prefers to play in the center; the hammer team prefers to play on the wing.** Most of the time, the non-hammer team will play to the center in order to steal or force the hammer team to play in the center. Likewise, most of the time, the hammer team will play to the wings to try to score multiple points. The hammer team, however, must be careful to maintain a path to the center, so it can bail itself out with last rock.

Rule of Thumb 2   **Play in front of the tee line.** Most of the time, both teams prefer to put rocks in front of the tee line rather than behind it. Otherwise, it's easy for the opposing team to freeze and be shot. ("Backing" can work as well as guards to keep rocks in play!)

Rule of Thumb 3   **Split the house.** "Splitting the house" is the tactic in which a team puts two rocks parallel to each other in the house, separated by enough distance that they are difficult to remove with a double takeout. The hammer team can use this tactic to score two points. The non-hammer team can use this tactic to force the hammer team to draw for one.

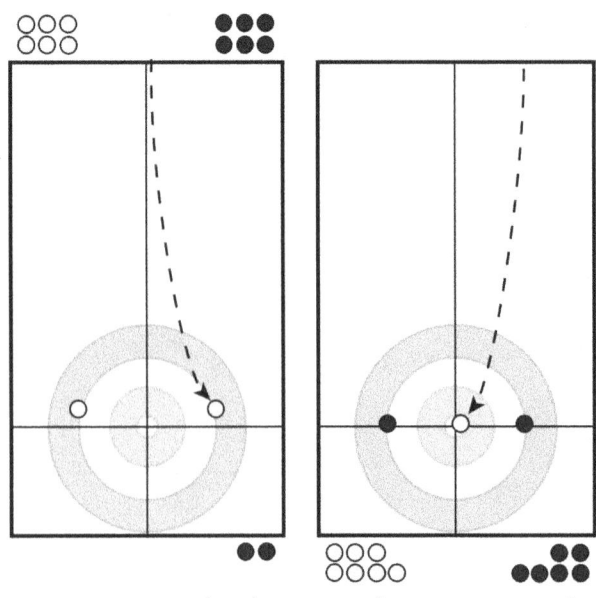

Hammer team splits the house to score 2

Non-hammer team splits the house to force 1

Simple End 2: "Throw Everything to the Pin!"

This time, let's imagine the non-hammer team puts its first rock in front of the house as a center guard. Since the rock closest to the center scores, the hammer team throws its first rock to the front of the button, behind the center guard.

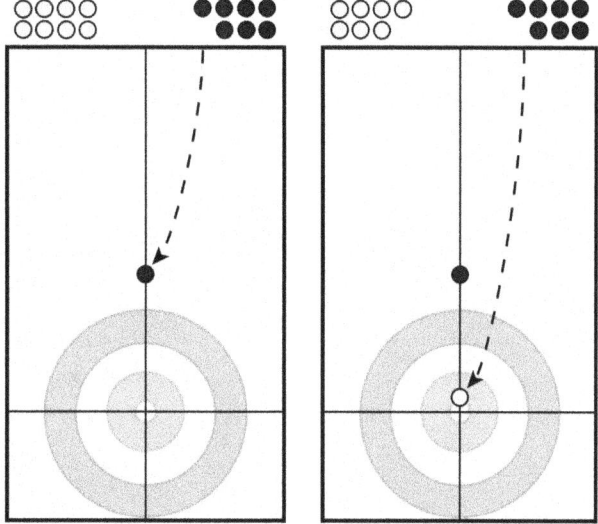

The non-hammer team wants to be shot, so it throws a tap-back and moves the hammer team's stone to the back of the house. The hammer team tries to do the same.

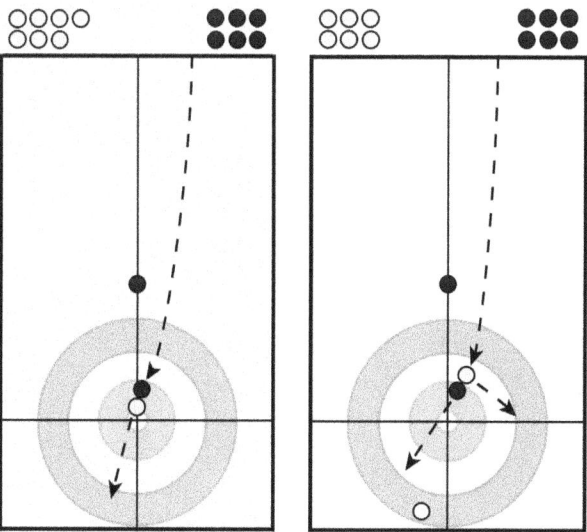

The teams continue to jostle for shot position. Here's an example of how it might play out with good but not perfect teams....

THREE TYPES OF STRATEGY   *INTRODUCTION TO CURLING STRATEGY*

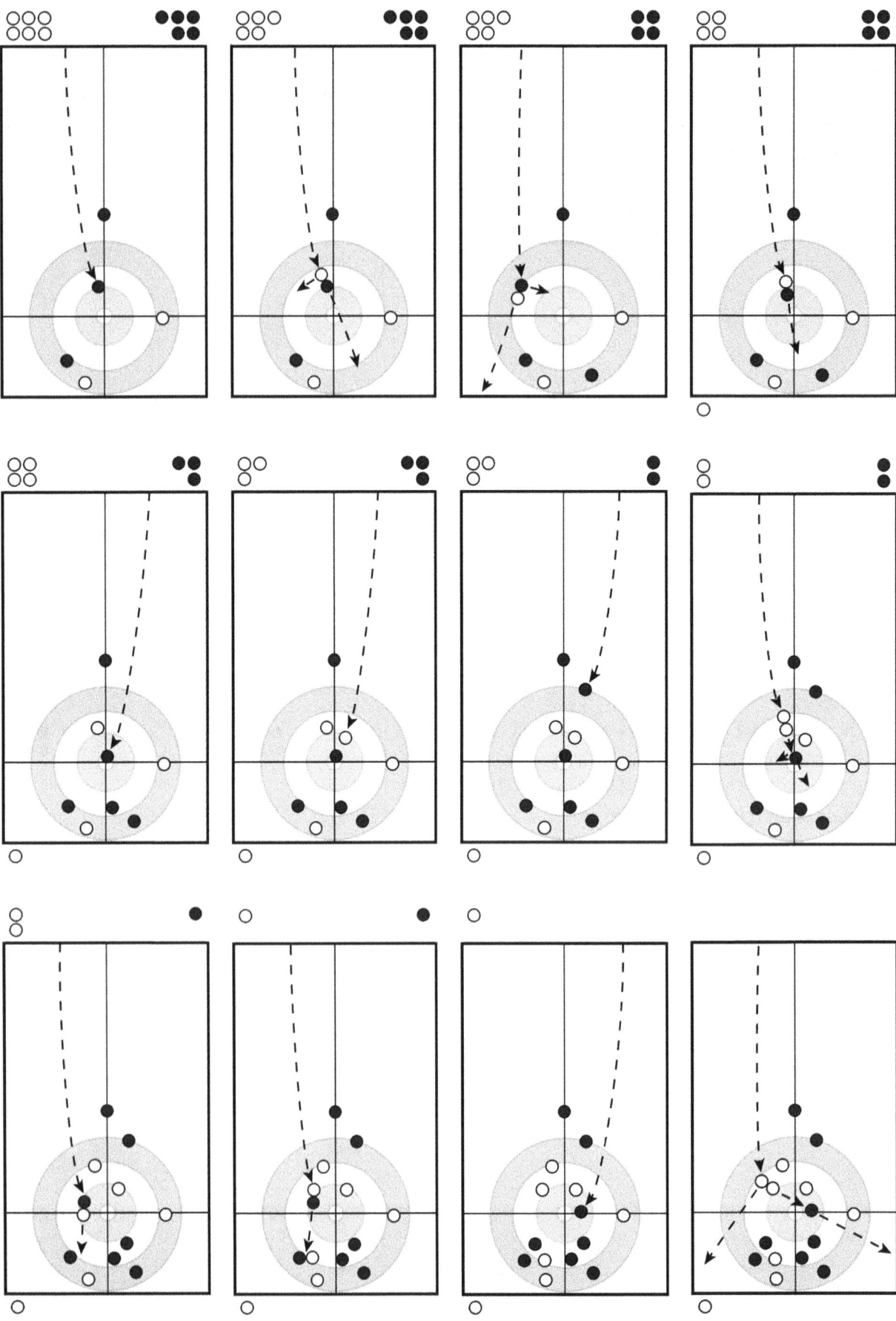

40

In that example, the hammer team had to make a very difficult double to get two points. It had no clear draw or hit for two, as it might have in "Simple End 1." Part of the reason for this is because there were so many rocks clustered around the center line and four-foot ring. This "junk" makes it difficult to maneuver. It also makes the effective scoring area small—meaning, in order for the hammer team's rocks to count as points, it needs them very close to the center of the target to out-count the nearest opponent stone.

This is also a riskier style of play for both teams. Because there are so many rocks in play, if the non-hammer team has a slight miss, the hammer team could score a big end. For example, in the last sequence, if the non-hammer team's last draw had been a little wide, the hammer team could have tapped for three points....

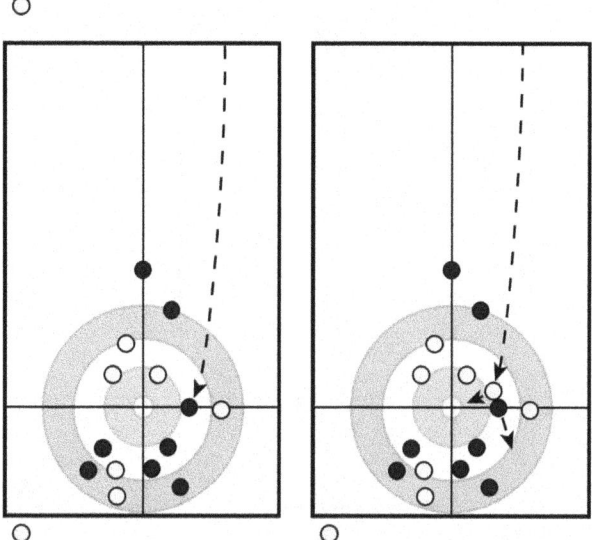

Or, if the non-hammer team's last draw had been a little high, the hammer team could have hit for three points.

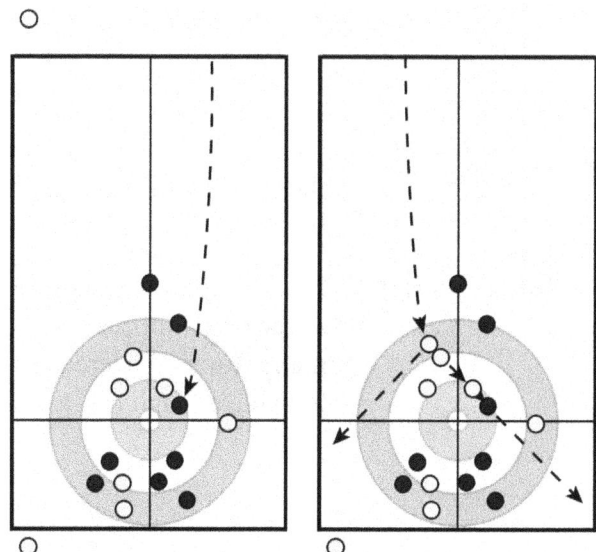

At the same time, in a situation like this with lots of rocks in play in the center, it is also easier for the non-hammer team to steal. (Remember that difficult angle takeout the hammer team had to make with its last rock to score two in the original scenario? There are not many teams that can make that shot consistently.)

VARIATION 1 *What if the non-hammer team wants to force one?*

One more thought before we leave this scenario, let's go back to the beginning and look at the non-hammer team's choice with its second rock. If the hammer team puts its first stone near the button, the non-hammer team could decide it's happy to force the hammer team to one point and freeze to hammer team's shot stone. Now the hammer team will need to do a lot of clever tapping and hitting to create enough space to get a second stone into the center.

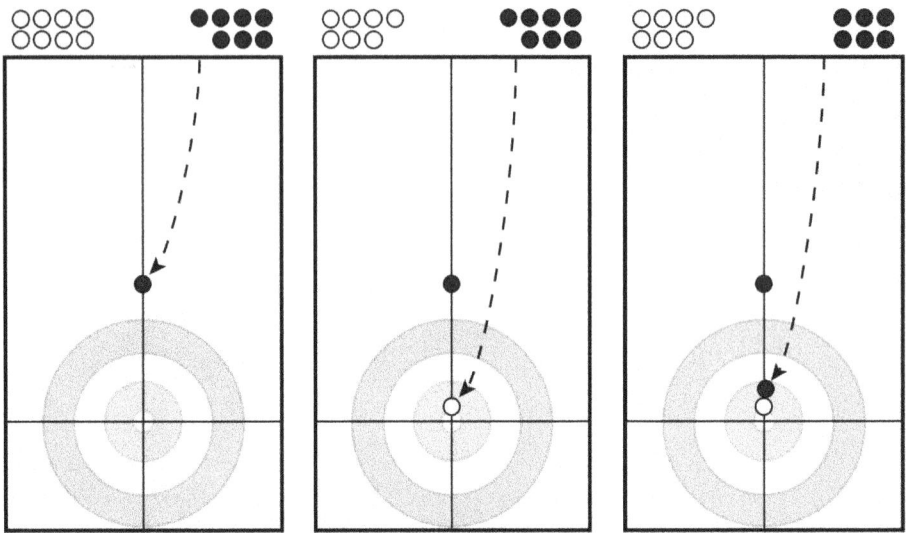

Rules of Thumb from Simple End 2

Rule of Thumb 4   **The more rocks in play, the more risk.** When there are more rocks in play, there's a greater chance the hammer team will score a big end. Also, when there are more rocks in play clustered in the middle, there's a greater chance the non-hammer team will be able to steal.

Rule of Thumb 5   **It takes space to score multiple points.** Very simply, rocks take up space, so scoring multiple points requires a bigger scoring area. If both teams have many stones clustered in the center, it can be difficult for the hammer team to make enough room to score multiple points.

Simple End 3: "The Non-Hammer Team Plays in the Middle, and the Hammer Team Plays on the Wing."

In this end, both teams put up guards and draw behind them.

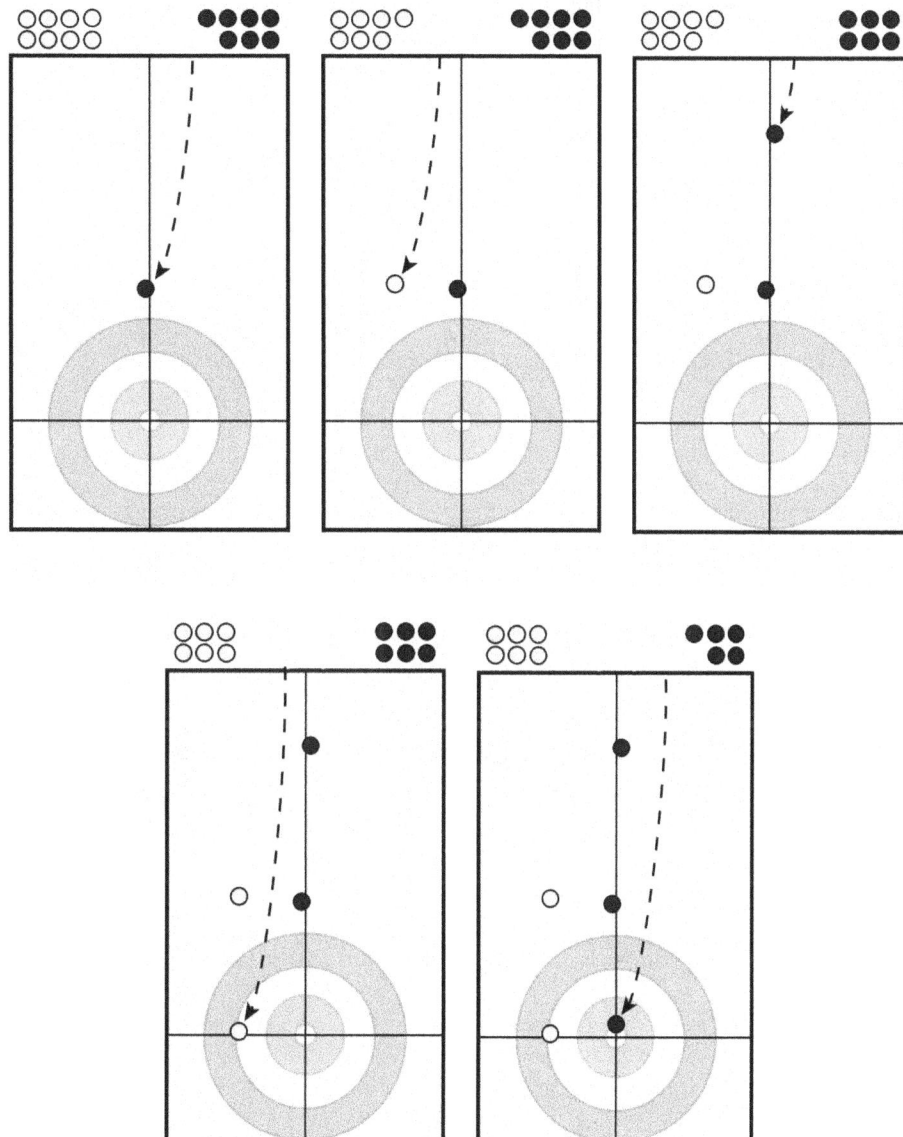

The non-hammer team controls the center and is set up to steal. The hammer team has established a protected rock on the wing as a possible second point. Both teams have gambled. By letting the hammer team set up a protected rock on the wing, the non-hammer team risks giving up multiple points if its steal attempt fails. By letting the non-hammer team set up a protected rock in the middle, the hammer team risks giving up a steal if it can't make a come-around hit to remove the rock near the button, or a double takeout to remove the center guards.

Here is an example of the difficult shots the hammer team will have to make to get out of trouble....

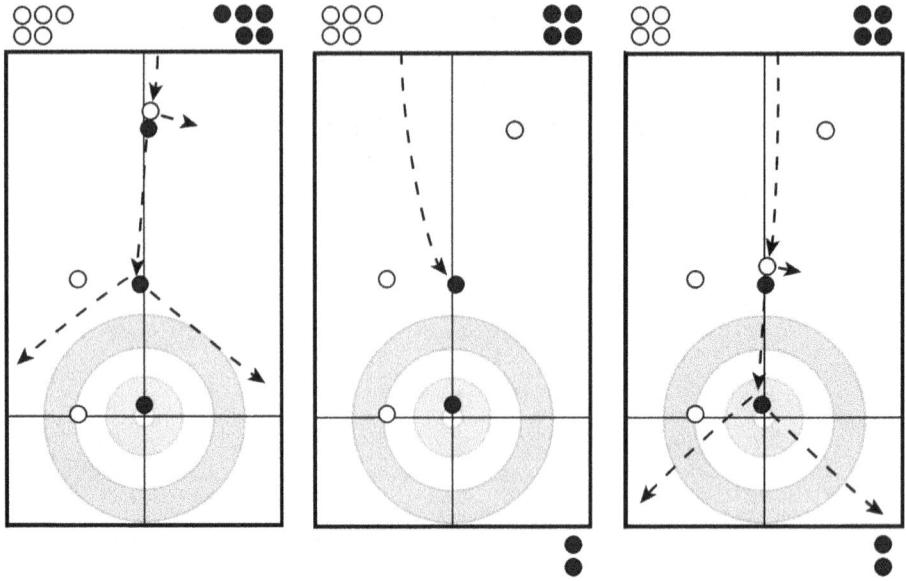

The hammer team will likely need to make at least two double takeouts to clear the non-hammer team's rocks from the front.

This is part of planning ahead in the "chess" strategy—the non-hammer team has to bet that it can do a better job replacing its guards or shot stones, than the hammer team can do making double takeouts to remove them. If you are the skip of the hammer team and you know your team doesn't hit well, you wouldn't choose this tactical plan, because you can't execute the shots required to make it succeed. Likewise, if you are the skip of the non-hammer team and you know your team doesn't feel secure with its draw weight, you should probably choose a different tactical plan that will rely more on hits than draws.

Rules of Thumb from Simple End 3

Rule of Thumb 6 **Make a plan you can execute.** When you pick a tactical plan, think about which shots you'll probably have to make in order for that plan to succeed. It doesn't matter how clever a strategist you are, if your team can't make the necessary shots, your plan won't work.

Aggressive vs. Conservative

One theme that appears in these three scenarios is the idea of risk versus reward. In "Simple End 1: Hit Everything!" there weren't many rocks in play. That meant it was difficult for either team to score multiple points, but at the same time, neither team risked giving up a big end. There was less chance of a very good outcome, but also less risk of a very bad outcome. That "less risk, less reward" choice is considered a "conservative" style of play.

In "Simple End 2: Throw Everything to the Pin!" there were more rocks in play. This meant there was a greater chance that the hammer team could score a big end and that the non-hammer team could steal. So, each team's chance of having a really good outcome went up, but so did each team's chance of having a really bad outcome. This "big risk, big reward" choice is a more "aggressive" style of play.

In "Simple End 3: The Non-Hammer Team Plays in the Middle, and the Hammer Team Plays on the Wings," the teams use an even more aggressive style of play. Not only are there lots of rocks in play, but there are multiple guards to protect them. The rocks are spread out, which means there is a bigger scoring area with more room for scoring stones—which increases the opportunity for the hammer team to score a big end. Also, the shots needed to remove rocks from the rings will likely be more difficult—long double takeouts, instead of open hits. This increases the odds the hammer team will have a costly miss and give up a steal.

So, tactically speaking, what did the teams do to create this risky scenario in "Simple End 3"? Both teams ignored their opponent's rocks for several turns while they set up their own offense. Setting up offense is good—it gives teams a better chance to score multiple points. However, the longer teams delay dealing with opponent stones, the more trouble they allow to build up, simultaneously increasing the risk of very good and very bad outcomes.

Another way to describe aggressive versus conservative play is by relating it to a team's commitment level to its plan. Let's say it's the last end of the game. The non-hammer team is down by one. If it doesn't score, it loses, therefore, it must be very aggressive and totally committed to stealing, no matter what the risk. If the hammer team draws a rock to the side of the rings, the non-hammer team will ignore it and keep setting up guards or drawing to the center. Even if the hammer team gets all of its rocks on the wings and is poised to score an eight-ender, a committed non-hammer team will ignore those rocks and keep drawing or guarding for the steal. It doesn't matter if the hammer team wins the game by one point or nine—if the non-hammer team don't steal, it loses.

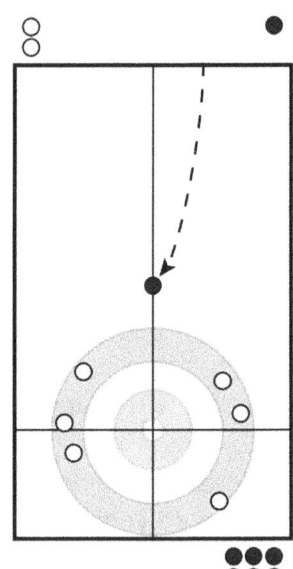

By contrast, if it were the first end of the game, the non-hammer team might want to try for a steal, but not at the risk of giving up a big end. In other words, even though its end plan is "steal," it would happily change it to "allow a blank," or "allow the hammer team to score one point," rather than risk the hammer team scoring two or more. For example, if the non-hammer team puts up a center guard and the hammer team draws to the side of the rings, the non-hammer team would forget about drawing behind its center guard and take out the hammer team's stone instead. (If it could roll behind the center guard to set up a steal, that would be a bonus, but its focus is more on preventing a very bad outcome than on creating a very good outcome.)

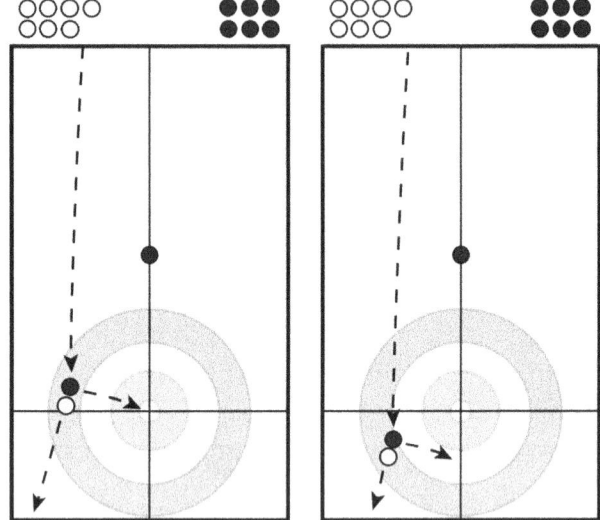

In the next section, I'll lay out a series of opening moves, arranged from conservative to aggressive. One theme you'll notice is that the more aggressive the tactical plan, the more shots the team spends setting up its own offense before attacking its opponent. A very aggressive team might ignore its opponent's stones for two turns or more while it sets up its own guards. A very conservative team, on the other hand, will react immediately to any opponent threat.

> **BEGINNER TIP** As one of my proofreaders pointed out, the idea of aggressive and conservative doesn't totally hold up beginners. Since most beginners miss a lot of hits, trying to hit to keep the house "clean" can be an easy way to give up four or five points. Beginners may always need to use junky "aggressive" tactics, regardless of the score, simply because those are the shots they can make. For more tactical tips aimed specifically at beginners, see the "New Curler Tactics" chapter.

PART 3
TACTICS IN DEPTH

Here are some opening tactics for a few common end plans (Deuce, Steal 1, Force 1) arranged from conservative to aggressive. This is a general guide aimed at introducing you to patterns and thought processes—it is not exhaustive, nor is it meant to provide absolute answers. The actual tactical plans you should choose will depend on the ice conditions, the skill level of your team and your opponents, and the style of play you prefer.

Deuces

Intro to Deuces

It's not easy to score two points, even with the hammer. Often, you need your opponent to miss—or at least make only half a shot—for it to be possible. There's also risk involved. If you push hard for the second point and wait to clear opponent stones from the center of the house, your opponent could steal. Thus, the tactics you use to try for a deuce will vary a lot depending on how badly you need the second point, and as always, on the ice conditions and the strengths and weaknesses of both teams.

I like to begin an end by thinking about how it will finish. Steals and forces usually need to happen near the center of the house, and tend to finish in fairly specific patterns. (More on that in the "Steals" and "Forces" chapers!) Deuces, on the other hand, can happen in diverse ways spread out across the rings. Here are some examples:

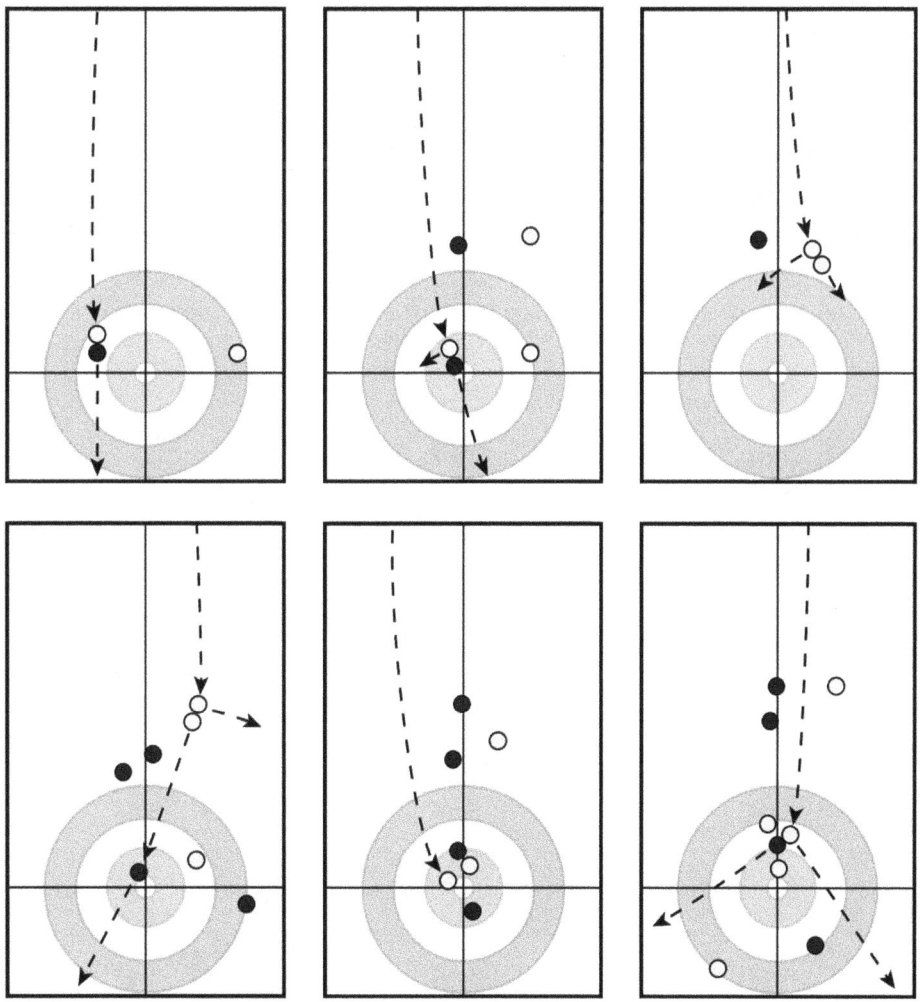

Deuces - The Big Picture

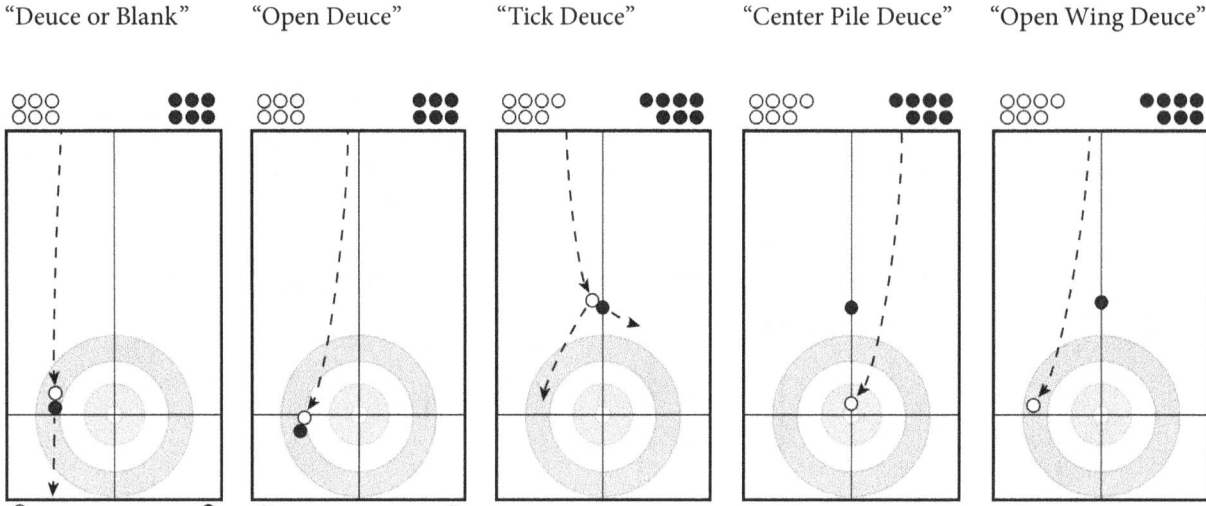

CONSERVATIVE
low risk of giving up a steal, low odds of scoring two

"Deuce or Blank"   "Open Deuce"   "Tick Deuce"   "Center Pile Deuce"   "Open Wing Deuce"

INTRODUCTION TO CURLING STRATEGY — DEUCES

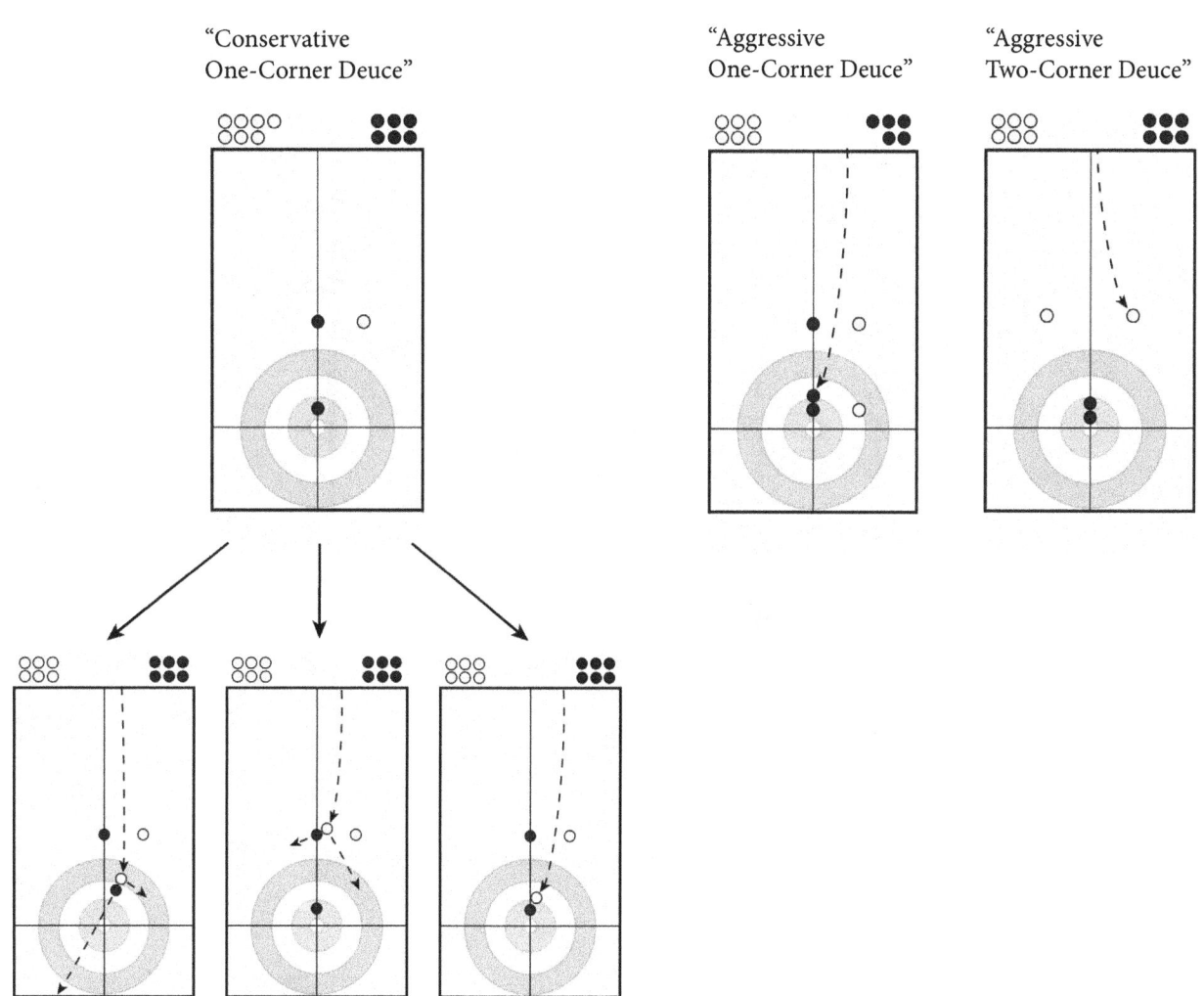

51

"Deuce or Blank"

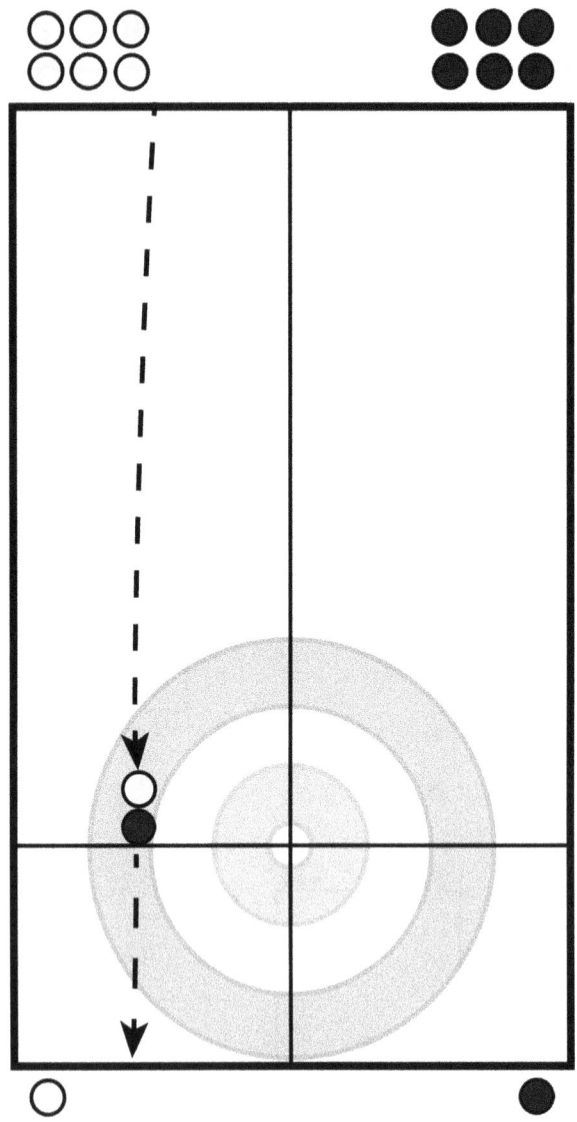

How it works:

The non-hammer team draws into the front center of the rings with its first stone. The hammer team hits and rolls to the wing. Then, the non-hammer team hits and rolls back to the middle. Both teams exchange hits and rolls for the rest of the end.

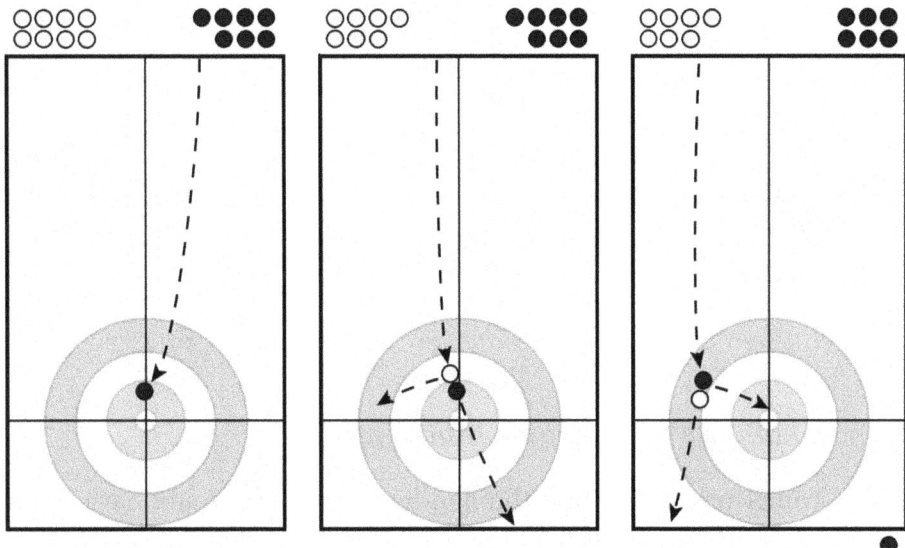

If both teams make all their shots, the hammer team can hit and roll out for a blank.

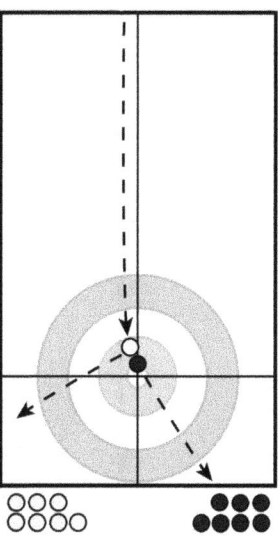

What happens if the non-hammer team misses a shot?

If the non-hammer team hits but stays on the wing, the hammer team will still take out that rock. (The alternative would be to use that rock to freeze or guard—we'll see that in the next section, "Open Deuce.") By hitting here, the hammer team keeps the blank option alive.

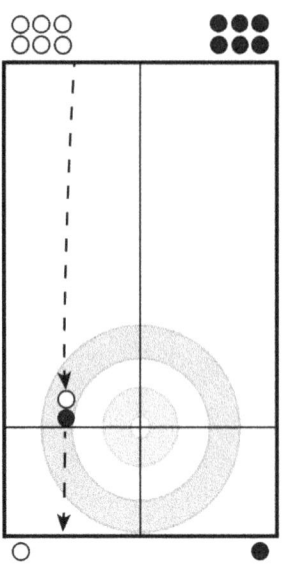

If the non-hammer team misses a hit completely, the hammer team can draw to the other side of the rings and "split the house" to set up a deuce.

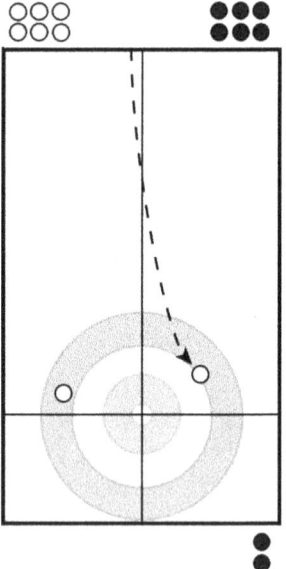

How does the non-hammer team recover from a miss?

To recover from a completely missed hit, the non-hammer team would have to make a double takeout. If it can't, a good alternative is to hit-and-roll to sit near or in front of one of the hammer team's stones. This could make the non-hammer team's rock difficult to take out. If the hammer team did make the takeout, the non-hammer team might have an easier double later. If that doesn't work, the non-hammer team will have to make a great freeze with its last rock to avoid giving up two.

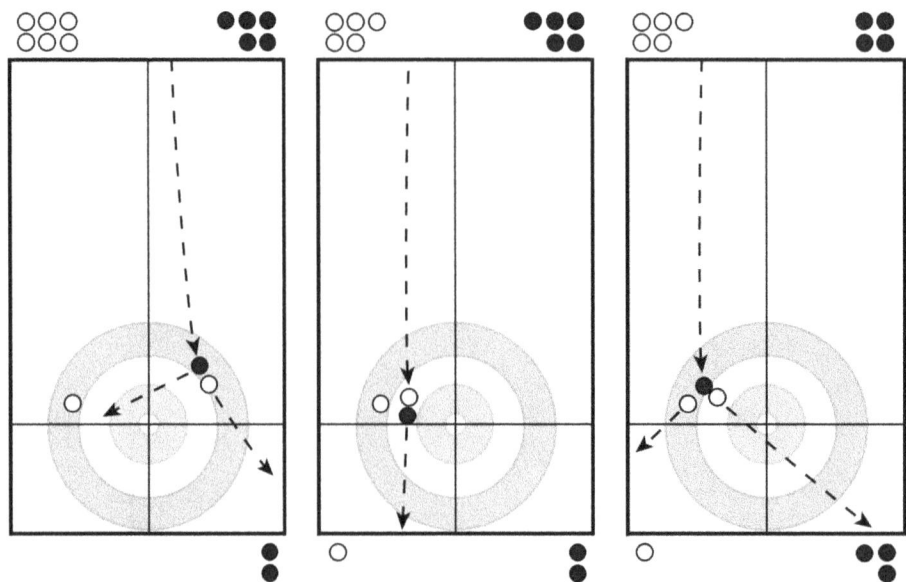

In this sequence, the non-hammer team attempts the double but only gets a hit-and-roll. The hammer team takes it out, but doesn't roll. Now, the non-hammer team has an easy double to save itself from giving up a deuce.

What happens if the hammer team misses a shot?

If the hammer team flashes a hit, the non-hammer team could guard its rock to steal or force one.

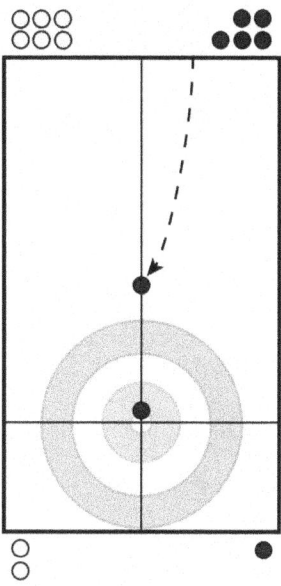

Why choose this tactic?

Some teams choose this approach early in the game when the score is close. They might do it for a number of reasons, including: to play quickly and bank time, to learn the ice, to break down fresh pebble, or to give themselves simple shots while they get through early-game jitters. Some teams also choose this tactic if they think they hit significantly better than their opponents. (This tactic has the nickname, the "Junior Deuce," for that reason. Often, juniors expect other juniors to miss lots of shots, so they don't worry about making moves to generate points, they just wait for their opponents to make a mistake.)

A hammer team that chooses this "Deuce or Blank" plan might have a goal chart that looks like this:

Hammer Team's Goal Chart
  Want: Score 2 or Blank
  Accept: Score 1
  Strongly Avoid: Steal

  Pros: Low risk of giving up a steal
  Cons: Low odds of keeping enough rocks in play to score two points

"Open Deuce"

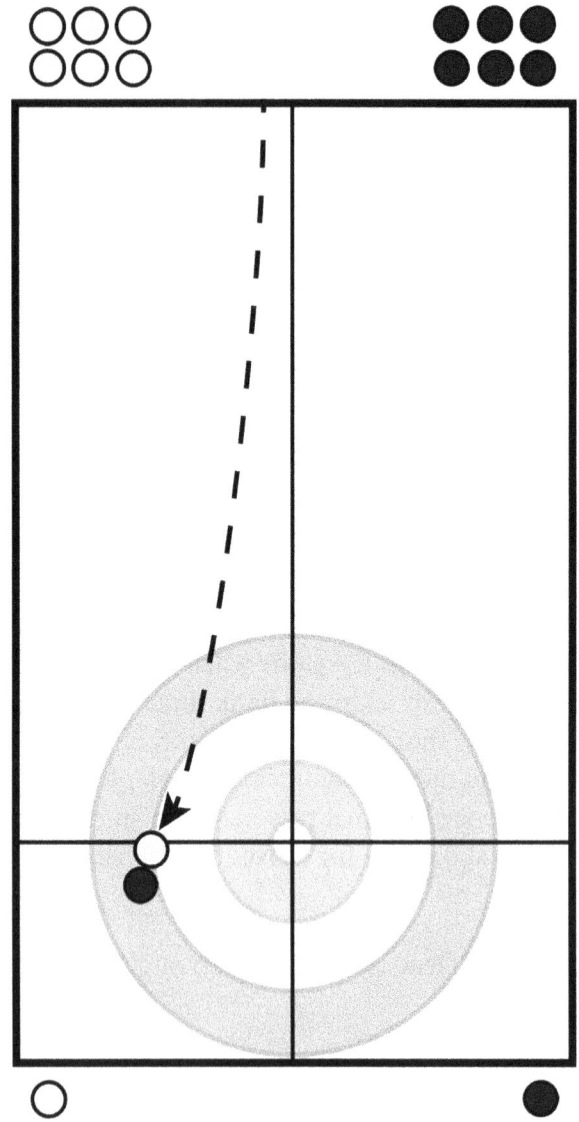

How it works:

The non-hammer team draws into the front center of the rings with its first stone. The hammer team hits and rolls to the wing. The non-hammer team hits and sticks on the wing or rolls behind the tee line. Now, instead of hitting, the hammer team freezes to the non-hammer team's stone to sit shot with backing.

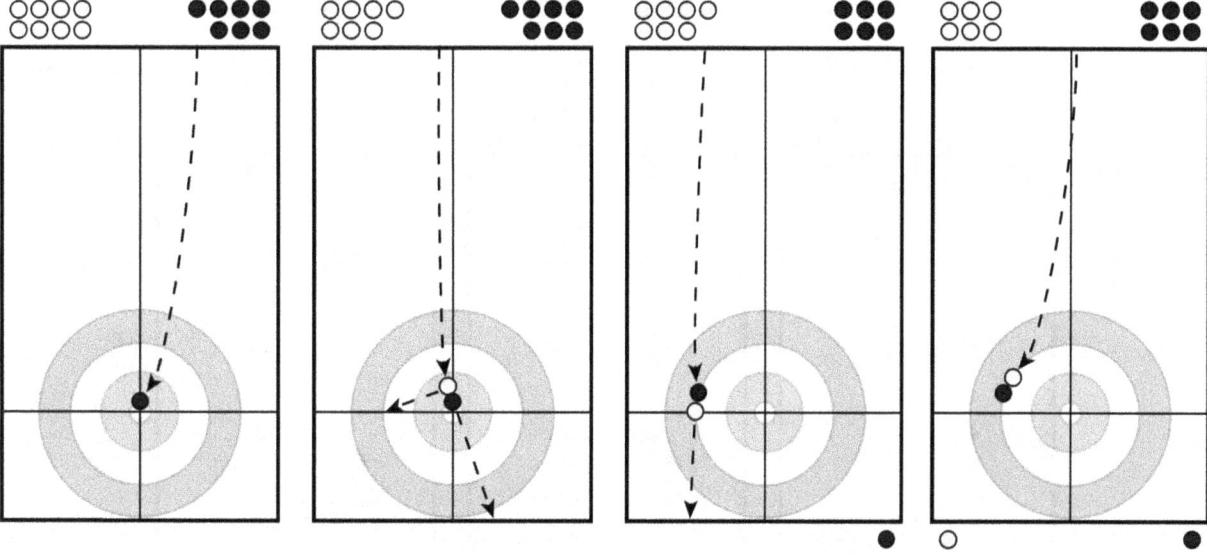

The non-hammer team hits, trying to take out the hammer team's rock or remove both stones. If the hammer team's freeze is good, its rock will likely stick around. The hammer team can then split the house to get two points.

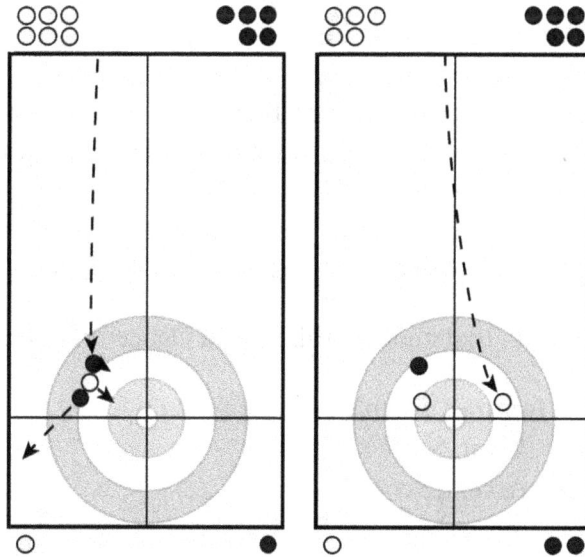

How does the non-hammer team recover?

The non-hammer team will have to make a double takeout to get the end back on track, or a good freeze with its last shot to avoid giving up two.

What happens if the hammer team misses?

If the hammer team doesn't make a good enough freeze, the non-hammer team can take its rock out and stay for second shot. The hammer team would then try freezing again. If the hammer team continues to miss, its skip could be forced to draw against multiple stones with the last rock.

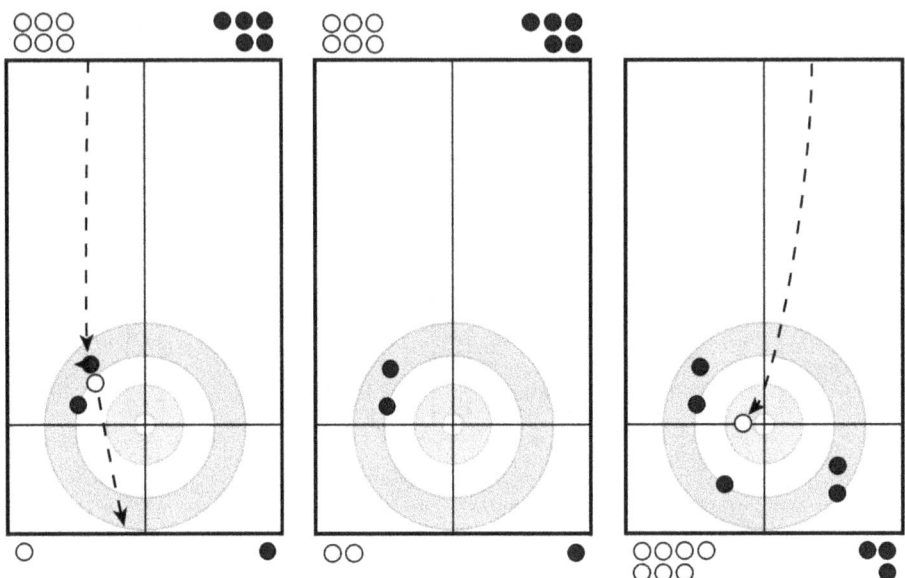

Why choose this tactic?

Why choose this tactic? This is a relatively low-risk way to score two, since the center stays clear and the hammer team's skip can bail out the end with a draw to the button. A hammer team might choose this tactic early in the game when the score is close—if its skip feels confident with his or her draw weight. This tactic can also help the hammer team members get a feel for draw weight, since they will be drawing while their opponents hit.

A team that chooses this "Open Deuce" plan might have a goal chart that looks like this:

<u>**Hammer Team's Goal Chart**</u>
    Want: Score 2 or Blank
    Accept: Score 1
    Strongly Avoid: Steal

  Pros: Relatively low risk of a steal since the center stays open
  Cons: The hammer team's skip had better have draw weight in case the team misses shots!

"Tick Deuce"

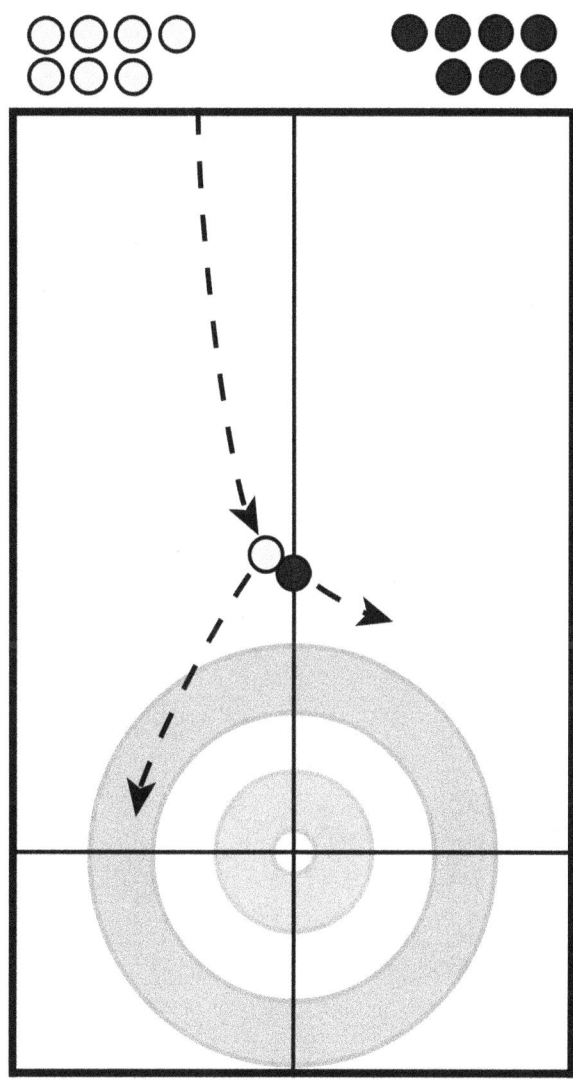

How it works:

The non-hammer team sets up a center guard with its first stone. The hammer team moves the non-hammer team's stone away from the center with a light hit or draw-weight tick shot.

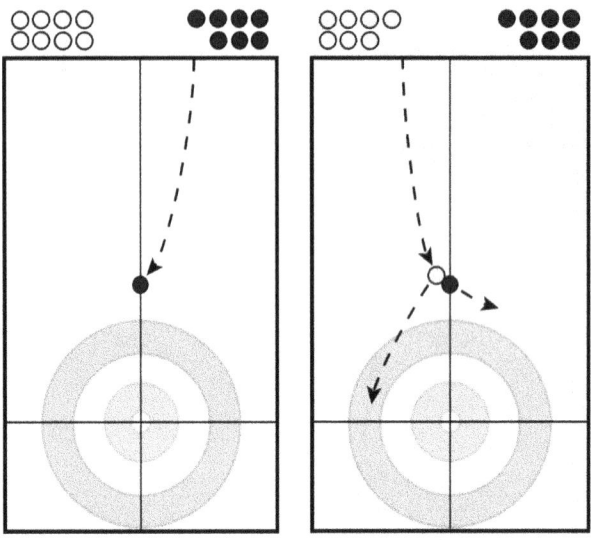

All of these ticks are helpful:

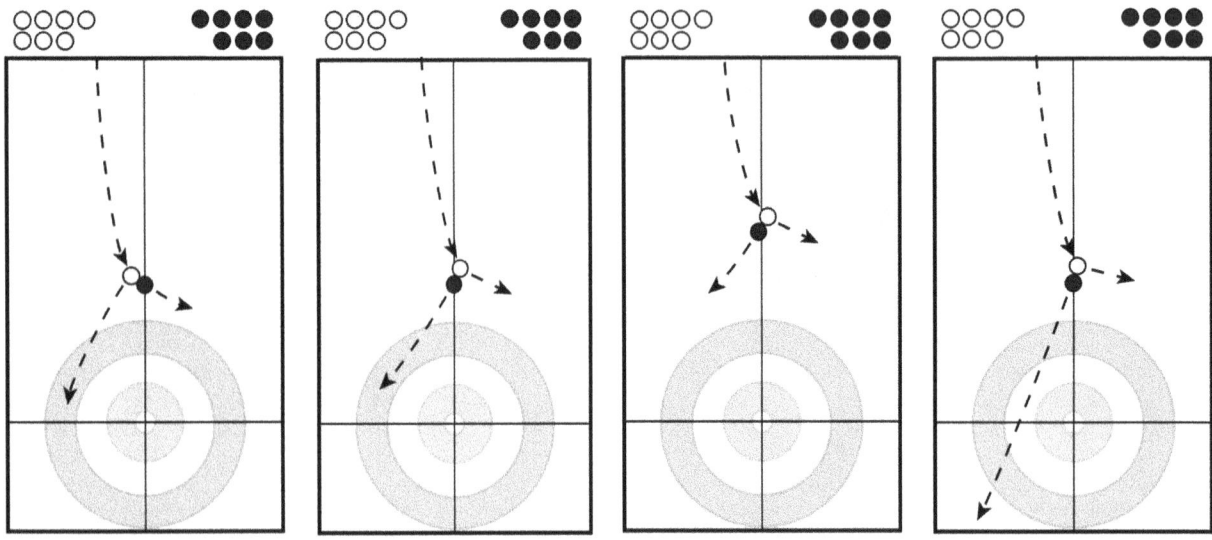

Why choose this tactic?

This tactic is used more often as a defensive "Prevent the non-hammer team from stealing" move than a play to get a deuce. However, it could be a good deuce plan for a team that is out-matched by its opponent and usually gives up a steal if its opponent is able to establish a center guard.

A hammer team that chooses this "Tick Deuce" plan might have a goal chart that looks like this:

Hammer Team's Goal Chart
    Want: Score 2 or Blank
    Accept: Score 1
    Strongly Avoid: Steal

Pros: If your team can execute the tick shot, this is a great tactic that can eliminate non-hammer team threats while simultaneously setting up offense.

Cons: Ticks are tough shots. If you miss, you could make things much worse. For example, if the shooter throws too much weight, the shot could miss the guard completely, or, if it made contact, it could take out the guard, violating the Free Guard Zone. In both those cases, the shot achieves nothing. Worse, if the hammer team uses a light weight, it risks accidentally tapping the guard straight back—giving its opponent shot rock behind a center guard.

"Center Pile Deuce"

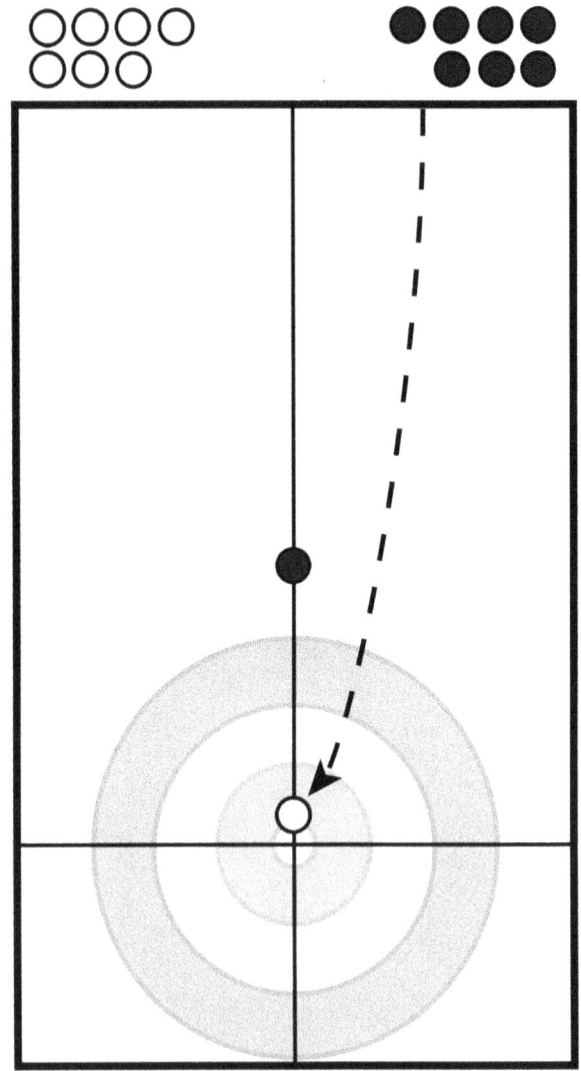

How it works:

The non-hammer team puts up a center guard. The hammer team draws around it in front of the button. Both teams continue to play to the center, mostly with draws and bumps. The hammer team hopes to make a good draw or hit with its last rock to score two. (To see details of how this might play out, see "Simple End 2" from the "Strategy Basics" section earlier in the book.)

This isn't an easy way to get a deuce, but by occupying the scoring spot on the button first, the hammer team can make it difficult for the non-hammer team to steal. That being said, because there are so many rocks in play, the hammer team might be able to score three or more if the non-hammer team misses a critical shot.

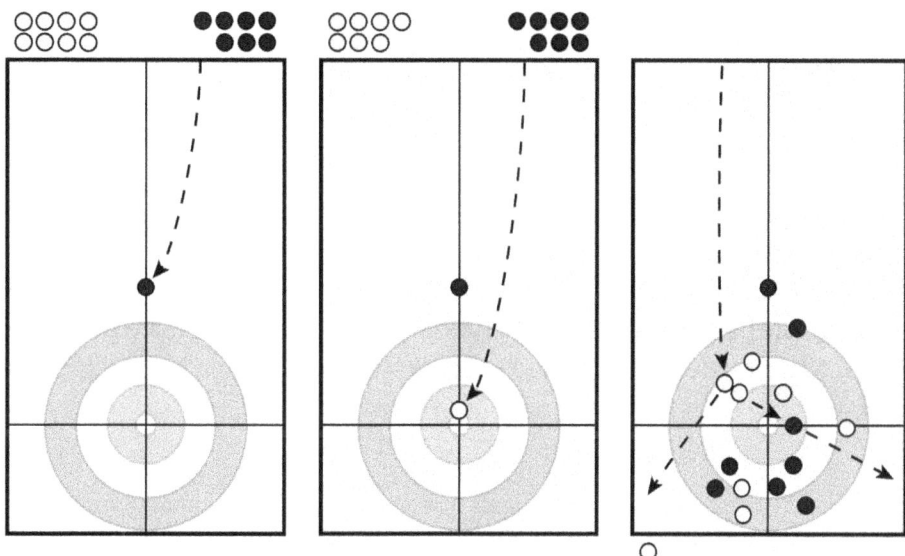

Why choose this tactic?

Two reasons a team might choose this tactic are: (1) At that point in the game, it is more important to prevent a steal than to score two points, or (2) The hammer team members don't hit well. Let's look at these reasons in more detail:

Reason 1: *"Don't allow a steal"*

In this case, the hammer team would like to score two points, but doesn't absolutely need to. Its goal chart might look like this:

> **Hammer Team's Goal Chart**
> Want: Score 2, Blank
> Accept: Score 1
> Strongly Avoid: Steal

By using this tactic and fighting for position in the center, the hammer team makes it hard for the non-hammer team to steal. At the same time, because rocks are accumulating in the rings, the hammer team may have a opportunity to make a good shot with its last rock to get two or more points.

Reason 2: *"The hammer team can't hit well"*

In this case, the hammer team really wants or needs to score two points. Normally, when a team wants to score two points, it uses more aggressive tactics (like those you'll see in a moment involving corner guards). However in this situation, the team members' range of tactical choices is limited by their shooting ability. (Remember "Simple End 3" from the "Strategy Basics" section earlier in the book? In that example, the hammer team spent time putting up a corner guard to develop its offense, while its opponent built up stones in the middle. The hammer team then had to throw double takeouts to get out of trouble. If the hammer team can't hit well, it won't do well with a strategy that relies on making those shots.)

So even though the hammer team's goal chart might look like this:

<u>**Hammer Team's Goal Chart**</u>
  Strongly Want: Score 2
  Accept: Score 1 or Blank
  Avoid: Steal

Practically speaking, the hammer team must choose a more conservative tactical plan, because the shots that plan requires are easier for it to execute—thus giving it a better chance at an acceptable outcome.

- **Pros:** Although this is a conservative tactic, it allows teams to get multiple rocks into play, which makes it possible to score multiple points.
- **Cons:** When both teams are fighting for a spot on the button, the scoring area becomes small and it can be difficult to get more than one rock into scoring position.

"Open Wing Deuce"

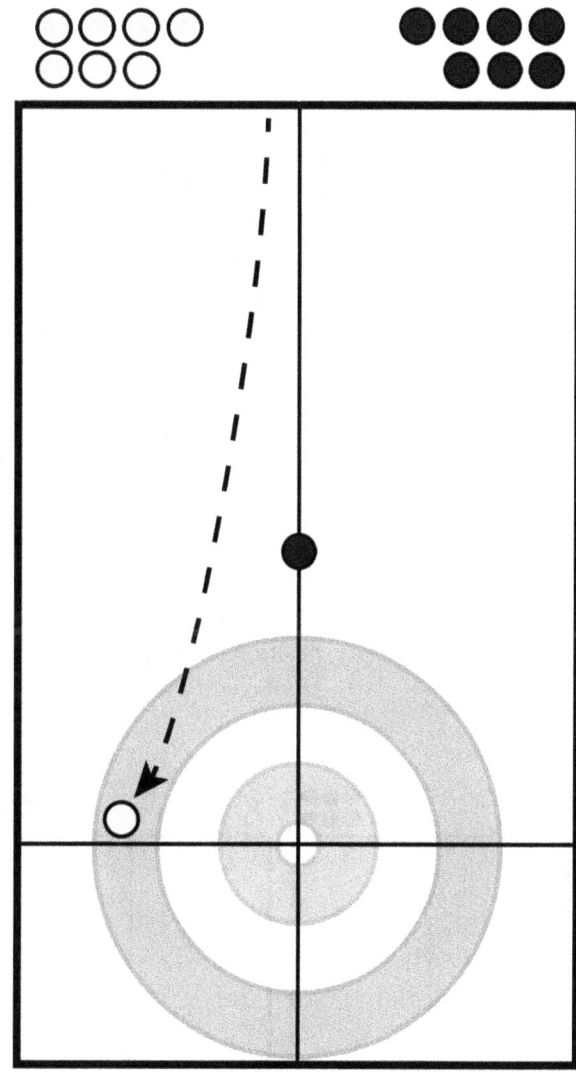

How it works:

The non-hammer team puts up a center guard. The hammer team ignores the threat and draws to the wing just above the tee line. (Alternatively, the hammer team could draw to the back corner.)

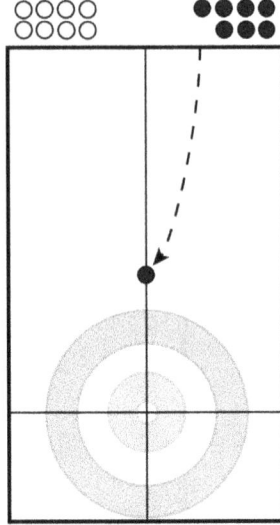

The non-hammer team puts up a guard with its first rock.

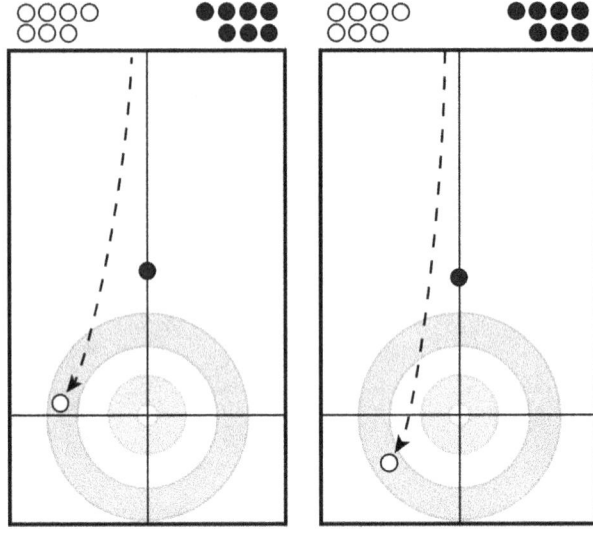

The hammer team could draw to the wing, either on or behind the tee line. The advantage of drawing behind the tee line is that the non-hammer team can't hit and roll off that rock to a good stealing position. The disadvantage is that the non-hammer team could freeze to that rock to out-count it.

Either way, this forces the non-hammer team to make a choice—play conservatively and hit the hammer team's stone to minimize the chance of giving up two, or play aggressively to steal by drawing behind the center guard or by putting up another center guard.

Let's look at how these choices could play out….

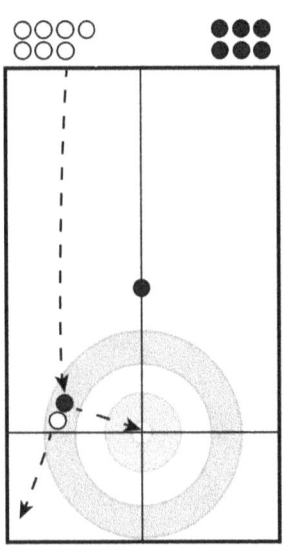

Conservative choice

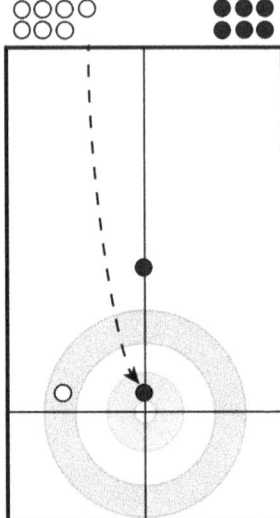

Moderately aggressive choice

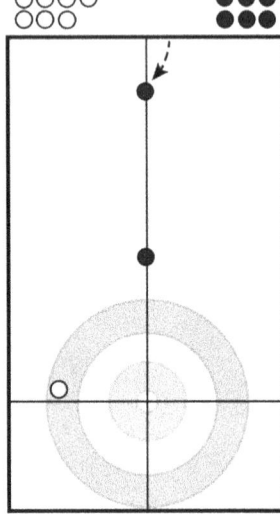

Highly aggressive choice

Non-hammer team responds conservatively

If the non-hammer team is playing conservatively, it would likely try to hit and roll behind the center guard. This tactic is considered conservative, because it is more focused on preventing the hammer team from scoring two than it is on helping the non-hammer team to achieve its goal to steal or force one. If the non-hammer team doesn't make a perfect roll, the hammer team could hit it and roll back to the wing.

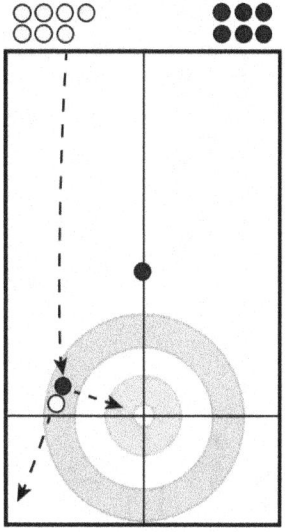
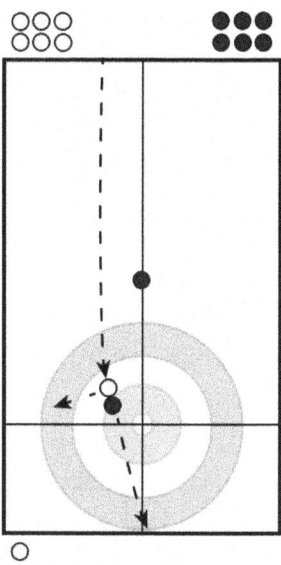

This a bit like the "Deuce or Blank" and "Open Deuce" tactics, but with one major difference. The non-hammer team could change tactics at any point and draw behind the center guard to steal or force. If the non-hammer team makes a great draw with its last shot, the hammer team could have a tough time scoring.

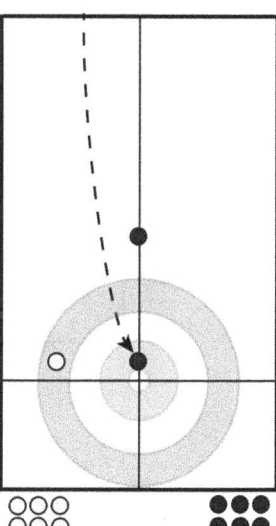

Non-hammer team responds moderately aggressively

If the non-hammer team is playing moderately aggressively to steal, it might draw in behind the center guard. Now the hammer team can play to that stone in the center the same way it might in the "Center Pile Deuce." The major difference now is that the hammer team has a rock stashed on the wing that it could use as a second point later.

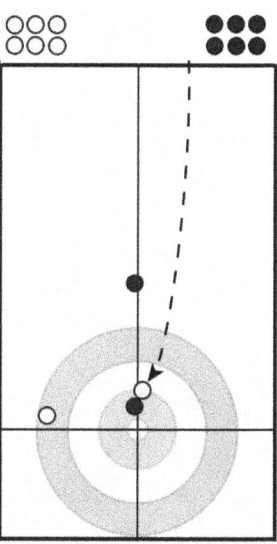

Non-hammer team responds highly aggressively

If the non-hammer team is playing highly aggressively to steal, it might put up a second center guard. The hammer team could respond conservatively and tick the top guard to begin clearing the front. The hammer team could respond moderately conservatively and draw behind the center guards to block the steal by occupying the button first. Finally, the hammer team could respond highly aggressively and draw to the side again to accumulate more possible scoring rocks. (Again, conservative is defined as focusing on foiling your opponent's plans, and aggressive is defined as ignoring your opponent while focusing on building your own offense.) Either way, the hammer team may eventually need to make some double takeouts to clear the front and prevent a steal.

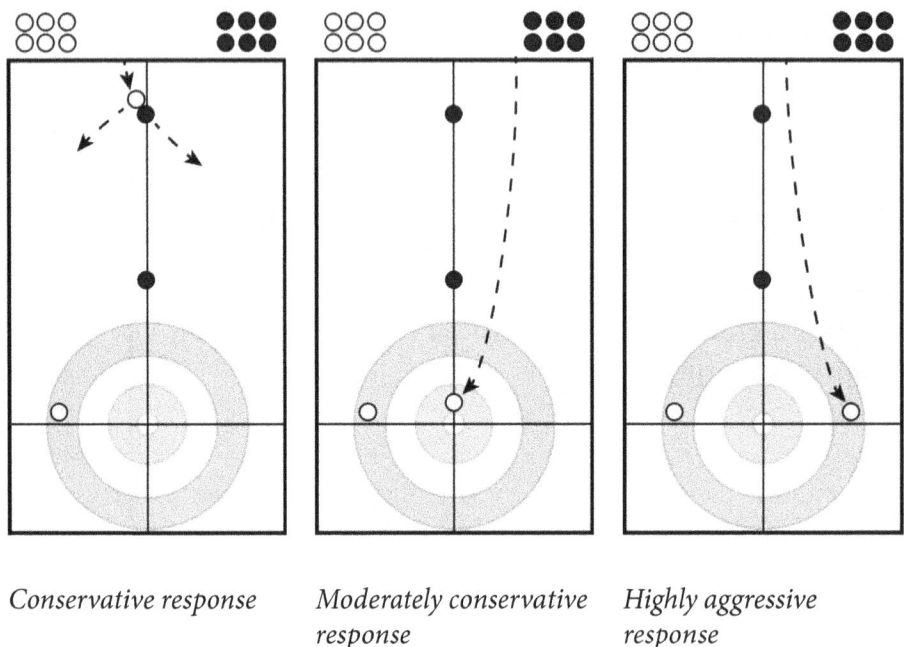

Conservative response   *Moderately conservative response*   *Highly aggressive response*

Why choose this tactic?

A hammer team might choose this tactic if it wanted to play a conservative end (like a "Blank," "Deuce or Blank," or an "Open Deuce") but the non-hammer team didn't oblige by putting its first rock in the rings.

Alternatively, a hammer team that knows its opponent is keen to steal and is very confident in its own ability to make double takeouts might use this tactic as a way to load the house with stones to score a big end.

Pros: This can be a way to pressure an otherwise aggressive non-hammer team back into a conservative mode.

Cons: This allows the non-hammer team time to put up a second center guard, which increases the risk of a steal.

"Conservative One-Corner Deuce"

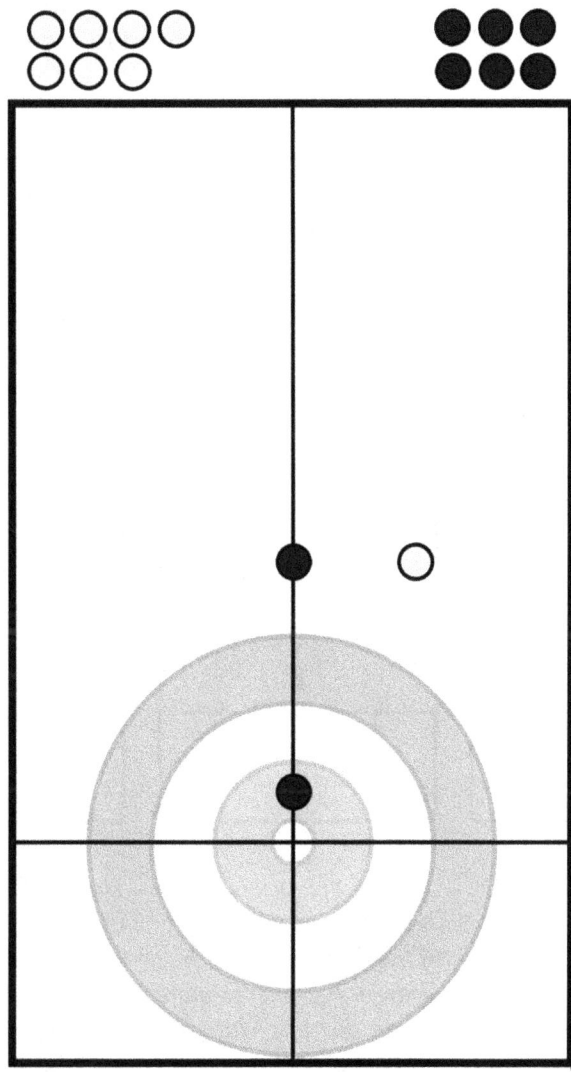

How it works:

The non-hammer team sets up a center guard and a rock near the button with its first two stones. (For this discussion, we won't worry about whether the non-hammer team threw the center guard or the rock on the button first. For more on how non-hammer teams make that decision, see the upcoming chapters on "Steals" and "Forces".)

The hammer team ignores the non-hammer team's first rock, and uses its own first rock to put up a corner guard. By doing this, the hammer team has developed its own offense, because the corner guard creates a place to hide rocks.

However, the hammer team doesn't wait too long to address the dangerous non-hammer team stones in the middle of the sheet. With its second rock, the hammer team makes one of the following three plays on the center, depending on the exact position of the non-hammer team's stones:

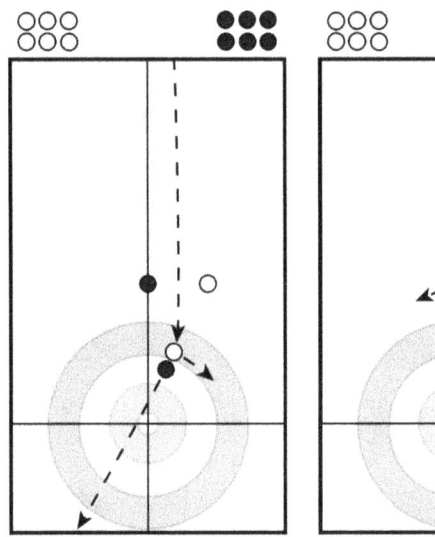

Hit-and-roll—if the rock is exposed

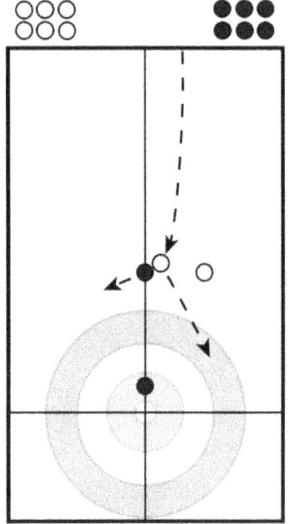

Tick—if the rock is buried (or as a "Plan B" if the shooter misses the draw or hit. There's more about "Plan Bs" later in the book!)

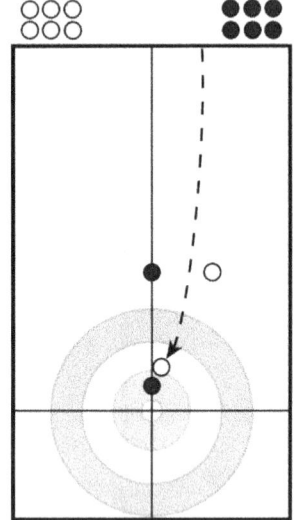

Draw—if the rock is buried and can't easily be moved. (This is the start of a very common shot sequence. For more on this, see the "Tips for Using Center Guards" section coming up!)

Notice that the hammer team doesn't necessarily plan to use its corner guard right away. The team set it up so it might have a chance to hit and roll behind it at some point in the end. It's possible the hammer team might never get to use that corner guard.

Why choose this tactic?

A hammer team might choose a "Conservative One-Corner Deuce" tactic when it wants to create a good opportunity to score two points, but doesn't want to wait a long time to attack the opponent stones in the middle and risk giving up a steal. The hammer team's end goal chart might look like this:

Hammer Team's Goal Chart
  Want: Score 2
  Accept: Score 1 or Blank
  Avoid: Steal

Pros: This is a flexible, middle-of-the-road tactic that uses shots which are relatively easy to execute (for example, single takeouts instead of double takeouts.)

Cons: The hammer team will probably need to make a very good hit-and-roll at some point in order to use the corner guard.

"Aggressive One-Corner Deuce"

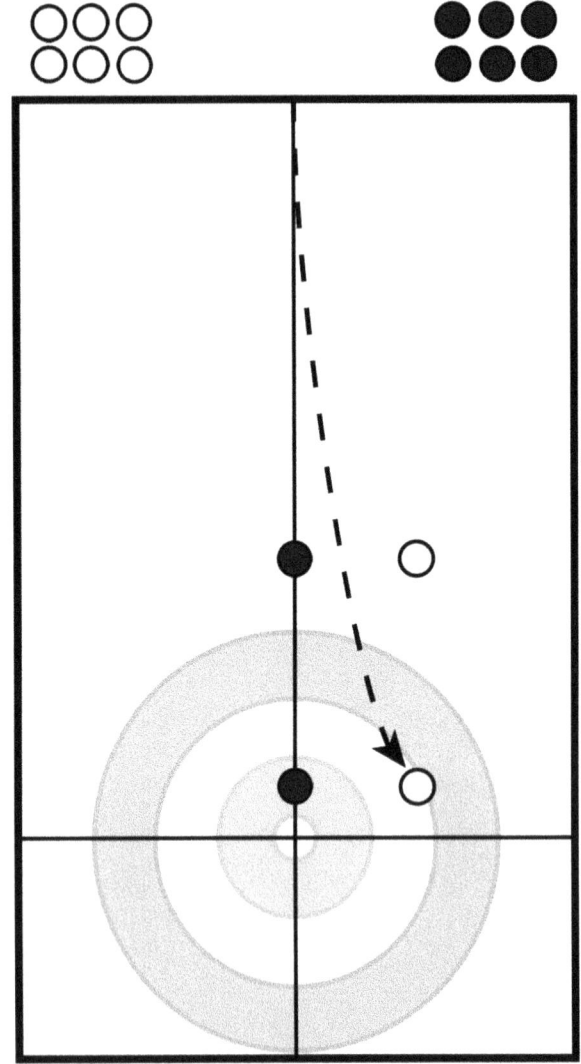

How it works:

The hammer team urgently needs two points and is very focused on setting up its own offense. While the non-hammer team establishes a center guard and rock near the button, the hammer team sets up a corner guard, then draws behind it. What happens next depends on the non-hammer team's goals and tactical choices. Let's look at a few possibilities:

If the non-hammer team wants to steal aggressively, it might put up a second center guard.

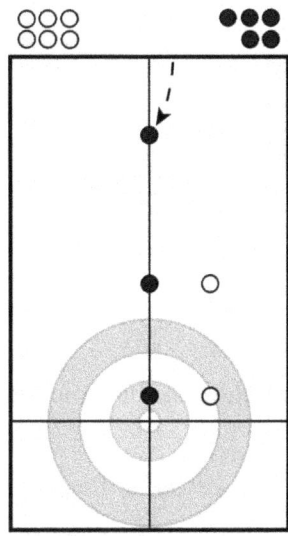

If the non-hammer team wants to steal a little more conservatively or force, it might freeze to its own rock near the button.

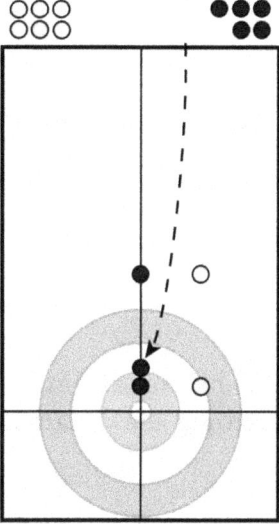

If the non-hammer team wants to force the hammer team to score one (or minimize the number of points it can score), it might hit or freeze to the hammer team's stone in the rings.

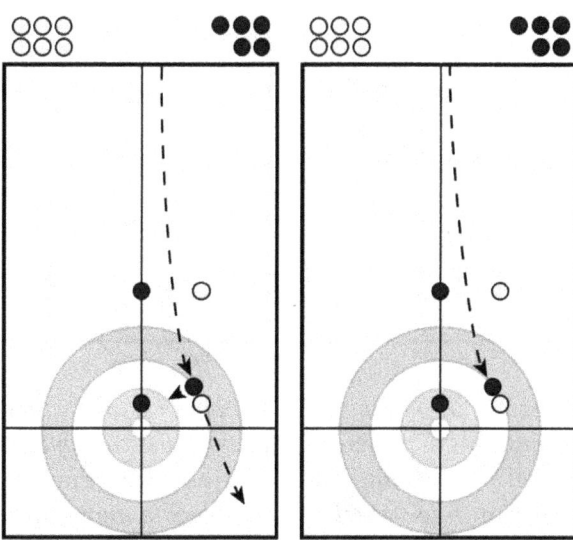

If the non-hammer team is focused on minimizing the number of points the hammer team can score, it might take out the hammer team's corner guard, or play a double takeout on both of the hammer team's stones. (The double is a good choice if the hammer team's stones are close together.)

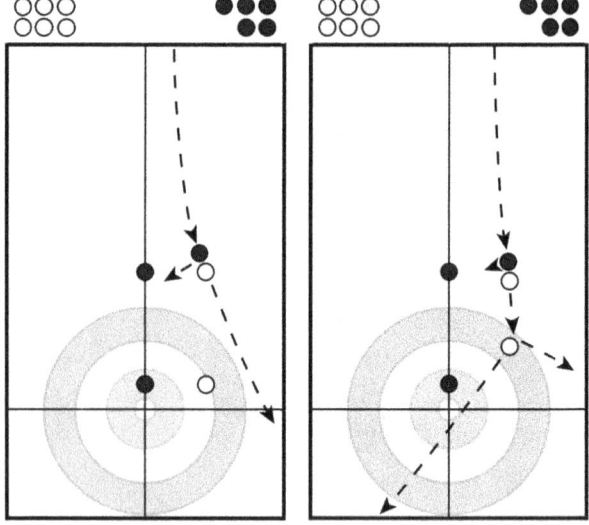

The hammer team's third shot will depend on what the non-hammer team has done, of course! Here are a few examples:

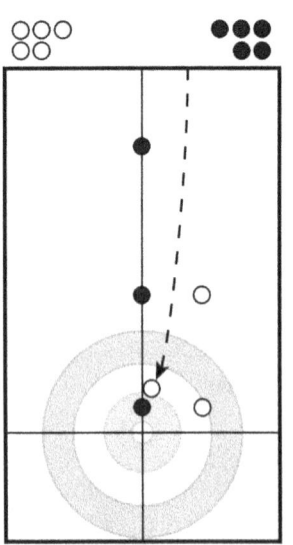 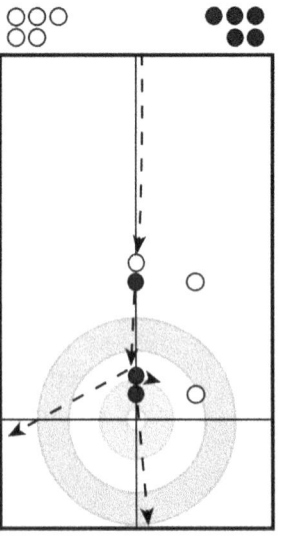 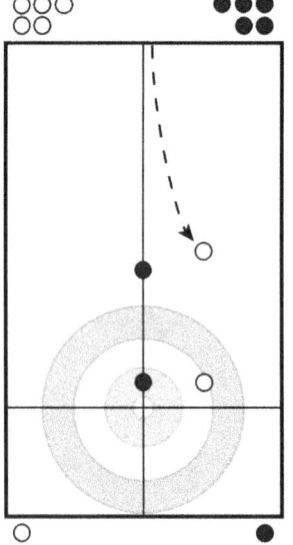 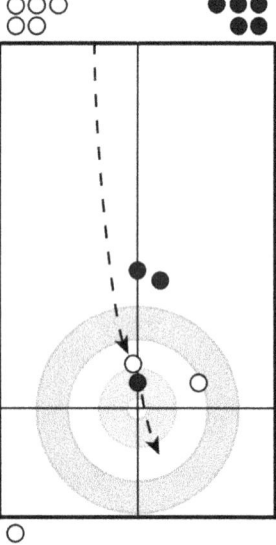

Freeze—if the hammer team wants to prevent a steal but can't hit well enough to clear the guards, or if it needs two points very badly and wants to use the opponent guards to protect its own rocks

Runback (or takeout the guard)—if it can't move the frozen stones by hitting or bumping them directly

Replace the guard—if the hammer team is significantly behind and absolutely must get two points

Tap the shot rock—if the non-hammer team is more worried about preventing a steal than scoring two, or if it thinks it can still get two without a corner guard

Why choose this tactic?

A hammer team would chose this tactic if it is significantly behind in points and is willing to risk giving up a steal for a better chance to get a second point. (Again, the paradox of aggressive tactics is that they raise the chances of very good outcomes and very bad outcomes at the same time. This is because both teams have more developed offensive positions and more rocks in play.)

The hammer team's goal chart might look like this:

Hammer Team's Goal Chart
Strongly Want: Score 2
Accept: Score 1
Avoid: Steal 1

Pros: This tactic does a good job of setting up a second point for the hammer team.

Cons: The hammer team will probably need to make at least one double takeout in the middle—or some very good taps around the center guard—to count that second point.

"Aggressive Two-Corner Deuce"

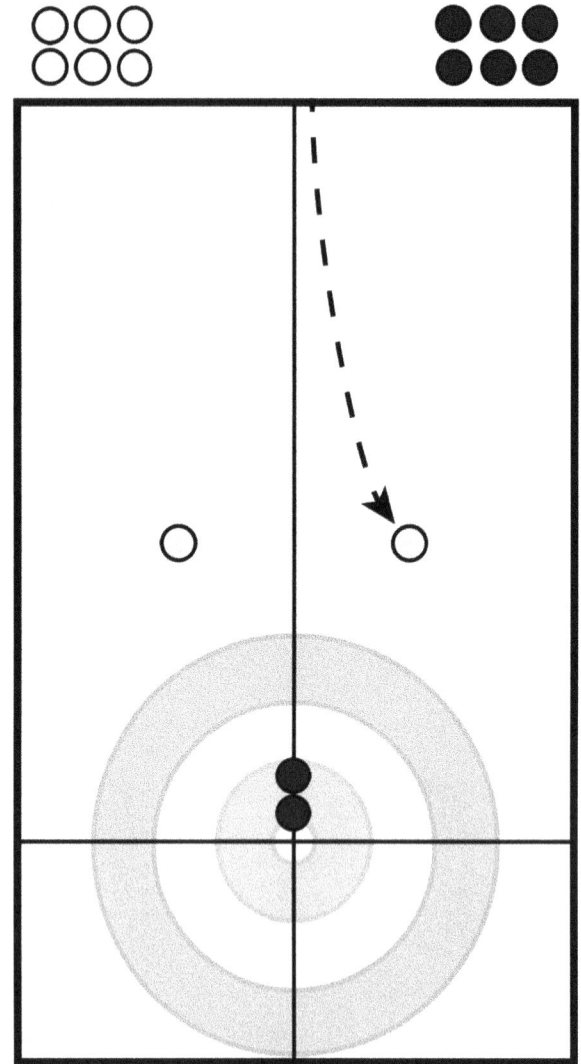

How it works:

A hammer team that chooses this tactic is desperate to score two (or more) points. In the main image, I've show the non-hammer team with two stones frozen in the middle. That is a common configuration when the non-hammer team has a two or three point lead and wants to prevent the hammer team from scoring more than one point. However, if the score or the non-hammer team's end goals are a little different, the non-hammer team may make different shot choices. Here are a few examples:

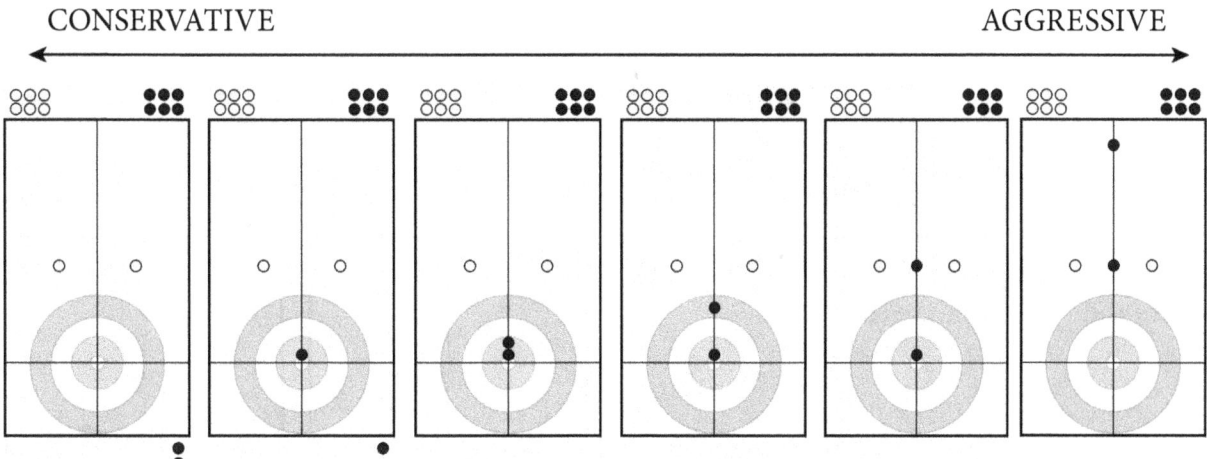

Non-hammer team's shot choices: On the very conservative end of the spectrum, a non-hammer team with a big lead (e.g., more than three points in the final end) might throw both rocks through the house so the hammer team can't use them for backing. On the very aggressive end of the spectrum, a non-hammer team might put up two center guards if it were desperate to steal or force.

Let's see how the main example might play out. The hammer team now has two problems—it needs to get at least two rocks into the rings, and it needs to move the non-hammer team's shot stones. In the meantime, the non-hammer team will remove the corner guards so the hammer team can't hide stones.

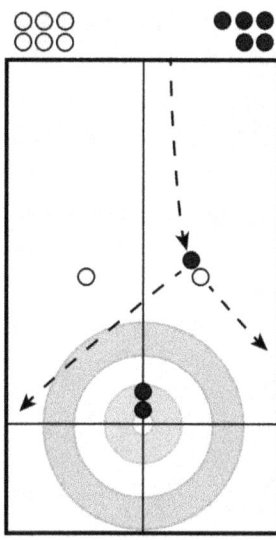

The hammer team would likely replace those corner guards for a few turns.

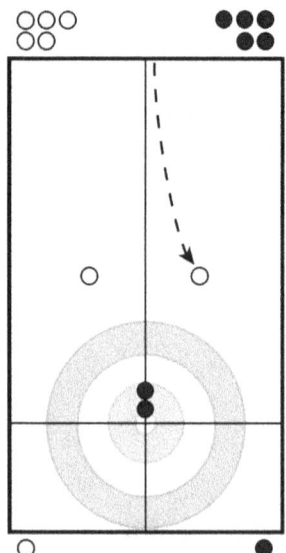

The hammer team must be careful to keep the guards level. If one is higher than the other, the non-hammer team can remove both with a double takeout.

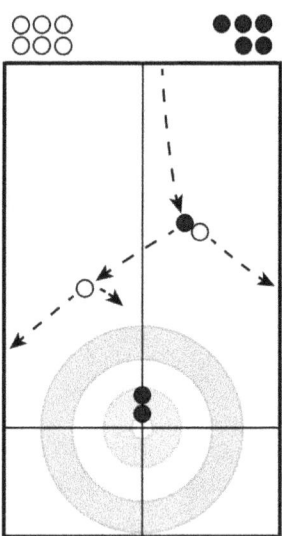

The hammer team is hoping the non-hammer team will miss by flashing a hit or by nose-hitting a corner guard. Then it can hit the shot stones and roll behind cover.

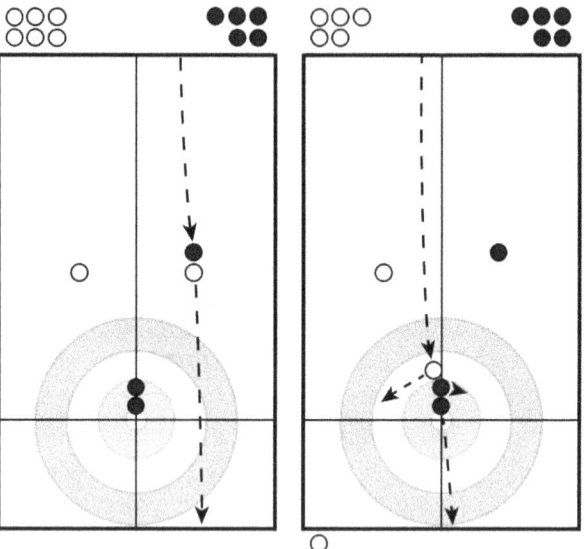

If after a few turns the hammer team doesn't get any breaks, it will have to stop replacing the guards and focus on getting rocks in the rings. The hammer team would then have to creatively use the non-hammer team's stones for backing to keep rocks in play. For example, the hammer team can try tapping them.

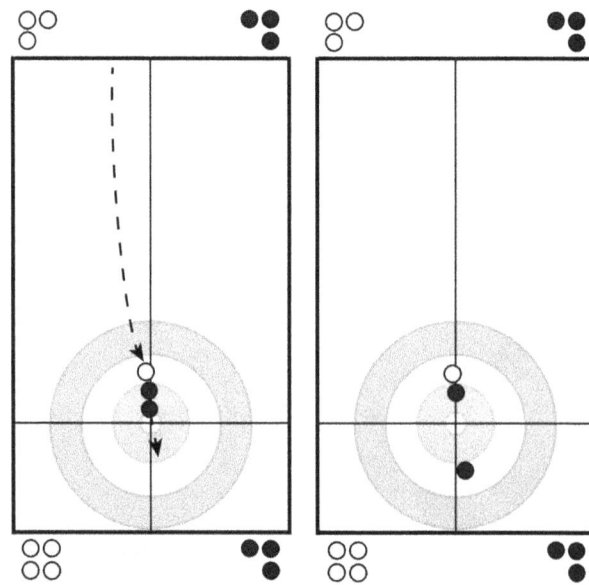

If the hammer team's rock is frozen, it will be difficult for the non-hammer team to remove. If the non-hammer team tries and fails, the hammer team can set up a deuce.

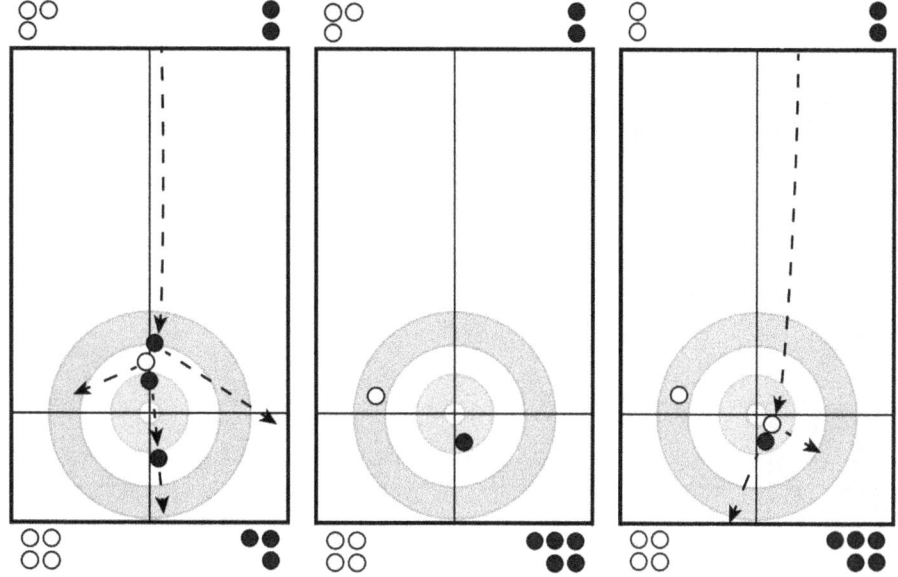

Why choose this tactic?

A hammer team would only choose this tactic if it were significantly behind and needed to take big risks to score two points.

The team's goal chart might look like this:

Hammer Team's Goal Chart
Strongly Want: Score 2
Accept: Score 1
Avoid: Steal

Or, if this were the last end of the game and the hammer team was down by two points, it might look like this:

Hammer Team's Goal Chart
Want: Score 3
Need: Score 2
Can't Accept: Any other outcome

Pros: Two corner guards mean lots of potential cover for the hammer team.
Cons: The hammer team will have a tough time keeping two rocks protected while removing the non-hammer team's shot stones.

Tips for Using Corner Guards

Good corner guards can be the key to success for hammer teams.

How can you use corner guards?

You can draw around them.

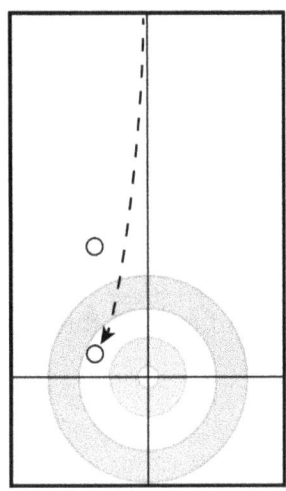

You can tap them into the rings.

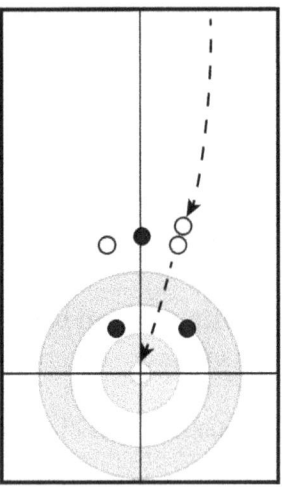

You can run back corner guards to remove rocks near the button.

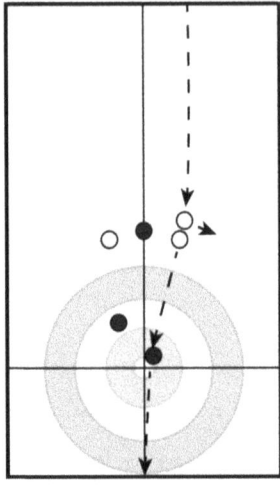

You can use corner guards to prevent your opposition from drawing to the middle.

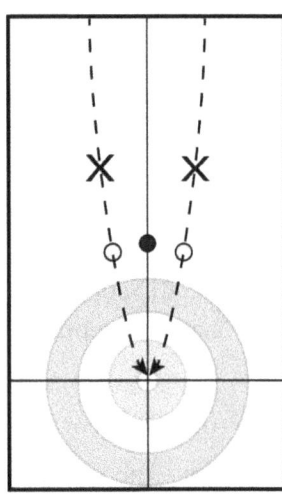

Where should you place corner guards?

Wide Corner Guards

Wider corner guards create a bigger scoring area. Here's how: Since the non-hammer team wants to score or minimize the number of points the hammer team can get, it will want to have shot rock inside the closest hammer team stone. If the hammer team puts up a corner guard and draws behind it, the non-hammer team (and thus the hammer team) will likely end up focusing play inside of the radius of that rock. Thus, the shot rock that scores—whether it belongs to the hammer team or the non-hammer team—will likely be located inside that area of play. So, the wider the corner guards, the more room the hammer team will have to maneuver and score its second point.

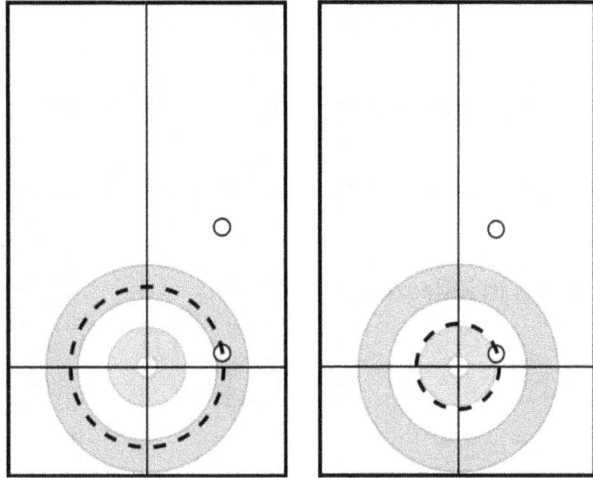

Narrow Corner Guards

There are, however, good reasons to put corner guards close to the middle.

For instance, corner guards that are close to the center line and the rings are more useful for taps, runbacks, and blocking draws to the button.

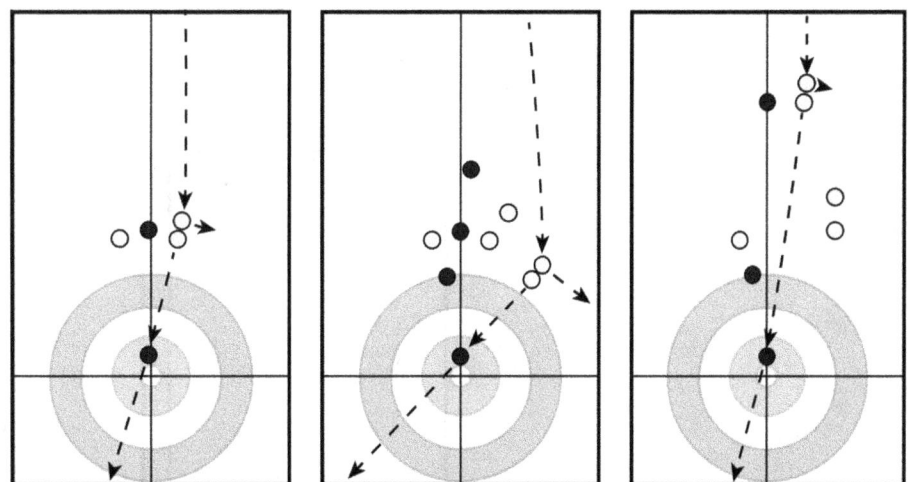

It's easier to run back a tight, narrow corner guard than a wide or high one, because the incoming rock can make contact with the first stationary stone over a wider area and still make the shot.

Corner guards that are closer to the center line can be used to control the draw paths to the button—both to help the hammer team score and to block the non-hammer team from scoring.

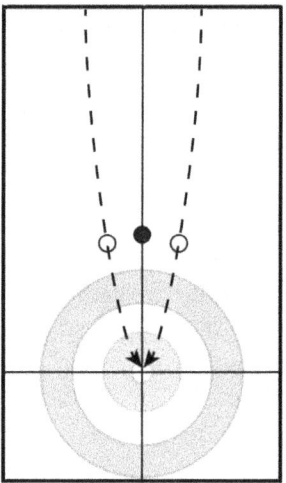

Corner guards that are closer to the center line have more room "behind" them to hide rocks...

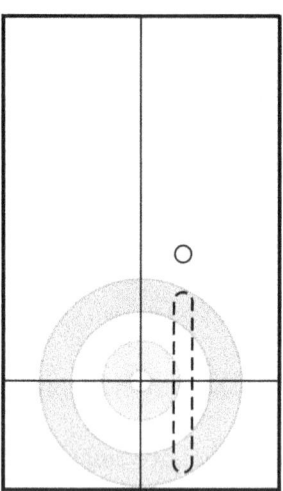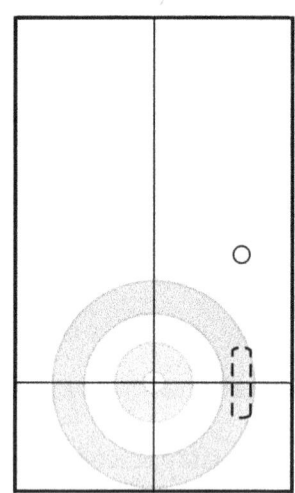

...and you can draw behind them from both sides.

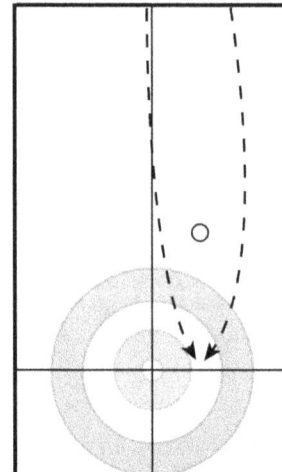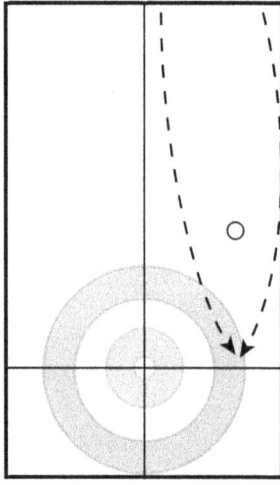

Corner guards that are closer to the center line are easier to roll behind. This is because they are closer to where most of the game play is likely to be, and short rolls are easier than wide rolls, because you can hit a wider area of the stone with a wider range of weights and still make the shot.

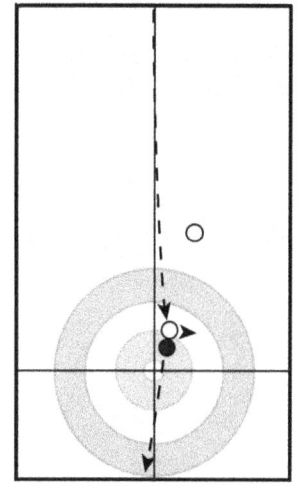 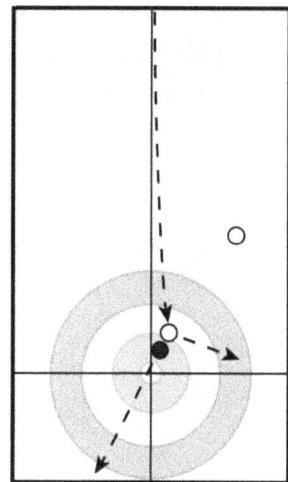

Where should you put a corner guard if you already have one rock in the rings?

Sometimes, when a team is trying to score a deuce, it gets a lucky break and already has a shot rock in place on the side of the rings as it starts its next turn. Where should it put its next rock?

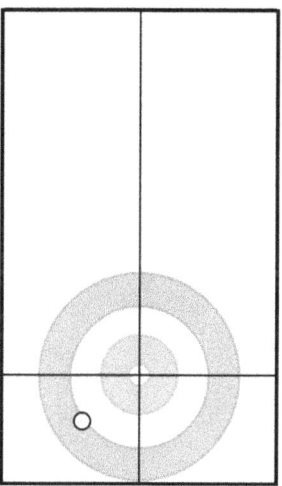

Most of the time, the hammer team will split the house. This makes sense, because the hammer team wants to score two points, and now it has two rocks in the rings!

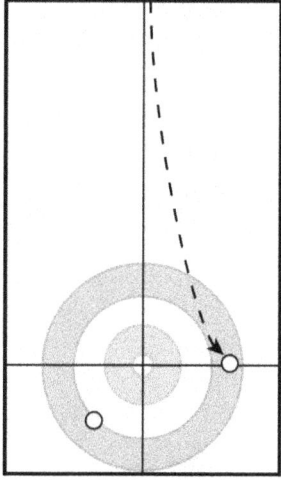

However, sometimes the hammer team feels it needs to put up a corner guard instead. It might do this because its opponent hits very well and could make a cross-house double takeout. Alternatively, the hammer team might decide that now is a good time to upgrade its goal and go for a three-point end.

Now the question becomes, on which side should it put the corner guard?

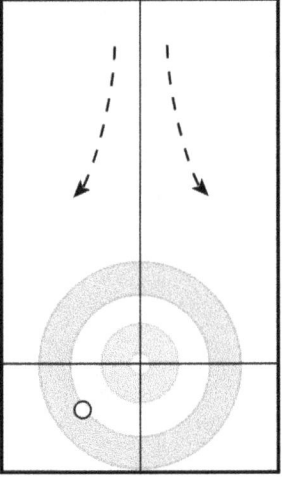

Guard on the Open Side

Guarding the open side is the more conservative choice. This is because it leaves the existing rock open, which might make it possible for the hammer team to blank later if things go wrong.

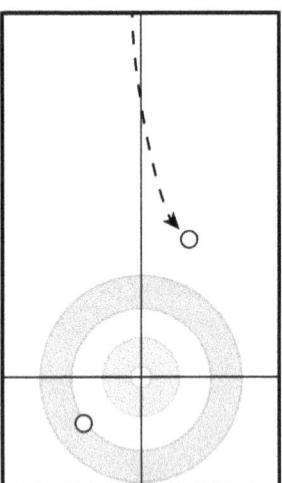

The non-hammer team will likely hit the open stone.

If the non-hammer team's stone stays far enough out, the hammer team can draw behind its guard and be shot.

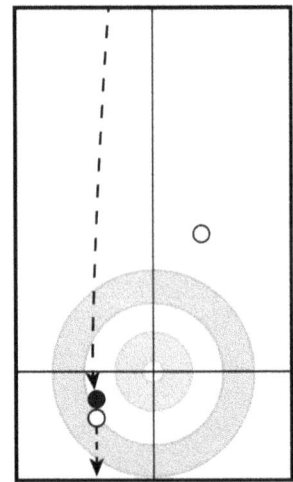
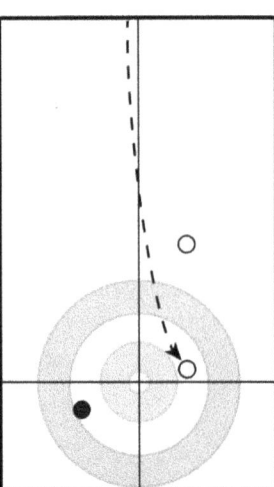

If the non-hammer team rolls closer in than the corner guard, the hammer team can hit that stone and roll behind the corner guard.

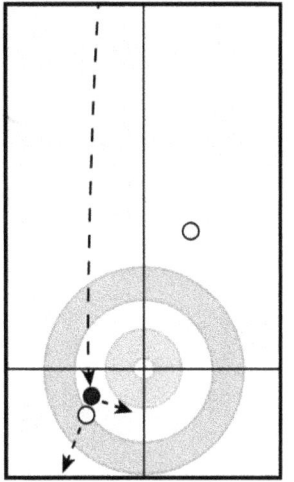 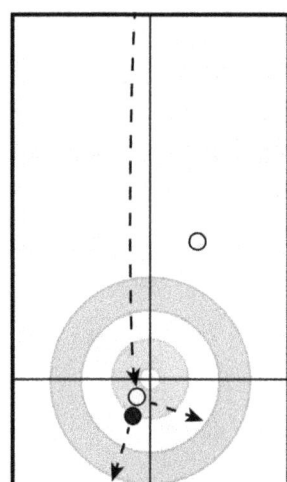

Guard on the Rock Side

Guarding the rock side is the more aggressive choice. By covering the rock in the rings, the hammer team makes it more likely that multiple rocks will still be in play at the end of the end. That improves the hammer team's chances of scoring multiple points, but lowers the odds the hammer team can bail out and change its plan to a blank if a deuce starts looking unlikely.

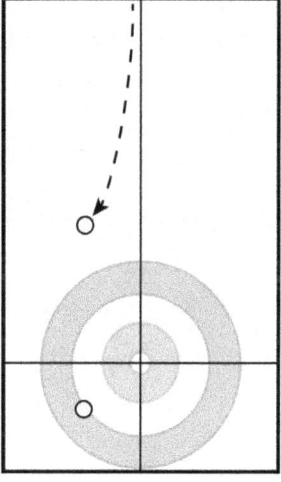

The non-hammer team has a number of choices, including: draw behind the corner guard to out-count the hammer team's stone in the back of the rings; take out the guard and roll out; and take out the rock in the rings. Let's look at them all in more detail....

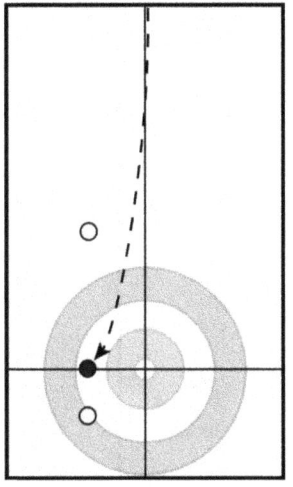 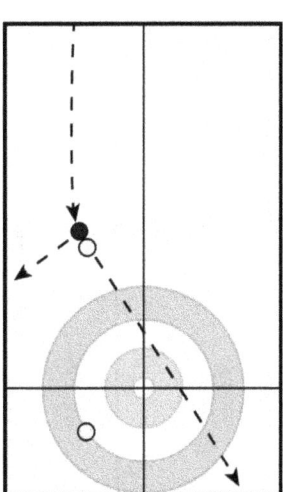 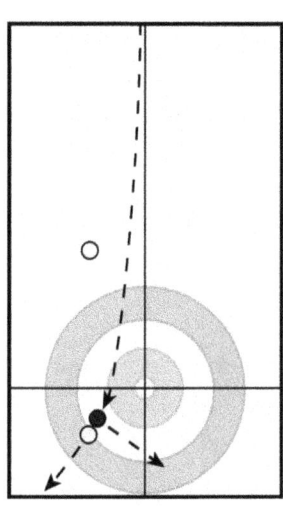

Choice 1: Draw

Let's look at the first choice—the draw. If the non-hammer team successfully draws to the tee line, the hammer team would likely tap that stone in hopes of eventually counting multiple stones.

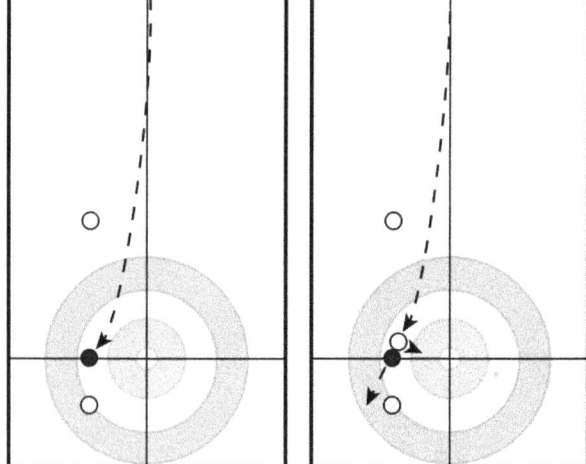

Alternatively, the non-hammer team could freeze to the hammer team's stone. The upside of this is that its rock could be difficult for the non-hammer team to move (though the hammer team could still try with a series of small bumps). The downside is that the hammer team could freeze on top of both stones and be shot.

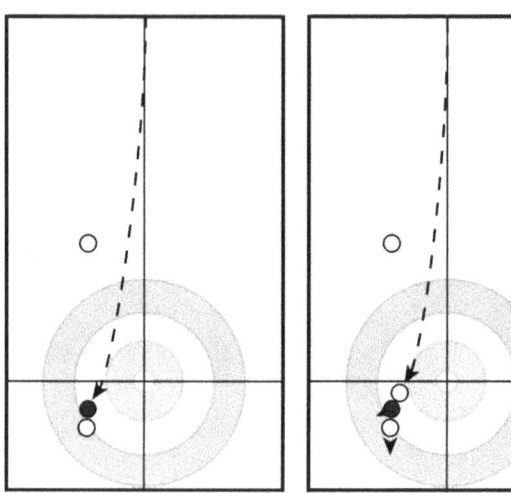

Choice 2: Take Out the Guard

Now let's look at shot choice two: the non-hammer team takes out the guard and rolls the shooter out. If the non-hammer team is successful, the hammer team can simply re-guard.

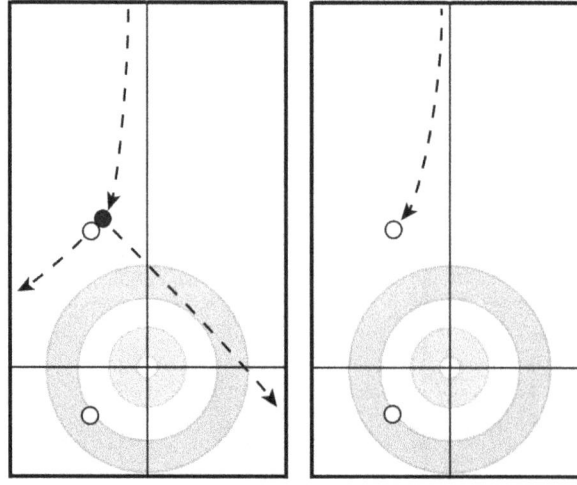

If the non-hammer team attempts to peel the guard and roll out, but misses the roll and leaves its shooter as a new guard, the hammer team can draw behind that rock. In the situation shown here, the end would play out like the "Center Pile Deuce," except that the hammer team has an extra rock on the wing that it could use later to score two or more points.

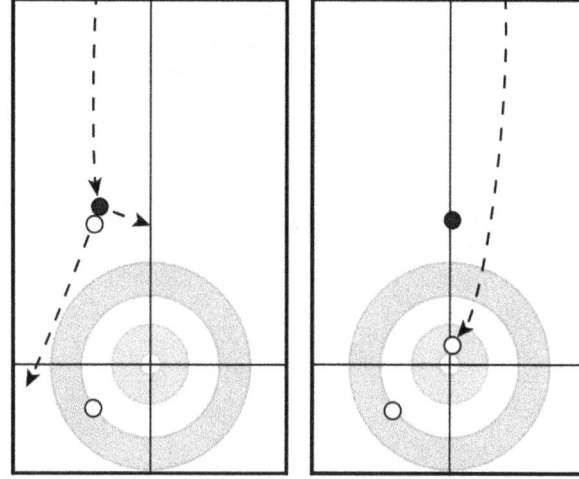

If the non-hammer team misses the hit altogether, the hammer team can go after a three-point end. (More on this in the next section, "How to use corner guards to get three points.")

Choice 3: Take Out the Shot Rock

Finally, let's look at what happens if the non-hammer team hits the shot rock.

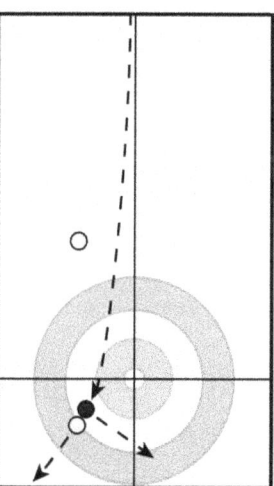

If the non-hammer team hits and stays on the rings, the hammer team can freeze to that stone. Alternatively, if the non-hammer team hits and stays far enough back, the hammer team can draw behind the corner guard for shot.

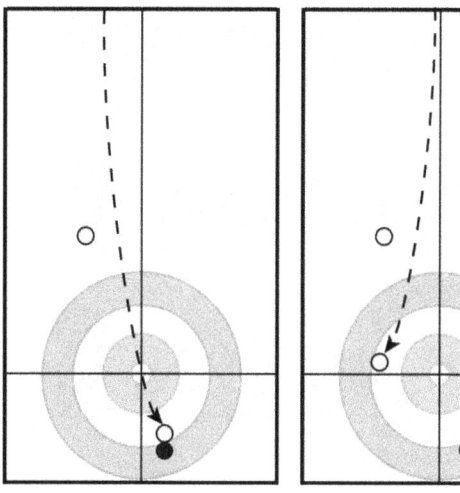

And, of course, if the non-hammer team hits and rolls out, the hammer team can draw behind its corner guard.

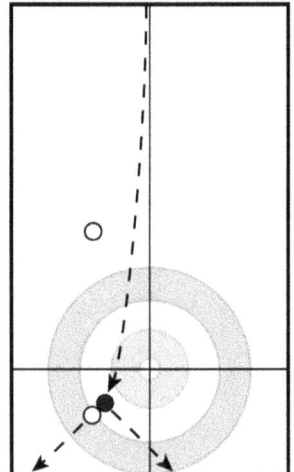 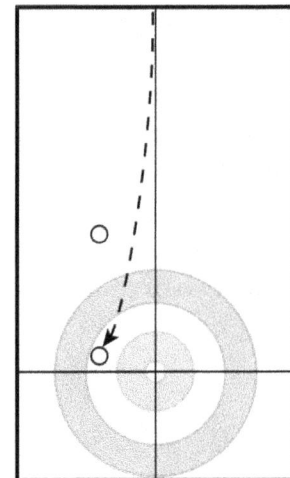

How to use corner guards to get three points

One reason to put up a corner guard on the rock side is to go for a three-point end. Here are two common configurations for this. It's not easy to get three points, and the hammer team will need its opponent to miss a few shots to be able to set it up.

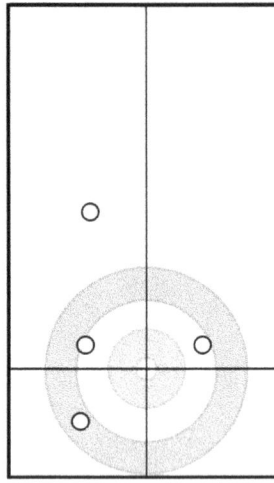 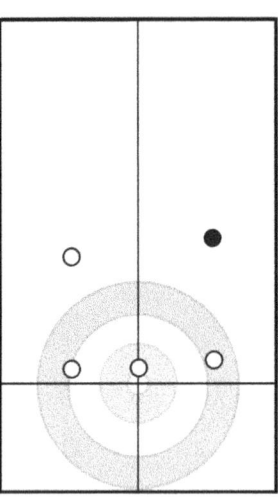

Why would a non-hammer team draw behind a corner guard?

There are several reasons a non-hammer team might draw behind a corner guard:

The non-hammer team may want to take that shot away from the hammer team.

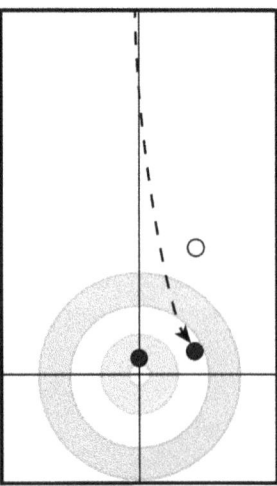

The non-hammer team may want to out-count the hammer team's stones further out on the wings.

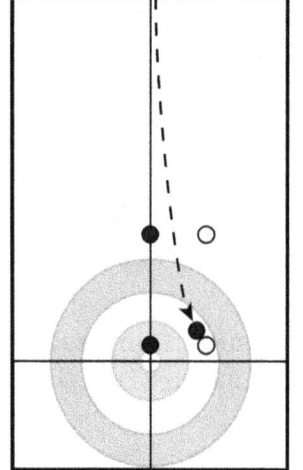 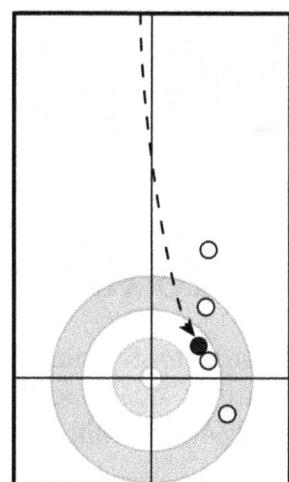

Or, the non-hammer team may want to force the hammer team to draw for one with its last rock.

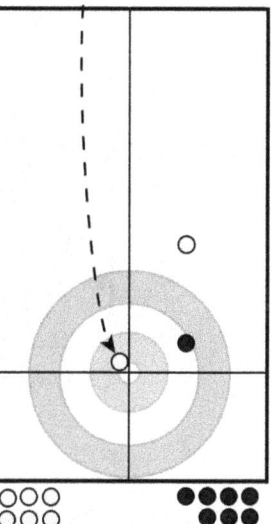

Notice in all of those scenarios, the non-hammer team is trying to force one or limit damage—not steal.

Steals

Intro to Steals

In order to steal, the non-hammer team usually needs a "quality shot rock" hidden behind a center guard. A "quality shot rock" means a rock that's very close to the button so the hammer team can't easily out-draw it.

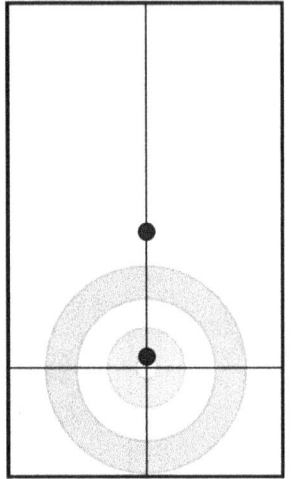 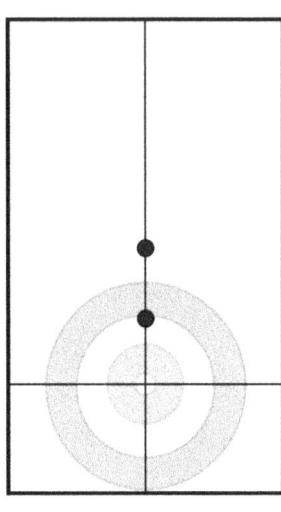 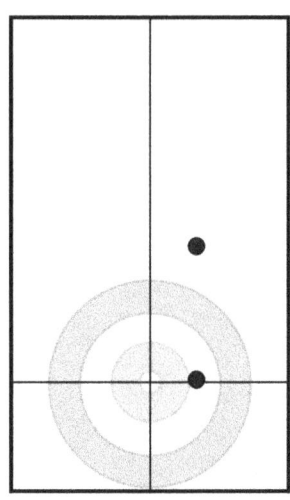

Good steal configuration — *Not a good steal configuration, because the hammer team can easily out-draw the non-hammer team's rock* — *Not a good steal configuration, because the hammer team can easily out-draw the non-hammer team's rock*

Of course, even if the non-hammer team sets up a center guard and quality shot rock, it could still face trouble. For example, the hammer team could make a double takeout to remove both rocks if they are close together...

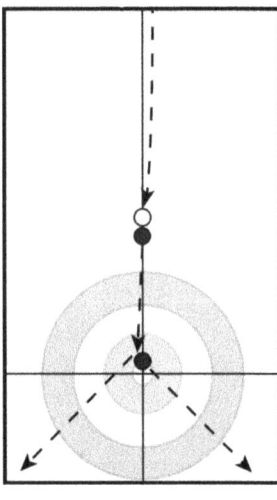

...or tap the shot rock off the button if the rocks are far apart.

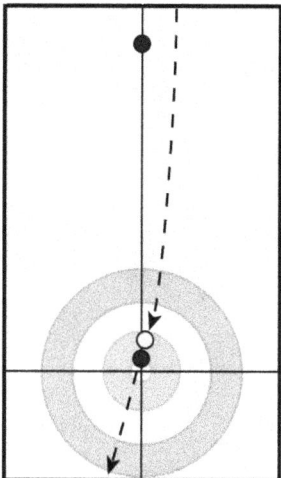

There are other configurations that are even better for stealing, for example, a high center guard, a tight guard, and a rock on the button.

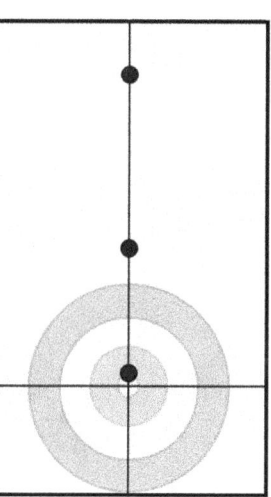

With that in mind, let's look at steal tactics....

Steals—The Big Picture

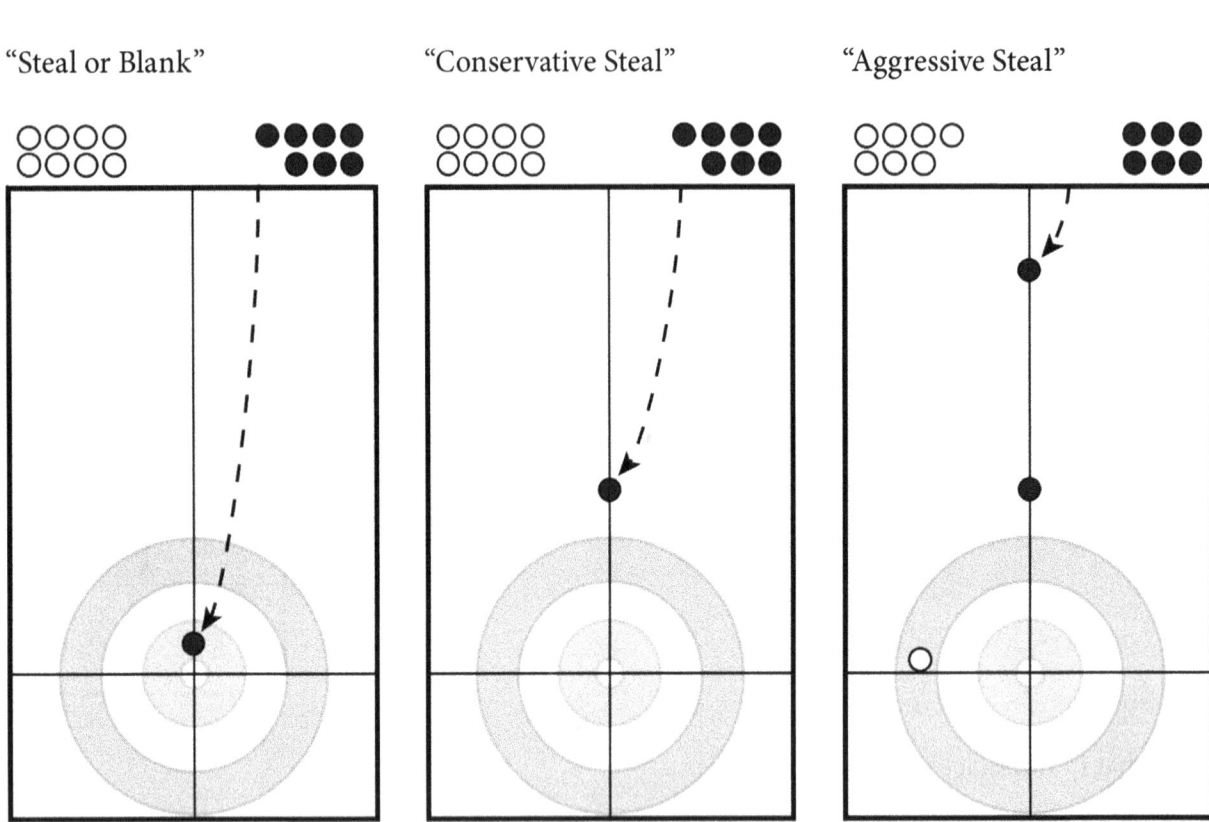

"Steal or Blank"

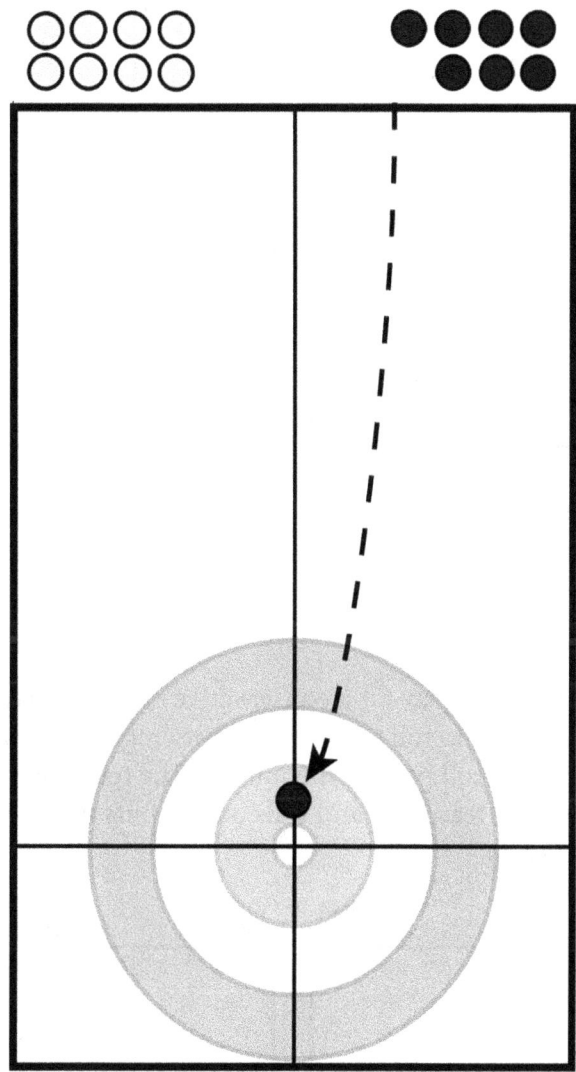

How it works:

The non-hammer team puts its first stone in the rings in front of the button. Depending on the hammer team's end goal and shot choices, this could play out a number of ways, including:

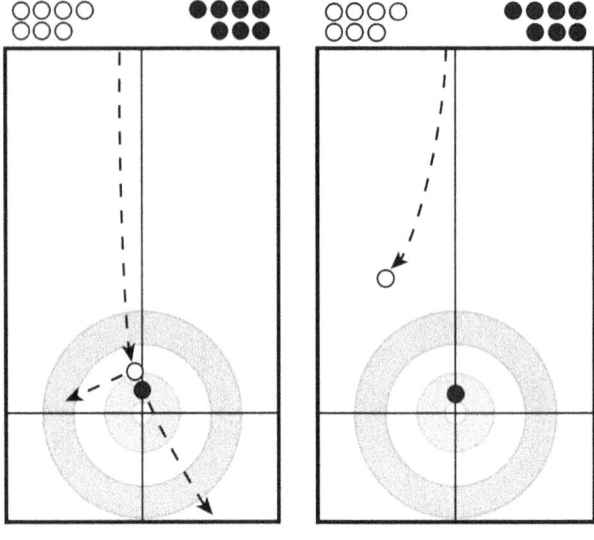

Conservative response *Aggressive response*

Conservative Response

If the hammer team's end goal is to play for a conservative deuce or blank, the hammer team will hit the non-hammer team's stone and roll to the side of the rings. Then, the non-hammer team will hit the hammer team's stone and roll back to the middle. The teams will exchange shots until one side misses, or until the hammer team hits and rolls out with its final rock to blank the end. (This is like the "Deuce or Blank" end.)

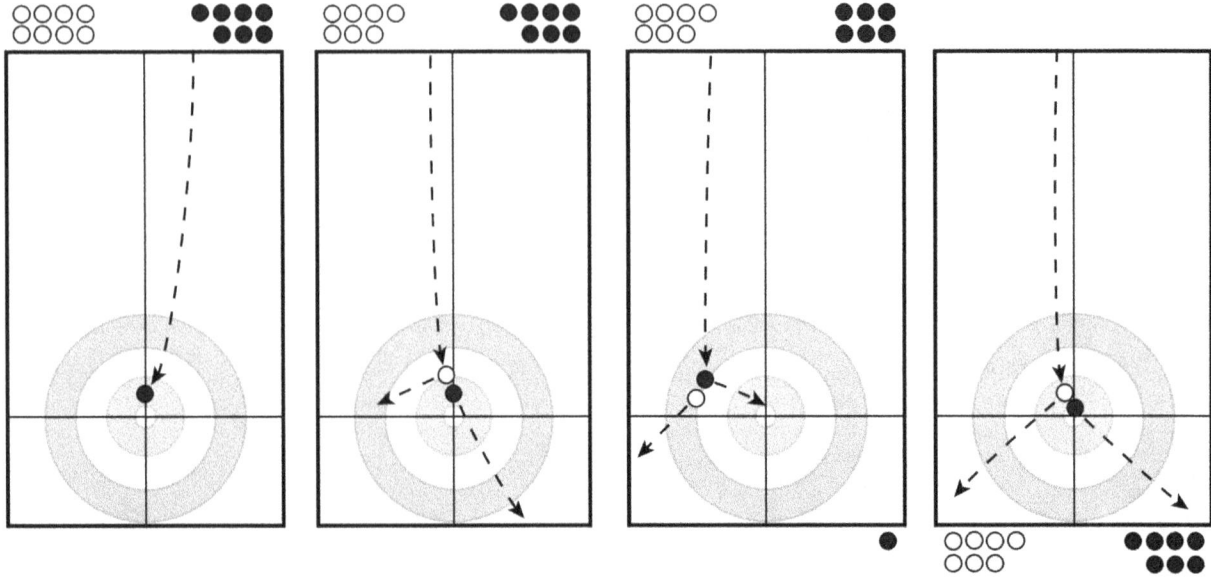

If the hammer team misses a hit, the non-hammer team can guard and go for a low-risk steal. (It's low risk, because there are no hammer team stones in the rings to create a multi-point scoring threat.)

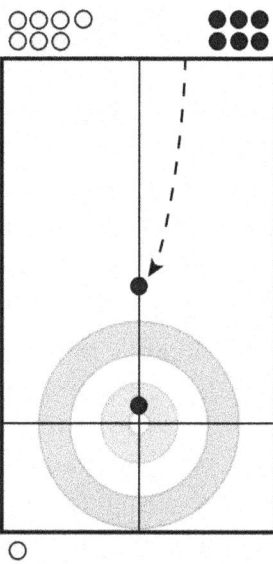

Aggressive Response

If the hammer team responds aggressively by putting up a corner guard, the non-hammer team has a low-risk opportunity to put up a center guard to steal.

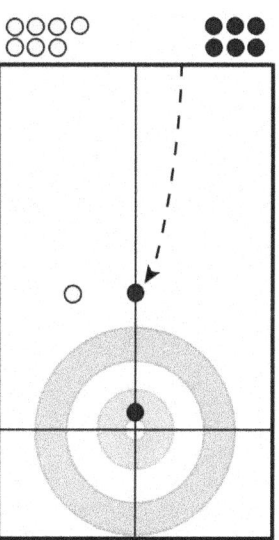

Why choose this tactic?

There are several reasons a non-hammer team might choose this conservative tactical plan, including to:

- **Avoid accidentally giving up a big end** - In an early end or when the score is close, the non-hammer team may not want to play complicated shots or risk giving up a big end by allowing lots of rocks to get into play.

- **Create a low-risk steal opportunity while playing with a lead** - If the non-hammer team has a lead in a middle or late end, it will likely focus on preventing the hammer team from scoring more than one point, rather than play aggressively to steal. By putting its first rock near the button, the non-hammer team puts immediate pressure on the hammer team and avoids giving the hammer team a guard to hide behind. If the hammer team blanks, that's okay. And, if the non-hammer team is eventually able to steal, that's a good result, too!

- **Overpower an opponent that doesn't hit well** - This could also be a good tactic for a non-hammer team that thinks it hits significantly better than its opponent. If the hammer team misses a hit, the non-hammer team will have a "free shot" to set up a guard and steal.

The non-hammer team's goal chart might look like this:

Non-Hammer Team's Goal Chart
    Want: Steal
    Accept: Force 1 or Blank
    Strongly Avoid: Hammer team scores 2 or more

  Pros: This is a low-risk way to steal.

  Cons: The odds aren't great that this will result in a steal. The hammer team can easily redirect this into a blank opportunity by hitting the non-hammer team's open rocks.

"Conservative Steal"

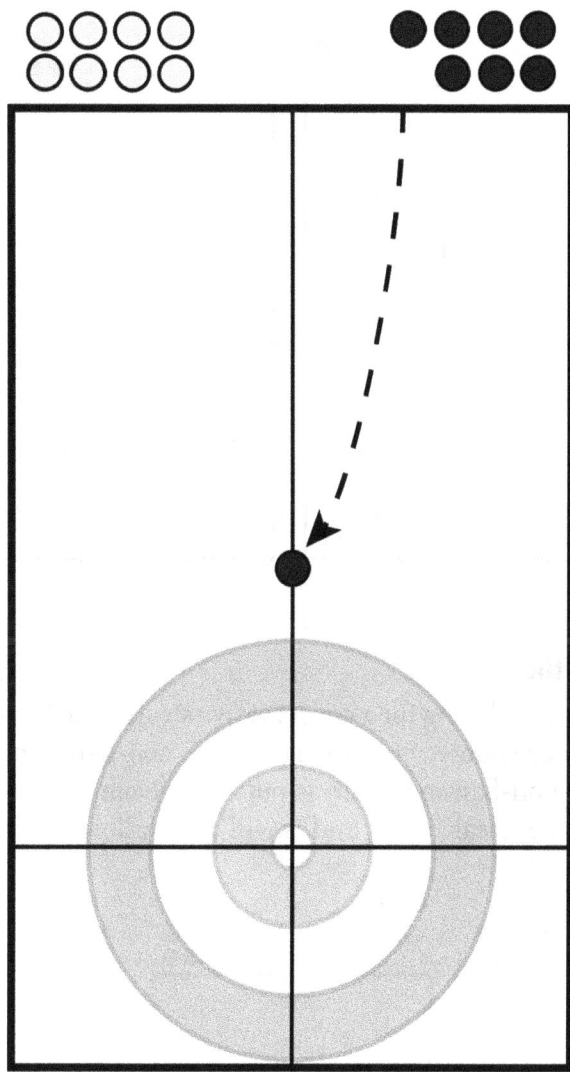

How it works:

The non-hammer team puts up a center guard with its first rock. Depending on the hammer team's end goal and shot choices, this could play out a number of ways, including:

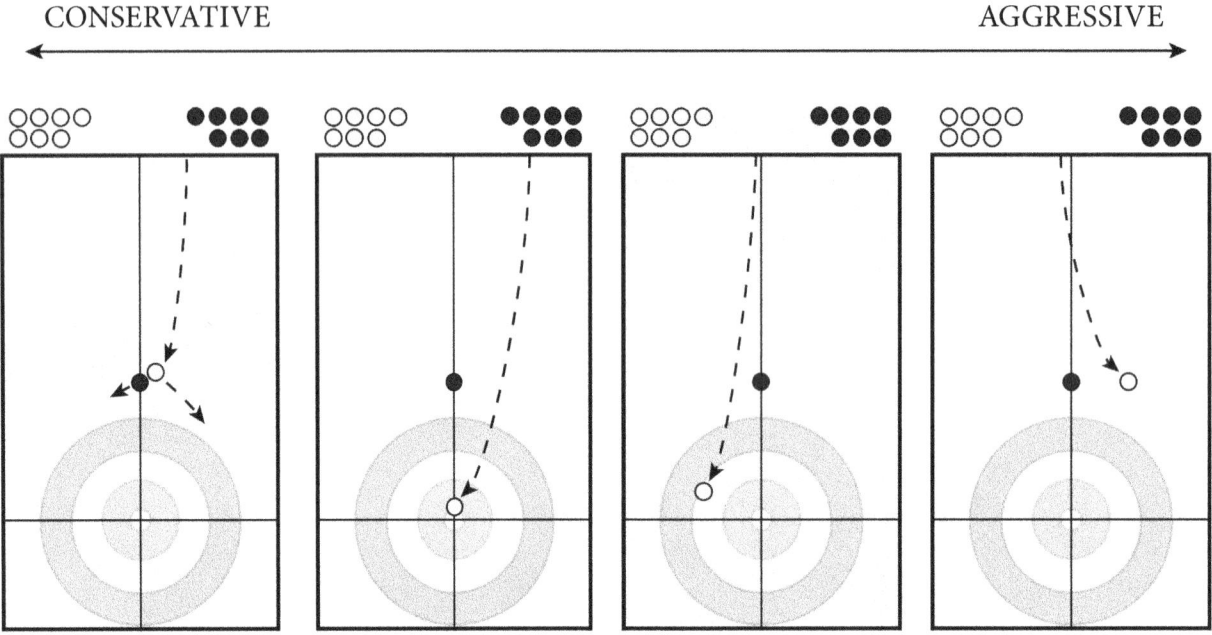

If the hammer team ticks the guard...

Since the non-hammer team is playing for a conservative steal, if the hammer team ticks the center guard to the side and rolls its shooter onto the rings, the non-hammer team would likely hit the hammer team's stone. The non-hammer team is putting the emphasis on the "conservative" part of its plan (rather than on the "steal" part), and is willing to allow a blank, rather than risk giving up two.

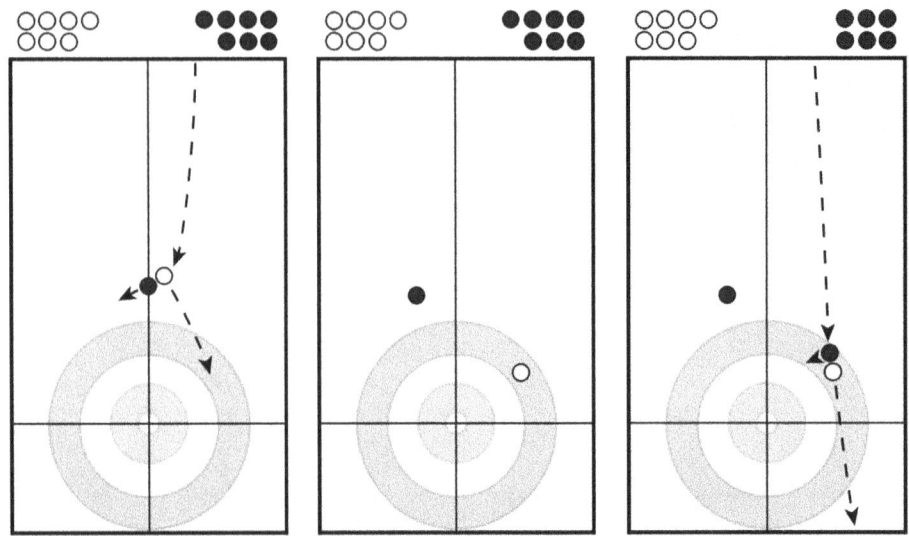

If the hammer team ticks the center guard to the side but doesn't roll onto the rings, the non-hammer team could replace the center guard and continue on towards the steal.

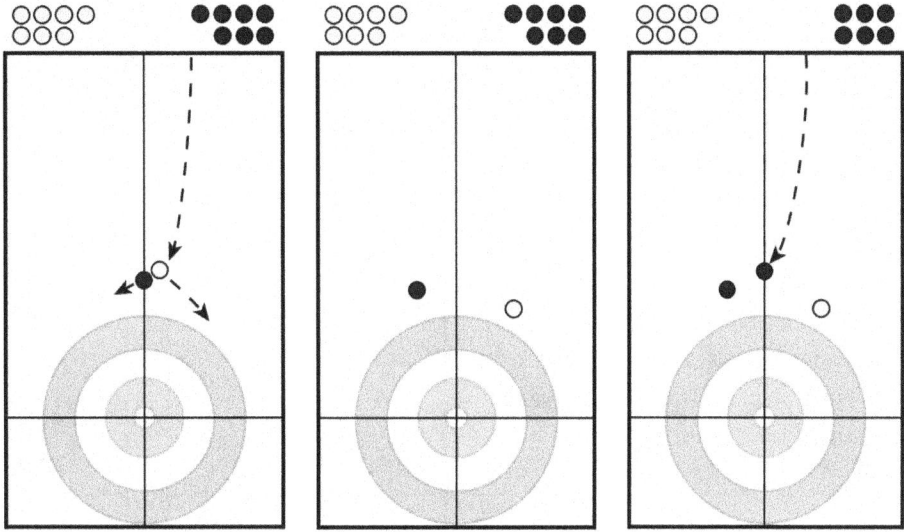

If the hammer team draws behind the center guard...

If the hammer team draws behind the center guard, the non-hammer team would likely play to that rock in some way. If the hammer team's rock is exposed, the non-hammer team could hit it out. If the hammer team's rock is buried, the non-hammer team could bump it back or freeze to it and try to hit it later. (This is like "Simple End 2." from the "Strategy Basics" section.)

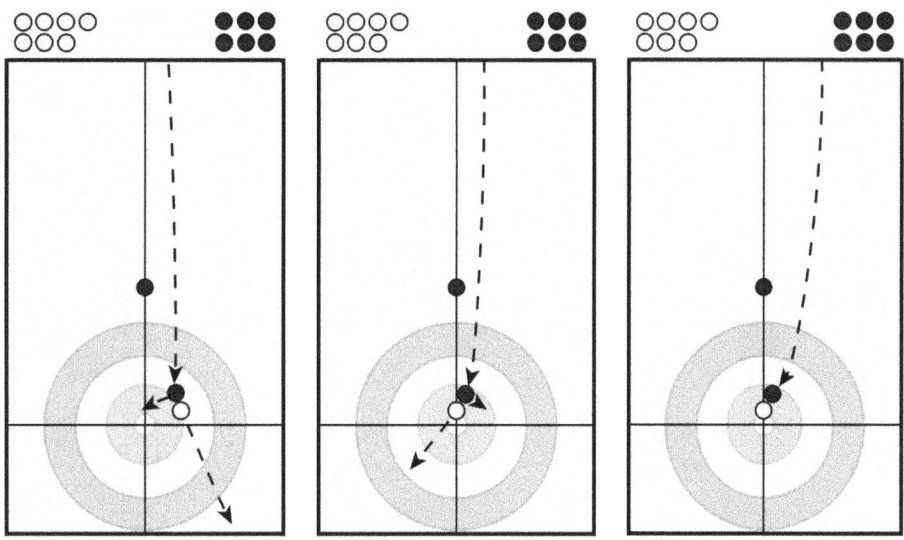

If the hammer team draws to the wing...

As we saw in the "Open Wing Deuce" part of the "Deuces" chapter, this can play out a lot of ways.

If the hammer team draws above the tee line, the non-hammer team can continue to play for a conservative steal by hitting and attempting to roll to the button. This is conservative because the non-hammer team is prioritizing eliminating the hammer team's stone to prevent a big end ahead of positioning its own stone for a steal. (Hit-and-rolls are tough to use to precisely position stones. It's usually easier to get behind a guard by drawing.)

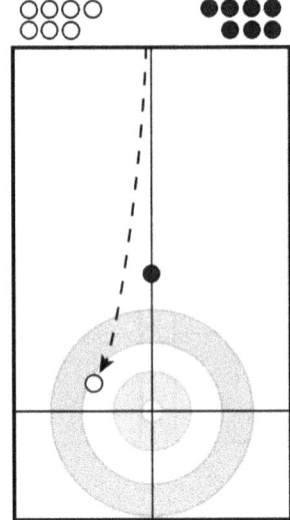 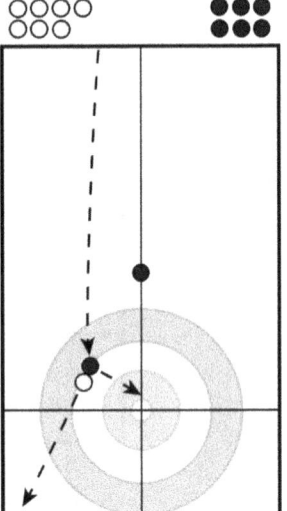

If the hammer team draws behind the tee line, the non-hammer team's choice is trickier.

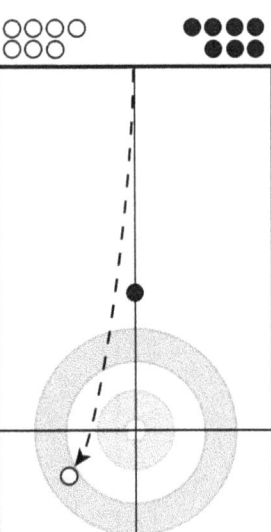

If the non-hammer team is playing very conservatively (prioritizing preventing a deuce above stealing), it will hit the hammer team's rock and roll to the middle, even though it can't roll to a good scoring position.

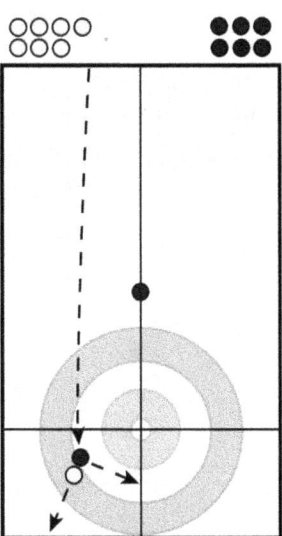

If the non-hammer team is willing to take on a moderate amount of risk, or thinks the hammer team's rock could be useful to it as backing later, it could ignore the rock and draw in.

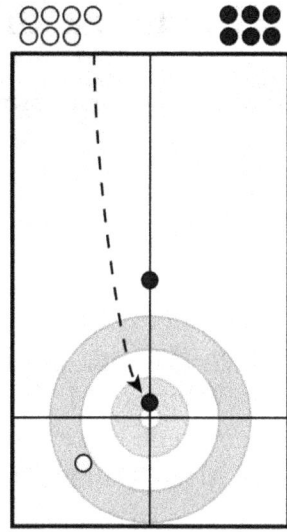

If the hammer team puts up a corner guard...

If the hammer team puts up a corner guard, the non-hammer team would likely ignore it and draw in with its second rock. By doing this, it puts pressure on the hammer team by setting up a steal in the middle. Later (after the Free Guard Zone ends) it might take out the corner guard to prevent the hammer team from setting up a deuce.

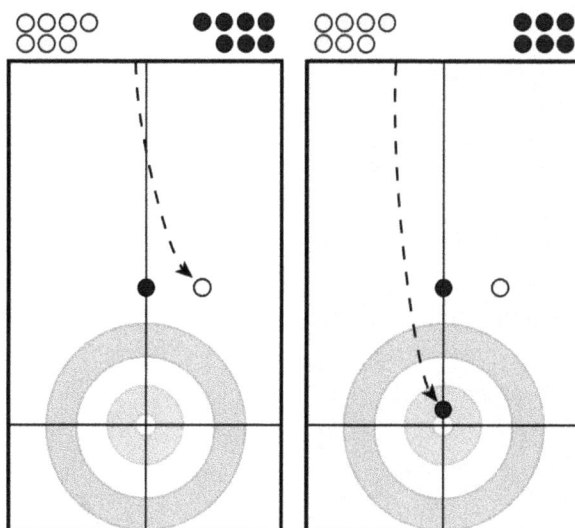

Why choose this tactic?

The non-hammer team's goal is to score one without taking major risks, such as allowing the hammer team to get lots of rocks in play. A non-hammer team might choose this tactic at a time in the game when it wants to steal, but doesn't absolutely have to (for example, early in the game when the score is close).

The team's goal chart might look like this:

Non-Hammer Team's Goal Chart
Want: Steal 1
Accept: Force 1 or Blank
Avoid: Hammer team scores 2 or more

Pros: This is a flexible plan with relatively low risk.
Cons: One guard isn't enough protection to steal when playing opponents who can make double takeouts.

"Aggressive Steal"

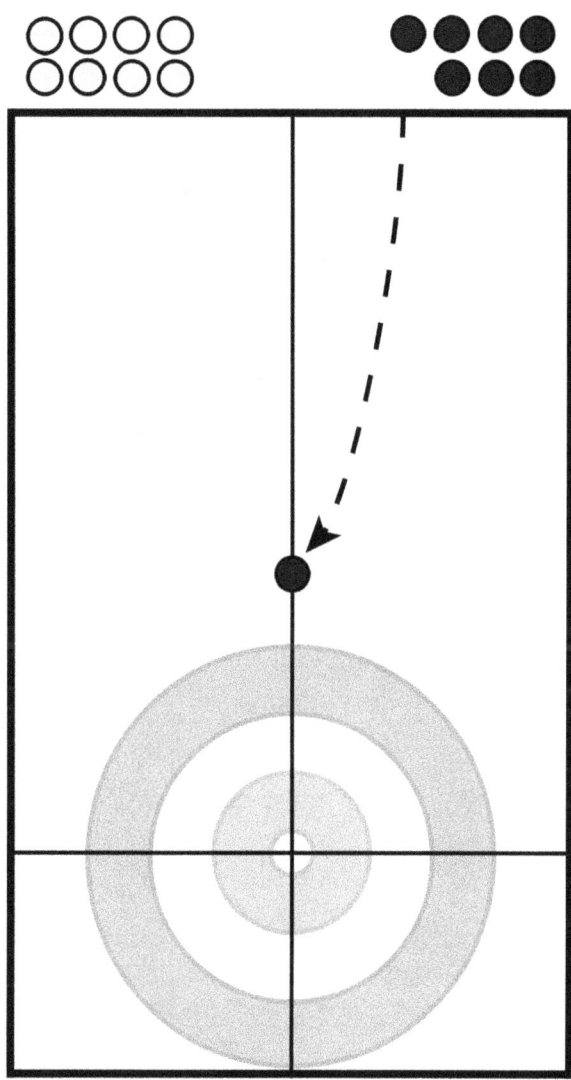

How it works:

Regardless of what the hammer team does, the non-hammer team will put up two guards. There are may things the hammer team could do, including:

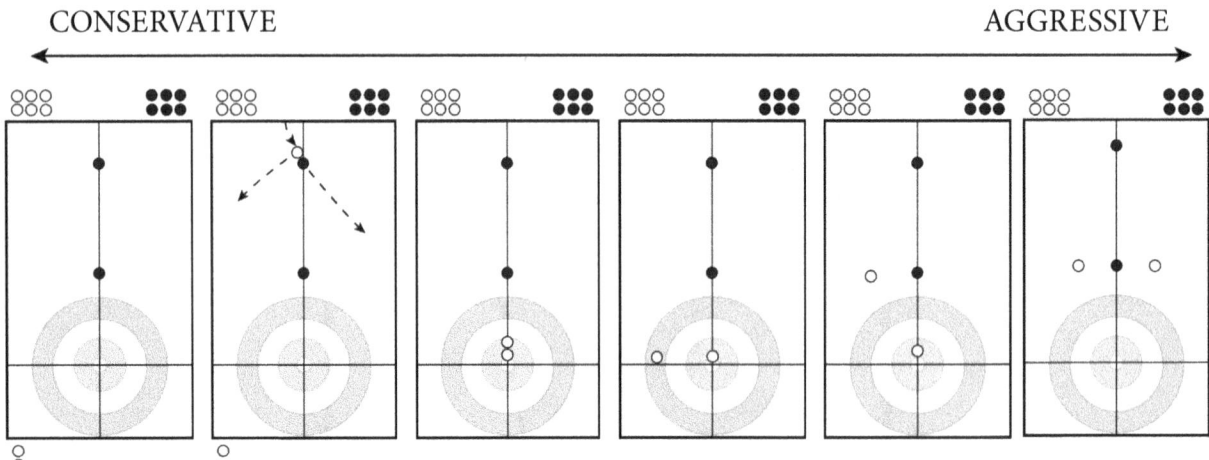

Hammer team's shot choices: On the very conservative end of the spectrum, a hammer team with a big lead (e.g., more than three points in the final end) might throw both rocks through the house so the non-hammer team can't use them for backing and so it can't jam on them when peeling the guards later. On the very aggressive end of the spectrum, a non-hammer team might put up two corner guards if it were desperate to score at least two.

In any of these cases, the non-hammer team will spend the rest of the end replacing guards as needed, and fighting to get shot rock on the button.

Why choose this tactic?

A non-hammer team would choose this tactic when it absolutely needs to steal. The two guards make it more difficult for the hammer team to clear the front, creating an opportunity for the non-hammer team to hide a rock on the button. However, the non-hammer team is taking on a lot of risk, because the hammer team could use its first two stones to draw to the button, which will make it difficult for the non-hammer team to get a rock there to steal.

If this were the middle of the game, the non-hammer team's goal chart might look like this:

Non-Hammer Team's Goal Chart
    Strongly Want: Steal 1 or more
    Accept: Force 1
    Avoid: Hammer team scores 2

Or, if this were the last end of the game, or if the non-hammer team were significantly behind in points, its goal chart might look like this:

Non-Hammer Team's Goal Chart
    Need: Steal 1 or more
    Can't Allow: Any other outcome

Pros: This tactic increases the odds the non-hammer team will still have at least one center guard left at the end of the end—which is important for a steal.

Cons: This tactic also increases the risk of the hammer team scoring multiple points, because the non-hammer team must ignore the hammer team's first shots while setting up the center guards.

Forces

Intro to Forces

A "force" happens when the non-hammer team forces its opponent to score one and only one point. It's a great tactic that doesn't get the love and respect it deserves. For example, if your team can score two points every time you have the hammer, and force your opponents to score one and only one point when they have the hammer, you will win easily—with no need to try risky steals.

There are times when a non-hammer team may not want to steal, even if it has the opportunity. For example, if the score is tied in the second-to-last end of a game, the non-hammer team may want to force its opponent to score one point, so it can have the hammer in the last end.

When you plan your force, think about how it might end. Most forces end one of two ways, as an "open-center force" or a "closed-center force."

"Open-Center Force"

In an "open-center force," the hammer team can make unobstructed shots in the middle of the rings. Despite this advantage, the non-hammer team's position on the sides of the rings is so strong, it prevents the hammer team from either scoring two or blanking, thus forcing one. Here are four examples:

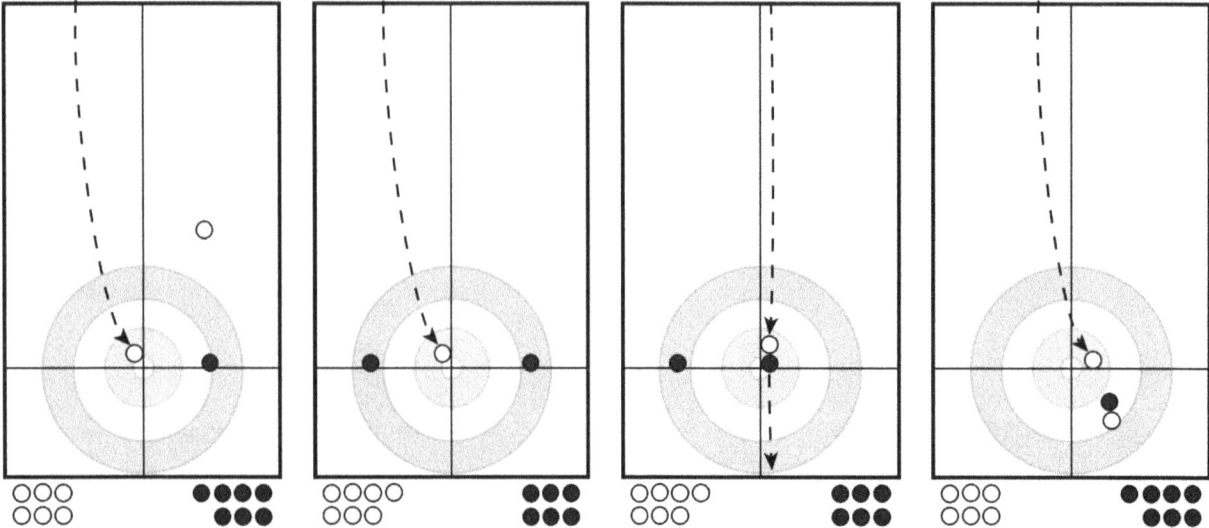

"Closed-Center Force"

In a "closed-center force," the non-hammer team closes off access to the center so the hammer team cannot shoot freely there. The non-hammer team also positions a stone near the button, so the hammer team can't move it to count multiple points or blank, or draw a second rock in to score two. This force works by reducing the scoring area. Here are two examples:

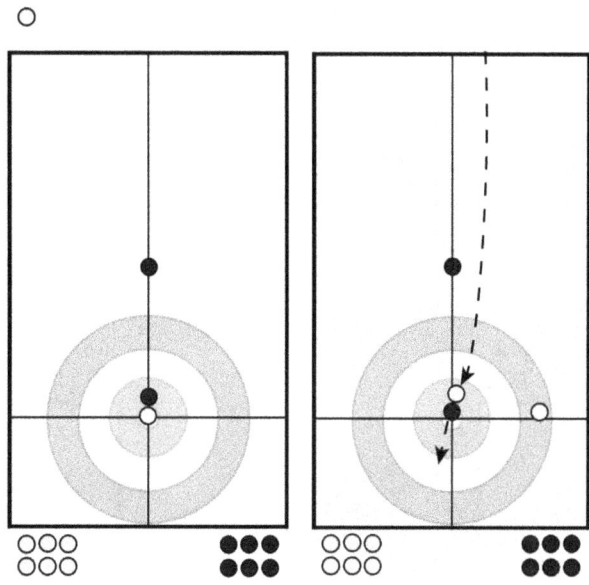

With that in mind, let's look at how forces begin....

Forces—The Big Picture

CONSERVATIVE
when a blank is okay, or the other team doesn't hit well

AGGRESSIVE
when you absolutely have to force

"Force or Blank"

"Aggressive Force"

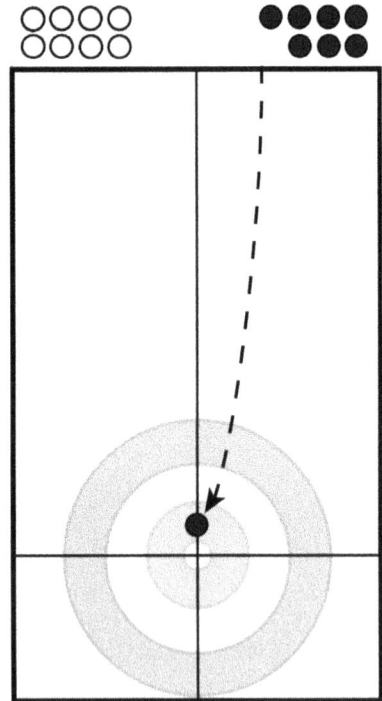
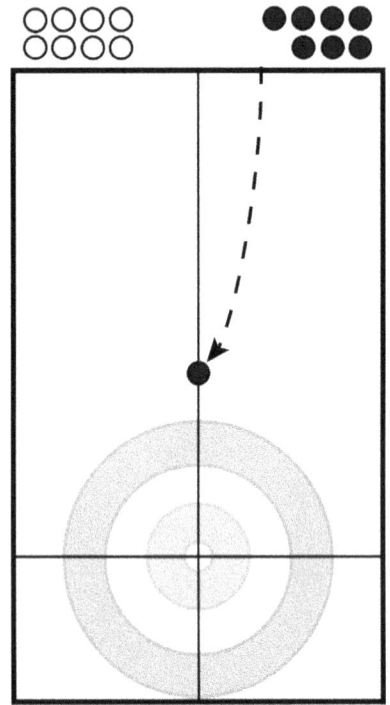

"Force or Blank"

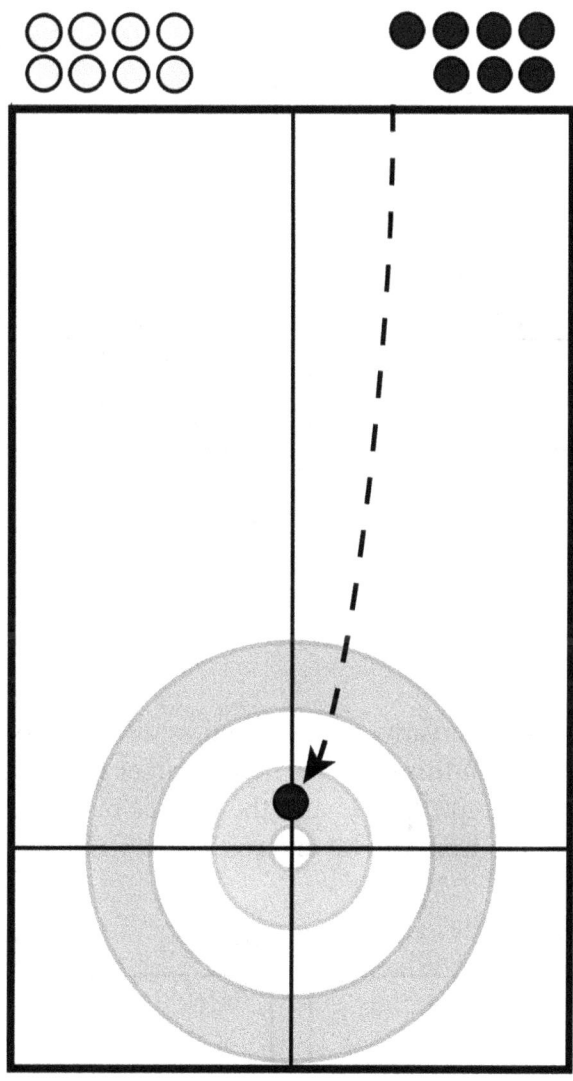

How it works:

The non-hammer team draws its first stone into the house in front of the button. Depending on the hammer team's end plan and shot choices, this could play out a number of ways, including:

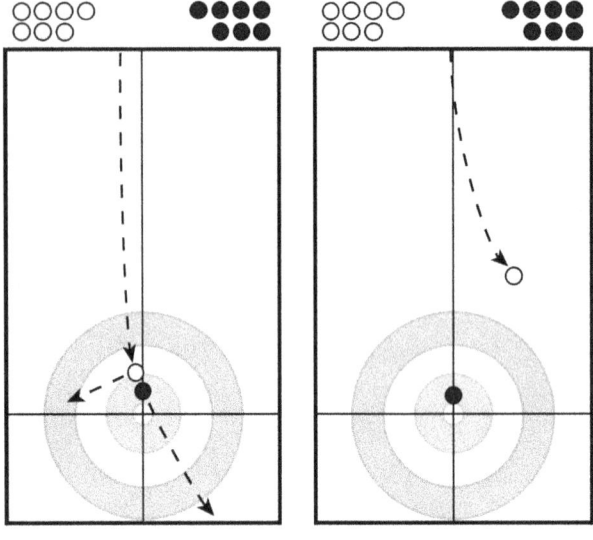

Conservative response   *Aggressive response*

Conservative Response

If the hammer team has a very conservative end plan and would be happy to blank the end, it would hit the rock and roll to the side. In this case, the non-hammer team would hit that rock and roll back to the middle—like the "Simple End 1" and the "Deuce or Blank" examples. If both teams make all their shots, the hammer team can hit and roll out to blank.

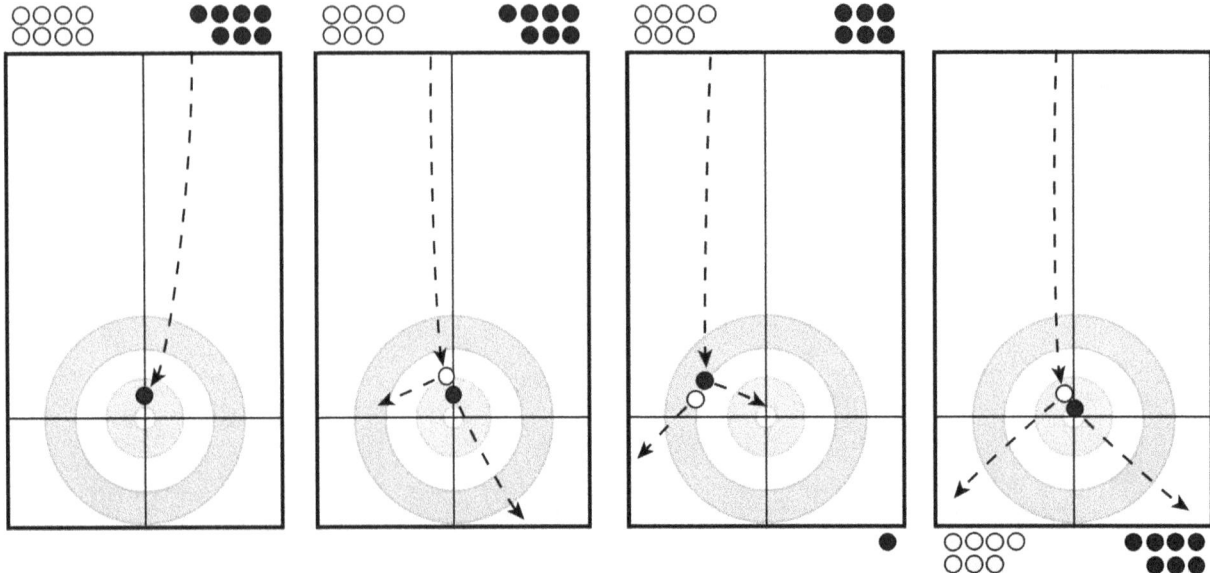

If the hammer team misses a hit, the non-hammer team could split the house.

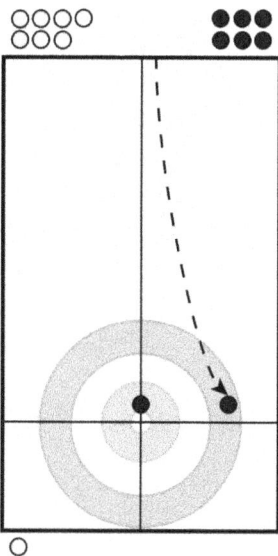

If the non-hammer team can keep its rocks spread out around the house through the rest of the end, the hammer team would likely be forced to draw or hit for one with its last rock. This would be an example of an "open-center force."

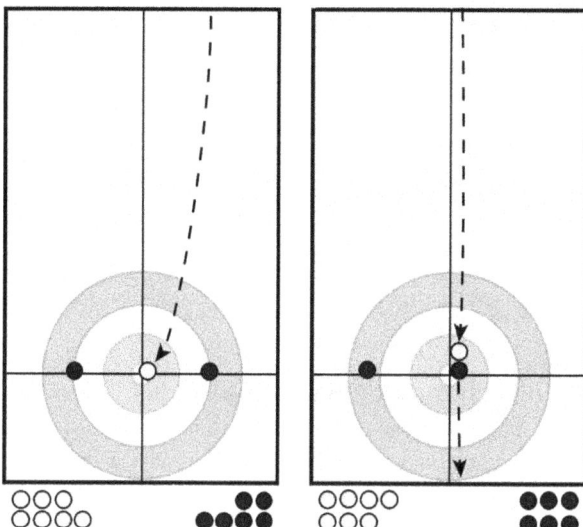

Conservative Response

If the hammer team has an aggressive end plan and wants to score multiple points, it might put up a corner guard.

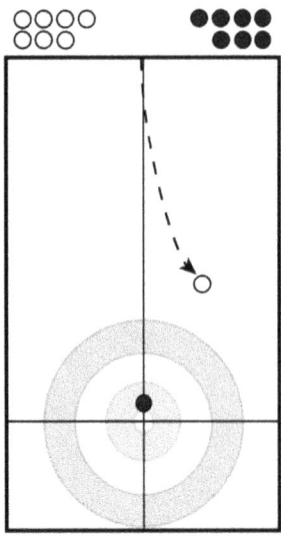

Since the non-hammer team's primary end goal is to prevent the hammer team from scoring two (and that's why the team is happy to blank or force 1), it might freeze a second rock onto the first. This will force the hammer team to spend shots clearing the center, which will give the non-hammer team time to take out any hammer team scoring threats.

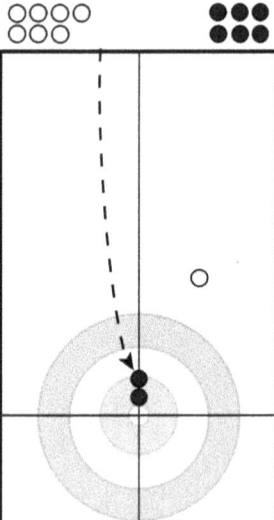

Why choose this tactic?

When the non-hammer team puts its first rock into the rings instead of out front, there's no guarantee of a force, since the hammer team could hit the rock and eventually blank the end. A non-hammer team would use this tactic to force in situations like these:

- A blank is okay
- The hammer team hits poorly
- The non-hammer team thinks the hammer team will choose not to hit for a tactical reason. (For example, if the hammer team is down by a lot of points, it will almost certainly put up guards instead of hitting with its first two stones.)

The non-hammer team's goal chart might look like this:

<u>Non-Hammer Team's Goal Chart</u>
Want: Force 1
Accept: Blank
Avoid: Hammer team scores 2 or more

Pros: This is a low-risk approach to forcing one.
Cons: This starting move doesn't guarantee a force, because the hammer team could hit the first stone and eventually blank the end.

"Aggressive Force"

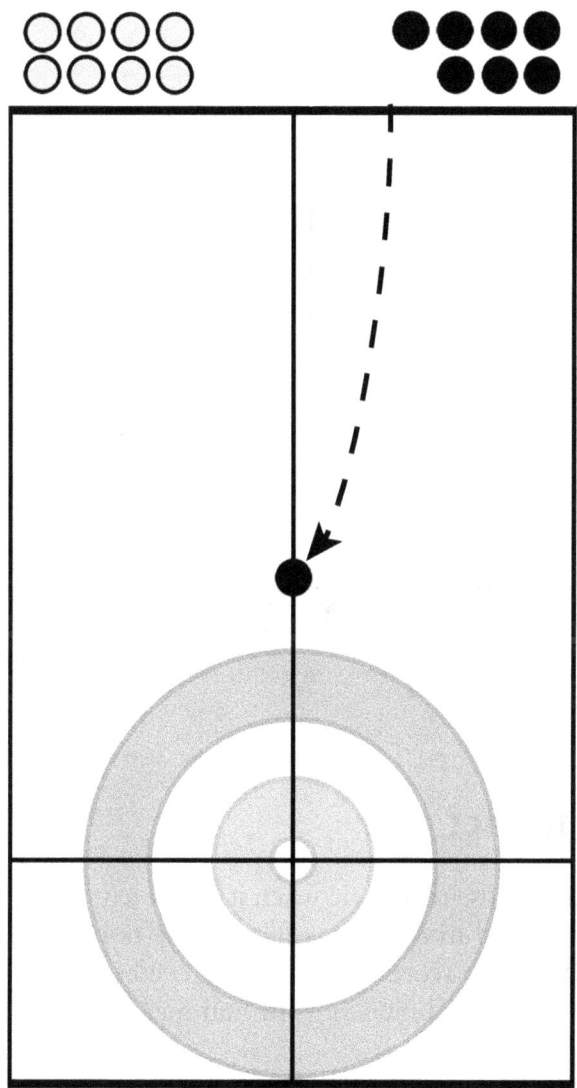

How it works:

The non-hammer team puts up a center guard with its first stone. The hammer team can make a number of different shot choices. The non-hammer team, on the other hand, will continue to play almost as though it is stealing—except that it will either trap one of the hammer team's stones on the button, or put its own stone there so that the hammer team can't move it enough to get more than one counting stone. The non-hammer team is aiming to finish this end as a "closed-center force." For example:

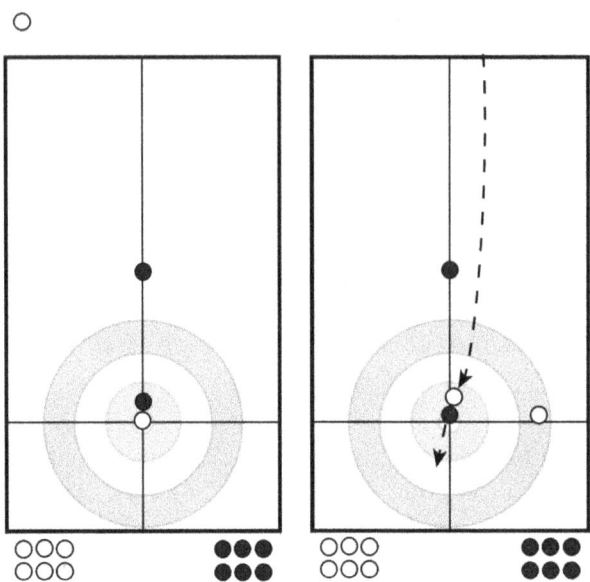

Why choose this tactic?

A non-hammer team would choose this tactic when it absolutely needs to force the hammer team to take a point. The center guard makes it possible for the non-hammer team to keep rocks in play, so some team will be forced to score in the end. The center guard can also make the potential scoring area small, and thus make it difficult for the hammer team to count more than one rock.

The non-hammer team's goal chart might look like this:

Non-Hammer Team's Goal Chart
    Strongly Want: Force 1
    Avoid: All other outcomes

Pros: By putting up a center guard, the non-hammer team can protect a rock near the pin, and prevent the hammer team from blanking the end.

Cons: Once guards are in play, the hammer team can hide rocks and possibly score multiple points.

Tips for Using Center Guards

How far from the rings should you place a center guard?

Most non-hammer teams will place a center guard as close to the rings as they can, while still being able to draw behind it. This makes it difficult for the hammer team to hit or bump any of the non-hammer team's rocks hidden behind the guard. For example, on ice that curls a lot, the non-hammer team might put up a "tight" center guard a foot in front of the rings. On ice that curls a medium amount, the non-hammer team might put up a "mid" center guard, in the middle of the Free Guard Zone. And, on ice that barely curls at all, the non-hammer team might put up a "high" center guard near the hog line.

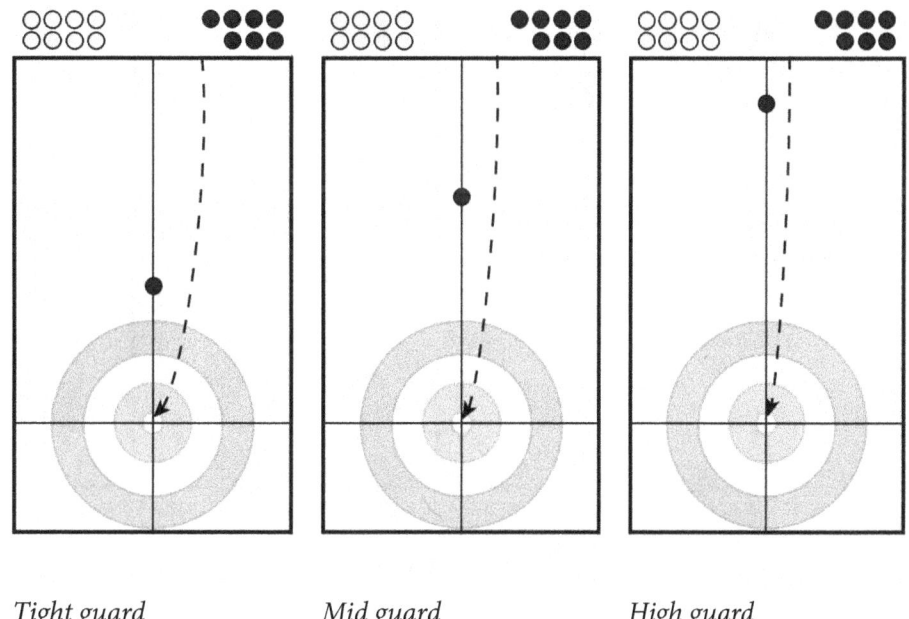

Tight guard   *Mid guard*   *High guard*

Alternatively, the non-hammer team might put up a tight center guard regardless of the ice conditions and plan to tap it back to get shot rock instead of drawing behind it.

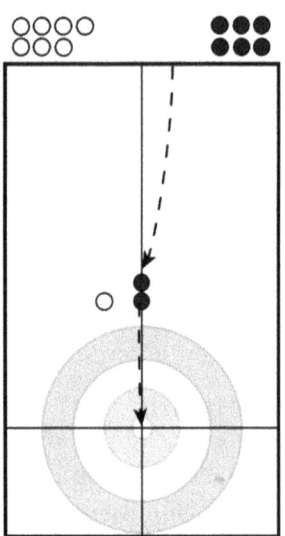

Close center guards are also easier for the non-hammer team to run back if it gets into trouble.

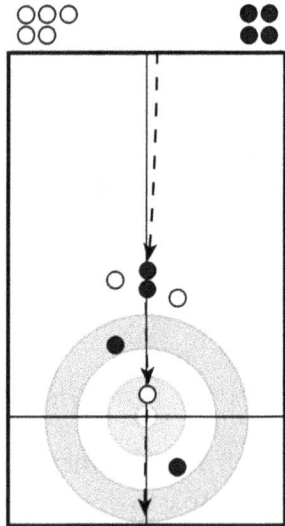

When should you use a double center guard?

Sometimes the opponent you are playing is so good, one guard isn't enough. For example, if you put up a tight guard and get a rock behind it, an opponent who hits well can remove both rocks with a double takeout. In that case, you need two center guards, far enough apart so they are not easy to remove with a double takeout.

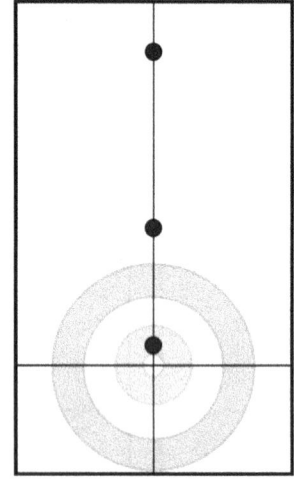 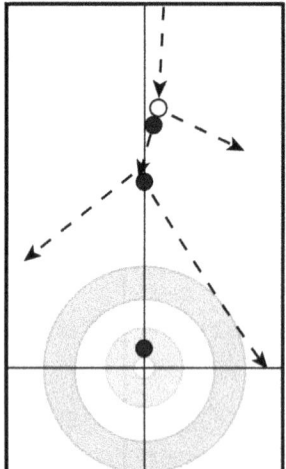

If you're planning to use two center guards, which one should you put up first?

It depends on your personal preference. Here are examples of how some teams make that decision.

High Guard First

Some non-hammer teams like to put up the high guard first. They do this for a few reasons, including: (1) If the lead throws light, the sweepers can bring the rock past the hog line, and if the lead throws heavy, the rock will be a tight guard, which is a good result. (If the lead was throwing a tight guard and was heavy, the rock would end up in the rings where it could be hit.) (2) If the lead throws heavy on his second shot (the tight guard) and the rock goes into the rings, the high guard will still be there to provide some protection.

Tight Guard First

Some non-hammer teams like to put up the tight guard first. Again, they do this for a few reasons: (1) In case they are only able to establish one guard (e.g., if the hammer team ticks one away), a tight guard is better for blocking direct hits than a high guard. (2) They might think it's easier to place a guard in front of an existing guard than behind it. This way, there's no risk of accidentally ticking their good guard off the center line if the second guard shot is off-line. (3) If a team's lead has been throwing tight center guards all game, it might be easier for him to throw that again, instead of guessing at a different weight.

Should center guards be perfectly aligned or staggered?

The advantage of perfectly aligned center guards is that if your opponent tries to remove them with a double takeout, there's a good chance (with non-World-level players) that the opponent's stone will remain somewhere in the front as a guard. (Some elite players can throw with enough weight and rotation that they can roll the shooter to the side under almost any circumstances.)

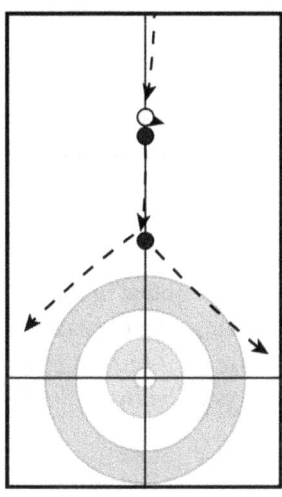 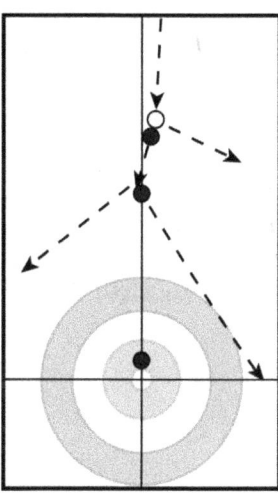

The advantage of slightly staggered guards is that they shelter a wider area in the middle, creating a bigger "scoring zone"—in other words, a bigger area where you can hide a rock.

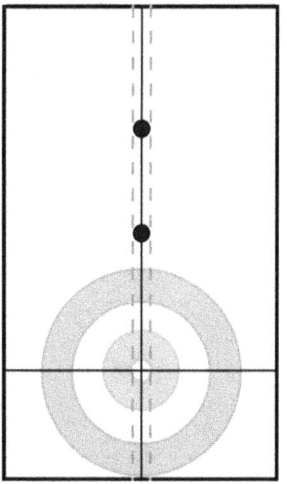 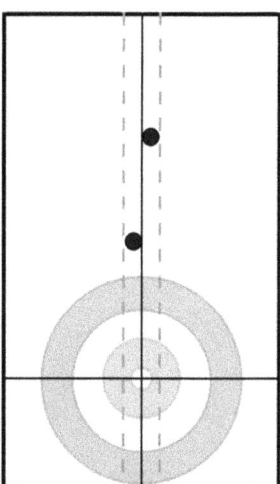

CENTER GUARDS — INTRODUCTION TO CURLING STRATEGY

How can a team move opponent stones protected by center guards?

If the ice is curling a lot or the stone isn't fully protected, you can bump or hit it. If it is well protected, you can corner freeze to it, then tap or hit both stones later. Here's an example of how that works:

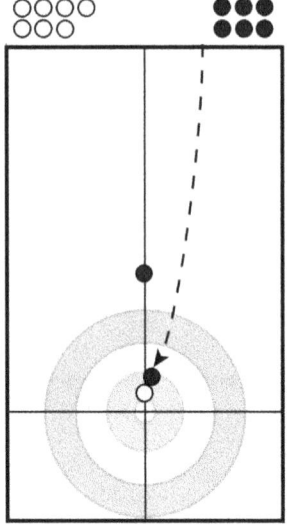 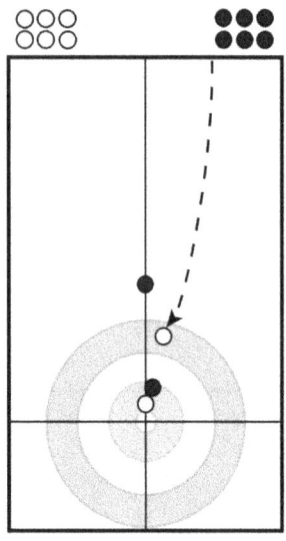 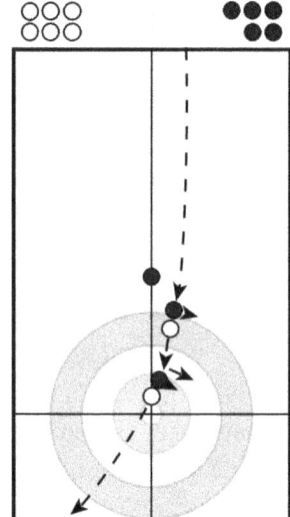 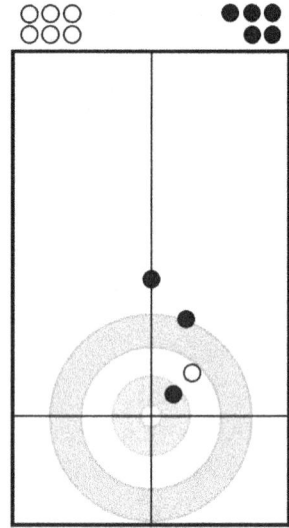

The non-hammer team freezes with intent to tap or hit later to get shot.

The hammer team guards its shot rock, but puts the guard in the house, so it will be easy to use for a raise later if things go badly.

The non-hammer team raises the hammer team's rock back into the pile and gets shot rock.

Even though the non-hammer team is shot now, the hammer team still has second shot in a good position. It could use that rock to attack the shot rock, or it could become a second point later if the hammer team can find another way to remove the shot rock.

This tactic is frequently used by both hammer and non-hammer teams.

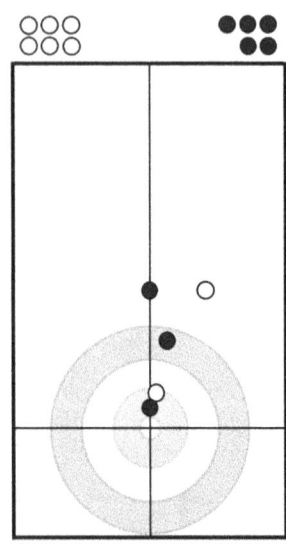

Sometimes teams load both sides before they begin to hit.

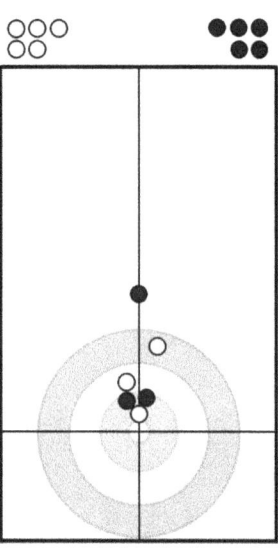

Alternatively, you can run back a center guard to clear threats in the middle.

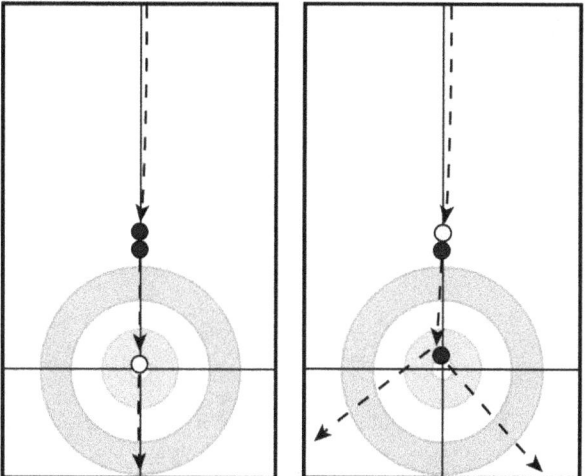

When should the hammer team use center guards?

Not all center guards are bad for the hammer team. For example, if the hammer team is significantly behind, center guards can help the hammer team get more rocks in play. While they do increase the risk the non-hammer team could steal or force, if the hammer team is significantly behind, it shouldn't waste shots removing center guards, it should draw or bump behind them to get more rocks in play.

Teams that don't hit well should also consider leaving center guards in place and playing around them, regardless of their end objective. It's better to choose the "second best" shot and make it, than to miss the perfect shot.

Finally, if the front is too cluttered to clear with two or three hits and you still have a path to the pin, it's probably time to forget your open-front plan and draw.

What's the best way to remove center guards?

There are two rules of thumb for clearing clusters of center guards:

Rule 1: Start at the top. Clear the highest guards first and work your way back. With luck, you may be able to run a high guard back into some others to clear multiple rocks in one shot.

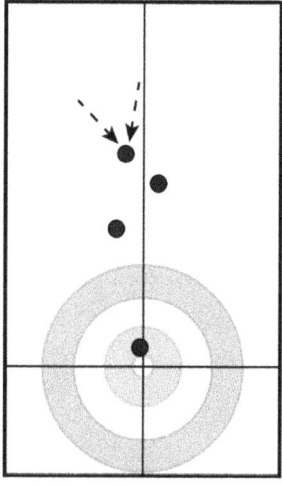

Rule 2: Early in the end, focus on clearing guards. Late in the end, consider running them back.

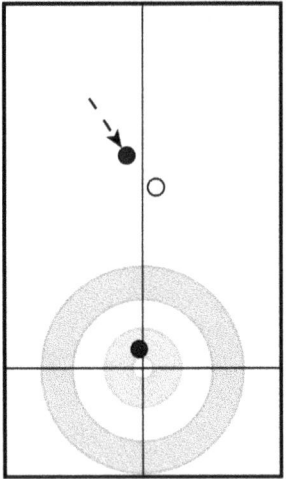

Early in the end, try to clear both guards—even if one is yours.

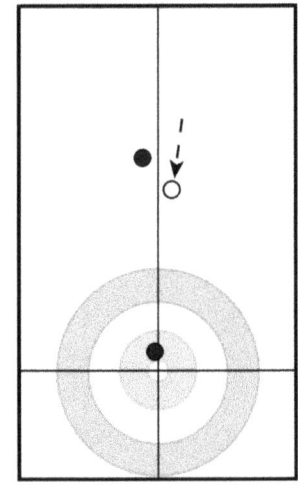

Late in the end when there's not much time left, consider a runback.

PART 4
STRATEGY SCENARIOS

Beginner Strategy Scenarios

Use Your End Goals to Make Better Shot Choices throughout the End

In the previous section, we talked about how to use end goals to choose opening moves. In this section, we'll focus on how to continue to use those goals to pick shots as you play through the rest of the end.

For the beginner scenarios, I provide the end goal and ask the reader to choose tactics to match. ***Unless I specify otherwise, assume the team has multiple rocks remaining and the Free Guard Zone time is over.***

For the intermediate scenarios, I provide information about the game (end number, rock number, score, hammer possession) and the reader needs to choose both the end goal and tactical plan.

In these scenarios, I present a set of choices. They are not the only choices a team could make in these situations. In fact, in many of the scenarios, there are several answers that could be "correct," depending on whether the team is playing conservatively, aggressively, or somewhere in between. The purpose of this section (and the book) is not to give absolute truths or answers, but to help curlers learn a structured logic for thinking about shot selection.

As a reminder, the hammer team has light stones and the non-hammer team has dark stones in all of these scenarios.

> **BEGINNER TIP** These situations are called "Beginner Strategy Scenarios" because they introduce some basic decision points that occur often in curling. They do not assume, however, that the people executing the shots are beginners! If your team can't consistently make hits or your ice conditions are bad, then in real life, you may need to make a different shot choice than what the "answer" is here. It's better to make the second best shot than to miss the best one!

Beginner Scenarios Overview

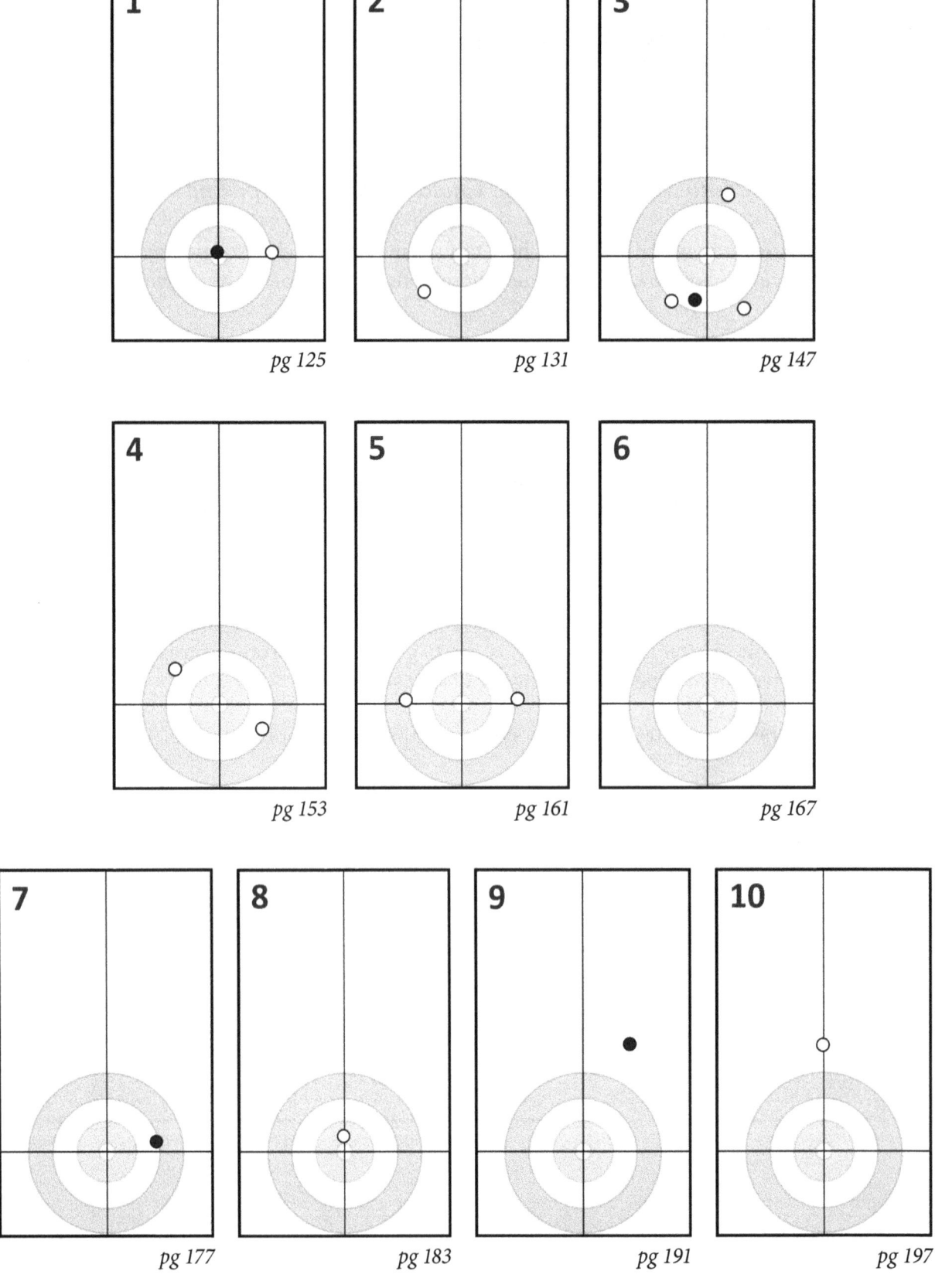

Beginner Scenario 1

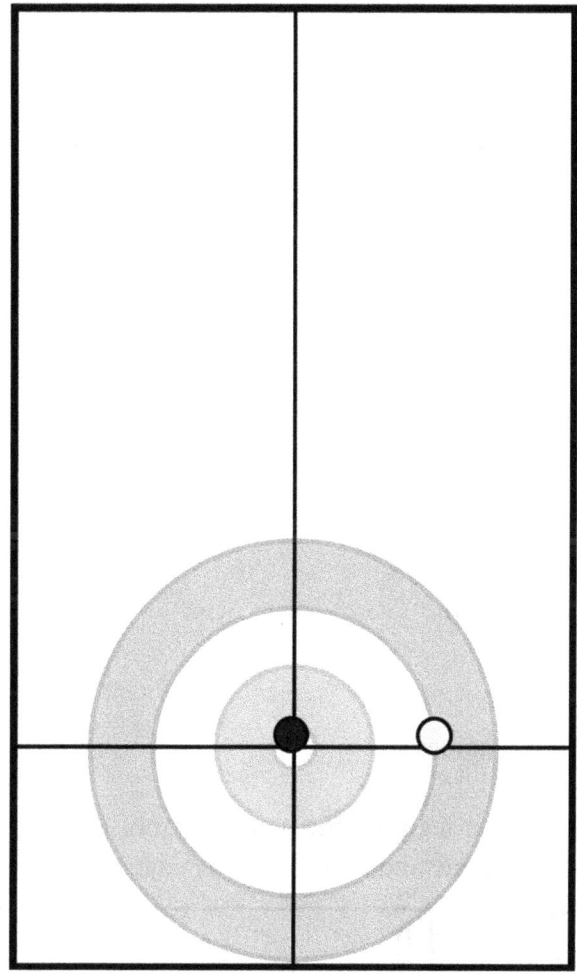

Beginner Scenario 1

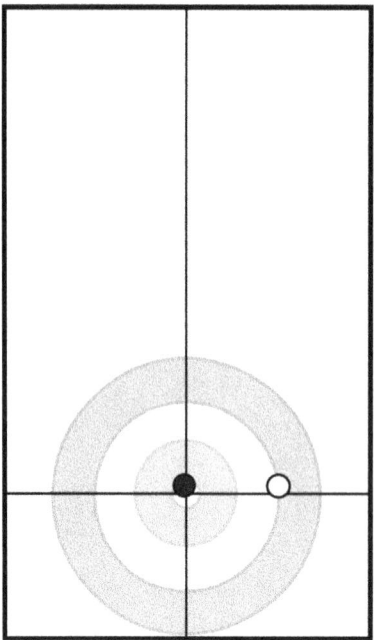

Questions

Non-Hammer Team

Which shot would you choose to:
- Force 1
- Steal

Non-Hammer Team's Shot Choices
  (A) Center guard
  (B) Freeze to the non-hammer team's stone on the button
  (C) Hit the hammer team's stone and and roll to the edge of the rings

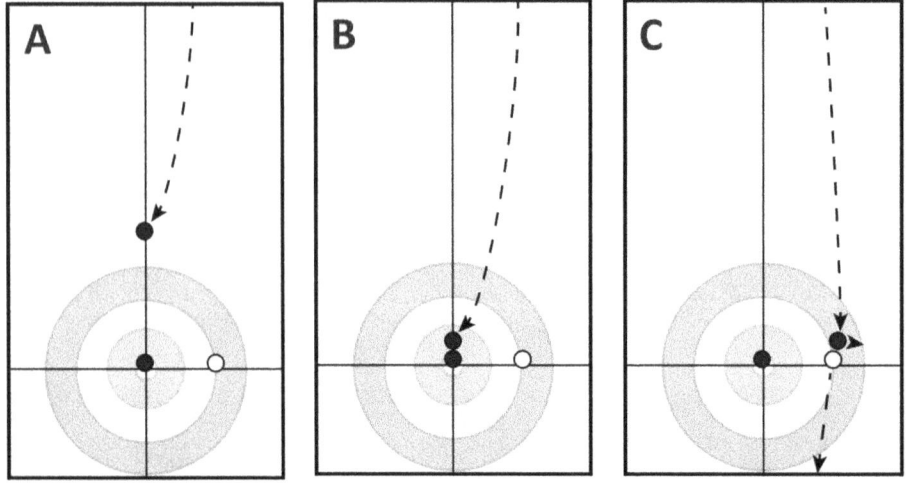

Hammer Team

Which shot would you choose to:
▸ Score 2

Hammer Team's Shot Choices
(A) Corner guard
(B) Hit the non-hammer team's stone and roll to split the house

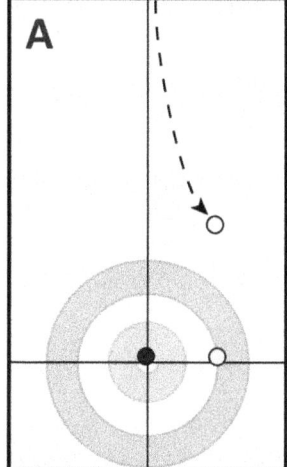 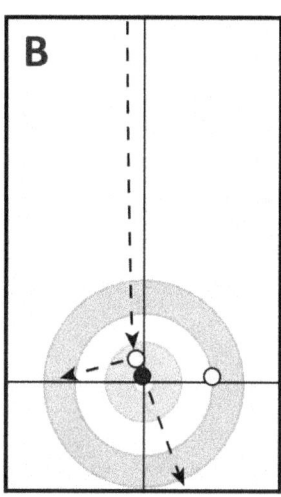

Discussion

Non-Hammer Team

Force 1

Conservative

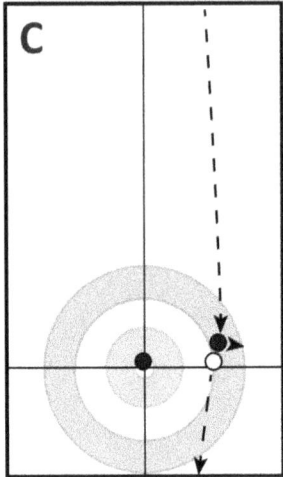

If the non-hammer team is playing conservatively to force the hammer team to score one and only one point, it would hit the hammer team's stone and roll to the edge of the rings (Option C). The hammer team can't score more than one point if it can't get more than one rock in play!

Remember—it's important for the non-hammer team's rock to stay on the rings in a spot where both non-hammer stones can't be removed with a double takeout. If the non-hammer team's stone rolls out, or rolls to a place where there's an easy double, the hammer team could blank the end.

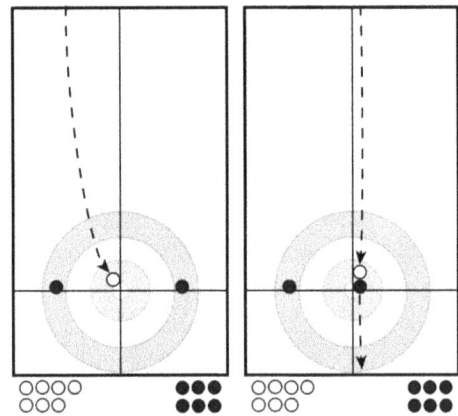

The non-hammer team is hoping the end will finish as an open-center force, in which the hammer team is forced to hit or draw for one.

This is a conservative way to force one because there's a chance the hammer team could blank, but very little risk the hammer team will score more than one.

Aggressive

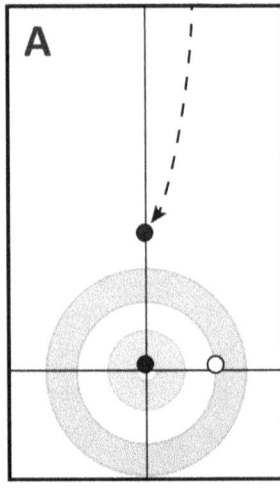

If the non-hammer team absolutely has to force one and needs to minimize the hammer team's chance of blanking, it can put up a center guard. Guards are good for keeping rocks in play—which means one team or the other will probably score in the end, minimizing the chance of a blank.

This is a risky, aggressive choice, because if the non-hammer team misses the guard shot, the hammer team may be able to hit the stone on the button and stay to set up a deuce.

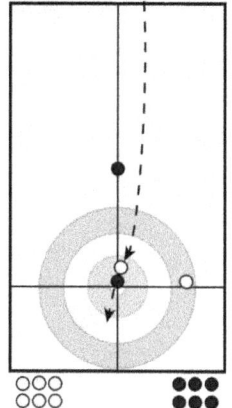

The non-hammer team is hoping the end will finish as a closed-center force, in which the hammer team is forced to draw or tap for one.

As with all aggressive tactics, as the odds of a good outcome increase, so do the odds of a bad outcome. By leaving the hammer team's stone in play, the non-hammer team risks giving up at least two points if its force plan doesn't work.

Steal 1

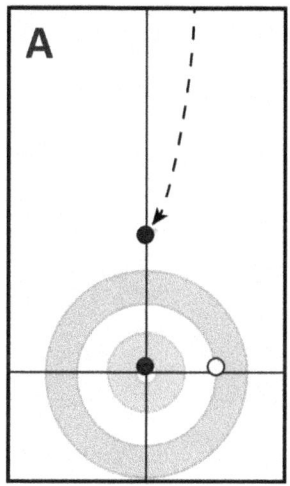

If the non-hammer team is trying to steal, then it should put up a tight center guard to protect its shot rock and ignore the hammer team's stone (Option A).

Hammer Team

Score 2

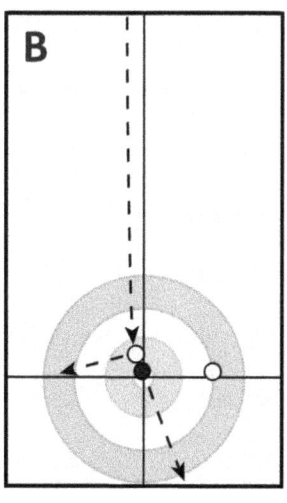

If the hammer team is trying to score two points, it would likely hit the non-hammer team's rock and roll to the left side to split the house (Option B).

Note: It's possible the hammer team could put up a corner guard (Option A) to score two—especially against an opponent that hits well. However, it's more likely that a hammer team would choose that tactic if it's desperate to score three and needs cover to keep more rocks in play.

Beginner Scenario 2

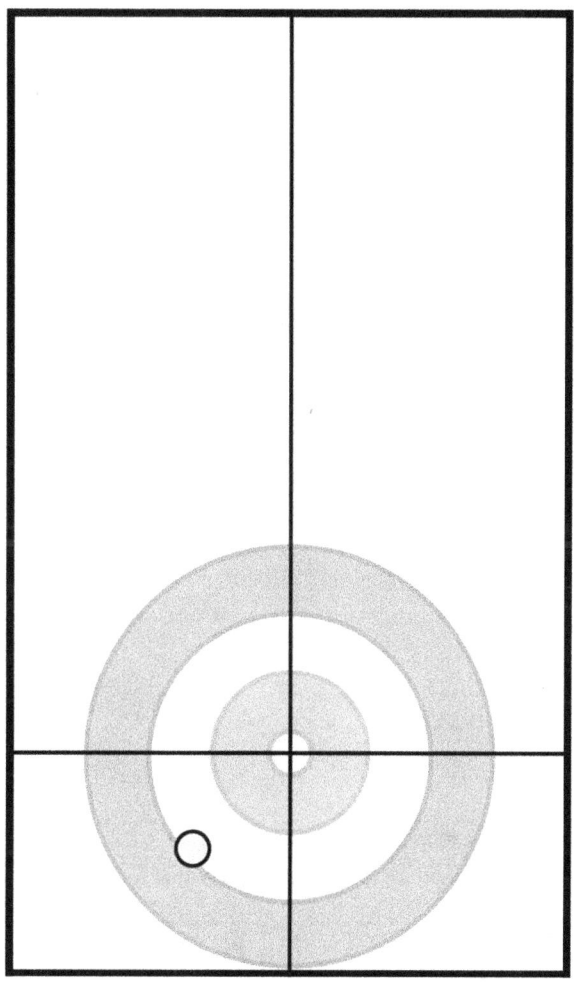

Beginner Scenario 2

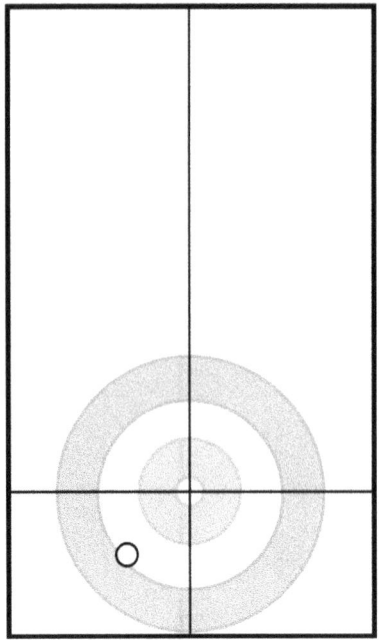

Questions

Non-Hammer Team

Which shot would you choose to:
- ▶ **Prevent the hammer team from scoring more than 1**
- ▶ **Force 1**
- ▶ **Steal 1**
- ▶ **Steal 1 (last rock)**

Non-Hammer Team's Shot Choices

(A) Center guard
(B) Draw to the button
(C) Freeze to the hammer team's stone
(D) Hit the hammer team's stone and roll to the center

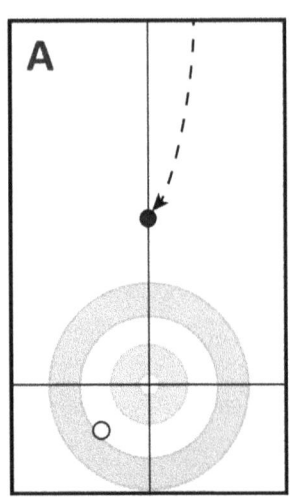
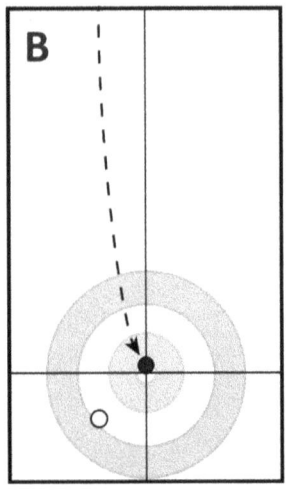
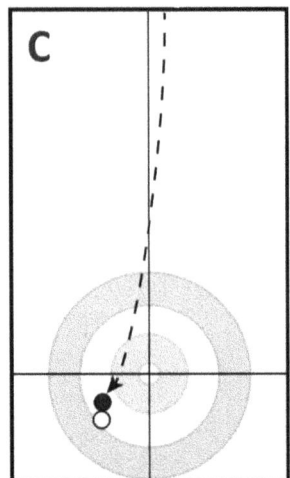
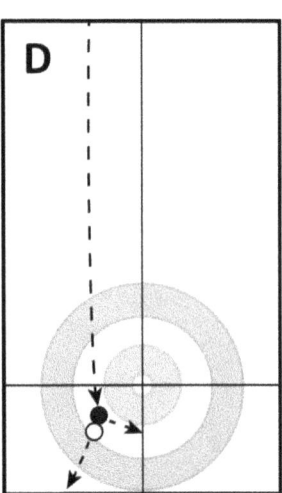

Hammer Team

Which shot would you choose to:
- Score 2
- Prevent the non-hammer team from stealing

Hammer Team's Shot Choices
(A) Corner guard
(B) Draw to the wing to split the house
(C) Take out own stone and roll out

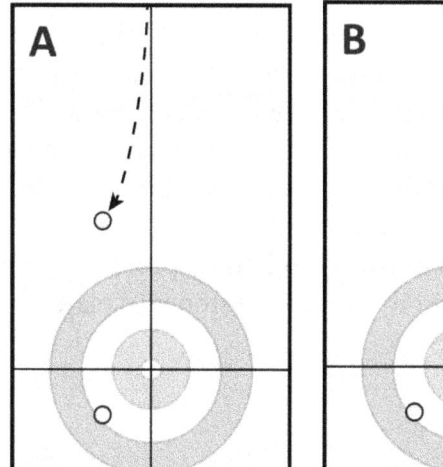
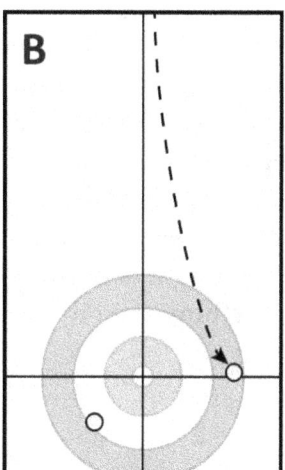
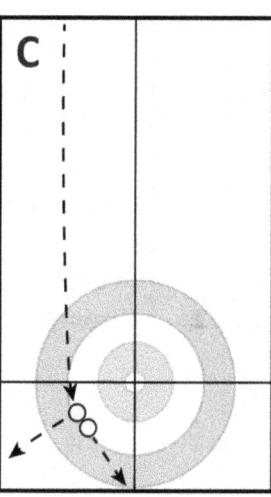

Discussion

Non-Hammer Team

Prevent the hammer team from scoring more than 1

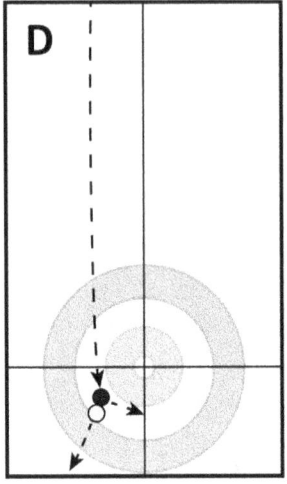

To prevent the hammer team from scoring more than one, the non-hammer team would hit the rock in the back of the rings and roll to the center (Option D). After all, the hammer team can't score two points if it doesn't have two rocks in play!

In this illustration, the non-hammer team rolls to the middle, likely with the goal of pressuring the hammer team to hit, since its rock is now near the four-foot and is a scoring threat. (As we discussed in "Simple End 1" in the "Strategy Basics" section, rocks near the center are more useful to the non-hammer team, and rocks on the wings are more useful to the hammer team.) However, if the non-hammer team were playing very conservatively, it might deliberately roll out to prevent the hammer team from having anything at all to use to keep stones in play.

Force 1

Conservative

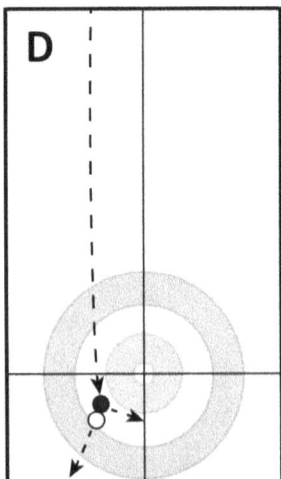

Hit through the middle of the end to keep the deuce risk low...

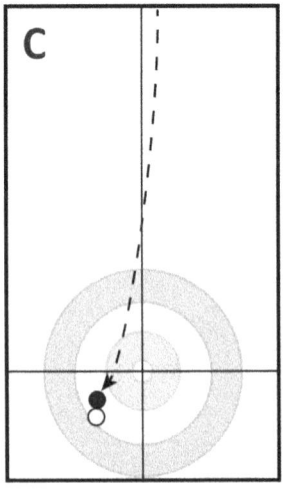

...then freeze on the last shot to prevent a blank.

A conservative non-hammer team would hit the hammer team's stone (Option D), until its own last rock and then freeze (Option C) to force the hammer team to draw for one. By playing hits through the middle of the end, the non-hammer team keeps the risk of giving up two or more low. Then by freezing with its last shot, the non-hammer team prevents the hammer team from blanking.

This is a bit of a gamble, because if the hammer team rolls out on its second-to-last shot, the non-hammer team won't have a place to freeze and the hammer team will have a chance to blank.

This choice is conservative because it focuses more on minimizing the possibility of a bad outcome (giving up multiple points) than it does on maximizing the possibility of a good outcome (forcing the hammer team to score one without a chance to blank).

Moderately Aggressive

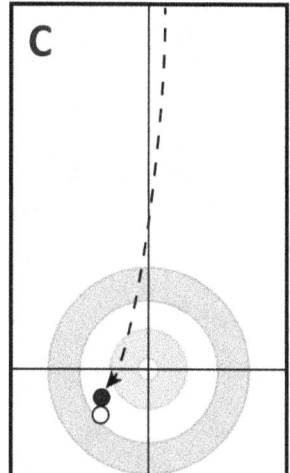

A moderately aggressive non-hammer team would freeze now. If the non-hammer team makes a perfect nose freeze, the hammer team will have a difficult time moving the non-hammer team's stone to count two. (Since both rocks are behind the tee line, the hammer team could freeze on top of both, in which case, the non-hammer team would have to freeze again, etc.)

If the freeze is not good, the hammer team might be able to pick out the non-hammer team's stone or simply remove both and play for a blank.

This choice is moderately aggressive because there could be multiple rocks in play at the end. That's a good thing, in the sense that it means the hammer team will likely be forced to score a point. However, that's also a risky thing, because the hammer team may have a chance to score multiple points. (And it's only moderately aggressive, because without guards to keep rocks in play, it will be easier for the hammer team to blank.)

Aggressive

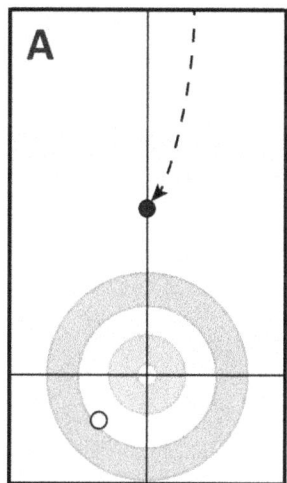

If the non-hammer team absolutely has to force and a blank is unacceptable, it would play aggressively and put up a center guard (Option A). Guards block hits, so they are the best way to ensure there will be rocks in play at the end of the end—thus forcing someone to score and preventing a blank. A center guard can also reduce the scoring area, making it more difficult for the hammer team to score more than one. (For more on this, see the "Aggressive Force" part of the "Forces" chapter.) However, by ignoring the hammer team's rock in the rings and putting up a guard, the non-hammer team will give the hammer team a "free turn" to draw another rock into the rings. The hammer team could even use the non-hammer team's guard for protection! This could allow the hammer team to eventually score two (or more) points.

This move is considered aggressive because it raises the odds of a good outcome (a force, not a blank) while it simultaneously raises the odds of a bad outcome (a deuce).

Steal 1

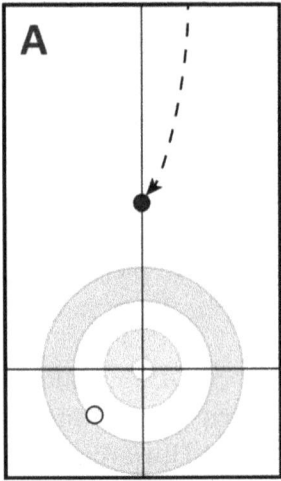

To steal, the non-hammer team would put up a center guard (Option A). The non-hammer team's best configuration for a steal is a shot rock on the button behind a center guard.

Since the Free Guard Zone time is over, the hammer team can take out that guard. The non-hammer team will probably need the hammer team to miss (either by flashing a hit or by nose-hitting and leaving its shooter as a new center guard) to be able to steal.

Steal 1 (last rock)

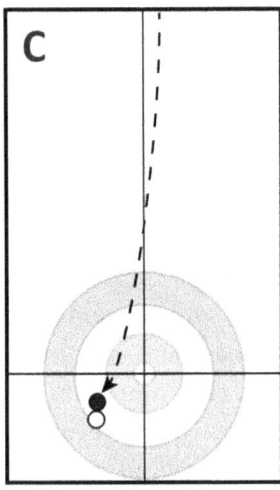

The non-hammer team has no guard to hide behind, so it would likely freeze its last rock to the hammer team's stone to make it difficult to remove (Option C). It's difficult to steal this way, since the hammer team's skip can easily out-draw those rocks to get one point, but that's the best the non-hammer team can do under the circumstances.

Non-Hammer Team

Score 2

Conservative

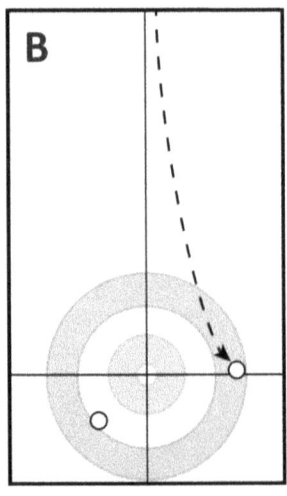

The conservative answer—and the most common play in this situation—is for the hammer team to split the house (Option B). The advantage of this choice is that the hammer team would have two rocks in the house—exactly what it needs to get two points! The downside is that the rocks are open and a very good non-hammer team might be able to remove both with a double takeout.

Aggressive

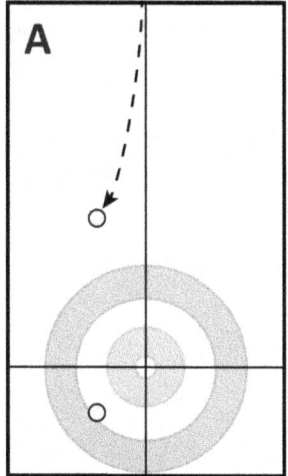

An aggressive hammer team might put up a corner guard (Option A).

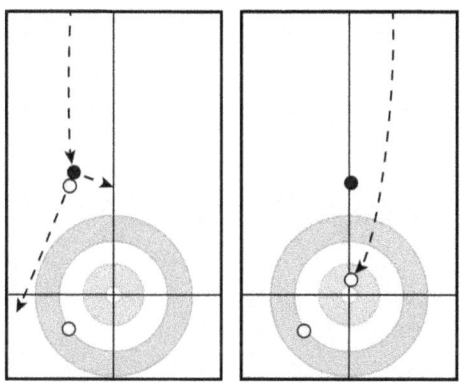

By putting up a corner guard over its existing stone, the hammer team hopes to make the non-hammer team's shots more difficult so it will get a miss or half-shot it can exploit for multiple points. For example, if the non-hammer team attempts to take out the guard and roll out, but accidentally leaves its shooter as a new guard, the hammer team can secure a second stone in the rings.

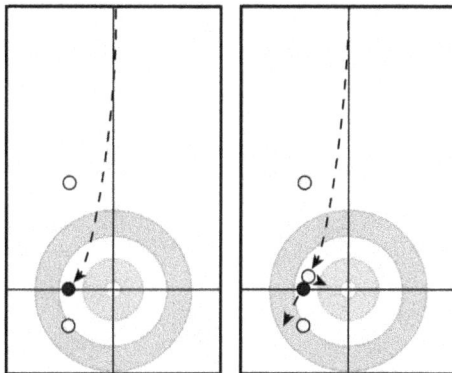

Or, if the non-hammer team tries to draw behind the guard to out-count the back stone, the hammer team may be able to bump it to sit two.

This choice is considered aggressive, because it gives the hammer team a better chance to score two (or more), while simultaneously giving the non-hammer team a better chance to force one by hiding a stone in a spot where the hammer team can't remove it.

Prevent the non-hammer team from stealing

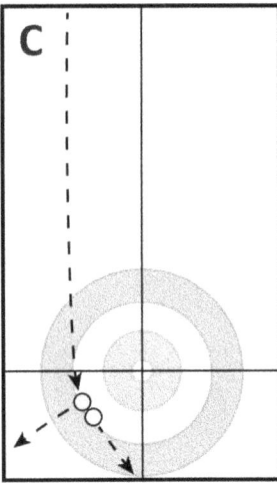

To prevent the non-hammer team from stealing, the hammer team would take out its own rock in the rings

The hammer team would do this because its stone in the back of the rings is a place where the non-hammer team can freeze and sit shot. The hammer team doesn't want to leave anything around that could help its opponent keep rocks in play.

Beginner Scenario 2—Variation 1

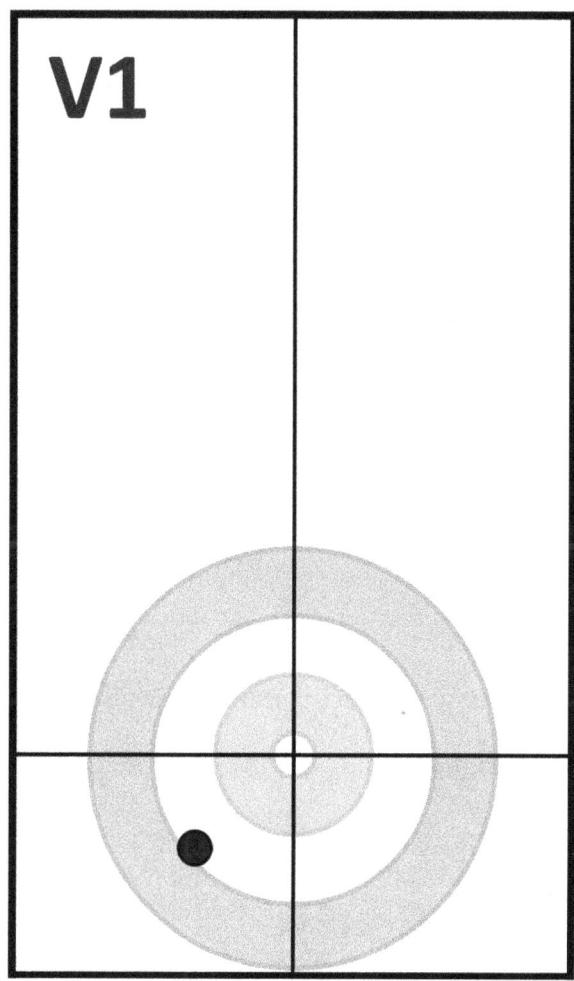

Beginner Scenario 2—Variation 1

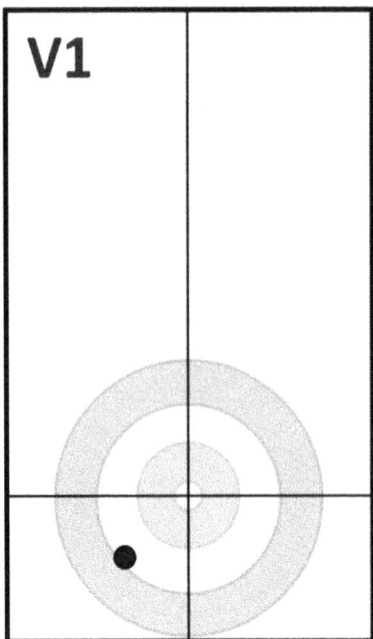

Questions

Non-Hammer Team

Which shot would you choose to:
- Steal 1
- Steal 1 (last rock)
- Prevent the hammer team from scoring more than 1

Non-Hammer Team's Shot Choices
(A) Center guard
(B) Draw to the eight-foot in front of its own stone
(C) Draw to the front four-foot
(D) Draw to the open side and split the house
(E) Take out its own stone in the back of the rings and roll out

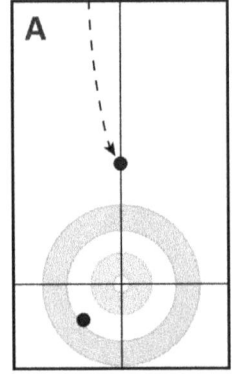 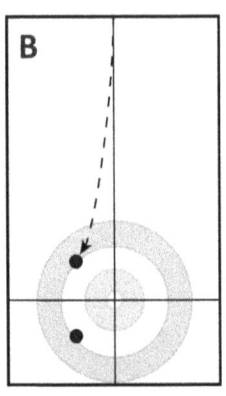 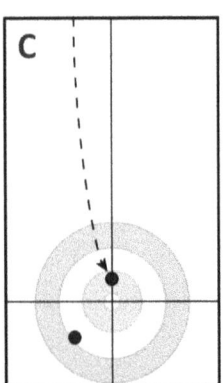 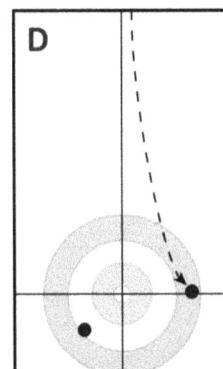 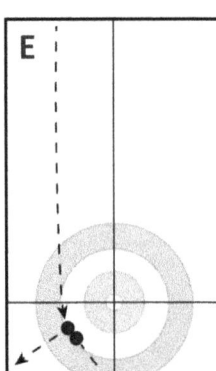

Hammer Team

Which shot would you choose to:
- Blank
- Score 2

Hammer Team's Shot Choices
(A) Corner guard on the rock side
(B) Corner guard on the open side
(C) Draw to the tee line in front of the non-hammer team's stone
(D) Freeze to the non-hammer team's stone
(E) Take out the non-hammer team's stone and roll to the wing

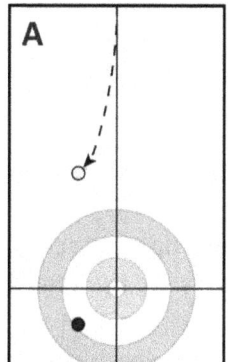
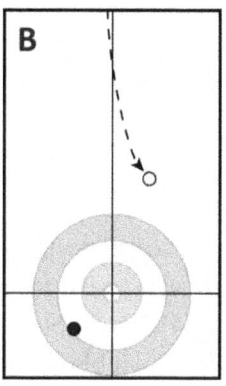
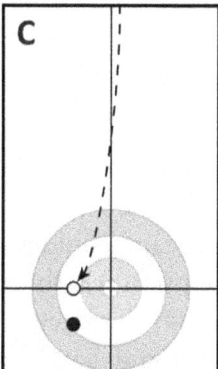
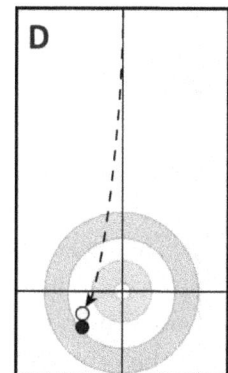
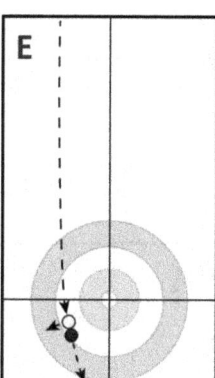

Discussion

Non-Hammer Team

Force 1

Conservative

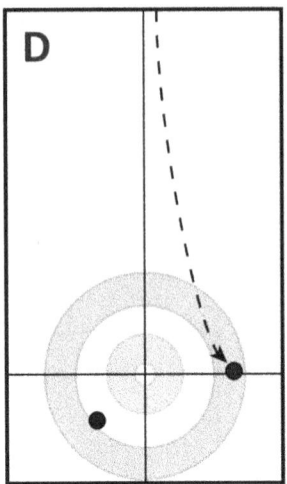

A conservative non-hammer team would "split the house" by putting another rock in the rings, far away from the existing rock so it would be difficult for the hammer team to make a double takeout (Option D). This is a conservative force because all the rocks are in the open, giving the hammer team a reasonable chance for a blank, but very little chance of scoring more than one.

Aggressive

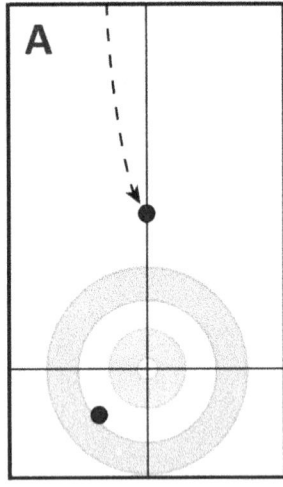

The non-hammer team would ignore its own stone in the rings and set up a center guard (Option A). This is an aggressive force because the guard will help the non-hammer team keep rocks in play, so that one team or the other will eventually have to score and a blank won't be possible.

Steal 1

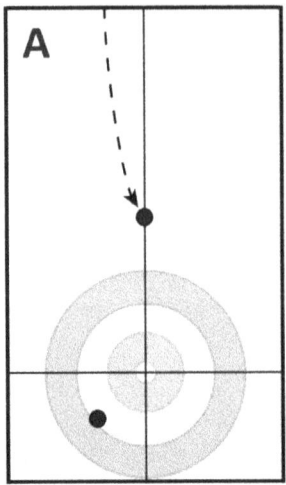

The non-hammer team should put up a center guard (Option A). (As we talked about in the beginning of the "Steals" chapter, non-hammer teams usually need a center guard and a quality shot rock near the pin to steal.)

Steal 1 (last rock)

The non-hammer team has an interesting choice here. It is not in a good position to steal—it doesn't have a center guard and its shot rock is not in good scoring position near the button. That means the hammer team will definitely have some kind of shot to score one. All the non-hammer team can do is make that shot as difficult as possible.

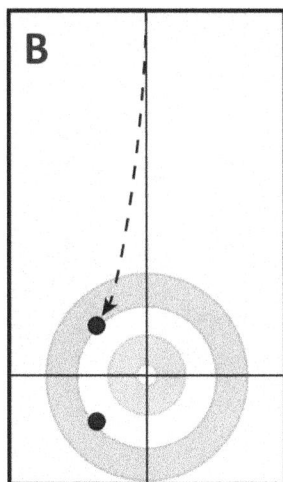

If the non-hammer team thinks the hammer team's skip is having trouble with draws, the non-hammer team might put its last stone in the top eight-foot in front of its own stone (Option B). That would make it difficult for the hammer team to hit and be shot, and thus force its skip to draw for the point. (Depending on the curl of the ice, the front rock could also make it difficult for the hammer team to use the back rock as backing for a draw).

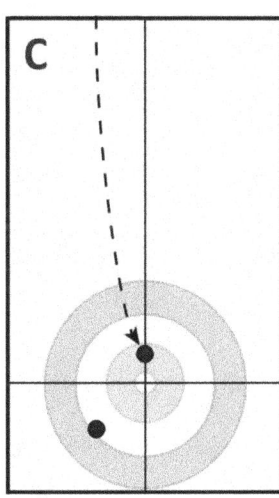

If the non-hammer team thinks the hammer team's skip has more difficulty with hits, the non-hammer team could put a rock in the front four-foot (Option C), so the hammer team has only a small area to draw to for the single point. This would encourage the hammer team to try the hit. (The hammer team could still conceivably try the difficult draw or a precise tap on the front rock.)

Prevent the hammer team from scoring more than 1

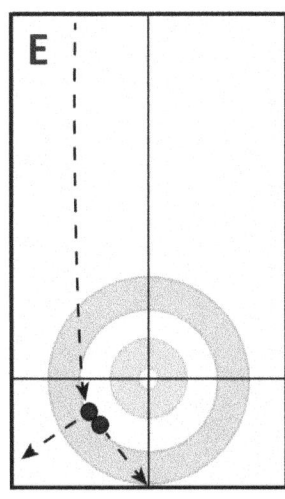

The non-hammer team should hit its own stone and roll out (Option E). The non-hammer team doesn't want to give the hammer team anything to use—guards or backing—to keep rocks in play.

Hammer Team

Blank

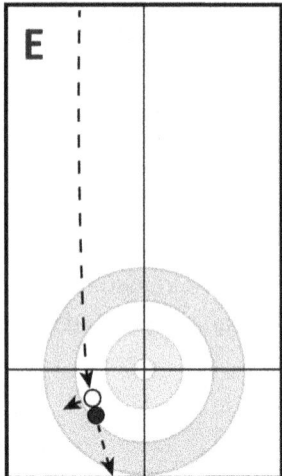

The hammer team should hit the non-hammer team's rock and roll to the side (Option E). Why roll? So the hammer team's stone is in a worse spot for a freeze, and so it's more difficult to hit. Most people have more trouble hitting stones on the wings because they find it difficult to push out of the hack at an angle.

Score 2

In this situation, the non-hammer team's stone in the rings is helpful to the hammer team. It's behind the tee line away from the four-foot, so it's not a scoring threat. It's not blocking a hammer team bail-out draw to the button. And, the hammer team could use it as backing to keep stones in play. Thus, the hammer team doesn't need to hit it.

Very Conservative

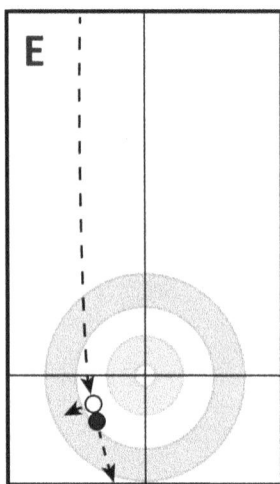

That being said, if the hammer team is playing very conservatively for a deuce, it could hit the non-hammer team's stone and roll to the side (Option E). If the non-hammer team attempts to hit but misses, the hammer team can draw to the other side and split the house. If not, then the hammer team can still blank the end.

Moderately Conservative

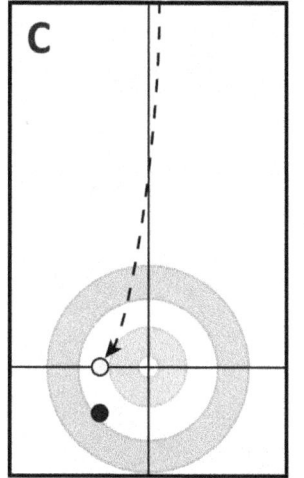 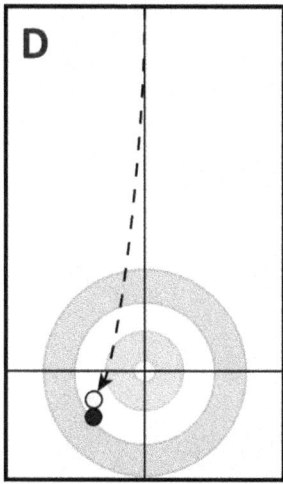

If the hammer team is playing moderately conservatively for a deuce, it could draw to the tee line in front of the non-hammer team's rock (Option C) or freeze to it (Option D), to make its own stone difficult to remove without jamming. The risk with the tee-line draw is that the hammer team's stone could be removed more easily. The risk with the freeze is that both stones would be behind the tee line, so the non-hammer team could freeze to them and sit shot.

Aggressive

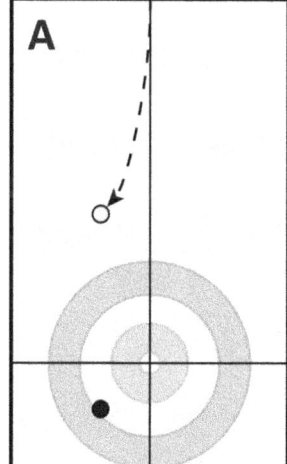 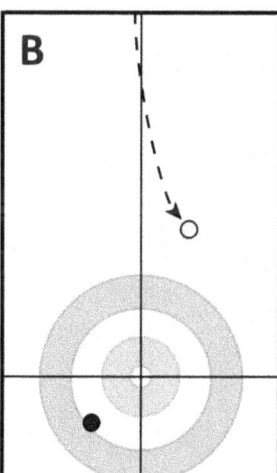

If the hammer team is playing aggressively for a deuce, it could put up a corner guard (Options A and B). As discussed in the chapter, "Tips for Using Corner Gaurds," the same-side guard (Choice A) is the more aggressive choice, and open-side guard (Choice B) is the more conservative choice. The advantage of the aggressive same-side guard (Choice A) is that it increases the odds rocks will remain in play, which could help the hammer team keep two stones on the rings. The advantage of the more conservative open-side guard (Choice B) is that—if worse comes to worse—the non-hammer team's stone would be open so the hammer team could hit it to blank.

Beginner Scenario 3

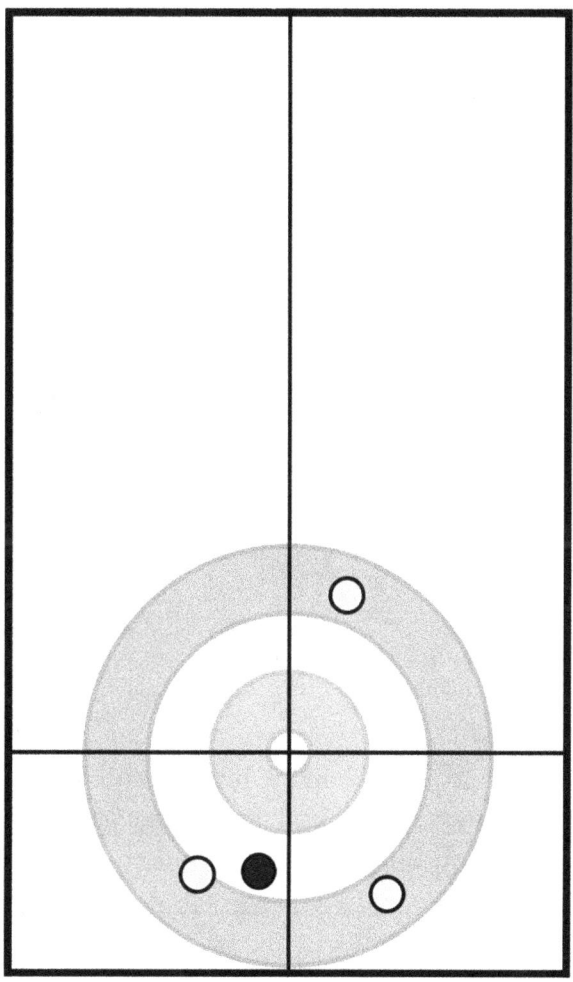

Beginner Scenario 3

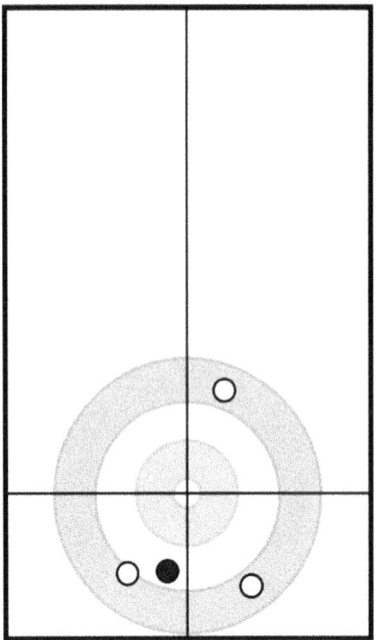

Questions

Hammer Team

Which shot would you choose to:
- **Score 2 or more**

Hammer Team's Shot Choices
(A) Draw to the tee line behind the rock in the top twelve-foot
(B) Bump the non-hammer team's stone back to the edge of the rings
(C) Take out the non-hammer team's stone

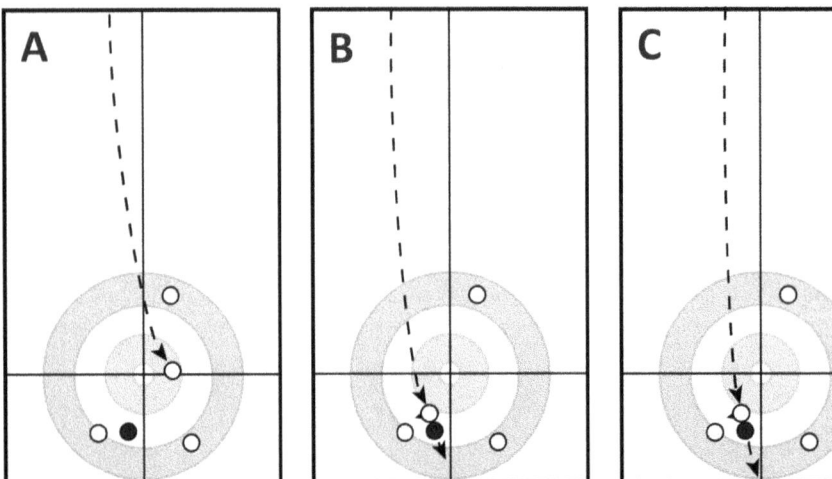

Non-Hammer Team

Which shot would you choose to:
- Avoid giving up a big end
- Steal 1
- Steal 1 (last rock)

Non-Hammer Team's Shot Choices

(A) Center guard
(B) Draw to the top eight-foot in front of its own stone
(C) Draw to the top four-foot slightly to the right of the center line
(D) Draw to the tee line behind the hammer team's stone in the top twelve-foot
(E) Draw in front of the hammer team's stone in the back right twelve-foot
(F) Double takeout

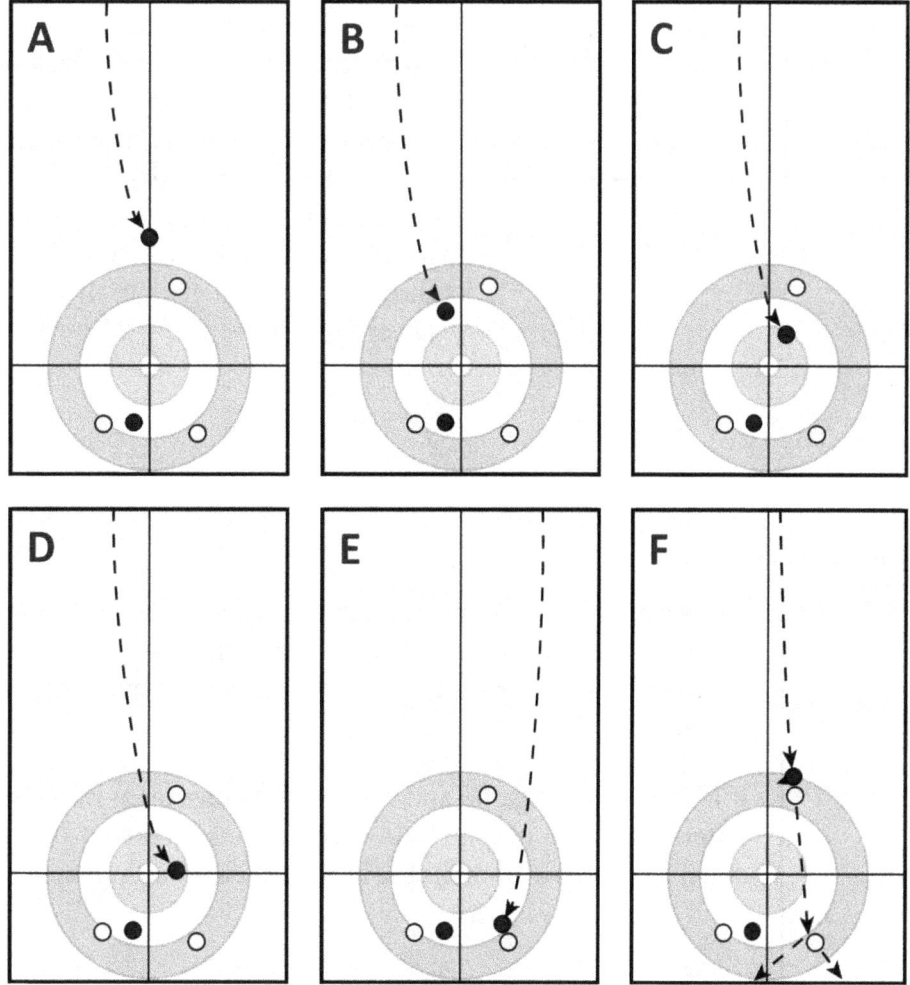

Discussion

Hammer Team

Score 2 or more

We just got through talking about when not to hit a lone opponent stone in the back of the rings, but here's an example of when it's good for the hammer team to break that rule.

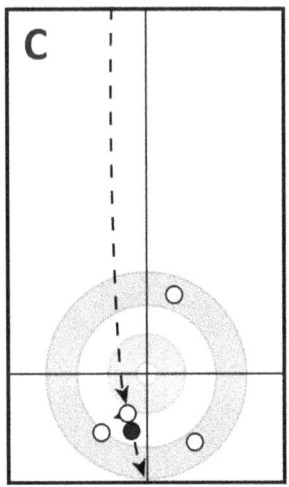
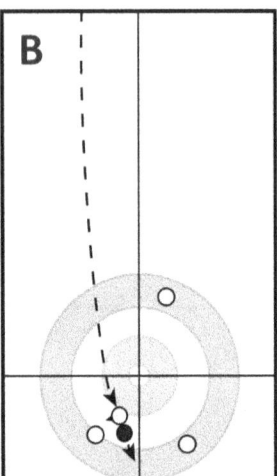

The hammer team's original goal for the end may have been to score two, but now it has an opportunity to score lots of points. Normally, the hammer team wouldn't hit a rock in the back of the rings—it would use it as backing to keep rocks in play. However, if the hammer team removes the non-hammer team's shot stone (Option C), or pushes it to the very edge of the rings (Option B), the hammer team would be counting four points. Even though the end could take more twists and turns (including the risk of the non-hammer team freezing to one of the hammer team's stones in the back of the rings), by removing the non-hammer team's shot rock from a counting position now, the hammer team gives itself a chance at a very big end.

Non-Hammer Team

Avoid giving up a big end

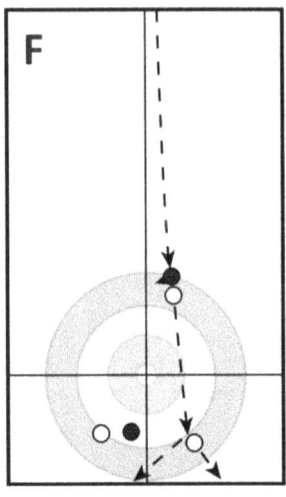

At the beginning of this end, the non-hammer team may have been planning to steal conservatively or force one, but that plan's gone out the window. Now all the team wants to do is avoid a disaster! The team has a couple of choices:

If it's early in the game and the non-hammer team members are expert hitters, the team might try to make a double takeout (Option F) to cut down the number of rocks the hammer team has in play.

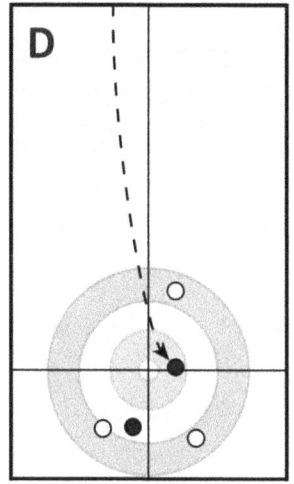 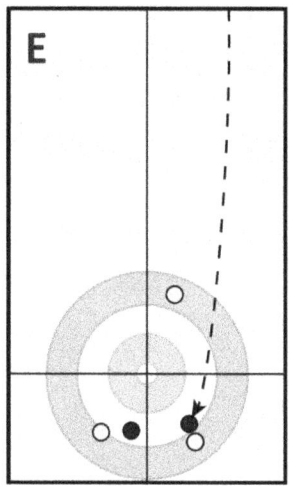

Alternatively, the non-hammer team could draw in for second shot, ideally behind the hammer team's top stone (Option D) or just in front of the hammer team's stone in the back right (Option E). The non-hammer team needs to place a rock in a spot where it would be difficult or impossible for the hammer team to remove both of its shot rocks.

Steal 1

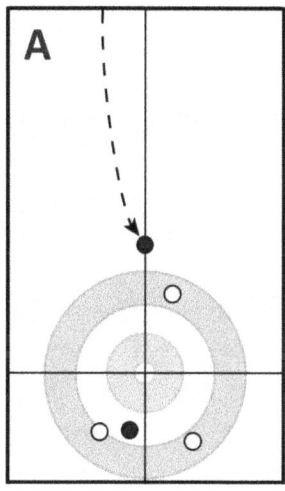

If the non-hammer team is down late in the game, it may need to steal to stay alive. Since the best way to steal is to have a shot rock on the button behind a center guard, the non-hammer team should put up a center guard (Option A).

Steal 1 (last rock)

The non-hammer team can no longer get that perfect steal configuration (shot rock on the button behind a center guard) so all it can do is make it as difficult as possible for the hammer team to score. The non-hammer team has a few reasonable choices:

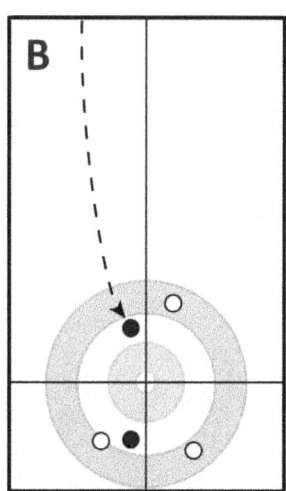 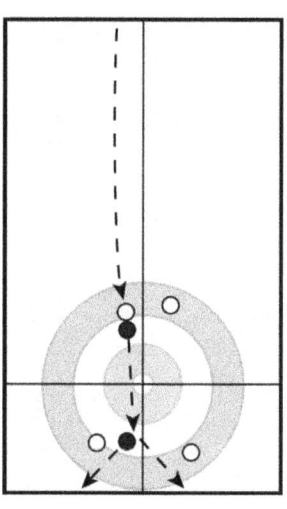

It could put a rock in the top eight-foot guarding its shot stone (Option B). The hammer team would still have a possible double takeout for four, or a very precise draw or tap for one.

This is an interesting choice point for the hammer team. The double is tough, so is the hammer team willing to risk giving up a steal to try for four? That's usually a worthwhile risk in the beginning of the game or if the hammer team is significantly behind.

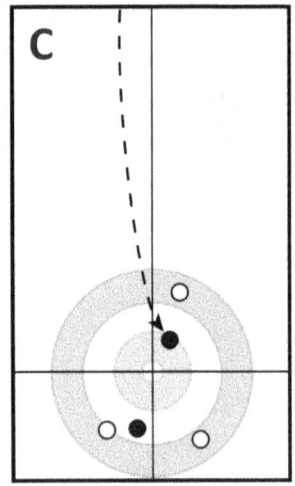
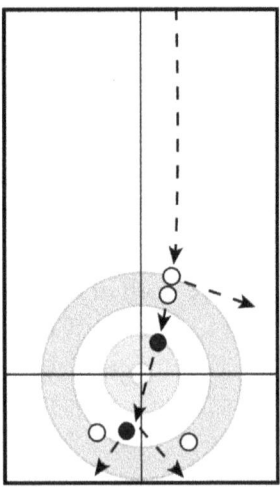

Alternatively, the non-hammer team could draw to the top four-foot slightly to the right of the center line (Option C). The hammer team would then have difficult runback double for three, or a draw for one.

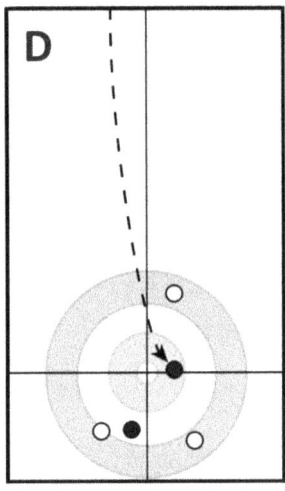

Finally, the non-hammer team could draw behind the hammer team's stone in the top twelve-foot (Option D). The hammer team's skip would then likely have to make a draw to the four-foot without backing to prevent the steal. The downside of this shot choice is that it's easy to out-draw—and it could even be backing for that draw. However, the big upside of it is that it would be very difficult for the hammer team to eliminate both of the non-hammer team's stones with one shot. Thus, it may not be the best steal option, but it would significantly reduce the risk of giving up a big end.

If this were the last end of the game and a "steal or lose" situation, the non-hammer team would choose which shot to play based on the ice conditions, and on which shot it thinks the opposing skip will find most difficult or stressful. It would not worry about the number of points it could potentially give up if the steal didn't work.

However, if this were an early end, the non-hammer team would likely pick the third choice, the draw behind the rock in the top twelve-foot (Option D), because it reduces the risk of giving up a big end.

Beginner Scenario 4

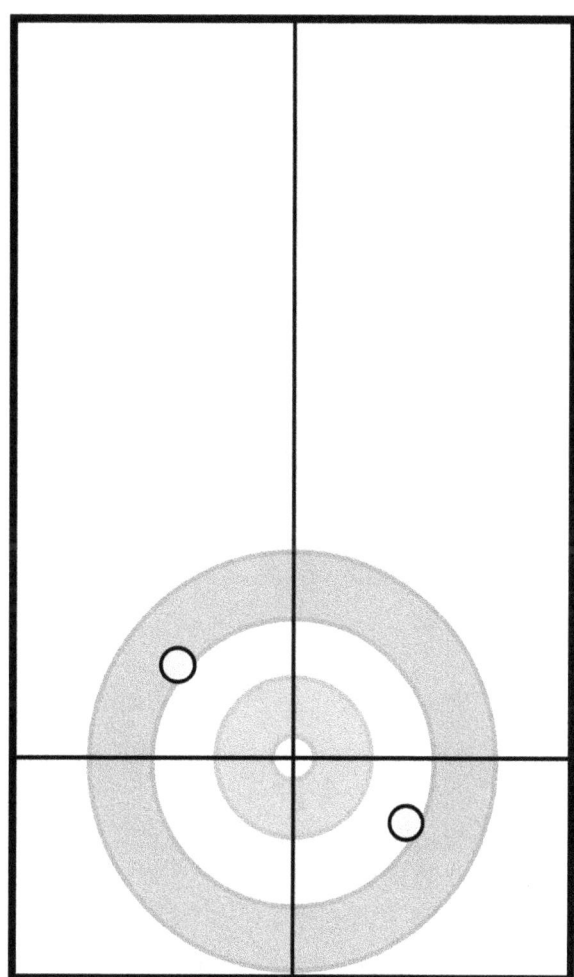

Beginner Scenario 4

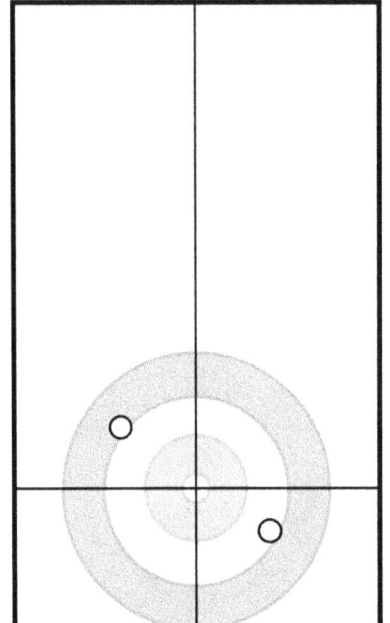

Questions

Non-Hammer Team

Which shot would you choose to:
- Force 1
- Force 1 (last rock)

Non-Hammer Team's Shot Choices
(A) Freeze to the stone in the back eight-foot
(B) Double takeout
(C) Hit and roll off the top stone
(D) Hit and roll off the shot stone

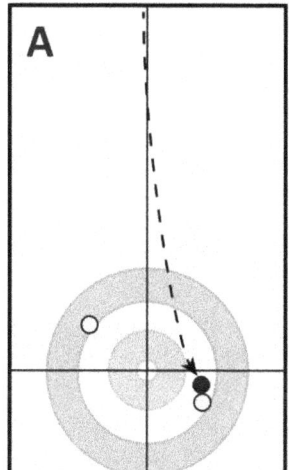 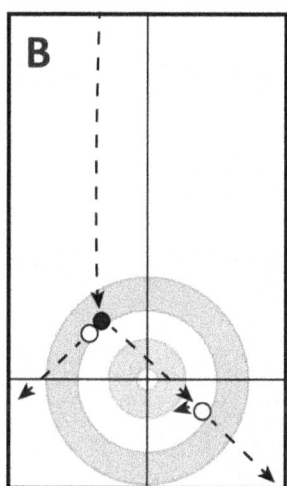 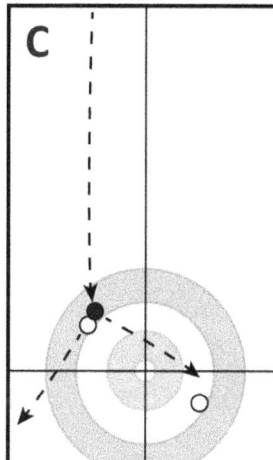 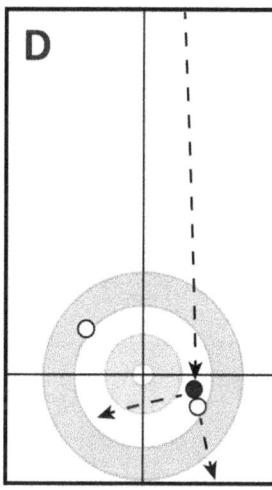

Discussion

Non-Hammer Team

Force 1

Conservative

The conservative non-hammer team wants to force one, but not at the risk of giving up a big end. So, first it would try to minimize the hammer team's opportunity for a big end, then it would work on forcing one.

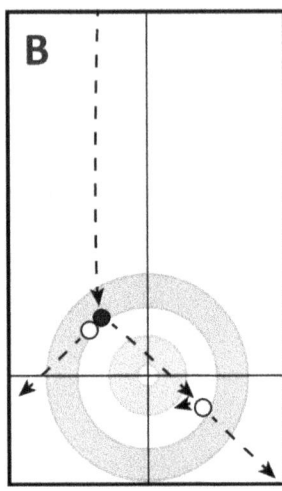

In this scenario, the hammer team is set up to score two. To absolutely prevent that, the non-hammer team needs to get rid of both of the hammer team's stones (Option B). The way the stones are positioned, the non-hammer team could make a double takeout, though that's a difficult shot.

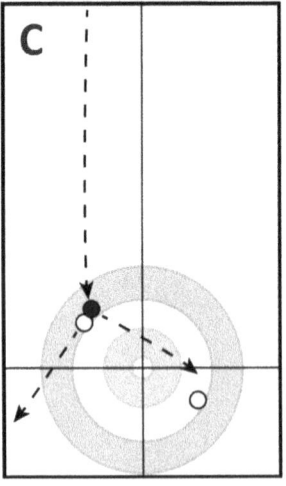

An alternative would be for the non-hammer to hit the higher stone and roll to sit shot in front of the lower stone (Option C).

This would force the hammer team to move the non-hammer team's rock to keep its deuce hopes alive. If the hammer team accidentally jams the non-hammer team's stone into the back stone, then the non-hammer team will be in a good position to force. Or, if the hammer team removes the stone, but leaves its shooter close to the back stone (shown below), the non-hammer team could have an easy double.

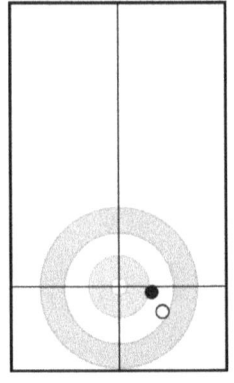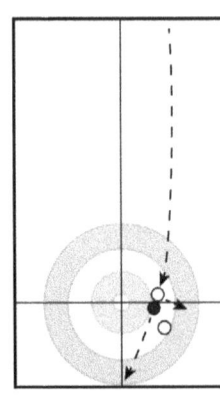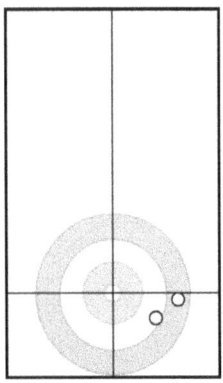

Once it eliminates the deuce threat, the non-hammer team could freeze with its last rock to force one.

156

Aggressive

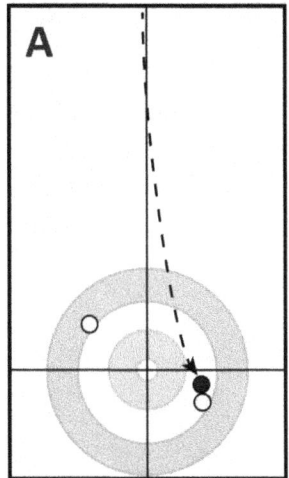

An aggressive team (or one with difficulty hitting) might choose to freeze to get shot (Option A).

This is a high risk shot, because if it's not perfect, the hammer team could tap it out and get three rocks in play. (If the non-hammer team tries to freeze multiple times and fails, it could give up a very big end!

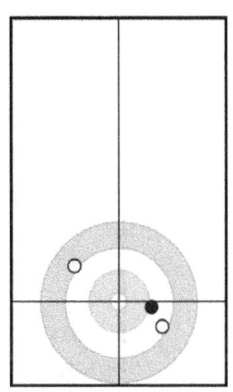 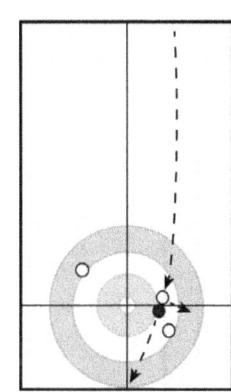 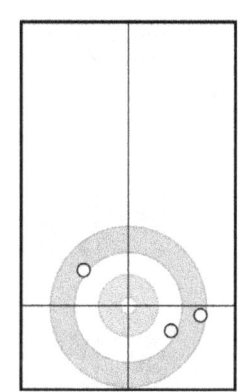

Also, even if the freeze is perfect, because the hammer team has multiple shots left, it could bump the pair of stones, then tap or hit the non-hammer team's stone later, possibly ending up with three or more stones in the rings.

Again, even though the hammer team is not yet set up for a big end, because it has lots of rocks in the rings, the potential is there.

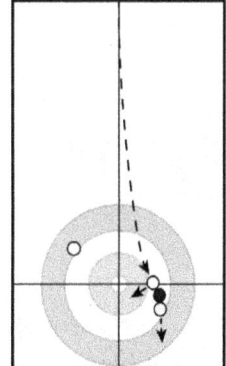 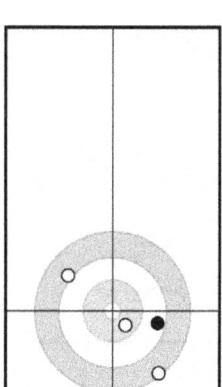

Force 1 (last rock)

Conservative

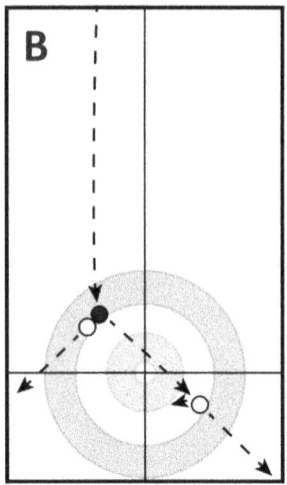

If the non-hammer team wants to force the hammer team to score one point, but can't afford to give up two or more points, it could attempt the double takeout. If the non-hammer team makes the double, the hammer team could blank. That's not a good outcome for the non-hammer team, but a conservative non-hammer team might prefer that to possibly giving up two or three.

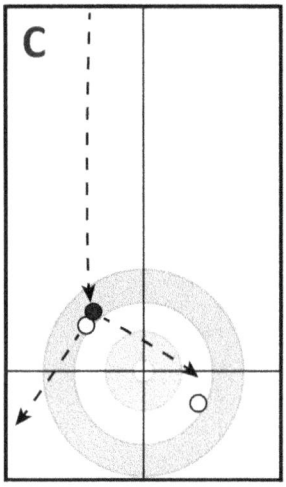 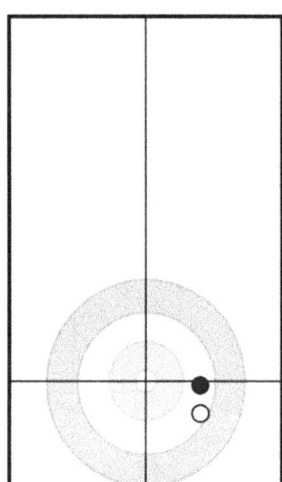

If the non-hammer team only manages to take out one stone but rolls in front of the hammer team's stone (Option C) to get shot rock, that is a good alternative. It will make it difficult for the hammer team to hit or bump and keep the shooter to score two points.

In general, the upside of making the conservative choice to hit is that the hammer team can't score more than two.

Aggressive

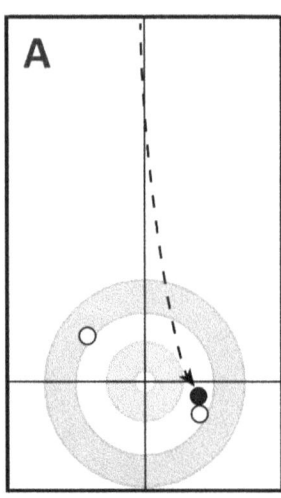

If the non-hammer team absolutely positively must force and can't risk a blank, it would freeze to the hammer team's shot stone. (This is also a good tactic for teams that don't hit well and aren't likely to make the double takeout.) If it works, it's a great shot, but if the non-hammer team doesn't make an excellent freeze, it could give up three points.

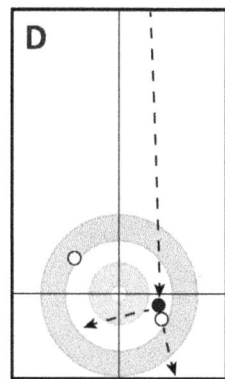

So why not hit the shot stone and roll behind the hammer team's stone in the front twelve-foot (Option D)? This is a possible option, but it's difficult to make a perfect roll and be totally hidden.

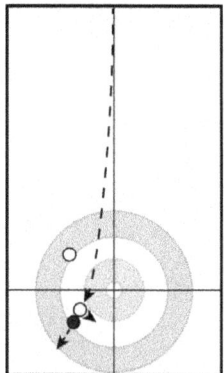 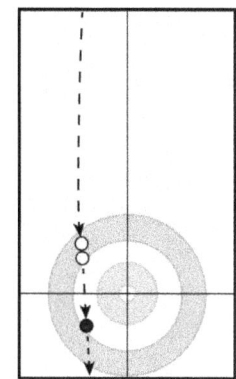

And even if the non-hammer team could do that, the hammer team might still be able to tap the non-hammer team's stone back, or run its own rock back onto the non-hammer team's stone to score two.

Beginner Scenario 5

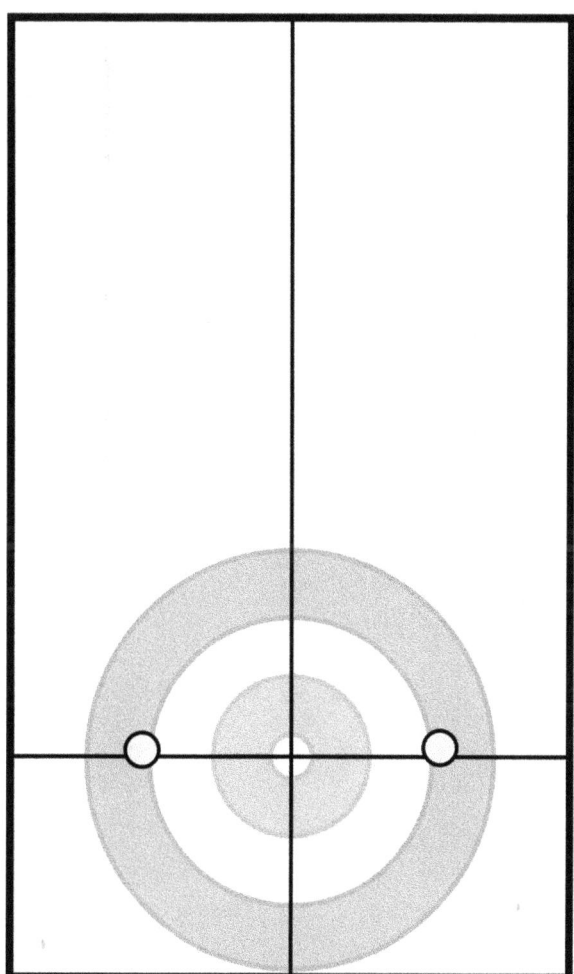

Beginner Scenario 5

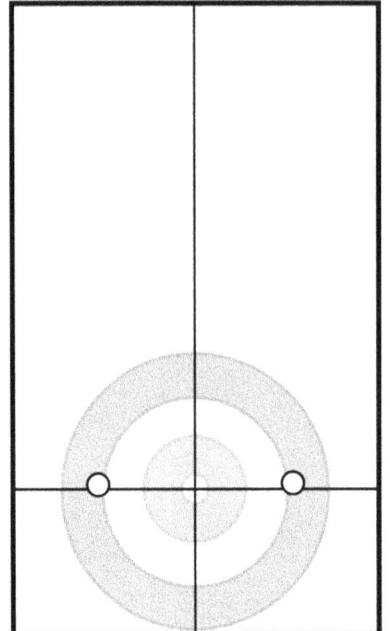

Questions

Hammer Team

Which shot would you choose to:
▸ **Score 3**

Hammer Team's Shot Choices
(A) Corner guard
(B) Draw to the edge of the twelve-foot, slightly outside the existing stone
(C) Draw to the button

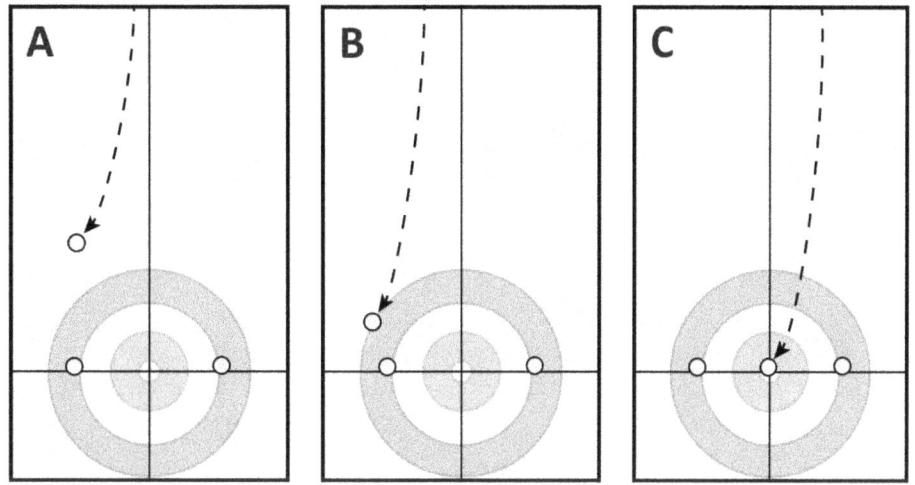

Discussion

Score 3

It's not easy to score a big end. The more rocks in play, the more opportunities the non-hammer team has to make double takeouts, or to hide or freeze a rock to force one.

All three of these shot choices could work, though they all have different pros and cons.

Option A

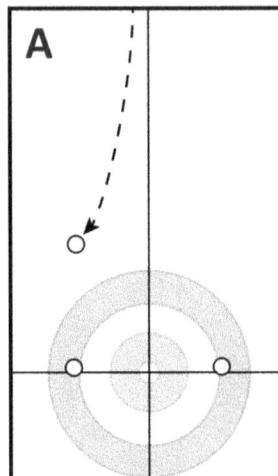

The advantage of putting up a corner guard (Option A) is that corner guards can be used to protect multiple stones.

Here's how it might play out:

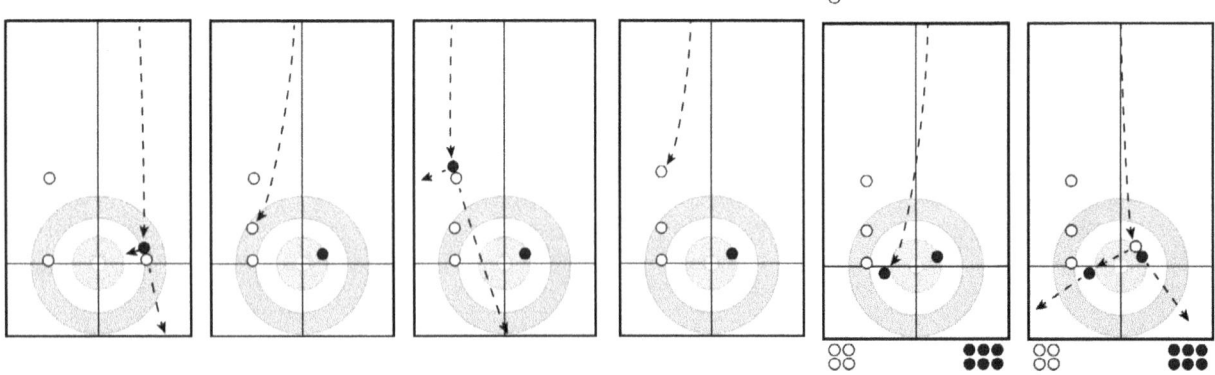

After the hammer team guards, the non-hammer team hits the open rock and takes shot position. The hammer team draws a second rock behind the guard. The non-hammer team peels the guard, and the hammer team replaces it. With its last shot, the non-hammer team tries to hit or freeze to one of the hammer team's stones in the rings and misses.

Finally, the hammer team has a shot for three.

There are two major risks for the hammer team:

The non-hammer team could freeze and out-count both of its stones in the rings….

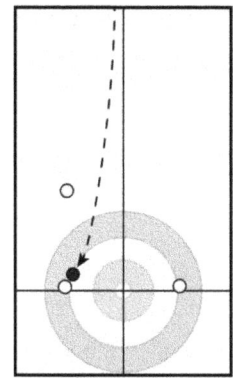

Or, the non-hammer team could make an amazing triple and eliminate all of the hammer team's stones.

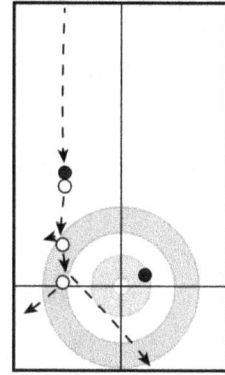

In either of these scenarios, the hammer team could be limited to scoring only one point.

(For more on how to use a corner guard to get three points, see the "How to use corner guards to get three points" section in the "Tips for Using Corner Guards" chapter.)

Option B

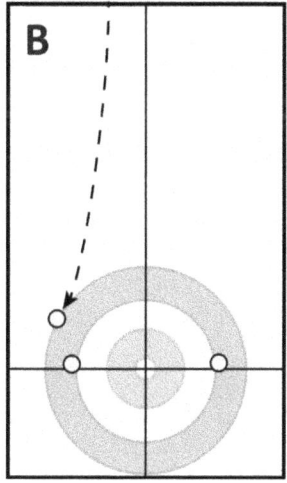

The advantage of drawing to the edge of the twelve-foot (Option B) is that if the non-hammer team tries to freeze, its rock won't be near the middle (where it would be tough to out-draw) or hidden by a guard (where it can't be hit).

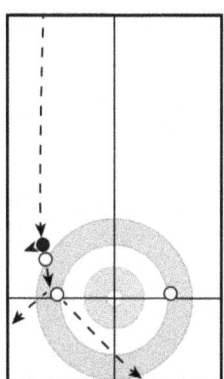

Also, if the non-hammer team attempts a double takeout on the two stones close together, it will roll out. That means the hammer team could still split the house to get two points.

Option C

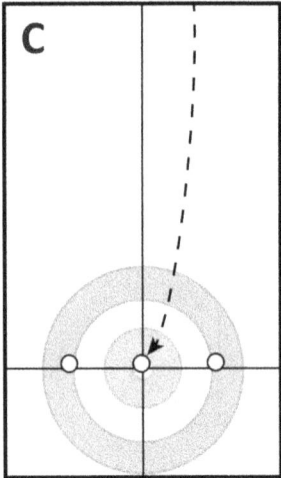

The advantage of the draw to the button (Option C) is that the non-hammer team can't make a double takeout, so the hammer team can keep more stones in play.

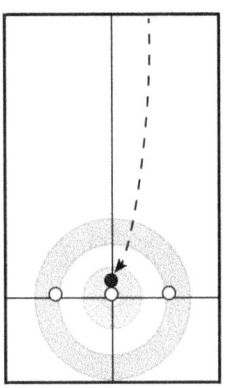

However, if the non-hammer team makes a good freeze to the rock in the middle, it will be difficult for the hammer team to remove that stone and score more than one.

Beginner Scenario 6

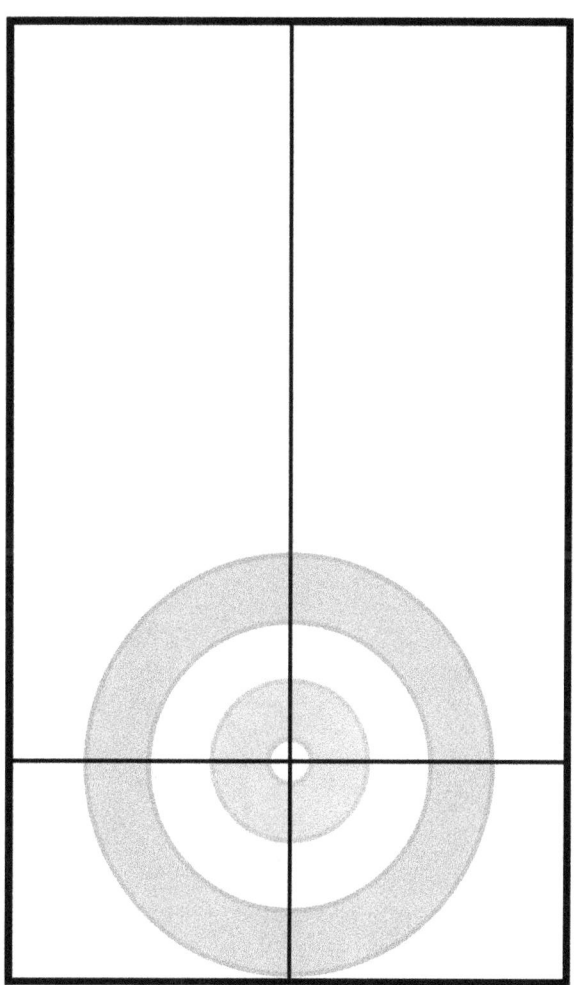

Beginner Scenario 6

It can feel a little odd to face an empty house halfway through an end. But remember your end plan and stay committed!

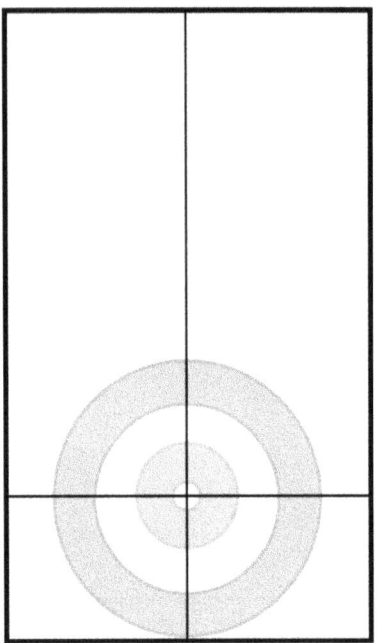

Questions

Non-Hammer Team

Which shot would you choose to:
- Steal 1
- Steal 1 (last rock)

Non-Hammer Team's Shot Choices
  (A) Center guard
  (B) Draw to the front four-foot

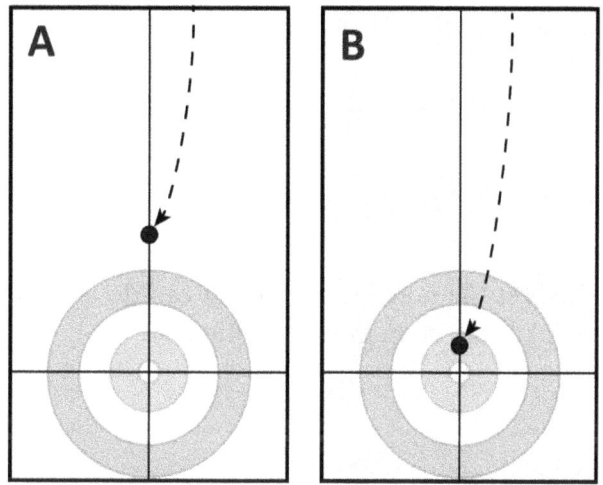

Discussion

Non-Hammer Team

Steal 1

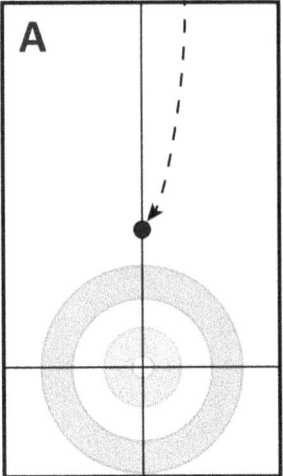

Since the best way to steal is to have a rock on the button behind a center guard, the non-hammer team should keep putting up guards (Option A). Because the Free Guard Zone time is over, the non-hammer team will need the hammer team to miss by either flashing or nose-hitting in order to steal.

Steal 1 (last rock)

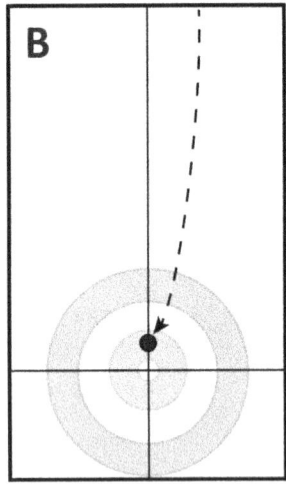

The best the non-hammer team can do is draw to the middle and hope the hammer team misses (Option B).

Beginner Scenario 6—Variation 1

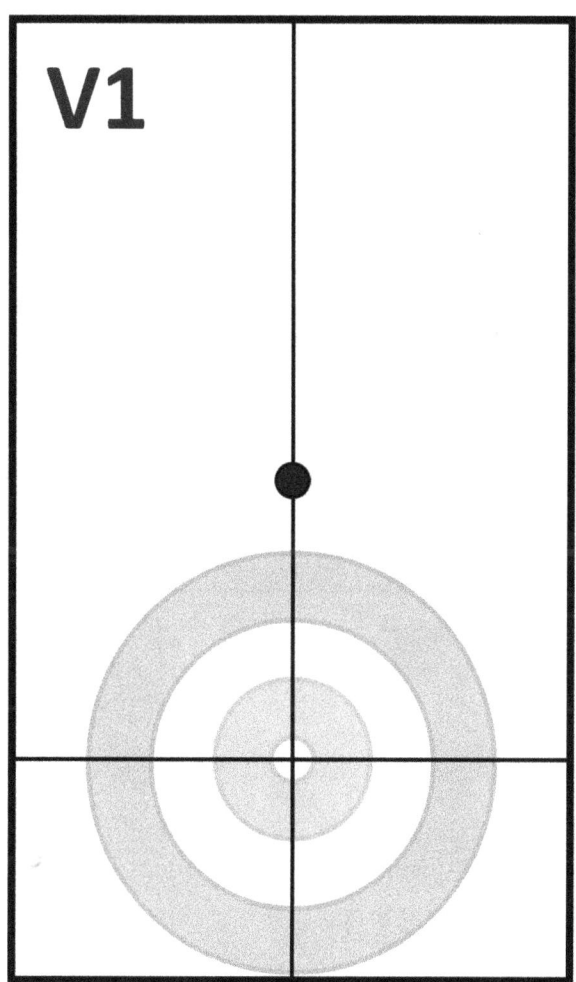

Beginner Scenario 6—Variation 1

Here's another example of an empty house during the middle of an end. In the first scenario, the non-hammer team was highly committed to stealing. Let's assume it is in this scenario, too.

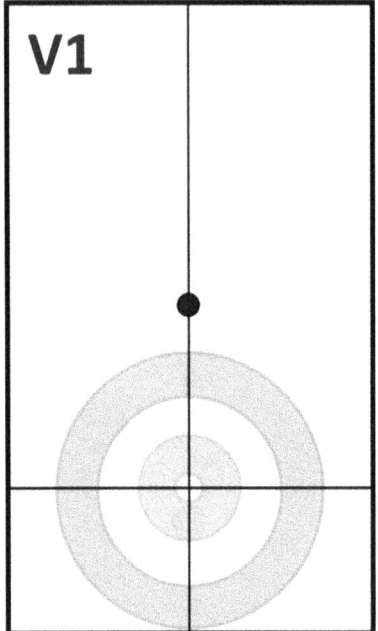

Questions

Hammer Team

Which shot would you choose to:
- **Prevent a steal**
- **Prevent a steal (Free Guard Zone in effect)**

Hammer Team's Shot Choices
(A) Draw in front of the button
(B) Tick the center guard
(C) Take out the center guard and roll the shooter out

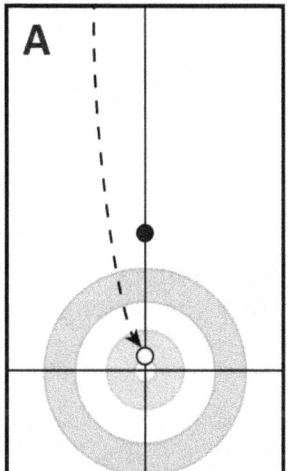 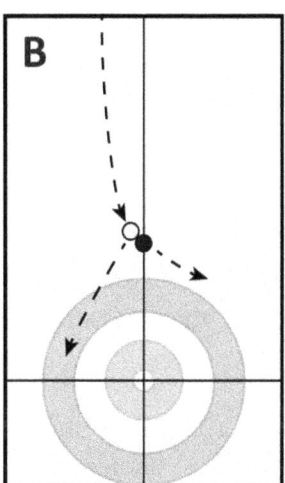 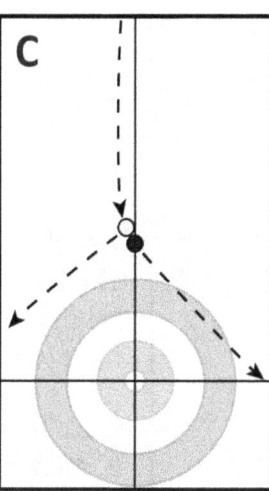

Discussion

Hammer Team

Prevent a steal

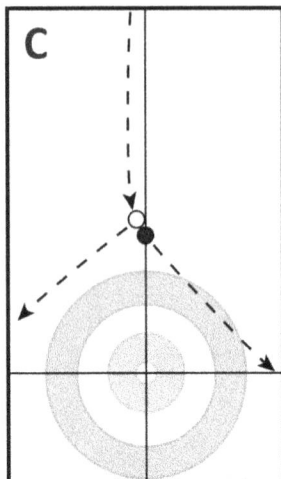

The hammer team should hit the guard and roll both rocks out (Option C). The hammer team does not want to give the non-hammer team a guard to hide behind or a rock in the rings to use for backing.

Prevent a steal (Free Guard Zone in effect)

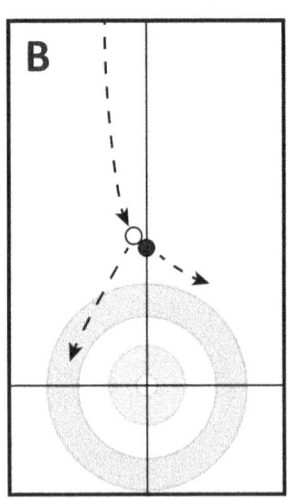

The Free Guard Zone is in effect, so the hammer team can either: draw behind the center guard (Option A), or tick the center guard to open the front (Option B).

Since the hammer team's primary goal is to prevent a steal, the tick shot (Option B) is the best choice. It opens the front, which will make it very difficult for the non-hammer team to steal.

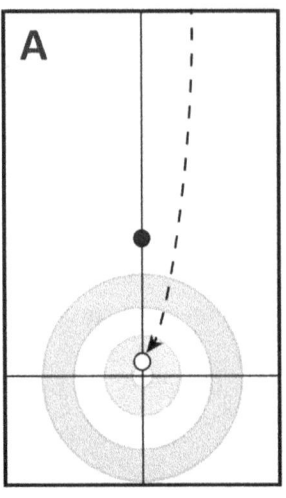

Most teams find it more difficult to throw tick shots than draws. This is partly because most teams don't practice ticks as often as draws, and also because the team won't likely have thrown many ticks earlier in the game. Also, there is relatively little margin for error on a tick shot—a "flash" or an accidental takeout achieves nothing, and tapping the opponent's guard straight back to the button makes things worse! (That being said, as of 2013, tick shots are in vogue in pro-level curling.)

For this reason, many teams choose the draw (Option A). The "pro-side" of the draw is that if the skip sets the broom tight (to give the draw the best chance of burying completely behind the guard), the draw might clip the guard rock and tick anyways.

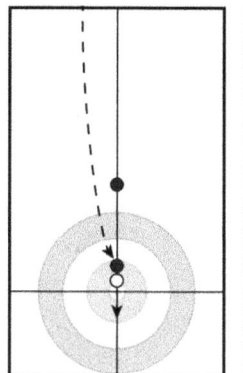 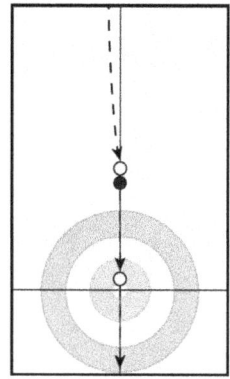

The danger with the draw is that it adds another rock into play that the non-hammer team could use as backing to steal. Also, if the hammer team does decide to clear the front later, there is a chance it could jam the non-hammer team's guard back onto its own rock in the middle and give the non-hammer team shot rock.

Sometimes good plans go terribly wrong. These next four beginner scenarios are about coping with common misses.

Beginner Scenario 7

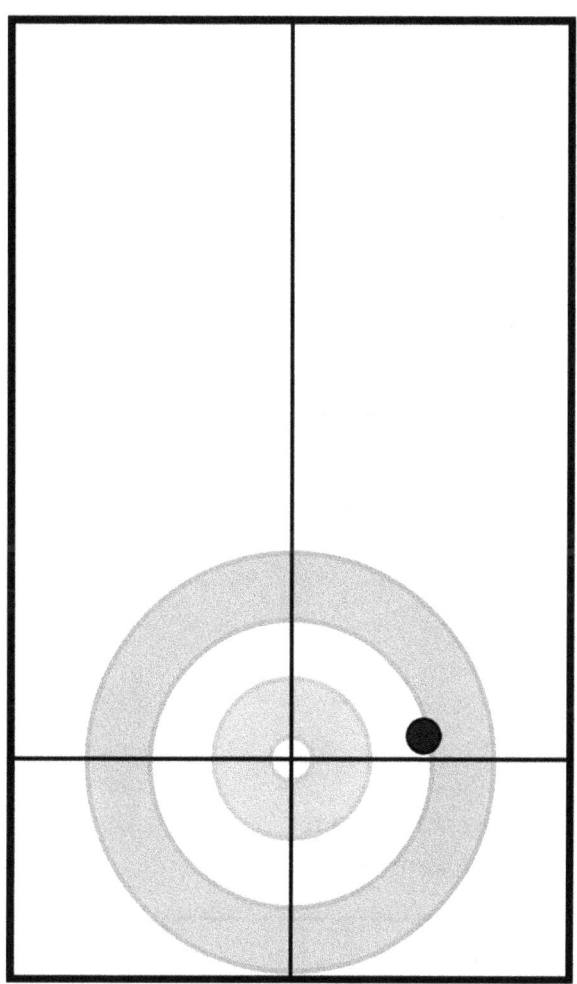

Beginner Scenario 7

The non-hammer team accidentally draws to the wing.

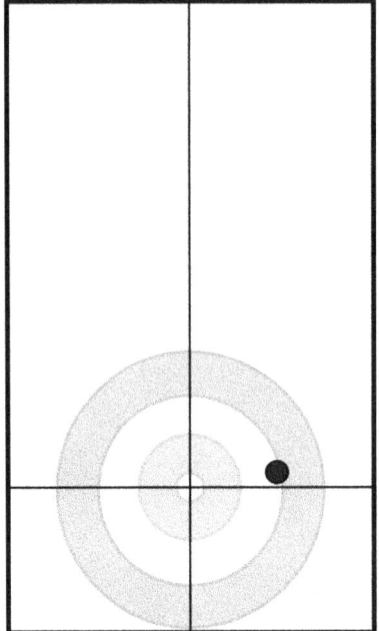

Questions

Hammer Team

Which shot would you choose to:
   ► Score 2

Hammer Team's Shot Choices
   (A) Corner guard
   (B) Freeze to the non-hammer team's stone
   (C) Take out the non-hammer team's stone

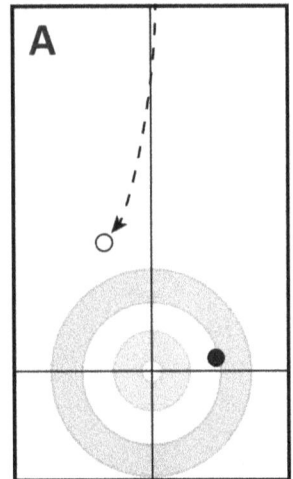 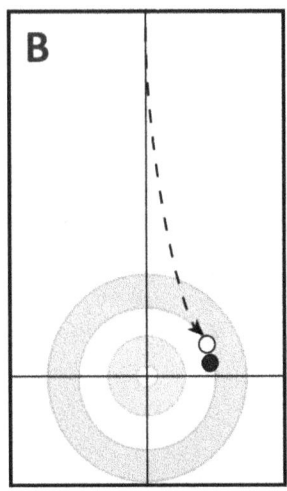 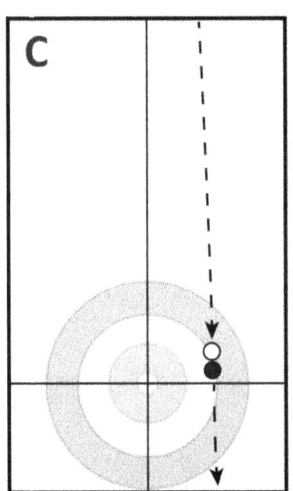

Non-Hammer Team

Which shot would you choose to:
- Steal 1
- Steal 1 (last rock)
- Force 1
- Prevent the hammer team from scoring more than 1

Non-Hammer Team's Shot Choices
(A) Center guard
(B) Draw to the front eight-foot
(C) Draw to the other wing and split the house
(D) Take out the non-hammer team's stone

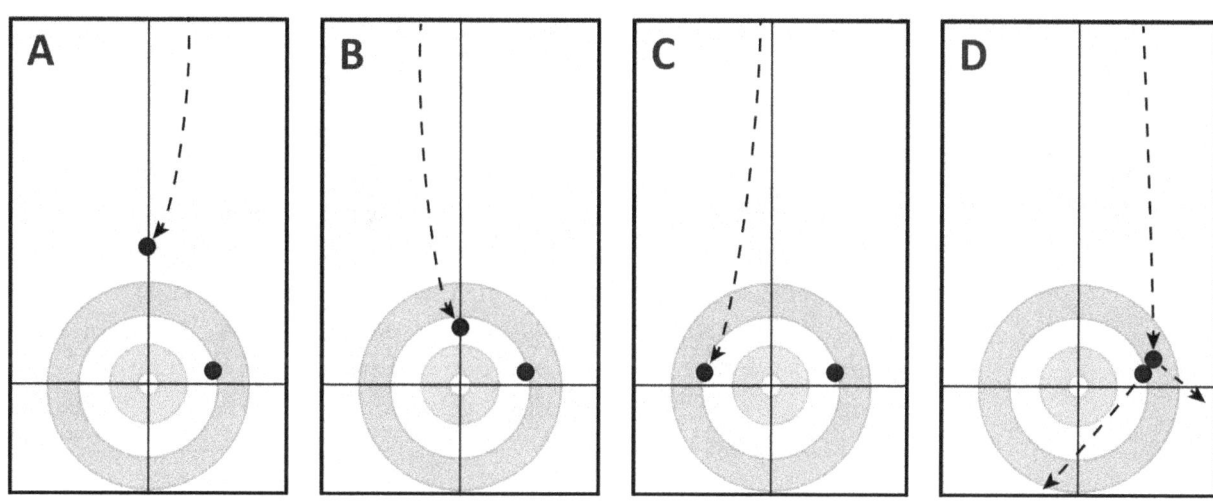

Discussion

Hammer Team
Score 2

Aggressive

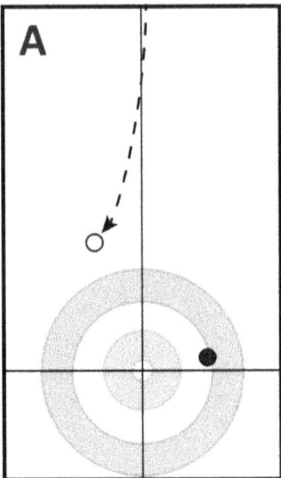

The non-hammer team's rock is far enough from the center that it's not a big scoring threat. Therefore, the hammer team can then either ignore it or use it to develop its offense. Since the Free Guard Zone is still in effect, the hammer team would likely put up a corner guard close enough to the center line that a rock behind the guard could be first shot (Option A).

Conservative

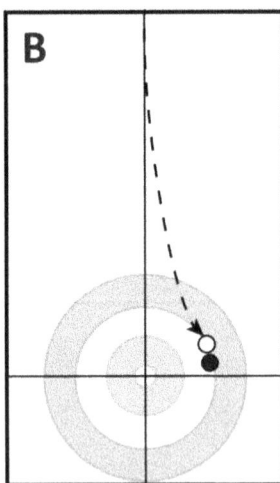

A hammer team that is playing conservatively might freeze to the non-hammer team's stone to sit shot (Option B). This is a more conservative choice because, with both rocks in the rings, the hammer team might still be able to blank if things go wrong, and there's less chance the non-hammer team will steal. This is also a good move when the hammer team is running low on stones, because it gets rocks onto the rings—where they need to be to count, of course!

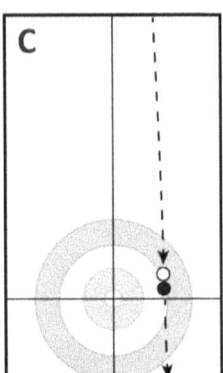

An ultra-conservative hammer team could choose to hit (Option C), as it would in a "Deuce or Blank." However, that's more of a plan to blank than to score two. The freeze (Option B) is nearly as conservative, and much more likely to produce two.

Non-Hammer Team
Steal 1

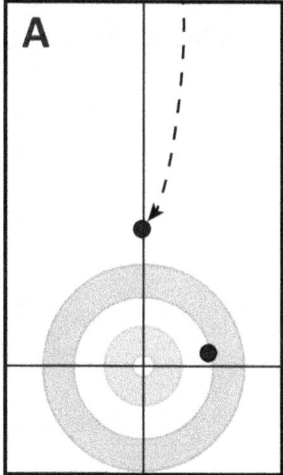

The non-hammer team should put up a center guard (Option A). Again, to have a good chance to steal, the non-hammer team needs a center guard and a rock near the button.

Steal 1 (last rock)

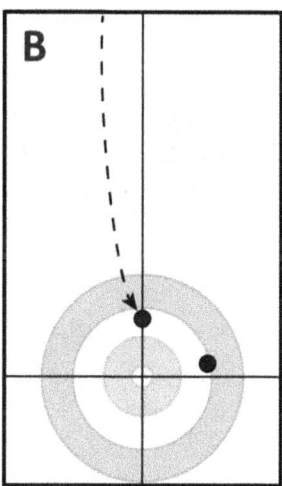

This is like "Beginner Scenario 2—Variation 1" earlier in this section. The non-hammer team can't guarantee a steal. All it can do is make the hammer team's shot as difficult as possible. The draw to the front eight-foot (Option B) is probably the best choice.

Force 1
Conservative

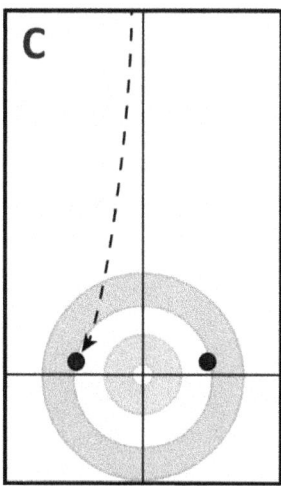

A conservative non-hammer team would draw to the left side of the rings and split the house (Option C). This makes it difficult or impossible for the hammer team to make a double takeout to save the end with a blank. It also minimizes the risk of giving up two, because there are no guards for the hammer team to hide behind. The non-hammer team is aiming for an open-center force.

Aggressive

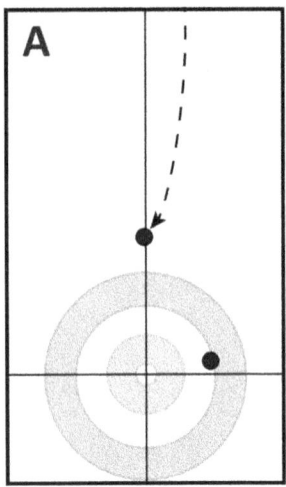

An aggressive non-hammer team would force by putting up a center guard (Option A). Guards increase the odds that there will be rocks left in play at the end of an end, forcing one team or the other to score and minimizing the chances of a blank. The non-hammer team is aiming for a closed-center force. (Remember, of course, that having more stones in play also increases the chances that the hammer team can score two or more!)

Prevent the hammer team from scoring more than 1

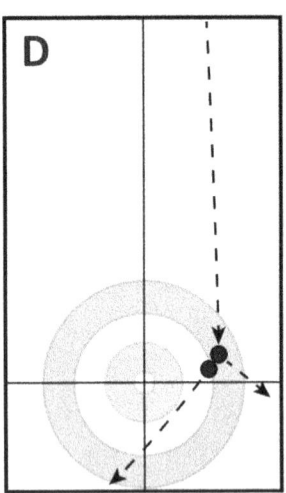

To prevent the hammer team from scoring more than one, the non-hammer team could take out its own rock and either roll to the middle, or roll out so the hammer team has nothing to freeze to (Option D).

Beginner Scenario 8

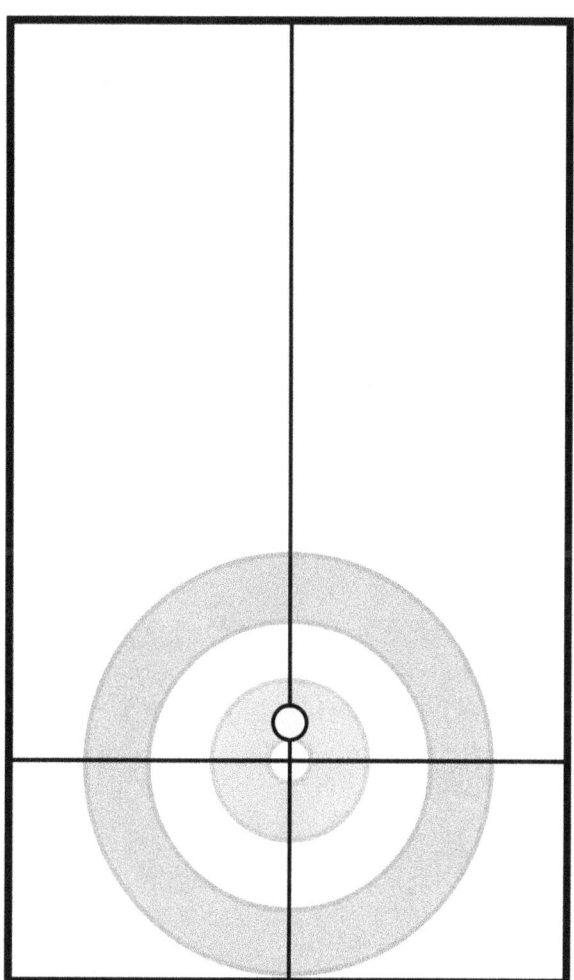

Beginner Scenario 8

The hammer team accidentally draws to the center.

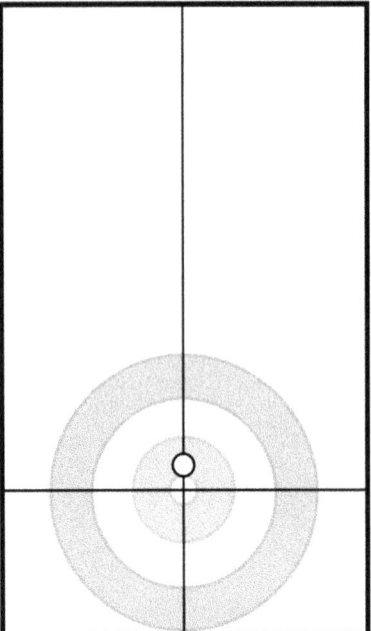

Questions

Non-Hammer Team

Which shot would you choose to:
- **Steal 1**
- **Steal 1 (last rock)**
- **Prevent the hammer team from scoring more than 1**

<u>Non-Hammer Team's Shot Choices</u>
(A) Center guard
(B) Freeze to the hammer team's stone
(C) Tap the hammer team's stone back to be shot
(D) Draw behind the hammer team's stone
(E) Take out the hammer team's stone

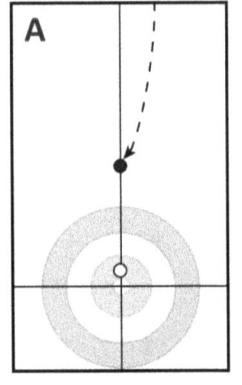 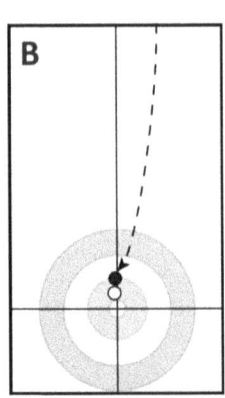 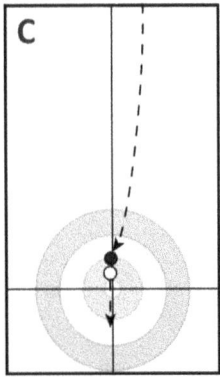 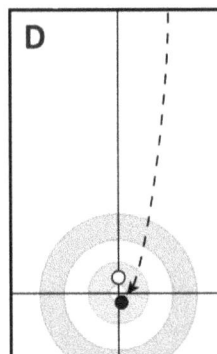 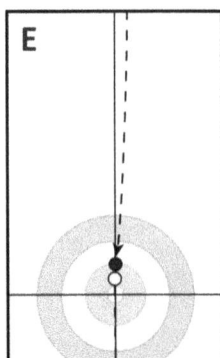

Hammer Team

Which shot would you choose to:
- **Score 2**
- **Prevent the non-hammer team from stealing**

Hammer Team's Shot Choices

(A) Corner guard
(B) Draw to the wing to split the house
(C) Take out own stone and roll out

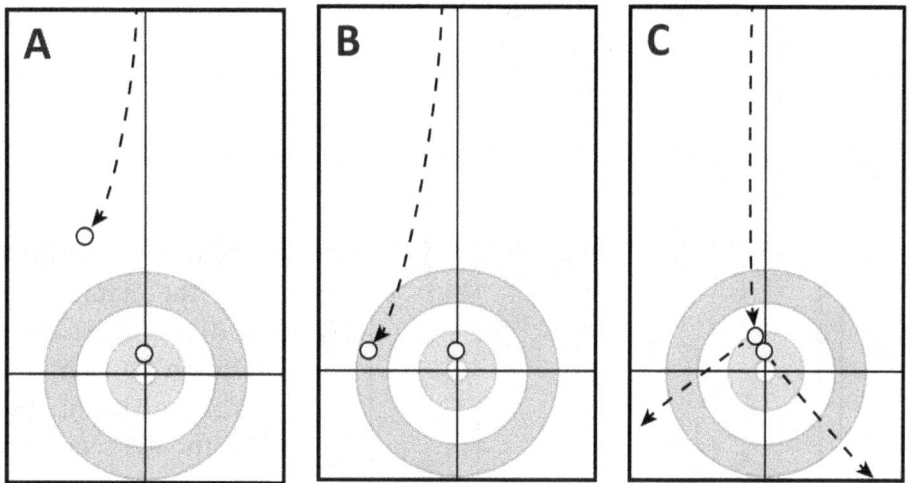

Discussion

Non-Hammer Team

Steal 1

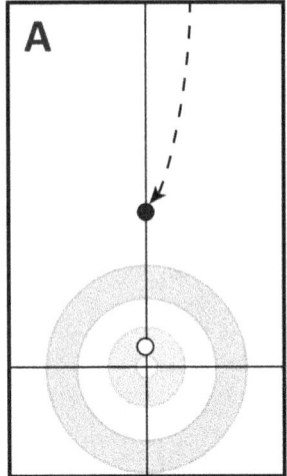

If the non-hammer team absolutely needs to steal, it should forget about the hammer team's stone near the button for a turn and put up a center guard (Option A).

Eventually, the non-hammer team can tap the hammer team's stone back to sit shot, or corner freeze to it, then tap or hit both rocks to get shot. The non-hammer team could even run its own center guard straight back to remove the hammer team's rock and have its own rock sit guarded in the front four-foot.

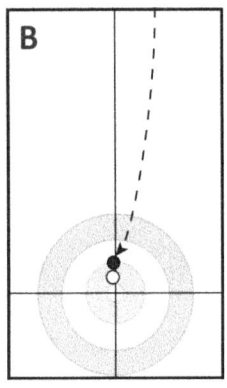 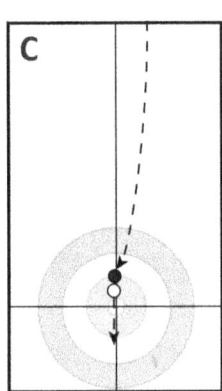 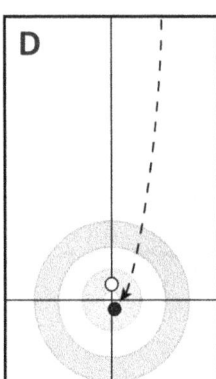

Why wouldn't the non-hammer team freeze to the hammer team's stone (Option B), tap it back (Option C), or draw (Option D) right away? It could, but against good teams, it's very difficult to steal without a center guard.

Steal 1 (last rock)

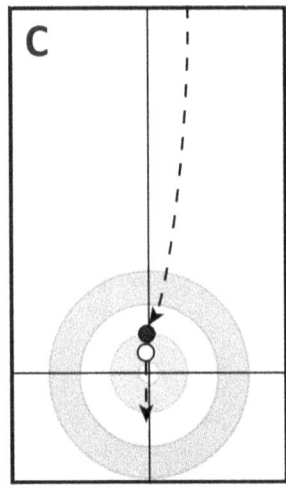

The non-hammer team has two choices: tap the hammer team's stone back to sit shot (Option C), or draw behind the hammer team's stone to sit shot (Option D).

The tap (Option C) is probably an easier shot to make, but it would leave the stones very far apart.

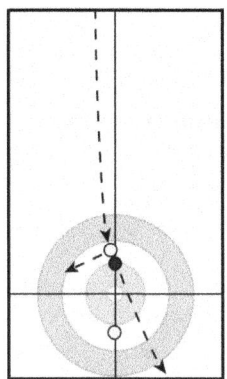

The hammer team would then have an easy takeout to score at least one point.

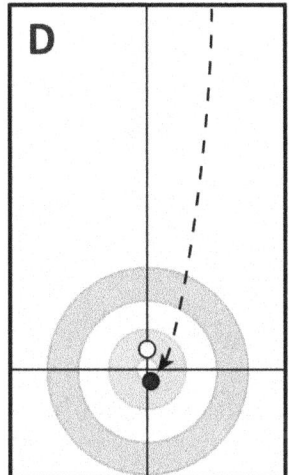

The draw (Option D) is the tougher shot to make.

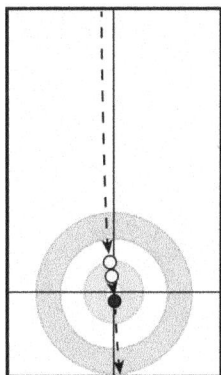

However, it forces the hammer team to make a more difficult shot to score. Instead of being able to simply hit an open stone, the hammer team now has to make a runback or tap to prevent the steal.

Prevent the hammer team from scoring more than 1

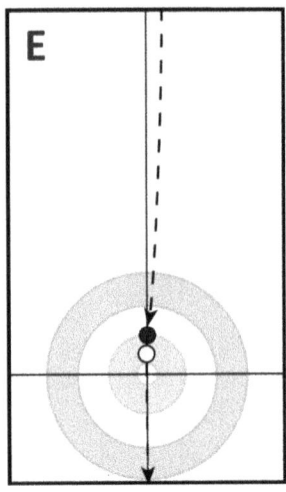

To prevent the hammer team from scoring more than one, the non-hammer team would take out the hammer team's stone and stay in its place (Option E).

Hammer Team

Score 2

Conservative

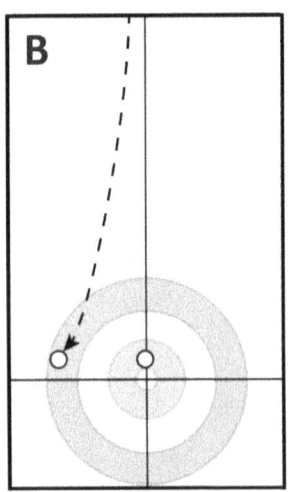

The conservative answer—and the most common choice—would be to draw to the wing to split the house (Option B).

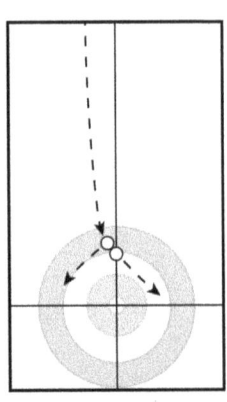

As a side note, if the hammer team's original stone were higher in the house near the center line, the hammer team could tap that rock to split the house. The split is a good choice in that situation because both rocks would end up in front of the tee line and away from the center line.

Aggressive

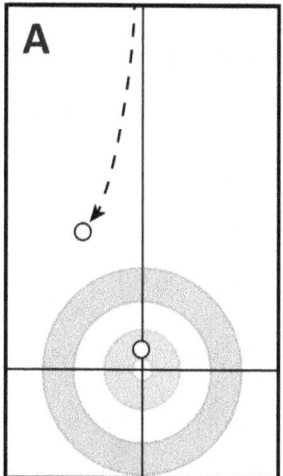

If the hammer team is concerned that the non-hammer team could make a double takeout on two rocks in the house, or if the hammer team would like to give itself a better opportunity to score three, it could put up a corner guard (Option A). (For more on how and why to do this, see the "How to use a corner guard to get three points" section in the "Tips for Using Corner Guards" chapter.)

Prevent the non-hammer team from stealing

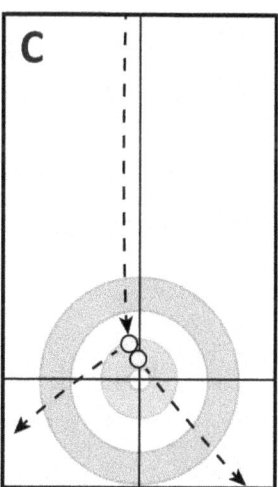

To prevent the non-hammer team from stealing, the hammer team should hit its own rock and roll out (Option C). If the hammer team clears the house, the non-hammer team won't have anywhere to hide or freeze.

Beginner Scenario 9

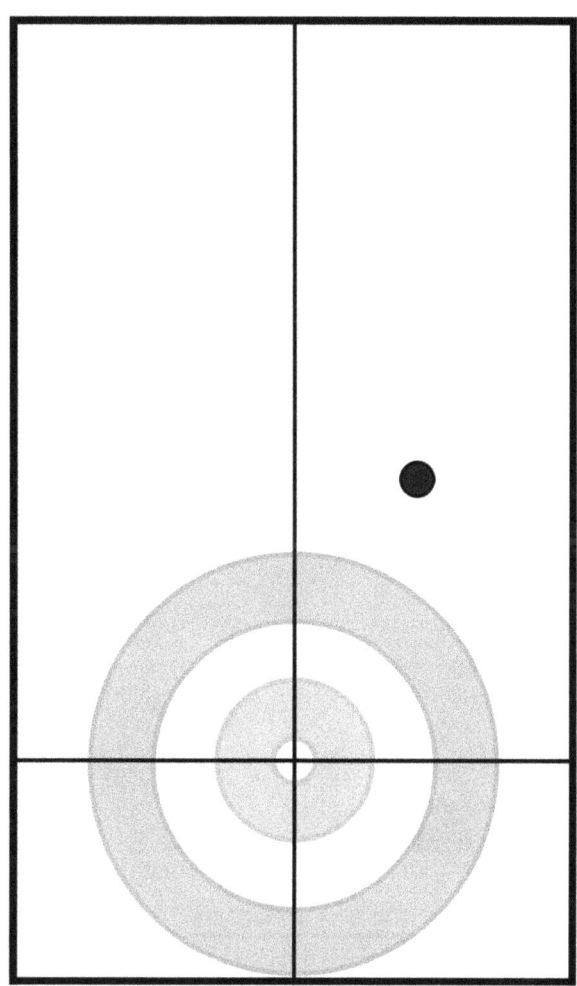

Beginner Scenario 9

The non-hammer team accidentally sets up a corner guard.

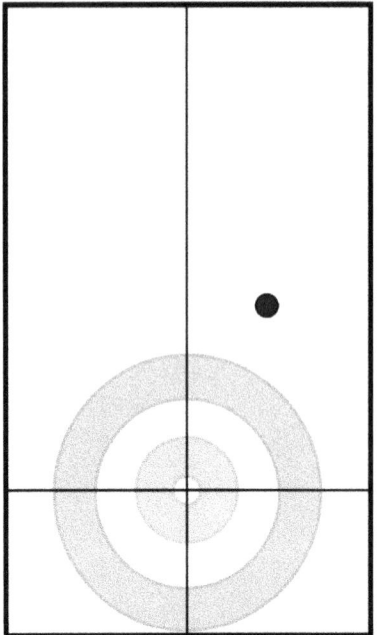

Questions

Hammer Team

    Which shot would you choose to:
        ▸ Score 2

Hammer Team's Shot Choices
    (A) Corner guard on the other side
    (B) Draw behind the corner guard
    (C) Draw to the open side

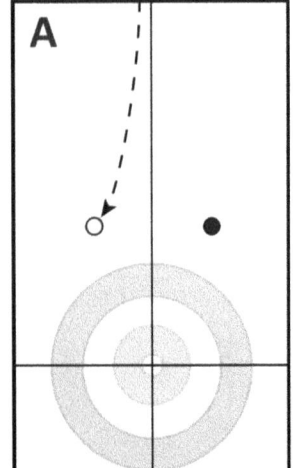 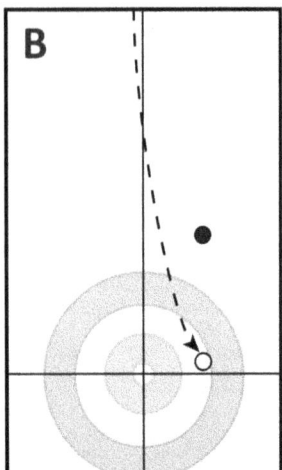 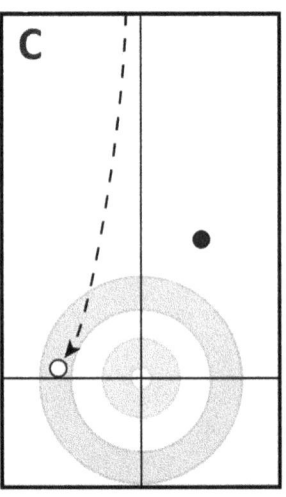

192

Non-Hammer Team

Which shot would you choose to:
- ▶ Steal 1
- ▶ Steal 1 (last rock)
- ▶ Prevent the hammer team from scoring more than 1
- ▶ Force 1 (last rock)

Non-Hammer Team's Shot Choices
    (A) Center guard
    (B) Draw behind the corner guard
    (C) Draw to the button
    (D) Take out the corner guard and roll out

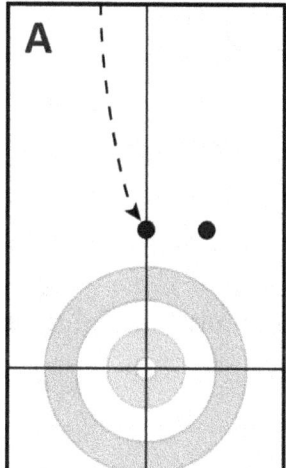
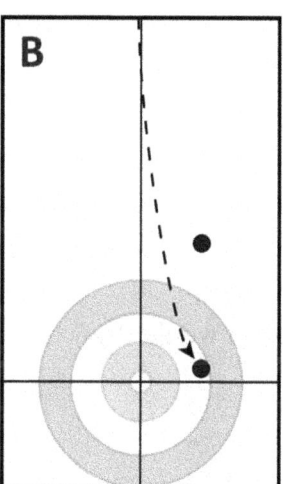
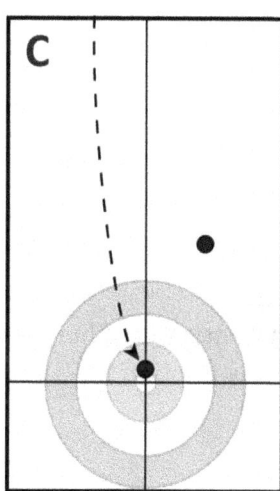
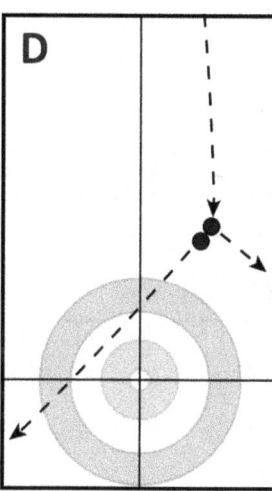

Discussion

Hammer Team

Score 2

Aggressive

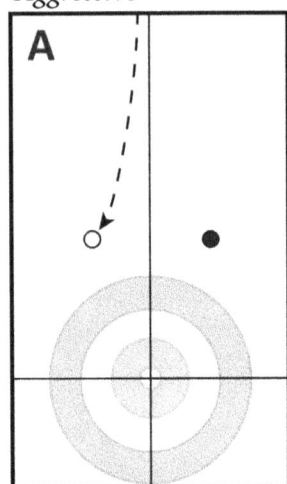

A very aggressive hammer team would put up a second corner guard (Option A). This will give it more places to hide rocks as the end progresses.

Conservative

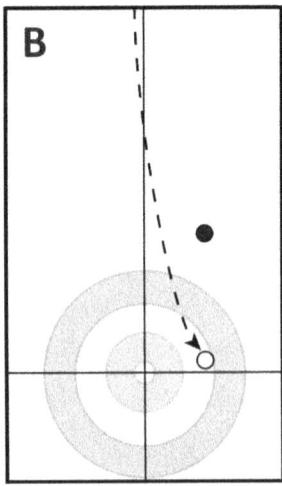

A conservative hammer team would draw behind the corner guard right away (Option B).

Non-Hammer Team

Steal 1

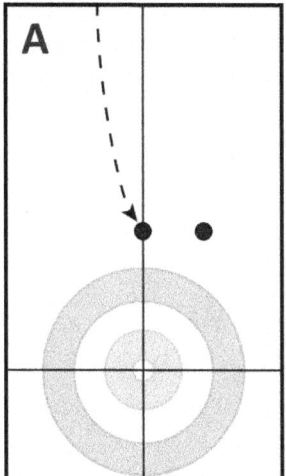

The non-hammer should put up a center guard (Option A). Again, the non-hammer team will likely need a center guard and a rock near the button to steal.

Steal 1 (last rock)

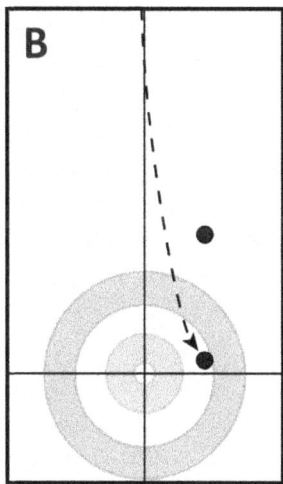

The non-hammer team is not set up well to steal because it doesn't have either a center guard or a rock near the pin. The best it can do is draw behind the corner guard (Option B) and hope the hammer team misses the open draw to the eight-foot.

Prevent the hammer team from scoring more than 1

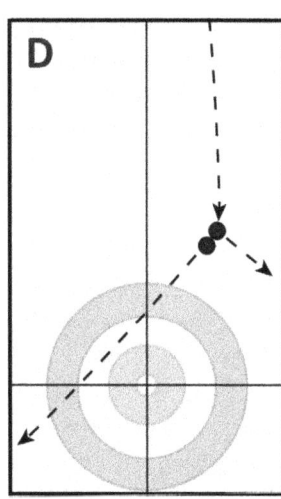

The non-hammer team should take out the corner guard and roll its own stone out (Option D). The non-hammer team doesn't want to give the hammer team any place to hide.

Force 1 (last rock)

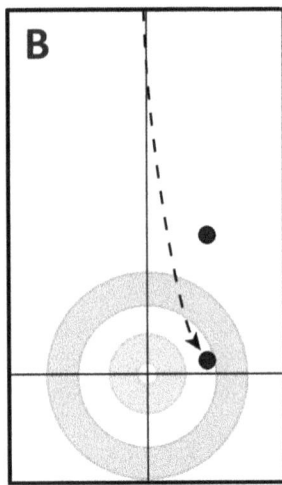

The non-hammer team should draw behind the corner guard (Option B). If that rock can't be removed, the hammer team will have to draw for one point.

Beginner Scenario 10

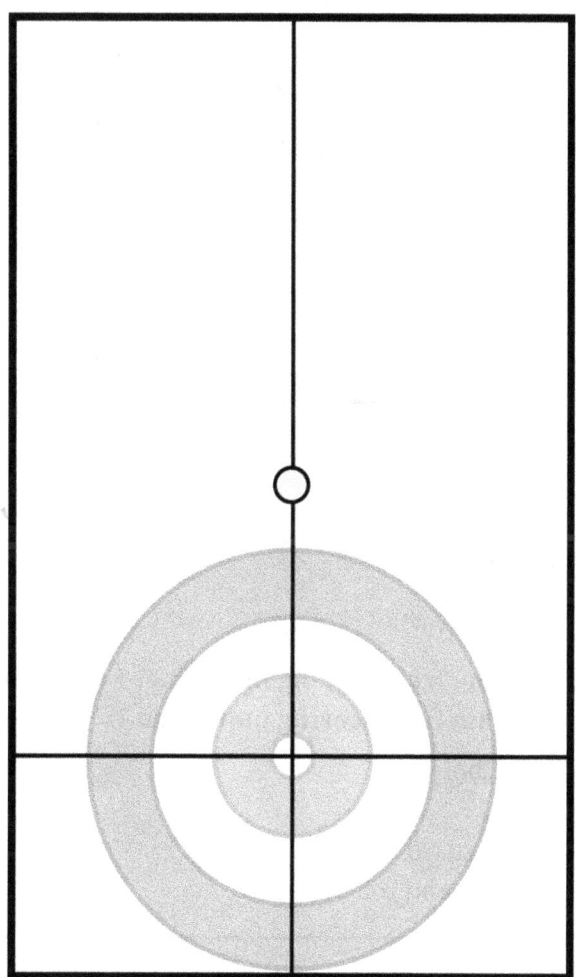

Beginner Scenario 10

The hammer team accidentally sets up a center guard.

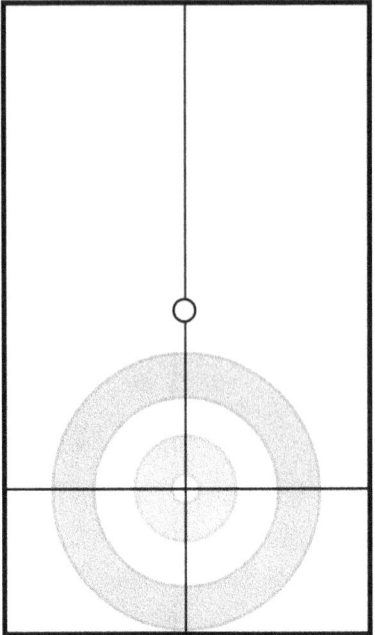

Questions

Non-Hammer Team

Which shot would you choose to:
- Steal 1
- Force 1
- Prevent the hammer team from scoring more than 1 (Free Guard Zone in effect)
- Prevent the hammer team from scoring more than 1

<u>Non-Hammer Team's Shot Choices</u>
(A) High center guard
(B) Draw behind the center guard
(C) Take out the center guard and roll out

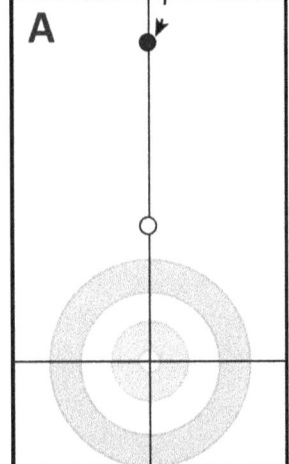
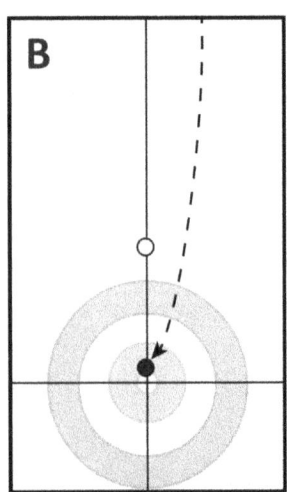
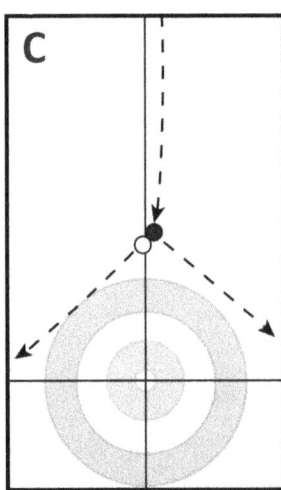

Hammer Team

Which shot would you choose to:
- Steal 2
- Prevent the non-hammer team from stealing

Hammer Team's Shot Choices
(A) Corner guard
(B) Split the center guard
(C) Draw to the wing
(D) Take out the center guard and roll out

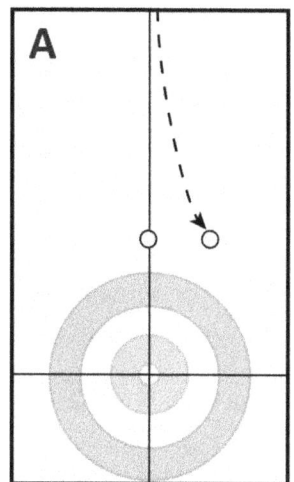 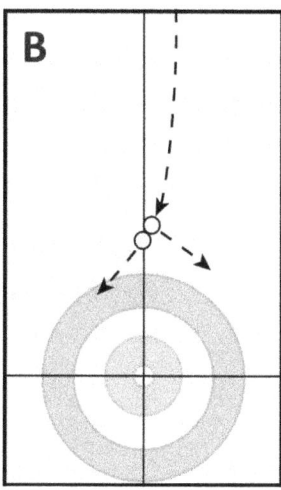 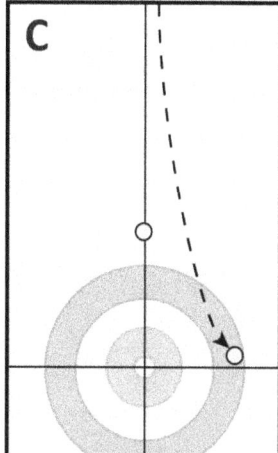 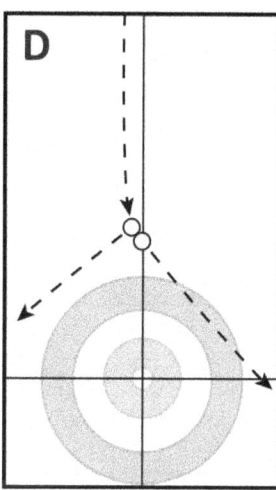

Discussion

Non-Hammer Team

Steal 1

Aggressive

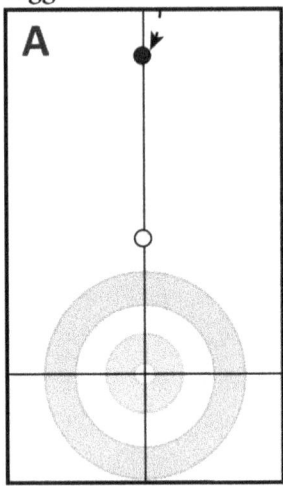

An aggressive non-hammer team would put up a second center guard (Option A). This gives the non-hammer team a better chance to steal by making it tougher for the hammer team to clear the middle. It also prevents the hammer team from running its guard back onto any rocks the non-hammer team might eventually put near the pin.

This tactic is considered aggressive because, with two guards in place, it will be difficult for the hammer team to clear the front, thus improving the non-hammer team's chance of stealing. At the same time, there is a bigger risk the hammer team could draw multiple rocks in—possibly beginning on its next shot—that would occupy the space near the button and make it difficult for the non-hammer team to get shot rock. Aggressive tactics increase the odds of very good and very bad outcomes at the same time.

Conservative

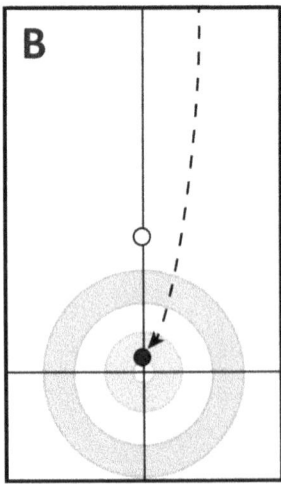

A conservative non-hammer team would draw in behind the center guard (Option B). This is a conservative choice because the non-hammer team will be first to the button and it won't have to worry as much about the hammer team getting a shot rock it can't move.

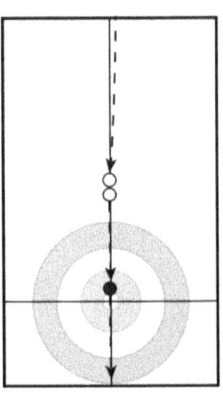

However, because there's only one guard, it will be easier for the hammer team to foil the steal by clearing the front or running back the guard. (A non-hammer team might also choose this tactic if it thought the hammer team didn't hit well and one guard would be enough protection.)

Force 1

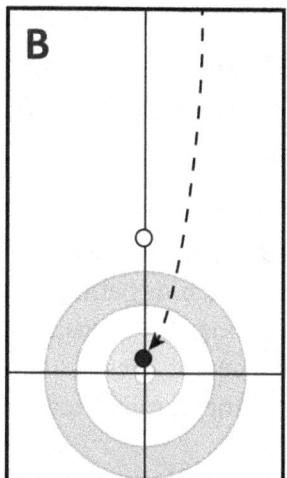

The non-hammer team would likely draw in (Option B). Because there is a center guard, both teams will be able to hide rocks. This makes it likely that one of the teams will have to score in this end, thus forcing a score to happen instead of possibly allowing a blank. (The non-hammer team's goal is to have this end like a closed-center force.

Prevent the hammer team from scoring more than 1 (Free Guard Zone in effect)

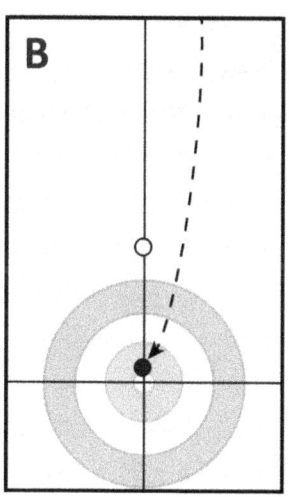

To prevent the hammer team from scoring more than one, the non-hammer team would likely draw behind the center guard (Option B). It can't take out the guard, so this is the best way to keep it from being useful to the hammer team. If the non-hammer team ticks the guard, it could accidentally create even more scoring opportunities for the hammer team by setting up corner guards.

Prevent the hammer team from scoring more than 1

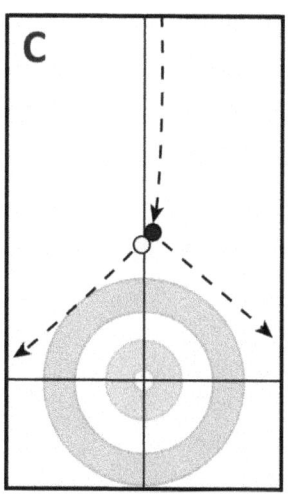

To prevent the hammer team from scoring more than one once the Free Guard Zone time is over, the non-hammer team should take out the center guard and roll out (Option C). Without guards, it will be difficult for the hammer team to keep more than one rock in play.

Hammer Team

Score 2

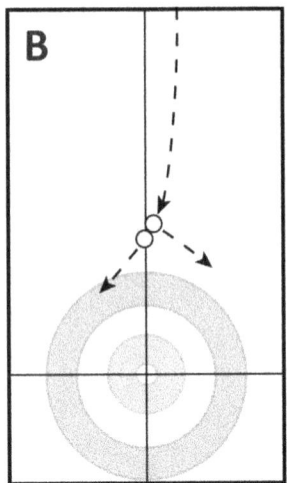 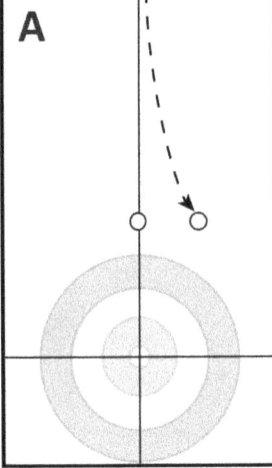

The hammer team's has two good choices: split the center guard to create at least one corner guard (Option B), or simply put up a corner guard (Option A). The advantage of putting up a corner guard is that there will definitely be two guards for the hammer team to hide behind. The risk is that the non-hammer team could hide behind the center guard to steal or force one. The advantage of the split is that it opens the center, even though it could move one or both of the hammer team's stones into the rings.

Prevent the non-hammer team from stealing

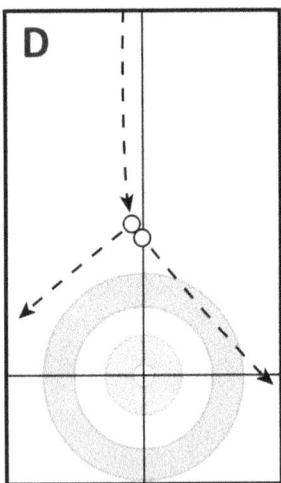

The hammer team should take out its own center guard and roll out so the non-hammer team has nothing to hide behind and nothing to freeze to (Option D).

Intermediate Strategy Scenarios

Use Your End Goals to Make Better Shot Choices throughout the End

We're going to take things up a notch for the intermediate section. In addition to making the game situations more complex, I will now ask you to pick an end plan as well as a tactical plan, based on the score, end number, rock number, and hammer possession.

As always, there are no correct answers or absolute truths, only choices that lead down different paths of risk and reward. When it's game time, you should make the choices that are right for your team and your ice conditions—perhaps even choices that are not included here.

As a reminder, the team with the hammer always has light stones and the team without the hammer always has dark stones.

Intermediate Scenarios Overview

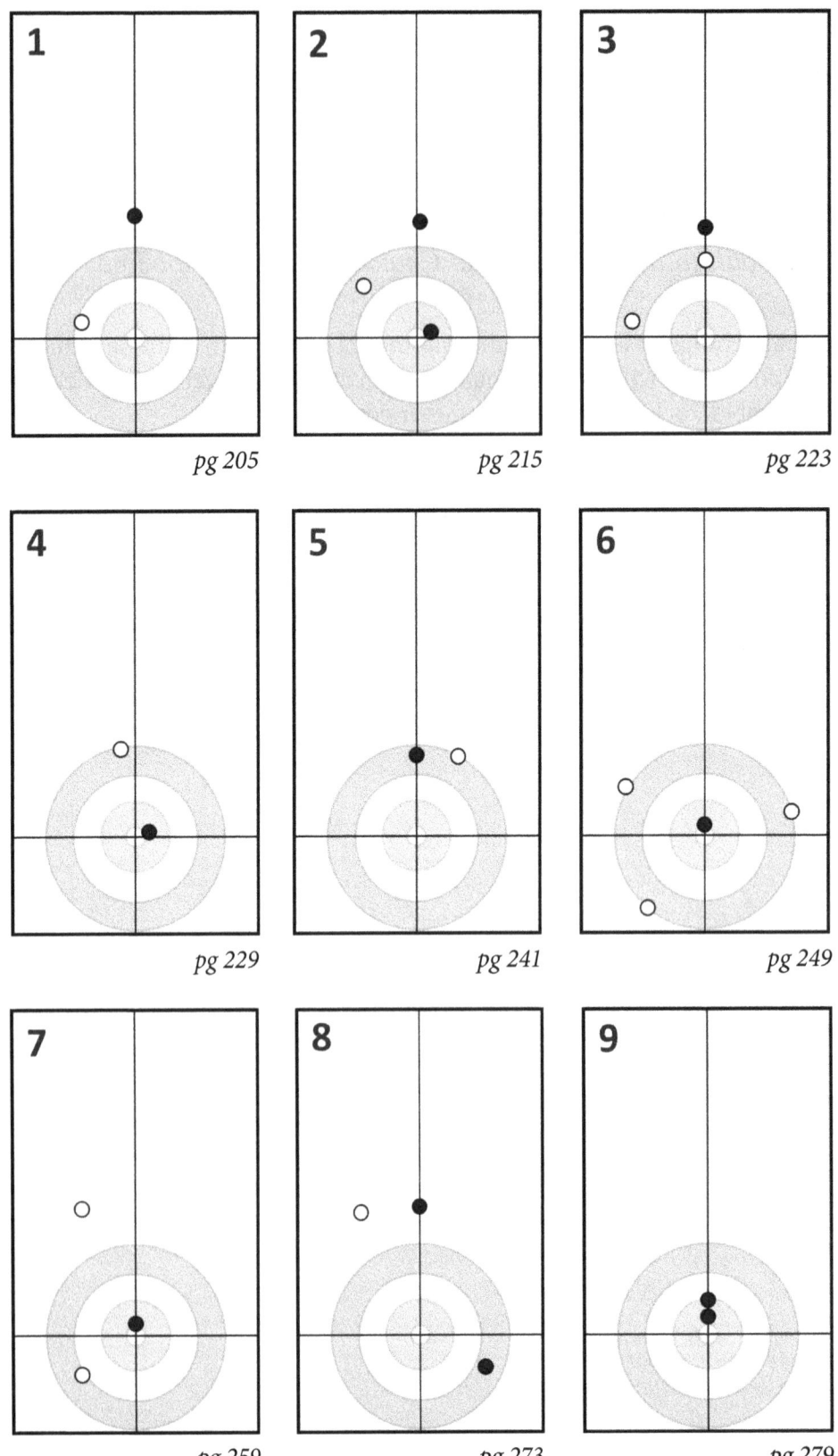

Intermediate Scenario 1

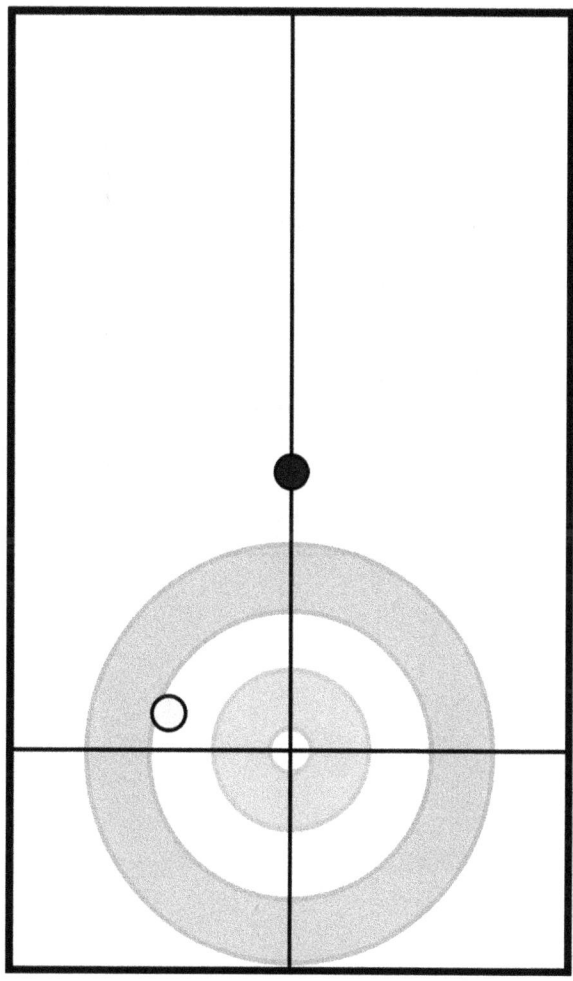

Intermediate Scenario 1

This scenario is similar to the "Open Wing Deuce" open from earlier in the book. However, it is such a common and critical choice point that, at the risk of being redundant, I'm including it here.

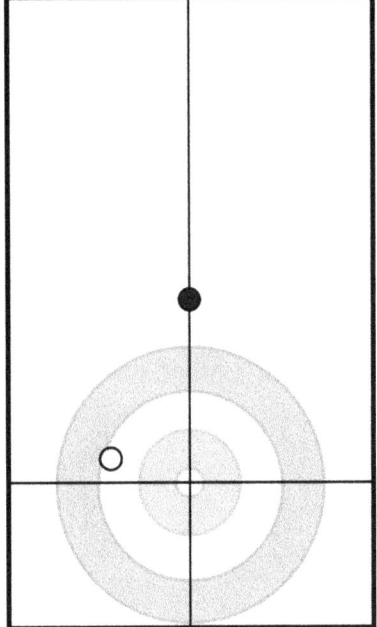

Questions

Non-Hammer Team

What end goal and shot would you choose:
- ▶ **Situation 1:** 8th end of 10-end game, tied score, non-hammer team's 2nd rock
- ▶ **Situation 2:** 8th end of 10-end game, non-hammer team down by 2, non-hammer team's 2nd rock

Non-Hammer Team's Shot Choices
(A) High center guard
(B) Draw to front four-foot
(C) Hit and roll behind the center guard

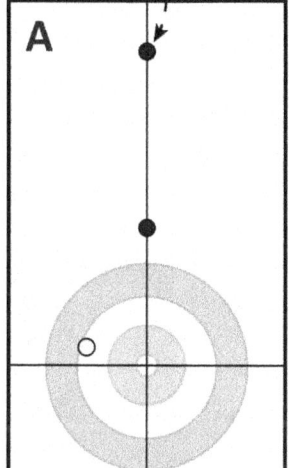
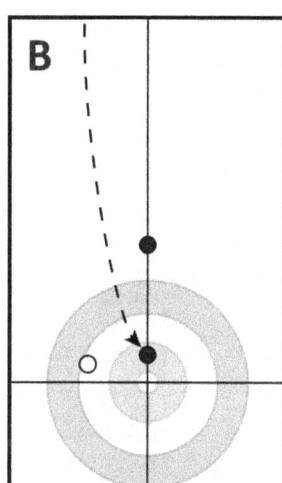
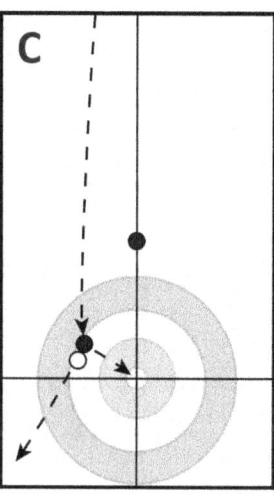

Discussion

Non-Hammer Team

Situation 1: 8th end of 10-end game, tied score, non-hammer team's 2nd rock

It's important for teams to have a plan at the beginning of each end. As they get closer to the end of the game, they should think about how they want to play all the remaining ends before they begin that final stretch. For example: In its team conference before the eighth end, the non-hammer team might decide that what it needs to do to win is steal in the eighth, force one in the ninth, and score one with the hammer in the tenth. Alternatively, the non-hammer team could force one in the eighth, score two with the hammer in the ninth, then either steal the tenth to win, or force one in the tenth to tie and have the hammer in an extra end. As a third option, the non-hammer team could allow a blank in the eighth and ninth, then steal in the tenth to win. Here's a chart of those options:

	8th End Primary Goal	9th End Primary Goal	10th End Primary Goal
Example Plan 1	Steal 1	Force 1	Score 1 with hammer to win
Example Plan 2	Force 1	Score 2	Steal 1 to win, or force 1 to get hammer in extra end
Example Plan 3	Blank	Blank	Steal 1 to win

Let's assume the non-hammer team chooses plan 1 (steal 1, force 1, score 1). That means the team has decided to steal in this end. Now the question becomes—how aggressive should the team be in pursuing that goal?

Very Aggressive

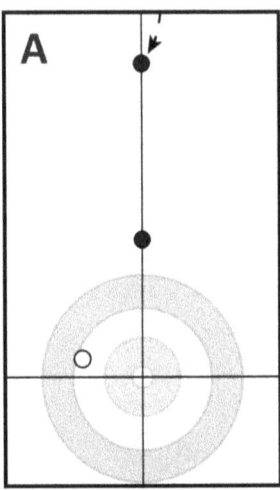

If the non-hammer team is very aggressive, it might put up a second center guard (Option A) so any shot rock it gets in the center will be well protected. This plan carries a lot of risk, however. The hammer team already has one rock in the rings, so it could score two or more. Also, if the hammer team throws its next rock to the button, it could be difficult for the non-hammer team to move it to get shot rock.

In this situation, the non-hammer team's goal chart might look like this:

Non-Hammer Team's Goal Chart
   Strongly Want: Steal
   Accept: Force 1 or Blank
   Avoid: Hammer team scores 2

Moderately Aggressive

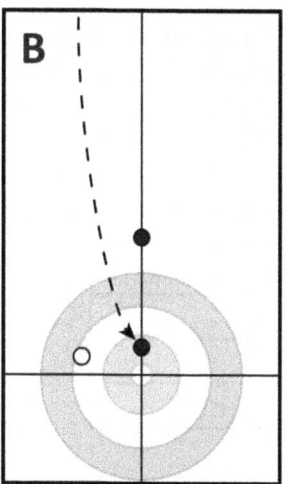

If the non-hammer team is moderately aggressive, it might draw in behind the center guard (Choice B). This sets up the steal right away and prevents the hammer team from drawing to the center.

The hammer team can hit, bump, or freeze to the non-hammer team's shot stone, depending on how buried it is. This could play out like "Simple End 2," except now the hammer team has an extra point on the wings to help it score two or more.

The non-hammer team's goal chart might look like this:

Non-Hammer Team's Goal Chart
  Want: Steal
  Accept: Force 1 or Blank
  Avoid: Hammer team scores 2

Conservative

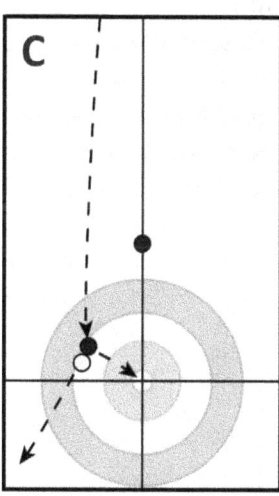

If the non-hammer team is conservative, it could take out the hammer team's rock and try to roll behind its center guard (Choice C). That's a difficult way to get behind a center guard and steal, but it is a very good way to prevent the hammer team from scoring two.

The non-hammer team's goal chart might look like this:

Non-Hammer Team's Goal Chart
  Want: Steal
  Accept: Force 1 or Blank
  Strongly Avoid: Hammer team scores 2

> ADVANCED TIP Since the non-hammer team had three goals it might want to pursue in this end (steal 1, force 1, or allow a blank) and only one outcome it really wants to avoid (allow the hammer team to score two or more) it might be best for the team to choose conservative tactics. That being said, conservative tactics may not be a very "pro-steal" choice. In other words, conservative tactics may be statistically far less likely to result in a steal than aggressive tactics in this situation. There are no published stats (that I know of) that show the relative effectiveness of conservative versus aggressive tactics. For example, if a non-hammer team chooses a very aggressive steal plan, it might be three times as likely to get a steal than if it chose a conservative plan, and only twice as likely to give up two. In that case, the math would favor using an aggressive steal plan. (Of course, aggressive tactics may be ten times as likely to result in giving up three points, which could be a devastating, game-ending result!)

Situation 2: 8th end of 10-end game, non-hammer team down by 2, non-hammer team's 2nd rock

As with the first situation, the non-hammer team would make plans for all three remaining ends before beginning the eighth. This time, instead of being tied, the non-hammer team is down by two points. There are only three ends left, so the non-hammer team does not have much time to maneuver. It has a few choices, including:

	8th End Primary Goal	9th End Primary Goal	10th End Primary Goal	Extra End (if necessary)
Example Plan 1	Steal 1	Steal 1	Steal 1	
Example Plan 2	Force 1	Score 2	Steal 2	
Example Plan 3	Force 1	Score 2	Steal 1	Steal 1

The easiest way through is probably to steal all three ends to win—a tough road!

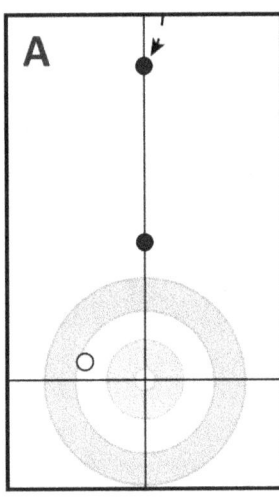

Now that the non-hammer team has an end plan (to steal), it needs to decide how aggressive to be as it pursues that goal. Since the game will become very difficult to win if the non-hammer team gives up even one more point, it will probably decide that it needs to "steal at all costs."

In that case, the non-hammer team would likely put up a high center guard (Choice A), as in the very aggressive steal plan in Situation 1.

Intermediate Scenario 1—Variation 1

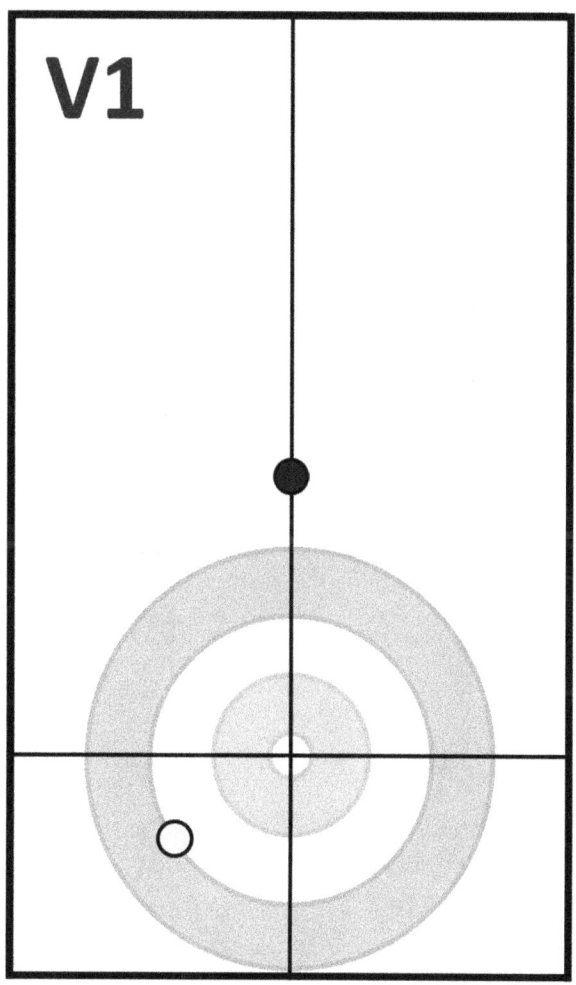

Intermediate Scenario 1—Variation 1

How would it affect the non-hammer team's tactical choices if the hammer team's stone were behind the tee line?

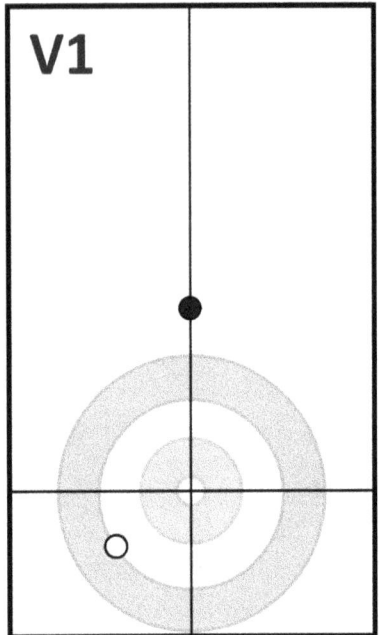

Questions

Non-Hammer Team

What end goal and shot would you choose:
▶ **Situation 1: 8th end of 10-end game, tied score, non-hammer team's 2nd rock**

Non-Hammer Team's Shot Choices
(A) High center guard
(B) Draw to front four-foot
(C) Hit and roll behind the center guard

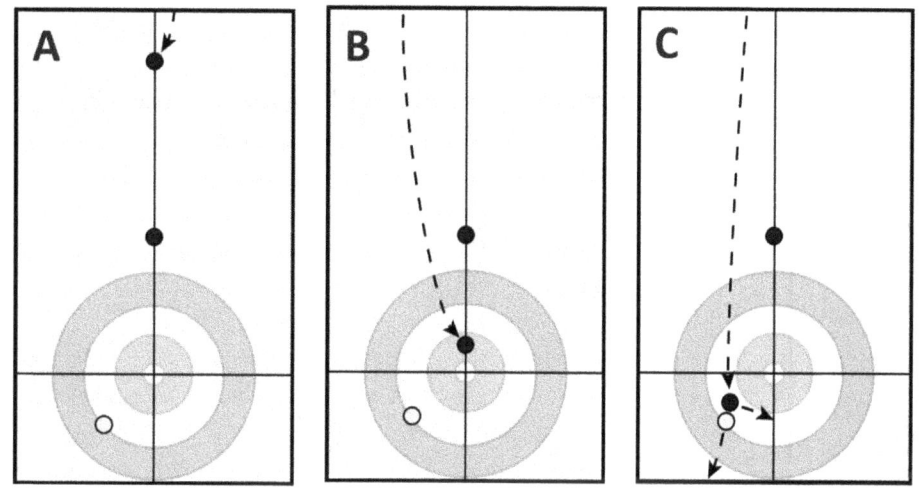

Discussion

Non-Hammer Team

Situation 1: 8th end of 10-end game, tied score, non-hammer team's 2nd rock

Let's return to Situation 1, in which the game was tied in the eighth end. However, this time, the non-hammer team can't hit and roll to a good position in front of the tee line. This makes the conservative hit option less attractive.

Very Conservative

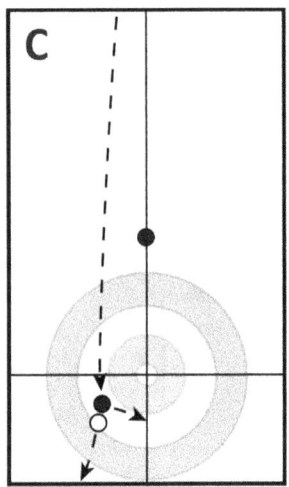

A very conservative team might still hit here (Option C), if it is significantly more interested in preventing two than stealing.

Aggressive and Moderately Conservative

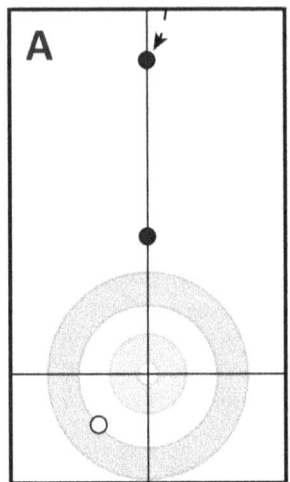 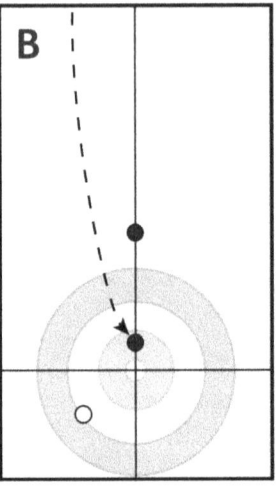

Even though these are still aggressive moves, the high guard (Option A) and the draw (Option B) might become more attractive options to moderately conservative teams. This is because the hit (Option C) is a less viable steal option now that the rock is in the back of the house.

Intermediate Scenario 2

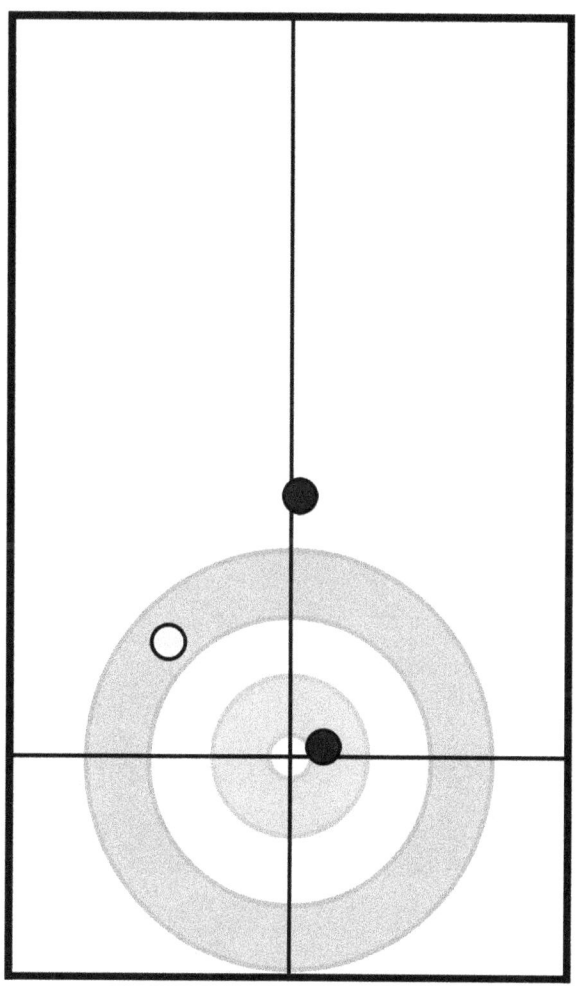

Intermediate Scenario 2

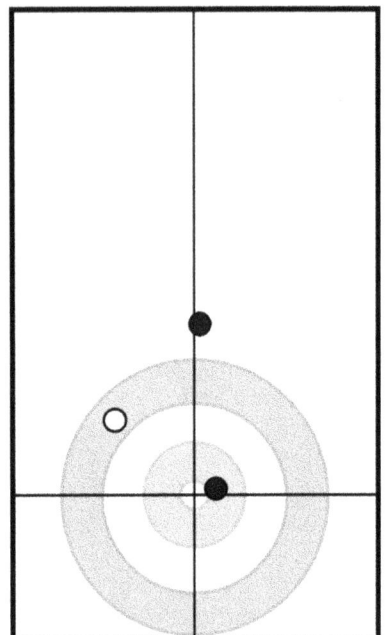

Questions

Hammer Team

What end goal and shot would you choose:
- ▸ Situation 1: Last end, tied score, hammer team's 3rd stone
- ▸ Situation 2: Last end, hammer team down by 1, hammer team's last stone
- ▸ Situation 3: Last end, hammer team down by 1, hammer team's 7th stone

Hammer Team's Shot Choices
(A) Corner guard
(B) Draw to the pin
(C) Remove the guard
(D) Double takeout
(E) Take out the rock on the button and stay on the rings
(F) Bump the rock on the button back to second shot

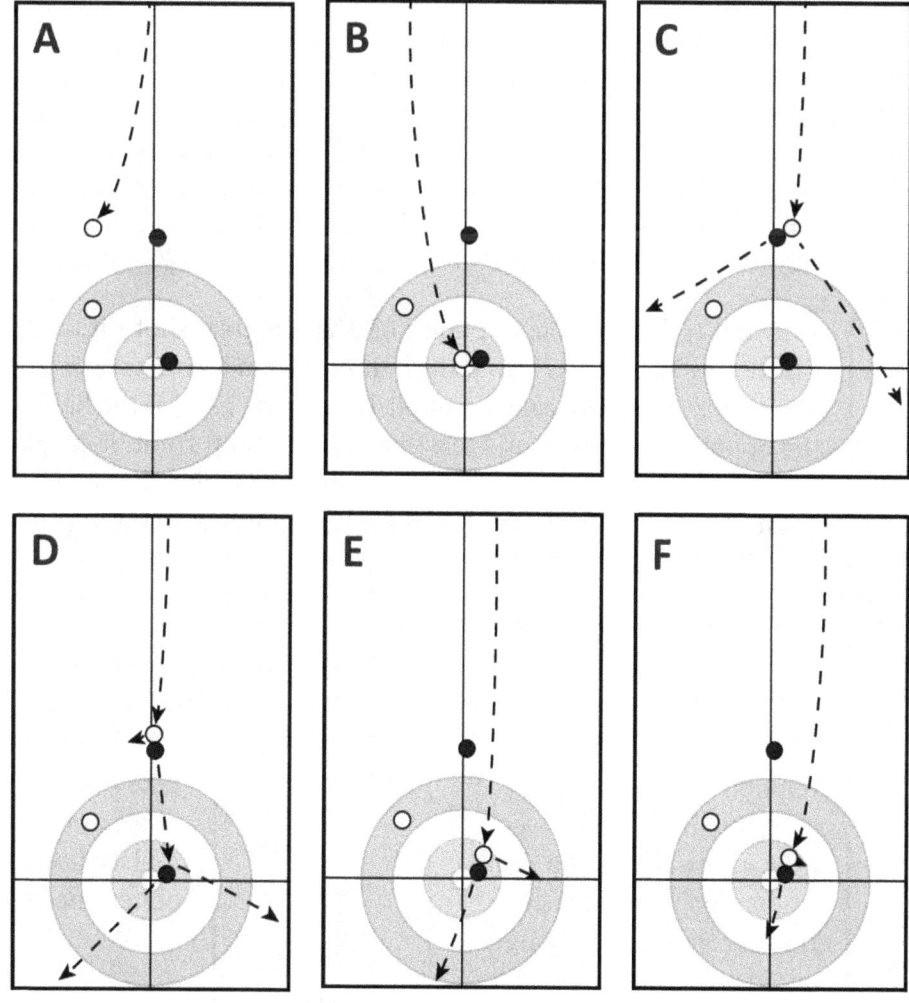

Discussion

Hammer Team

Situation 1: Last end, tied score, hammer team's 3rd stone

The hammer team's primary goal in this end is to prevent the non-hammer team from stealing. The hammer team's goal chart might look like this:

Hammer Team's Goal Chart
   Want: Score 1
   Accept: Blank
   Can't Allow: Steal

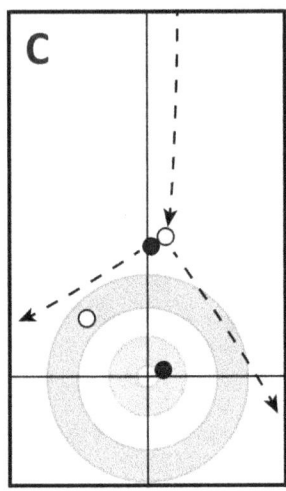

In order to prevent a steal, the hammer team needs to get rid of the guard and shot rock. Since it's early in the end and the non-hammer team has only one guard, the hammer team would probably choose to take the guard out and roll its own stone out (Choice C).

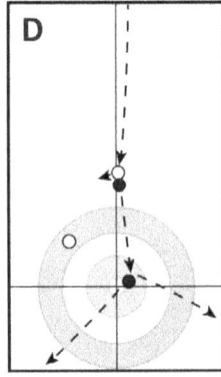

Why not try the double (Option D)? That's a great shot—if the hammer team can also roll its shooter out. If the hammer team leaves its own rock in the front as a center guard, it hasn't accomplished much. (And if the hammer team tries the double a few times and leaves a few rocks up front, it could have trouble accessing the button later.) Center guards are major threats in this situation, because they make it possible for the non-hammer team to protect a rock for a steal.

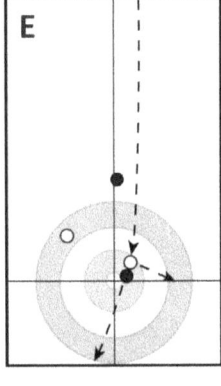

Why not hit the shot rock (Option E)? That's a good shot, too, if the rock is very exposed on the button. Most teams won't play that shot till later in the end, though, because the center guard is extremely well positioned—better, even, than the rock near the button.

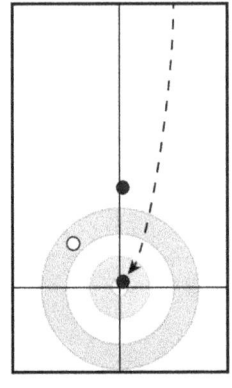

If the hammer team does take out the shot rock, the non-hammer team could replace it with an even better one.

Alternatively, the non-hammer team could put up a high center guard. That would make it even tougher for the hammer team to clear the front. If the hammer team does give up clearing and draws in, but doesn't make the shot perfectly, it could be in a lot of trouble!

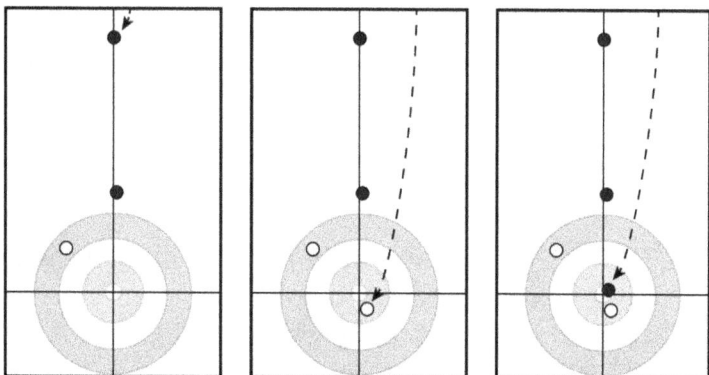

It may seem like a futile plan to remove a guard, then have your opponent replace it repeatedly while they've got a point counting on the rings that is, ultimately, the real scoring problem. However, it's not easy for most non-hammer teams to replace a perfect center guard five turns in a row. If the non-hammer team misses the line for the guard, the hammer team will have a clear shot on the rock in the rings. If the non-hammer team misses the weight and accidentally draws into the rings, the hammer team can double both rocks out.

Author's note: I've shown the hammer team playing the takeout from the right, because it gives the hammer team's second the widest range of angles through which he can miss and still make a useful shot. For example: If the shooter misses wide, he could take out the shot rock on the rings (Option E). If the shooter misses narrow, he could get the double (Option D). While it's true there is a bigger jam possibility when hitting from the right side (i.e., the hammer team could accidentally hit the non-hammer team's guard into its rock on the left), that's not a big deal. This end is all about control of the button—that rock won't likely be important at the end. Finally, if the team is really committed to the double takeout, it may be easier to make it from the left side, because the incoming stone will change impact angles more slowly when it approaches curling from that side, so it will be easier for the skip to call the line.

Situation 2: Last end, hammer team down by 1, hammer team's last rock

The hammer team is down by one, so it must score at least one point to force an extra end. However, if the hammer team can find a way to score two points, it can win the game now. The hammer team's goal chart might look like this:

Hammer Team's Goal Chart
  Want: Score 2
  Accept: Score 1
  Can't Allow: Blank or Steal

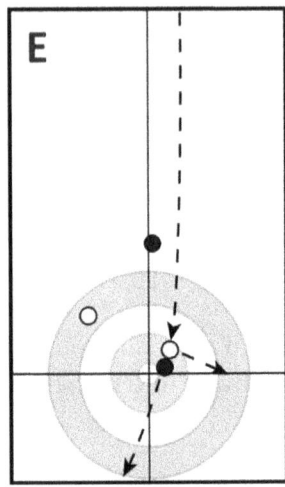

There is only one shot choice that will allow the hammer team to win the game now: take out the non-hammer team's rock near the button and keep the shooter on the rings (Option E).

There are three other shots that will allow the hammer team to tie the game and force an extra end: draw to the pin (Option B); throw a double takeout (Option D), and bump the non-hammer team's rock back to second shot (Option F).

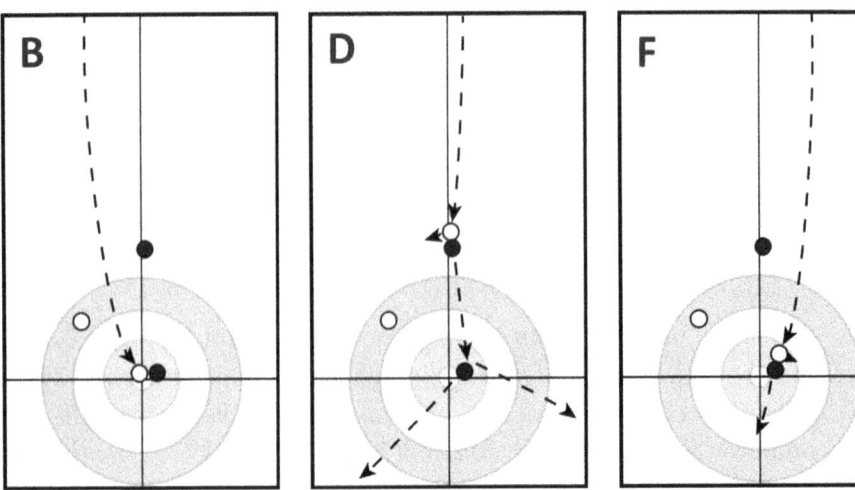

Thus, the hammer team should choose the only option it has to win—the hit-and-stay (Option E), assuming it thinks it can make the shot given the ice conditions in that game. (In this book, we make the assumption that the ice has good curl everywhere, but obviously that's not the case in real life.) If not, the hammer team will need to pick the shot it feels is the most makeable to tie the game.

The upside of the hit and stay on the rings (Option E) is that there are good "pro-side" options with the shot—in other words, if the skip doesn't throw the shot perfectly, there are still good alternative outcomes that are possible. For example, if the skip errs a little heavy and hits and rolls out, the team will still score one and tie. Alternatively, if the skip is a little light and only pushes the non-hammer team's stone back to second shot (Option F), the hammer team will still score one and tie.

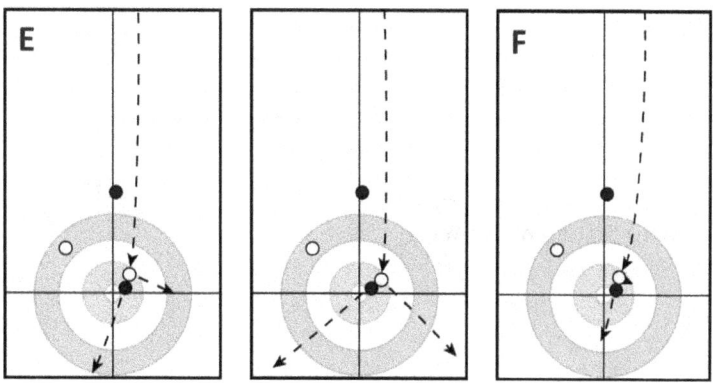

Situation 3: Last end, hammer team down by 1, hammer team's 7th stone

In this situation, the hammer team needs to be very clear on what its top priority end goal is—and what it's willing to risk (or give up) to get it.

Aggressive

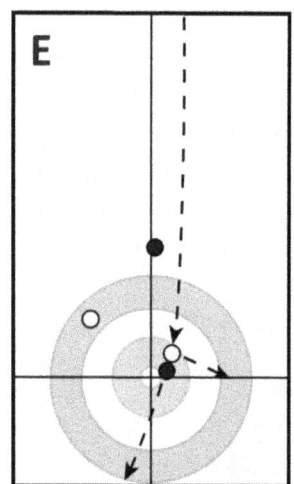

If the hammer team is aggressive and willing to risk all for a deuce to win, then it would take out the non-hammer team's rock on the button and keep the shooter on the rings (Option E).

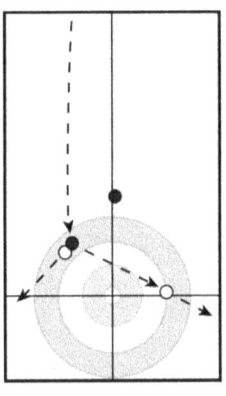 The non-hammer team could then respond by either attempting to double off both of the hammer team's stones to hold the hammer team to one point and force an extra end.

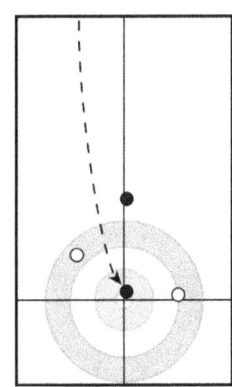 Alternatively, it could draw behind the center guard to either win by stealing, or force an extra end by reducing the hammer team's scoring area.

If the non-hammer team doesn't make the perfect double or draw, the hammer team will have enough rocks left in play to score two to win.

Conservative

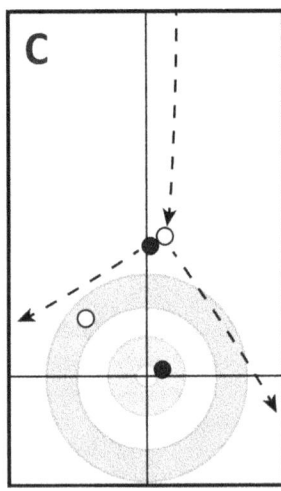 If the hammer team is conservative and wants to focus on preventing the steal to be sure it lives to fight in an extra end, it could peel the center guard (Option C).

The non-hammer team then has two choices:

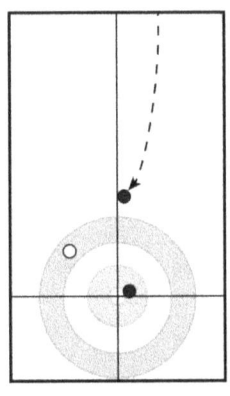 An aggressive non-hammer team would replace the guard to steal or to set up a "closed-center" force.

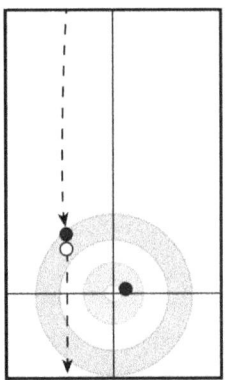 A conservative non-hammer team would hit the hammer team's open stone to force an extra end.

Intermediate Scenario 3

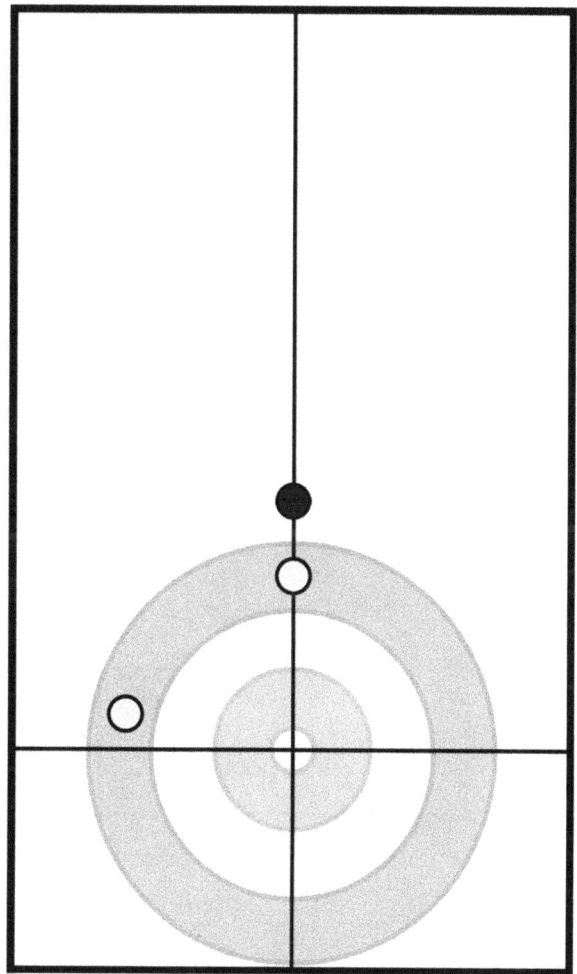

Intermediate Scenario 3

In the last scenario (Intermediate Scenario 2), we touched on one of curling's classic strategy questions: "What should you do if you're up one in the last end without the hammer?" Should you try to "steal at all costs" to win the end and the game, or should you force one so you can try to win in an extra end with the hammer? And if you decide to force 1, should you use aggressive tactics that clog the middle and reduce the scoring area, or conservative tactics to keep the house clear? Those questions will be the focus of this scenario.

There are no correct answers to those questions—you must choose based on your team's strengths and weaknesses, your opponent's strengths and weaknesses, the ice conditions, and your team's preferred style of play. You might even choose different answers in different games.

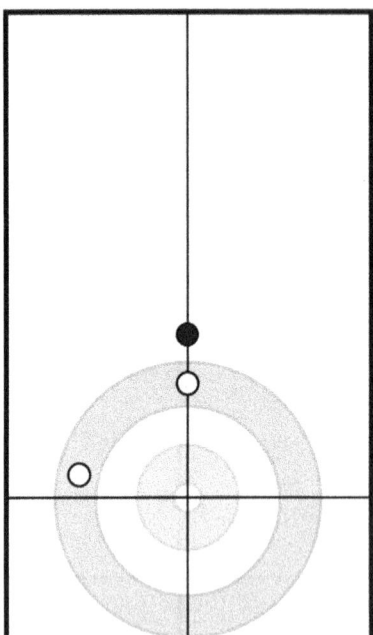

Questions

Non-Hammer Team

What end goal and shot would you choose:
- ▸ **Situation 1: Last end, non-hammer team up by 1, non-hammer team's 4th stone**
- ▸ **Situation 2: Last end, non-hammer team up by 1, non-hammer team's 7th stone**

Non-Hammer Team's Shot Choices
- (A) Put up a second center guard
- (B) Draw to the front button
- (C) Hit the open stone and roll towards the middle

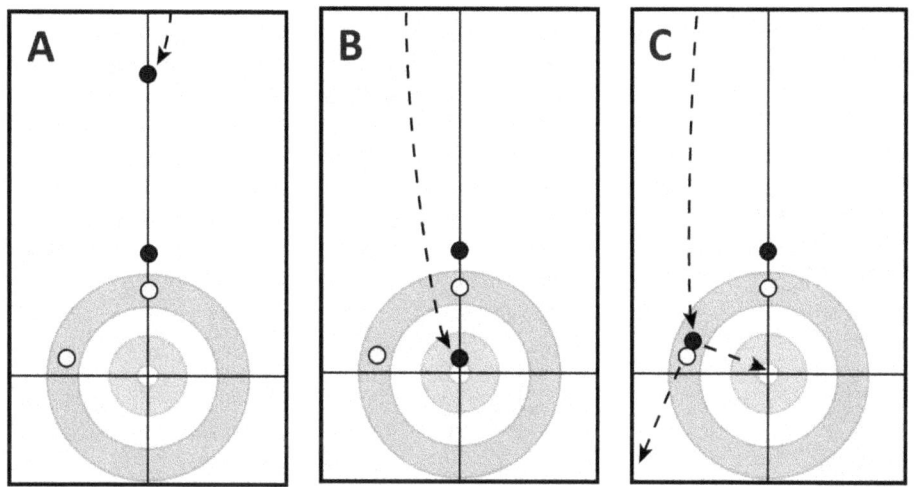

Discussion

Non-Hammer Team

Situation 1: Last end, non-hammer team up by 1, non-hammer team's 4th stone

Aggressive

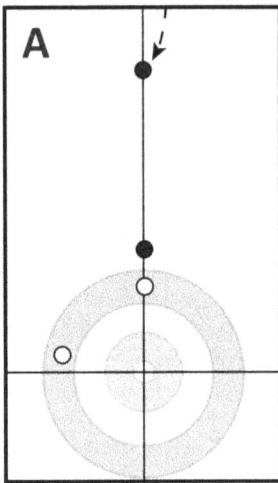

If the non-hammer team is highly committed to an aggressive steal or force, it would put up a second center guard (Choice A). Once that guard is in place, it will be very difficult for the hammer team to clear the front. The end will likely become a scramble for control of the middle.

Moderately Aggressive

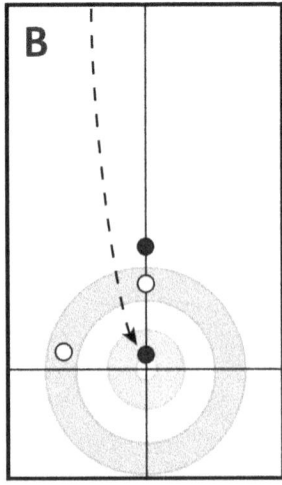

If the non-hammer team is moderately aggressive (or thinks the hammer team doesn't hit well), it would pick Choice B, the draw to the front button. The danger with this choice is that if the hammer team did manage to make a good hit, it could take out the two stones at the top of the house, or even run back the rocks in the center onto the non-hammer team's rock near the button. Once the center guard is gone, there's no protection for a steal or a closed-center force.

Conservative

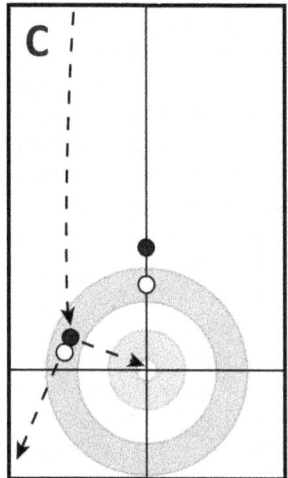

If the non-hammer team has chosen to play for a conservative force, it would choose the hit-and-roll (Option C). It is gambling that it can do one of two things: (1) Make a hit-and-roll behind the guard, or…

(2) Hit and roll close to the center. Exchange hits and rolls until either the non-hammer team succeeds in rolling behind the center guard, or until the hammer team misses by flashing or rolling out. Then the non-hammer team would run the center guard back to eliminate the one remaining hammer stone.

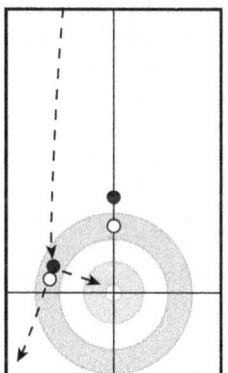 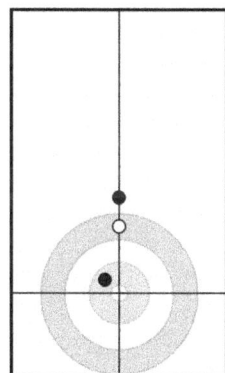 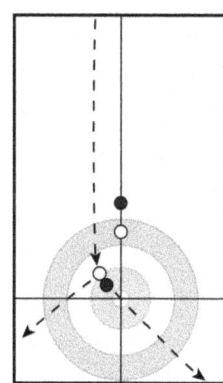 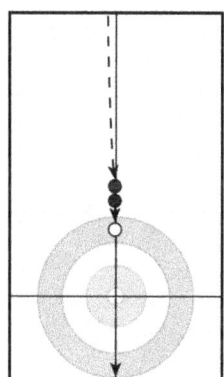

Situation 2: Last end, non-hammer team up by 1, non-hammer team's 7th stone

Now the non-hammer team has only two shots left. Should it stay committed to the same end goal and tactical plan and make the same shot choice as it did in earlier in the end? Or, is it time to bail out to a different plan? Again, this is a personal choice for your team.

> ADVANCED TIP When skips know there's a good chance they'll have to make a game-saving draw with their last rock, they will often draw with their first rock—even when that's not the ideal tactical choice. This gives the team a chance to test draw weight and find out how much the ice is curling before the game is on the line.

227

Intermediate Scenario 4

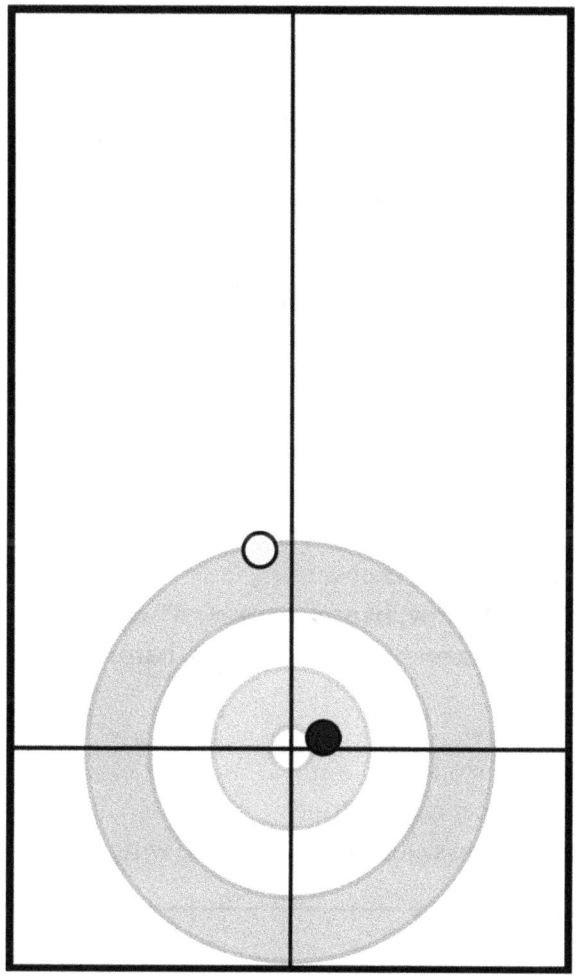

Intermediate Scenario 4

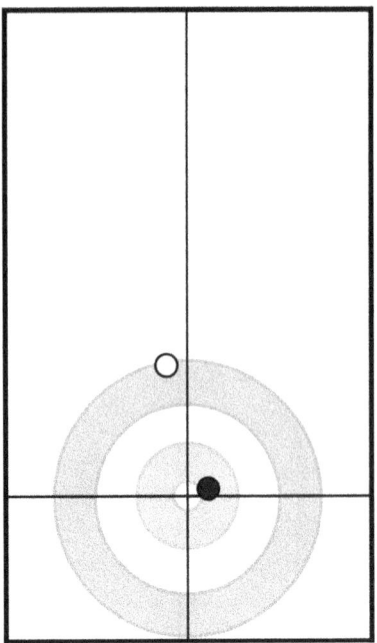

Questions

Hammer Team

What end goal and shot would you choose:
- Situation 1: 4th end, tied game, hammer team's 5th rock
- Situation 2: Last end, hammer team down by 3, hammer team's 5th rock

Hammer Team's Shot Choices
(A) Center guard over own stone
(B) Freeze to the non-hammer team's stone
(C) Hit the non-hammer team's stone and roll to the wing

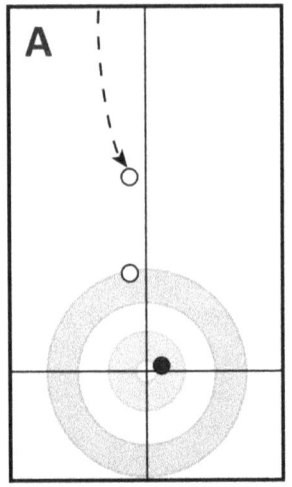
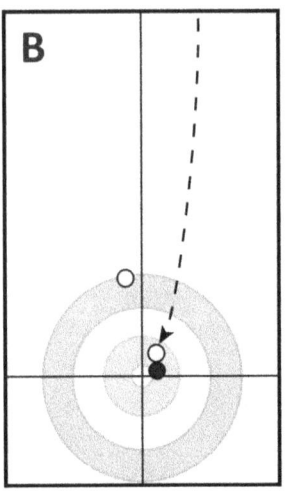
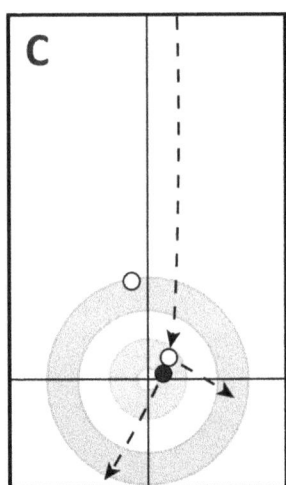

Non-Hammer Team

What end goal and shot would you choose:
▶ **Situation 1: Last end, tied game, non-hammer team's last rock**
▶ **Situation 2: First end, non-hammer team's last rock**

Non-Hammer Team's Shot Choices
(A) Hit and roll to remove the hammer team's stone and guard its own shot rock
(B) Guard the shot rock
(C) Draw in to a "Christmas tree" position for second shot
(D) Freeze to the shot stone
(E) Draw to the side for second shot

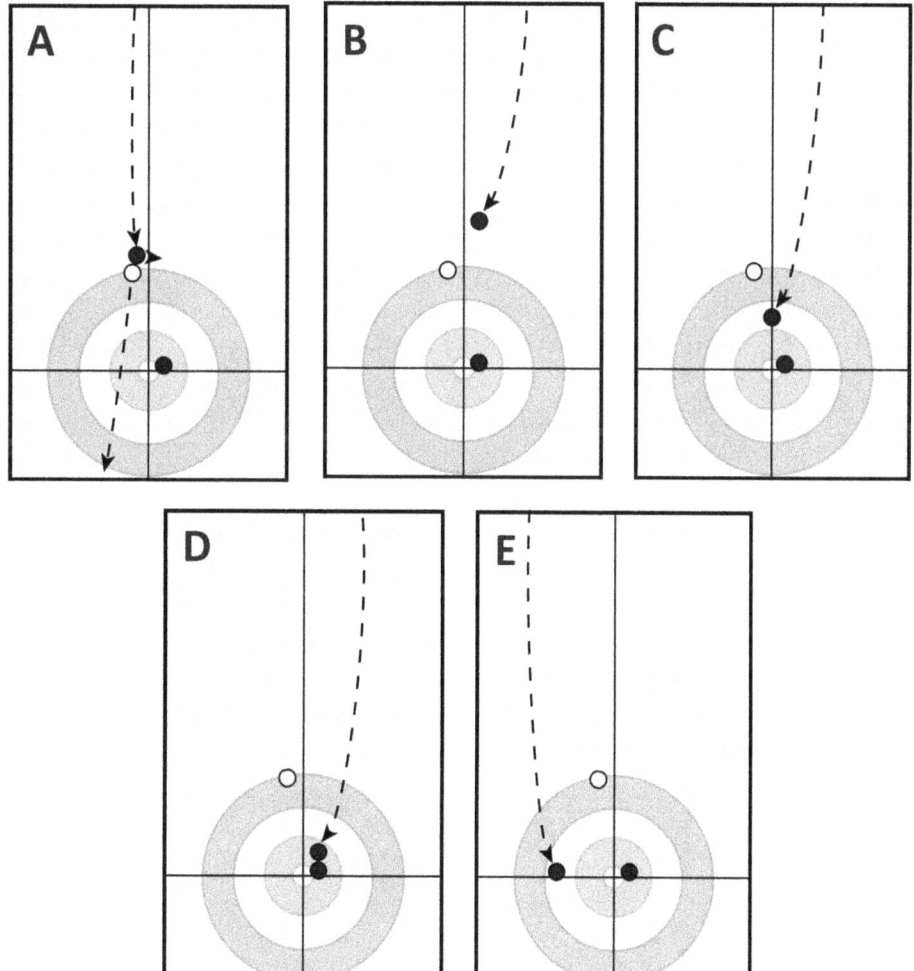

Discussion

Hammer Team

Situation 1: 4th end, tied game, hammer team's 5th rock

It's early in the game, the game is tied, and it's an even end, so this is a great time for the hammer team to try to score two. The hammer team's goal chart might look like this:

Hammer Team's Goal Chart
  Want: Score 2 or Blank
  Accept: Score 1
  Avoid: Steal

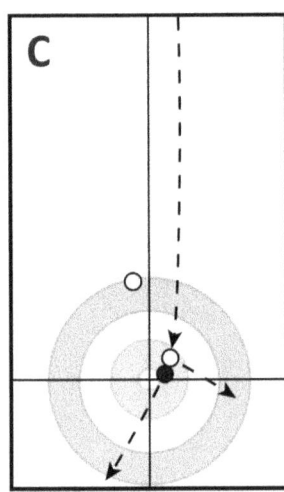

Happily, the hammer team is set up well to accomplish its deuce goal. The team can hit the non-hammer team's stone and roll to the side (Option C). Ideally, the hammer team should leave its own rock far out on the wing so it will be difficult for the non-hammer team to make a double takeout and remove both stones.

Situation 2: Last end, hammer team down by 3, hammer team's 5th rock

The hammer team is in trouble. It needs to score three to stay alive but it has no corner guards and only one of its own rocks in play. It's also getting low on rocks (it needs three points but only has four stones left to throw). The hammer team's goal chart would look like this:

Hammer Team Goal Chart
Want: Score 4
Need: Score 3
Can't Allow: Any other outcome

Option 1

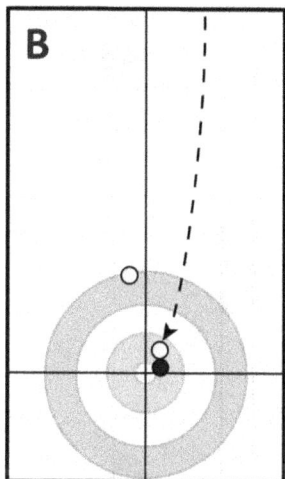

The hammer team's number one goal is to get more rocks in play, so, for the moment, it needs to find a way to use its opponent's stone, rather than worry about removing it. Therefore, the hammer team could freeze to its opponent's stone (Option B). This will make it difficult for the non-hammer team to remove both stones with a double takeout. After that, the hammer team would likely continue to freeze and tap (and hope for a few misses or half-shots by the non-hammer team). Here's an example of how this might play out:

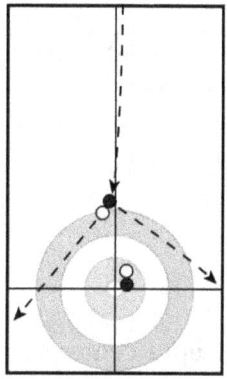 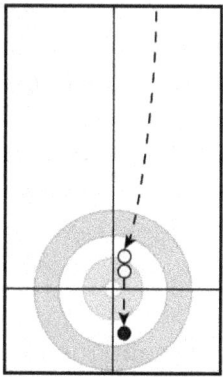 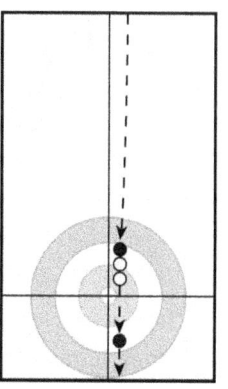 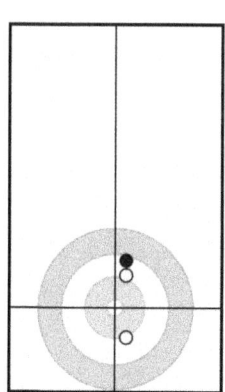

After the hammer team freezes, the non-hammer team takes out the open stone. After all, the non-hammer team's primary goal in this end is to avoid giving up four points!

The hammer team could then tap the frozen stones, pushing the non-hammer team's stone far enough back that both of the hammer team's stones would out-count it.

The non-hammer team tries to take out at least one of the hammer team's stones. The hammer team would need the non-hammer team to have a slight miss, like a jam, to get enough rocks in play.

INTERMEDIATE SCENARIOS   INTRODUCTION TO CURLING STRATEGY

After this, the hammer team has a couple of choices:

The hammer team could draw a third rock in and hope that the non-hammer team will miss one of the two possible doubles.

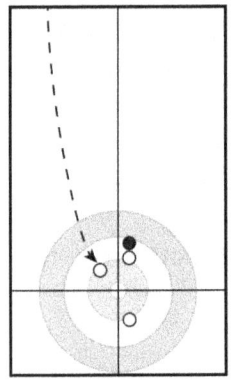
Hammer team draws

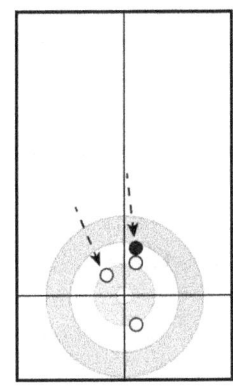
The hammer team needs the non-hammer team to miss a double.

Alternatively, it could guard the line of rocks and hope the non-hammer team misses a takeout or freeze on the back rock.

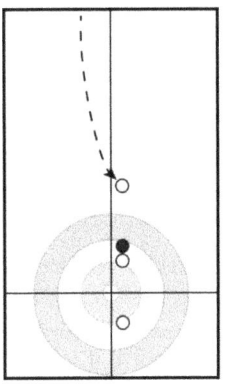
Hammer team guards

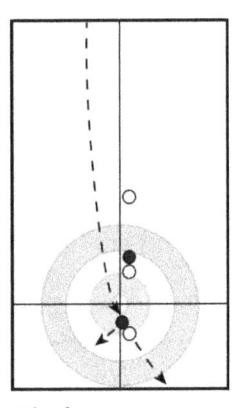
The hammer team needs the non-hammer team to miss a hit...

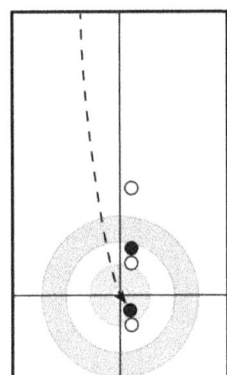
...or a freeze.

Option 2

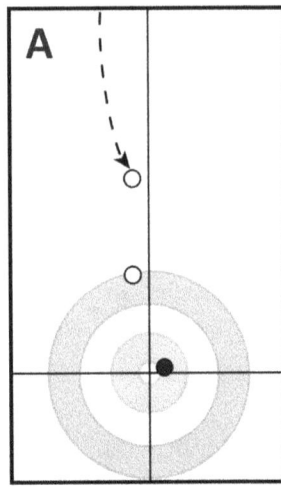

The hammer team's second option is to put up a center guard over its own stone (Option A) instead of freezing. Normally, the hammer team wouldn't put a guard so close to the center line, but now it needs to preserve the rock it does have and create a space that can safely hold more counting stones.

After this, the hammer team would have three rocks left to play, so all would have to go—and stay—in the house for the team to win. Again, the hammer team would need some lucky breaks to succeed.

234

Non-Hammer Team
Situation 1: Last end, tied game, non-hammer team's last rock

It's "steal at all costs" time. The non-hammer team needs to focus exclusively on stealing and not worry about giving up multiple points. The team's goal chart might look like this:

<u>Non-Hammer Team's Goal Chart</u>
  Strongly Want: Steal 1
  Accept: Blank
  Can't Allow: Hammer team scores 1 or more

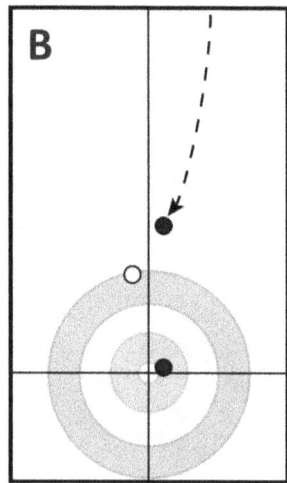

The non-hammer team's best choice is to guard the shot rock (Option B). It doesn't make sense to hit and roll to create the guard (Option A), since the hammer team's rock is actually helping by serving as a partial guard for the non-hammer team's shot rock. This still leaves the hammer team a draw to the pin or a runback to score one, but those are both very difficult shots because the margin for error on those shots is very small.

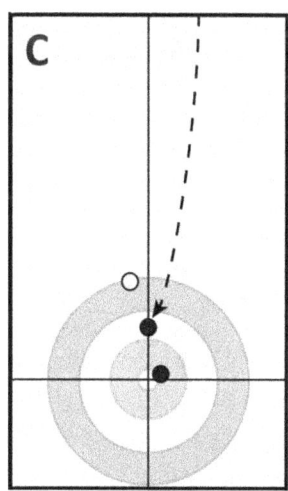

Alternatively, the non-hammer team could draw for second shot in a "Christmas tree" formation (Option C).

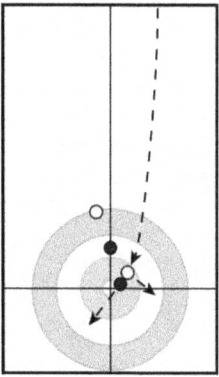

If the non-hammer team makes that draw perfectly (Option C), it will be difficult or impossible for the hammer team to remove the shot rock without losing its shooter (or having its shooter roll too far to count). The hammer team could still draw to the pin or make a triple takeout to score, but those are also very difficult shots.

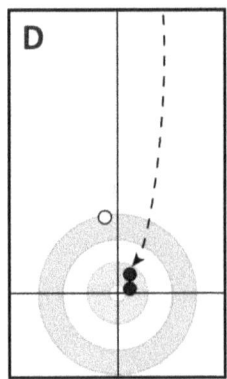

The freeze (Option D) is an okay choice here, but it has to be absolutely perfect. Otherwise, the hammer team could make a double takeout to win. And, as with the other choices, the hammer team can still draw to the pin to win.

Situation 2: First end, non-hammer team's last rock

The choice the non-hammer team makes here depends on its end plan: Is the non-hammer team trying for an "aggressive steal," in which it would be willing to risk giving up two for a chance to steal one? Is the non-hammer team trying for a "conservative steal" in which it would like to get one, but doesn't want to risk giving up two? Or is the non-hammer team trying to "force 1" in order to get the hammer in the next end and have an opportunity to score two points?

Steal 1

Aggressive Steal

If the non-hammer team's plan is an "aggressive steal," its goal chart might look like this:

<u>**Non-Hammer Team's Goal Chart**</u>
   Strongly Want: Steal 1
   Accept: Force 1 or Blank
   Avoid: Hammer team scores 2

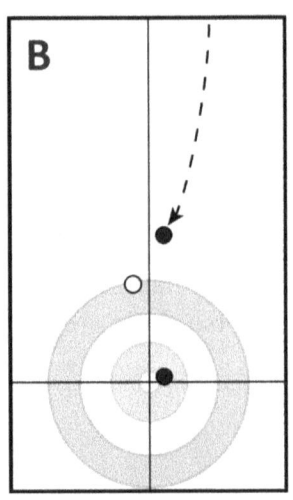 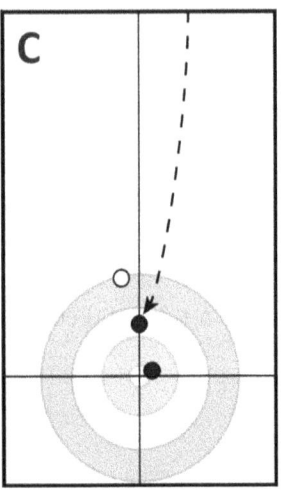

Even though its goal chart is slightly different than the "steal at all costs" goal chart in Situation 1, the non-hammer team would likely use the same tactics (Choice B or C).

Conservative Steal

If the non-hammer team were trying for a "conservative steal," its end goal chart might look like this:

Non-Hammer Team's Goal Chart
    Want: Steal 1
    Accept: Force 1 or Blank
    Strongly Avoid: Hammer team scores 2

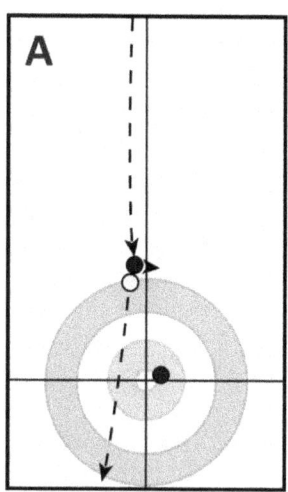

If the non-hammer team's plan is a "conservative steal," it would likely choose to hit and roll (Option A). If the non-hammer team makes the shot perfectly, it will have a chance to steal. If it makes the hit but not the roll, the hammer team can blank or score one, but has no chance for a deuce.

Force 1

Conservative Force (Blank okay)

Non-Hammer Team's Goal Chart
    Want: Force 1
    Accept: Blank
    Strongly Avoid: Hammer team scores 2

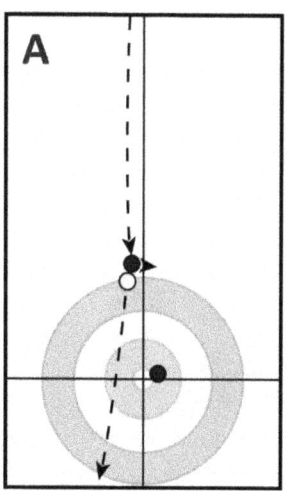

If the non-hammer team were trying for a very conservative force, it would hit and roll (Option A).

If the non-hammer team makes the shot perfectly, it will be set up for a closed-center force.

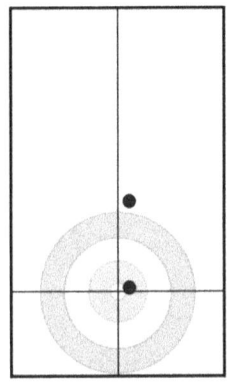

If it rolls onto the rings, it will be set up for an open-center force. If it rolls out, the hammer team could blank.

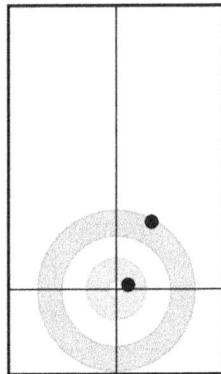

This approach is as much a "Prevent the hammer team from scoring more than 1" plan as it is a "Force 1" plan.

Moderately Aggressive Force

This is a committed force plan in which the non-hammer team is willing to risk giving up two points to ensure that the hammer team must score one and only one point in the end. The non-hammer team's goal chart might look like this:

Non-Hammer Team's Goal Chart
    Strongly Want: Force 1
    Accept: Hammer team scores 2
    Avoid: Blank

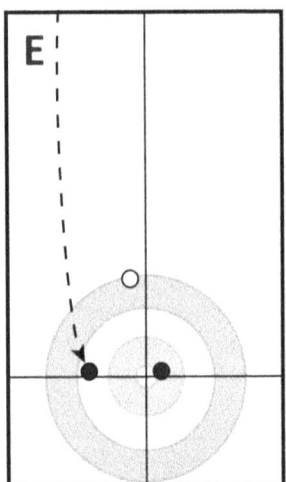

The non-hammer team draws to the side of the rings in a position where there is no double takeout (Option E). This is an open-center force.

Highly Aggressive Force

The non-hammer team could also take a very aggressive force approach that also gives a possibility of a steal.

Non-Hammer Team's Goal Chart
    Want: Force 1 or Steal 1
    Accept: Hammer team scores 2
    Avoid: Blank

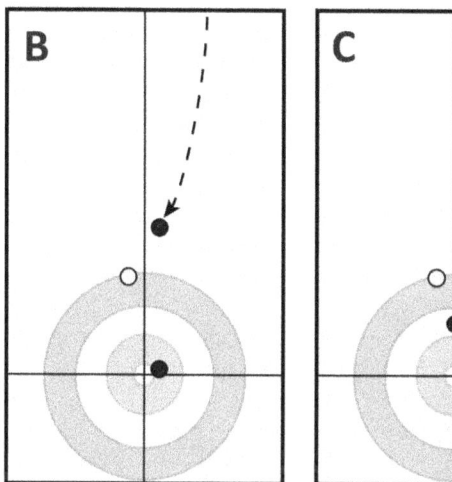

In this case, the non-hammer team would choose the same tactics as an aggressive steal (Options B and C). The downside of these tactics is that the risk of giving up a deuce is higher, because if the non-hammer team has a slight miss, the hammer team could have an easy shot for two. (By contrast, there is a bigger margin for error on the "moderately aggressive steal" plan (Option E), because the rocks are more spread out in the house, making a double in which the hammer team can keep the shooter more difficult.)

The upside of these tactics is that they also make a steal possible if the hammer team has a slight miss. (The hammer team would need to have a major miss—like a flash—to give up a steal if the non-hammer team plays a more conservative option, like Options A and E.)

Intermediate Scenario 5

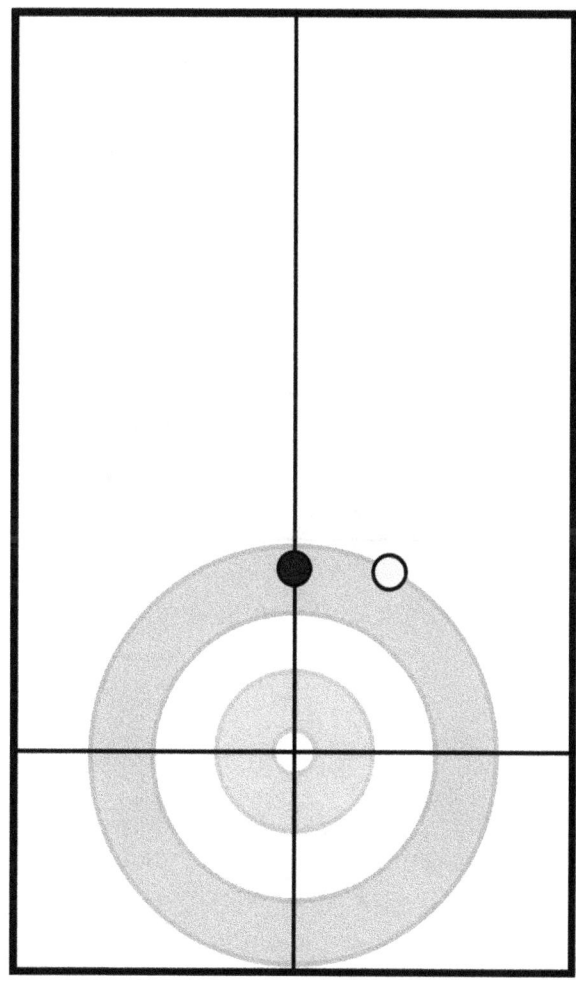

Intermediate Scenario 5

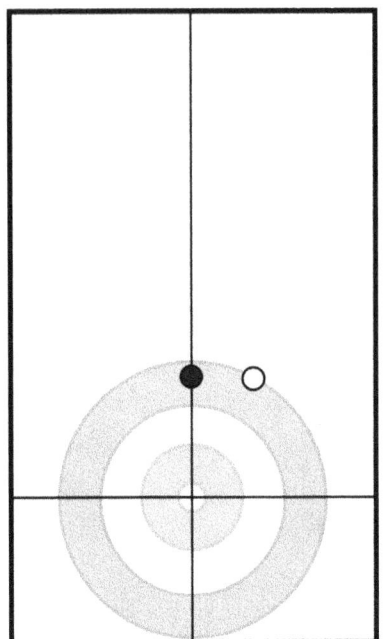

Questions

Non-Hammer Team

What end goal and shot would you choose:
- Situation 1: Last end, tied game, non-hammer team's 4th stone
- Situation 2: Last end, tied game, non-hammer team's last stone
- Situation 3: Last end, tied game, non-hammer team's 7th stone
- Situation 4: Last end, non-hammer team up by 1, non-hammer team's 3rd rock

<u>**Non-Hammer Team's Shot Choices**</u>
- (A) Center guard
- (B) Draw to the button
- (C) Tap own stone back to the button
- (D) Take out the hammer team's stone

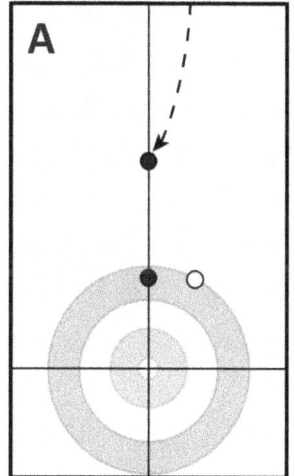 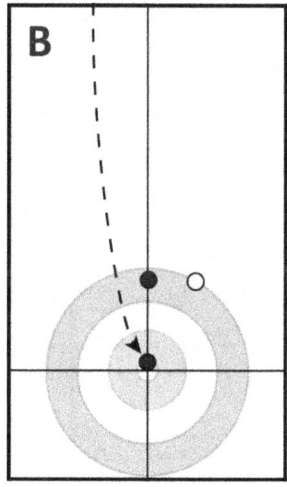 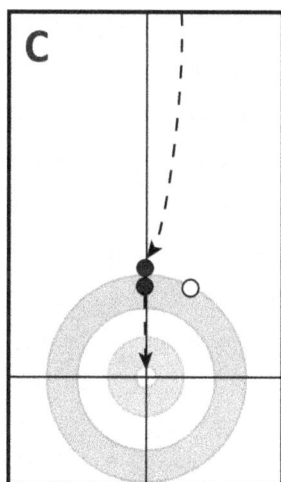 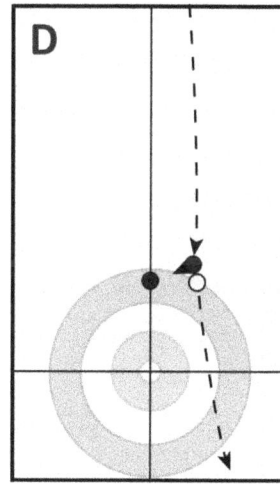

Discussion

Non-Hammer Team

Situation 1: Last end, tied game, non-hammer team's 4th stone

The non-hammer team's goal for this end would be to "steal at all costs."

> **Non-Hammer Team's Goal Chart**
> Need: Steal 1
> Can't Accept: Any other outcome

In order to have a good chance to steal, the non-hammer team needs two things: a guard and a quality shot rock. Right now, it doesn't have either. The non-hammer team's rock at the top of the rings is far from the button, so it would be easy for the hammer team to out-draw it with its last rock. Alas, that rock is also not a very good guard, because it is too close to the button. (If the non-hammer team got a quality shot rock behind it, the hammer team could make a relatively easy double takeout to remove both.)

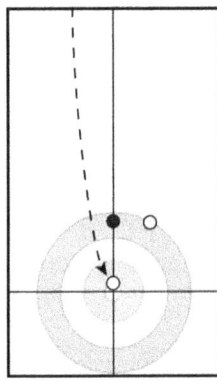 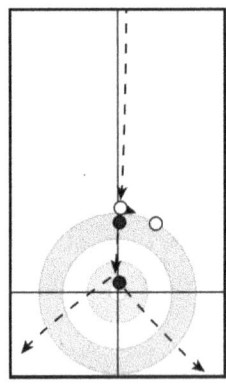

The non-hammer team's rock is easy to out-draw... *...and too close to be a good guard.*

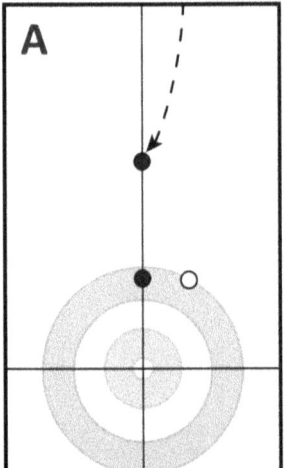

Fortunately, it's still early in the end, so the non-hammer team has time to set up a better guard (Option A).

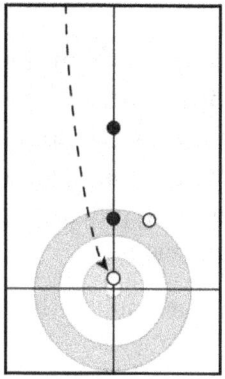

So what happens if the hammer team draws around the non-hammer team's rocks to the button? Won't that rock be difficult to remove? This is a risk. However the non-hammer team could tap that hammer team's stone, or freeze to it and hit the pair of rocks later to get shot stone. (For more on this, see the "How to remove rocks behind center guards" section.) For most non-hammer teams, it's easier to solve that problem than it is to steal without a good guard. Also, in this situation, most hammer teams would be focused on clearing the front to make sure their skip will have a draw or hit path to the button with the last rock. Again, all the hammer team needs to do to win is score one.

Situation 2: Last end, tied game, non-hammer team's last stone

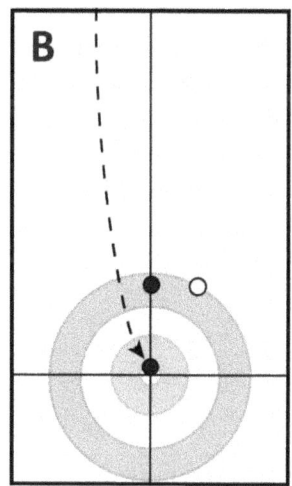
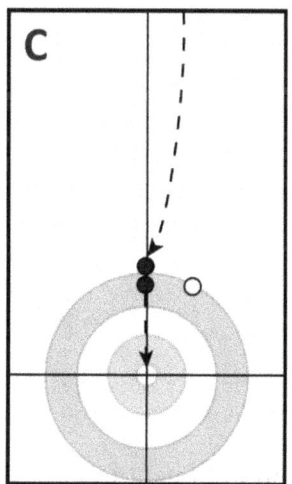

Again, the non-hammer team's end plan is to "steal at all costs." This time, the non-hammer team doesn't have time to set up both a good guard and a quality shot rock. Now, getting a quality shot rock is most important. So, the non-hammer team would draw or tap to get a quality shot rock (Options B and C). While it's true the hammer team could make a double takeout to win, that's a tougher shot for most hammer teams than a draw to anywhere in the eight-foot ring or closer.

Situation 3: Last end, tied game, non-hammer team's 7th stone

Once again, the non-hammer team is in a "steal at all costs" situation. In Situation 1, early in the end, it made sense for the non-hammer team to put up a guard. In Situation 2, the last rock of the end, it made sense for the non-hammer team to draw or tap to get a quality shot rock. The only question remaining is—at what point in the end should the non-hammer team switch from trying to set up a good guard, to trying to get a quality shot rock? This is a personal choice and it depends on the ice conditions and the strengths and weaknesses of your team and your opponent.

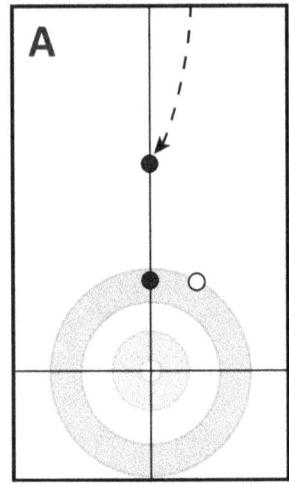

If your opponent is good at takeouts and likely to make the double, then you may want to put up another guard (Option A).

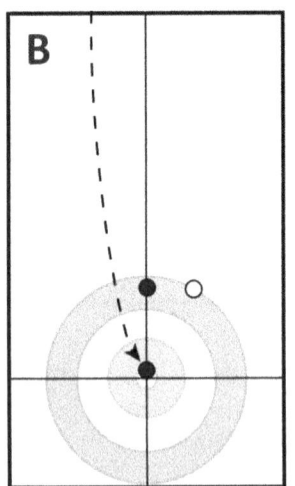 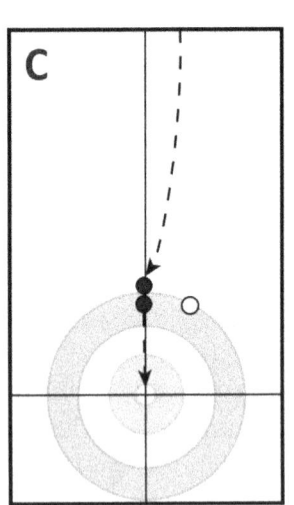

If not, you may want to draw (Option B) or tap (Option C).

Another reason to draw or tap now is to prevent your opponent from drawing to the button. If you choose to guard and your opponent then draws, with only one shot remaining, it may be difficult for you to both bump that opponent stone out of its shot rock position and sit shot behind cover.

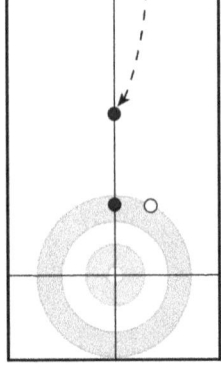 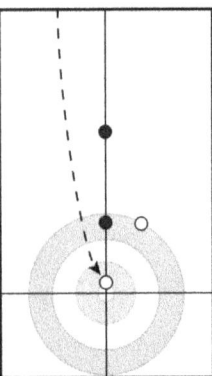 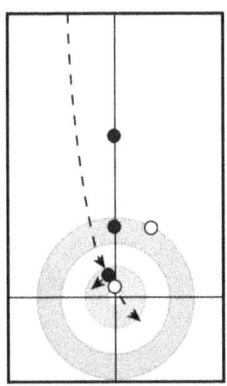

Situation 4: Last end, non-hammer team up by 1, non-hammer team's 3rd rock

As we talked about in "Intermediate Scenario 3," the "non-hammer team up by one in the final end" situation is a classic strategy problem—and one that different teams solve in different ways.

Aggressive (Steal)

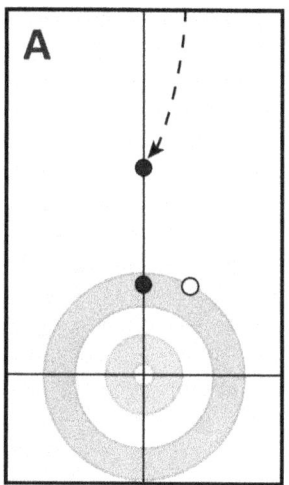

If the non-hammer team is aggressive and playing to "steal at all costs", this would be like Situation 1 above, and the non-hammer team would put up a center guard (Option A). The risk with this choice is that by leaving the hammer team's stone on the side, the hammer team could eventually score two points to win.

Non-Hammer Team's Goal Chart
Strongly Want: Steal 1
Accept: Force 1 or Blank
Can't Allow: Any other outcome

Conservative (Force)

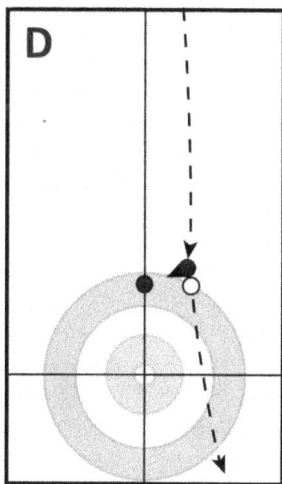

If the non-hammer team is conservative and playing to force one (or to prevent the hammer team from scoring two points to win), then it would take out the hammer team's rock (Option D). After all, the hammer team can't score two points if it can't get two rocks in the rings!

Non-Hammer Team's Goal Chart
Want: Force 1
Accept: Steal 1 or Blank
Can't allow: Any other outcome

Intermediate Scenario 6

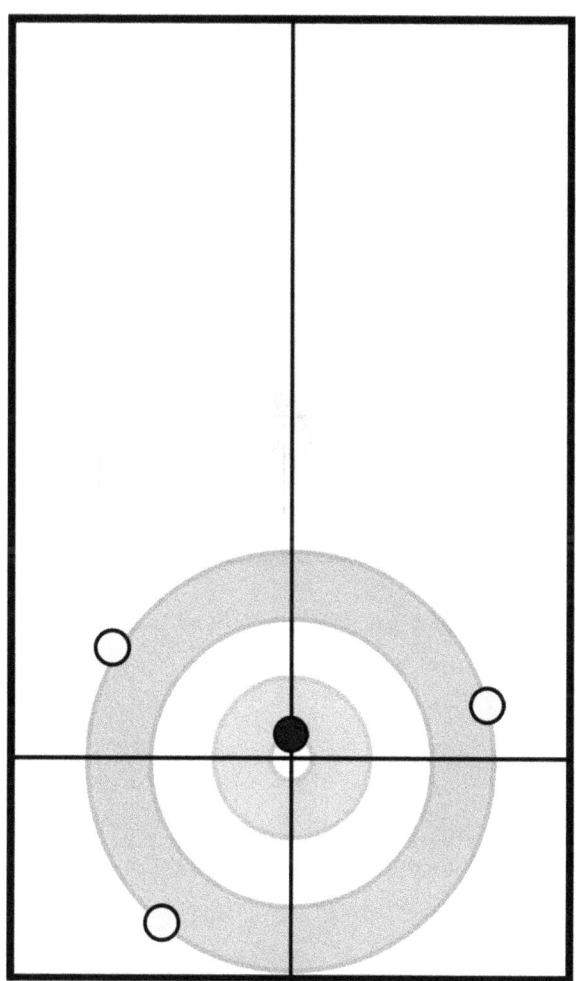

Intermediate Scenario 6

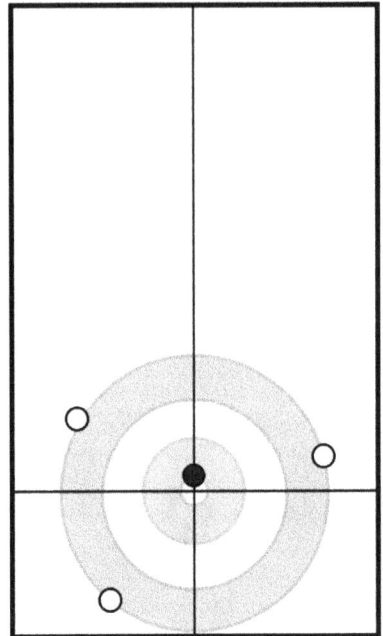

Questions

Non-Hammer Team

What end goal and shot would you choose:
- **Situation 1: Last end, tied score, non-hammer team's last rock**
- **Situation 2: Last end, non-hammer team leads by 1, non-hammer team's last rock**
- **Situation 3: First end, non-hammer team's last rock**
- **Situation 4: Last end, non-hammer team leads by three points, non-hammer team's last stone**

Non-Hammer Team's Shot Choices
(A) Center guard
(B) Freeze to the shot stone
(C) Freeze to an opponent stone to get second shot
(D) Draw to the wing
(E) Hit and roll a very short distance for second shot
(F) Double takeout

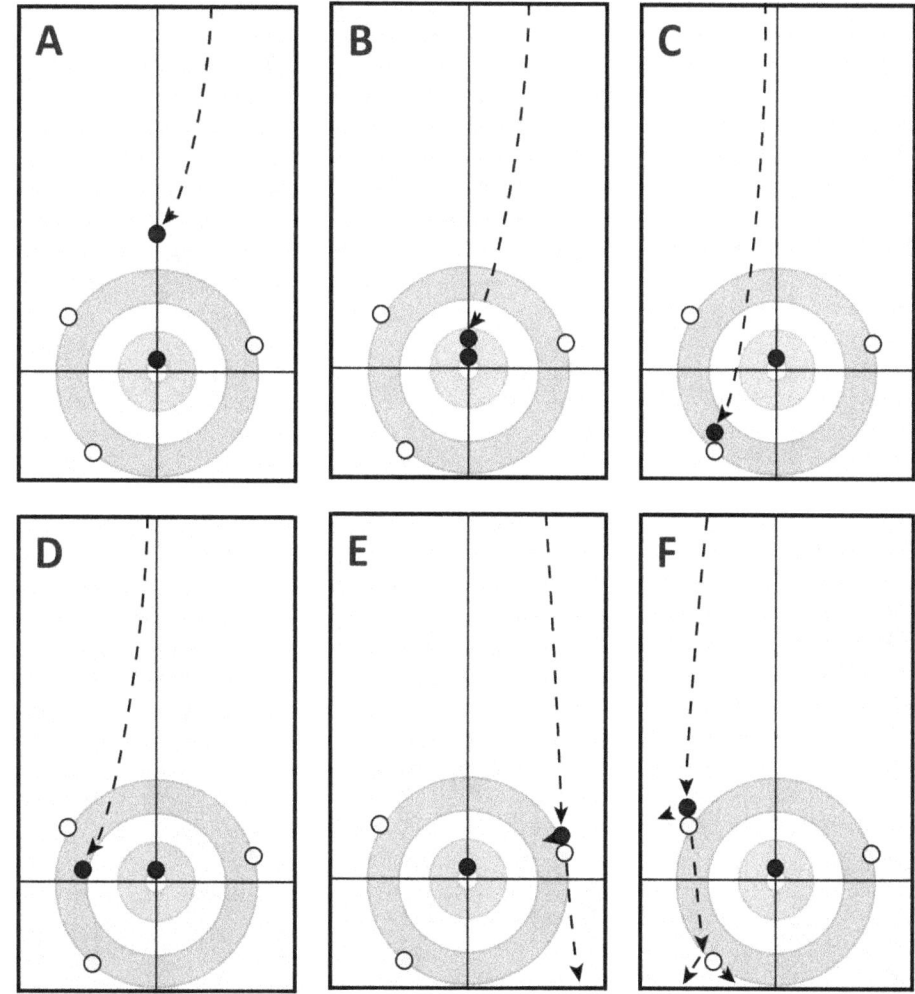

Discussion

Non-Hammer Team

Situation 1: Last end, tied score, non-hammer team's last rock

The non-hammer team must steal to stay alive, so its end goal is simple: "Steal at all costs."

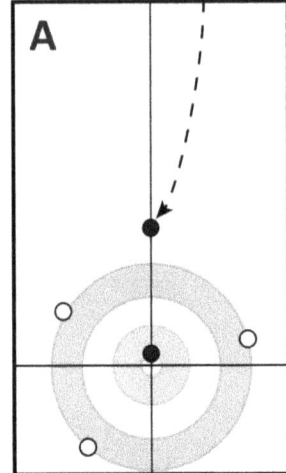

Its best hope is to put up a center guard (Option A) that's far enough out to make a double difficult, but close enough to prevent the hammer team from tapping the shot rock back to win.

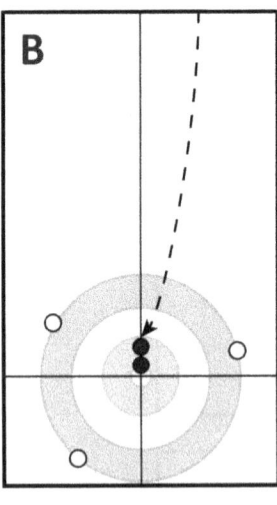

Alternatively, the non-hammer team could freeze to its shot stone (Option B). The freeze would have to be absolutely perfect so the hammer team couldn't make a double to remove both.

In my experience, most non-hammer teams would choose to play the center guard because there's a bigger margin for error. For example, if the center guard is a foot short of the perfect position, it will still offer good protection.

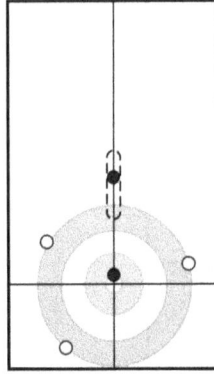

If the freeze is a foot short, the hammer team will have an easy double to win.

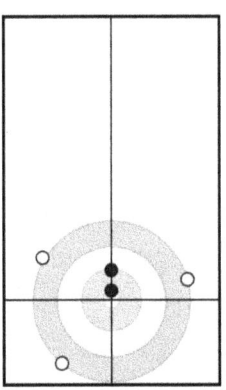
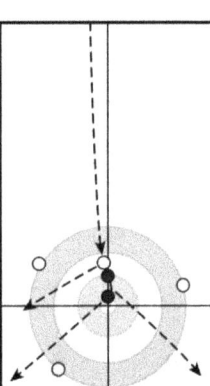

Situation 2: Last end, non-hammer team leads by 1, non-hammer team's last rock

Once again, we're in the classic "non-hammer team up by one in the final end" situation. (We saw this earlier in Intermediate Scenarios 3 and 5.) The non-hammer team must first decide if it wants to steal to win, or force 1 to play an extra end with the hammer. Then, it will choose a tactical plan to go with that end goal.

Aggressive (Steal)

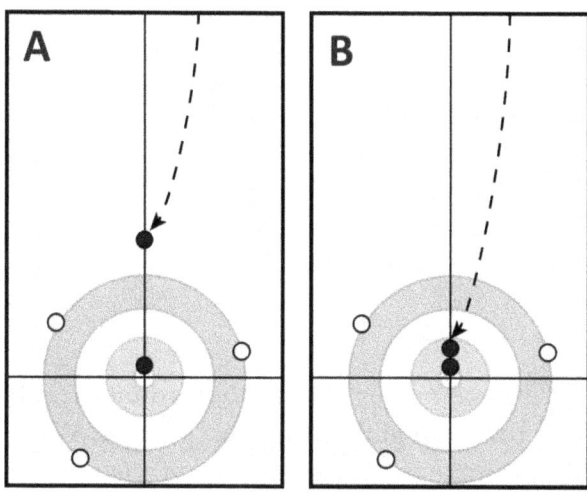

If the non-hammer team's end goal is to steal, it would put up a center guard (Option A) or freeze to its own rock (Option B) as in Situation 1.

Conservative (Force)

There are several ways the non-hammer team could force 1:

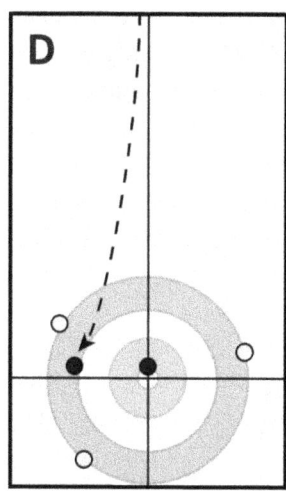

Draw for second shot

The non-hammer team could force one by drawing a rock onto the side of the rings for second shot (Option D). The non-hammer team would need to position its rock so the hammer team would not be able to throw a double takeout and remove both stones. Then, the best the hammer team could do is bump or hit the non-hammer team's stone in the center to get one point. (In my experience, most non-hammer teams would choose this shot because it has the biggest margin for error.)

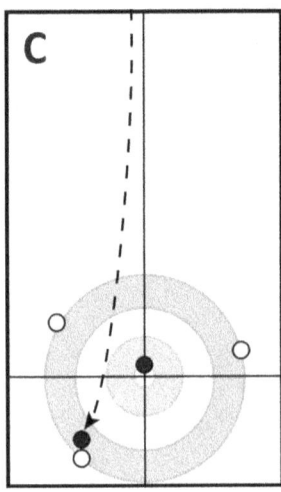

Freeze for second shot

The non-hammer team could freeze to one of the hammer team's stones to get second shot (Option C). It would be difficult for the hammer team to make a double to remove both stones, thus, it would be forced to play for one.

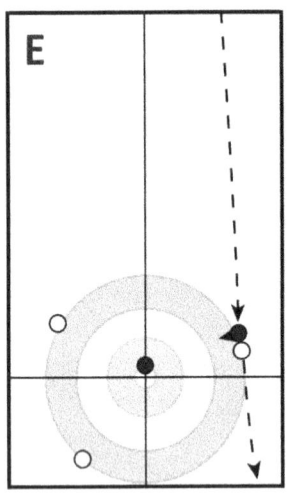

Hit and roll for second shot

The non-hammer team could force one by hitting the hammer team's stone on the right wing and rolling slightly in for second shot. While it is possible for this tactic to work, in this situation, very few teams would choose this option. Why? First, there's nothing to be gained from removing one of the hammer team's stones, since the hammer team would still have more than enough rocks left in the rings to get two points to win. (In an early end, it might make sense to use a cut-down tactic like this to avoid giving up a four-ender.) Second, the hit-and-roll is a very precise shot. The non-hammer team needs to hit the hammer team's stone in exactly the right spot in order to roll to a place where its rock will be second shot, but won't give the hammer team an easy double. There is virtually no margin for error. With the draw, the non-hammer team could draw to either side, and it could be off by a foot or so in any direction and still have a good result.

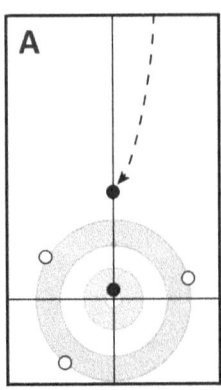

Technically, the hammer team could guard (Option A) for an aggressive "closed-center" force. However if it's going for a force instead of a steal, it's probably looking for a lower-risk option than this!

So why would the hammer team ever force when it could steal? There are two main types of reasons: strategic ones (e.g., the non-hammer team would rather force than steal to get the hammer in the next end), and tactical ones (e.g., the shot to force has a much greater chance for success than the shot to steal). We'll talk about the strategic reasons in the next section (Intermediate 7). Let's look at the tactical ones now, since they apply to the example above.

In this scenario, imagine that the ice is curling an extreme amount (e.g., 6 ft/2 m) with a lot of curl at the end. The non-hammer team might worry that it would be difficult or even impossible to put up an effective guard to steal. (In other words, the non-hammer team might worry that the guard could over-curl by six inches and leave the shot stone exposed. Or, it might worry that if the guard were on-line but a little short, it would be easy for the hammer team to throw a light-weight hit and curl around the guard to remove the shot stone.) Thus, the non-hammer team might decide that since there is a bigger margin for error on the draw to the wing, it should play that shot to give itself a better chance to win the game in the long run. This is a bit like "laying up" in golf.

Situation 3: First end, non-hammer team's last rock

Yikes! There is an expression in curling: "You can't win in the first end, but you can lose in it," and this is a scenario in which that could happen. If the non-hammer team misses with this final shot, it could give up four points—which would give the hammer team a huge, and possibly insurmountable, lead. The non-hammer team has a number of ways to try to get out of this mess. Let's look at them:

Aggressive (Steal)

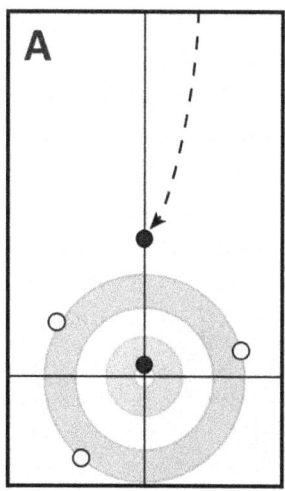

The non-hammer team could try an aggressive move to steal its way out of trouble. It has a rock near the button, so it is well positioned to steal—all it needs to do is put up a good center guard (Option A). A steal would be a great outcome. However, if the guard is a little off line, or a little too light, the hammer team could have an easy shot for four. That would be a very, very bad outcome.

Conservative (Force)

The non-hammer team could take a conservative approach and try to force one as a safer way to get out of trouble. (Again, you don't need to score in every end, and sometimes giving up one or two points—instead of four—is a major victory.) As in Scenario 2, there are multiple ways the non-hammer team could force conservatively: It could draw to the wing for second shot (Option D). It could freeze to a rock in the back for second shot (Option C). Or, it could hit and roll just a little for second shot (Option E).

In Scenario 2, there wasn't much value to hitting and rolling (Option E), however, here, there is some upside, since it would limit the hammer team to three points, at most. As bad as it is to give up three, it's a lot better than giving up four!

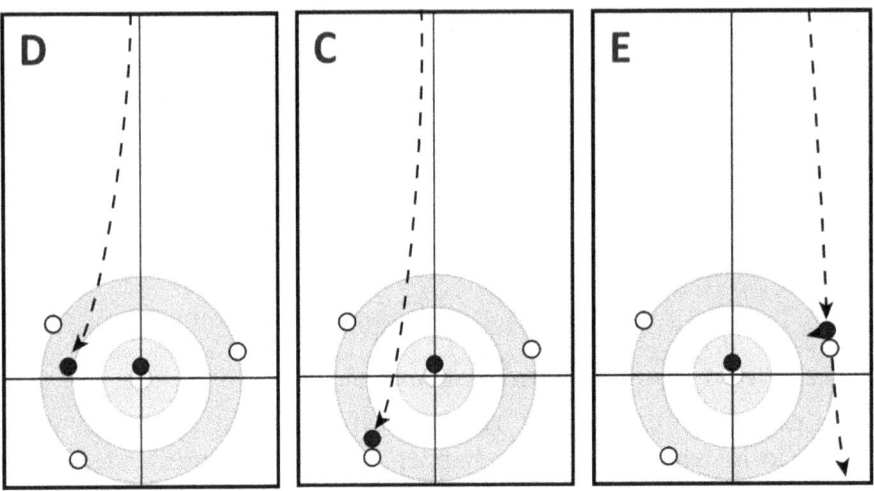

Conservative (Prevent the hammer team from scoring 3 or more)

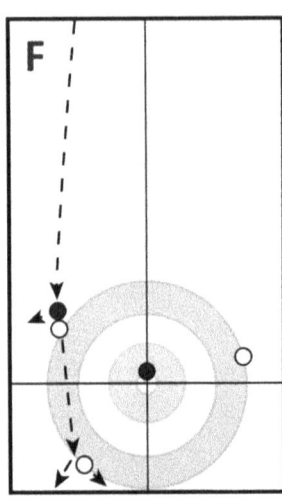

The only way the non-hammer team can be sure to avoid giving up a big end is to make a double takeout (Option F). In this scenario, all of the double takeouts are long and difficult, so this wouldn't be a good option for most teams.

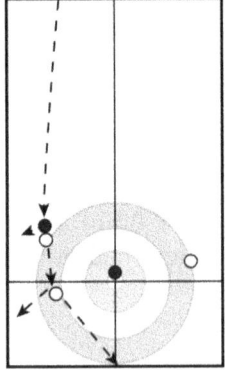

However, if the hammer team's stones were closer together, it might make sense to play a double, minimize the damage, and move on.

Situation 4: Last end, non-hammer team leads by 3, non-hammer team's last rock

Aargh! The non-hammer team built itself a three-point lead and is now in danger of giving that up, and more! Again, it has a range of choices to get itself out of trouble, depending on whether it wants to be aggressive and try to win now, or play it safe and force an extra end.

Aggressive (Steal)

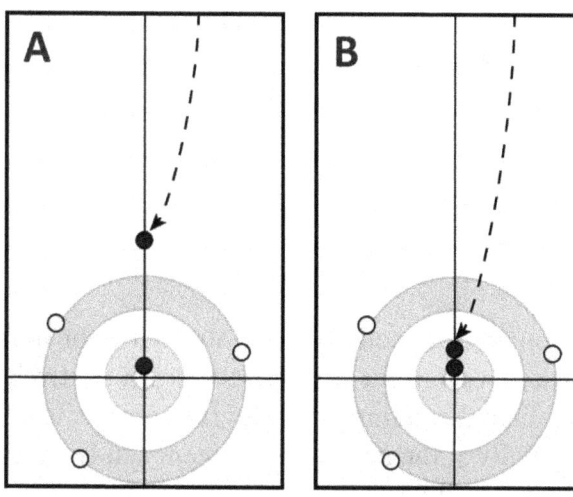

An aggressive non-hammer team might try to steal to win, regardless of the fact that it could force an extra end simply by removing one of the hammer team's stones. In that case, it would likely put up a center guard (Option A), or possibly freeze to its shot rock (Option B).

Moderately Aggressive (Force 1)

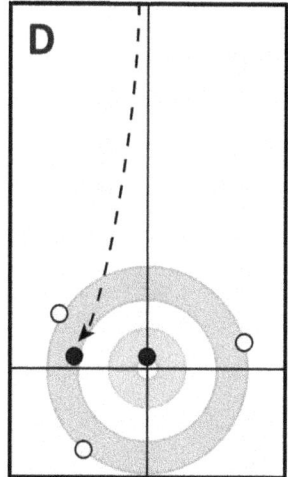 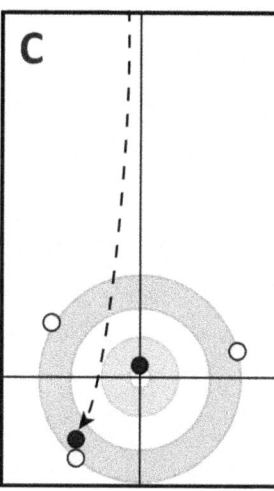

A moderately aggressive non-hammer team could draw (Option D) or freeze (Option C) for second shot. This is like the force plans discussed in previous examples. This is moderately aggressive, because it comes with some risk. If the non-hammer team makes a good shot, it will win now. If not, the hammer team could have a chance to score four to win.

257

Conservative (Prevent the hammer team from scoring more than 2 or 3, or Force 1)

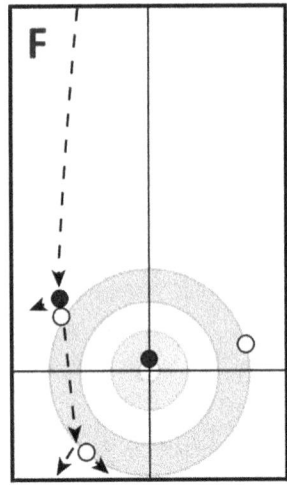

The non-hammer team could guarantee victory by making a double takeout (Option F). However, because the hammer team's stones are far apart, that is a difficult shot for most teams. The upside of attempting this shot is that if the non-hammer team only eliminates one of the hammer team's stones, it will still force a tie and have the hammer in the extra end.

This is conservative because as long as the hammer team makes at least a half-shot (i.e., a single takeout) it won't lose in this end.

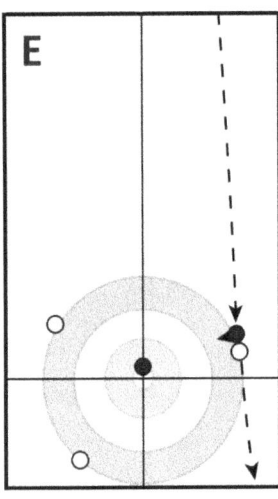

The single hit-and-roll (Option E) is a good choice in its own right (not just as a Plan B). There are three reasons for this: First, this is a relatively makeable shot. Second, this shot makes it impossible for the hammer team to score four points to win. Finally, if the non-hammer team can leave its shooter far from its shot stone, it still has a good chance of winning the game in this end, because it will be difficult for the hammer team to make a double and keep its shooter to tie.

Intermediate Scenario 7

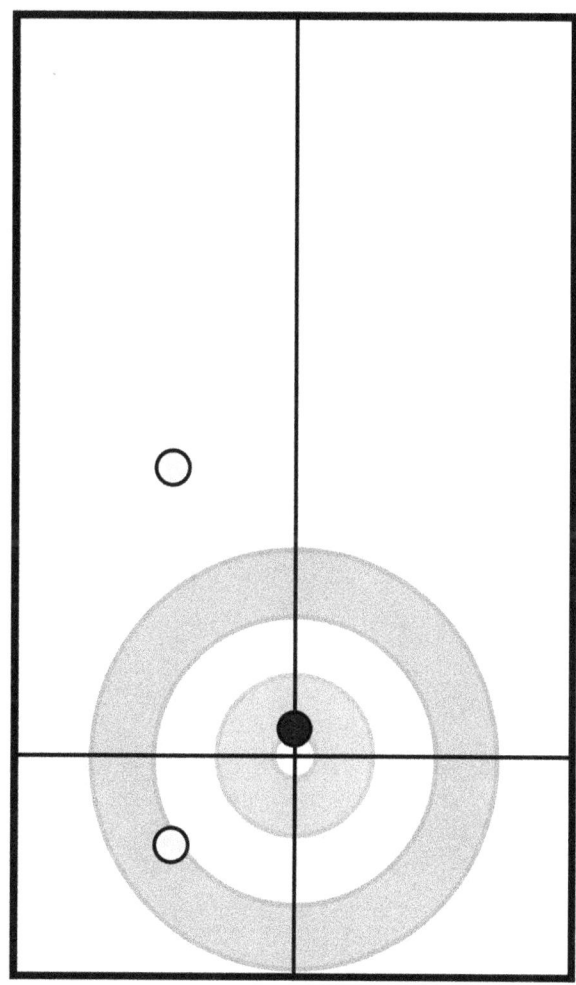

Intermediate Scenario 7

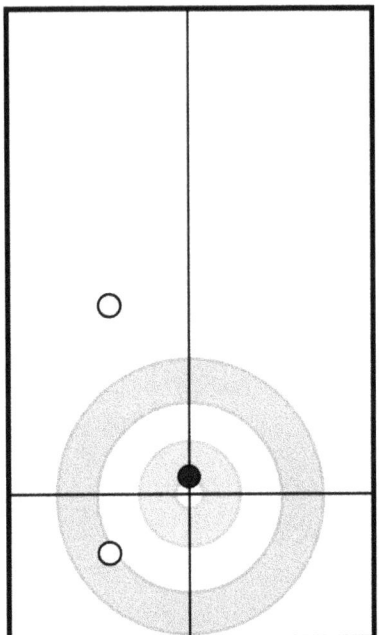

Questions

Non-Hammer Team

What end goal and shot would you choose:
▶ **Situation 1: 9th of 10 ends, non-hammer team leads by 1, non-hammer team's 5th stone**

Non-Hammer Team's Shot Choices
  (A) Center guard
  (B) Draw behind the corner guard
  (C) Freeze to the rock in the back
  (D) Take out the hammer team's stone in the back of the rings
  (E) Take out the corner guard and roll for a center guard
  (F) Take out the corner guard and roll out

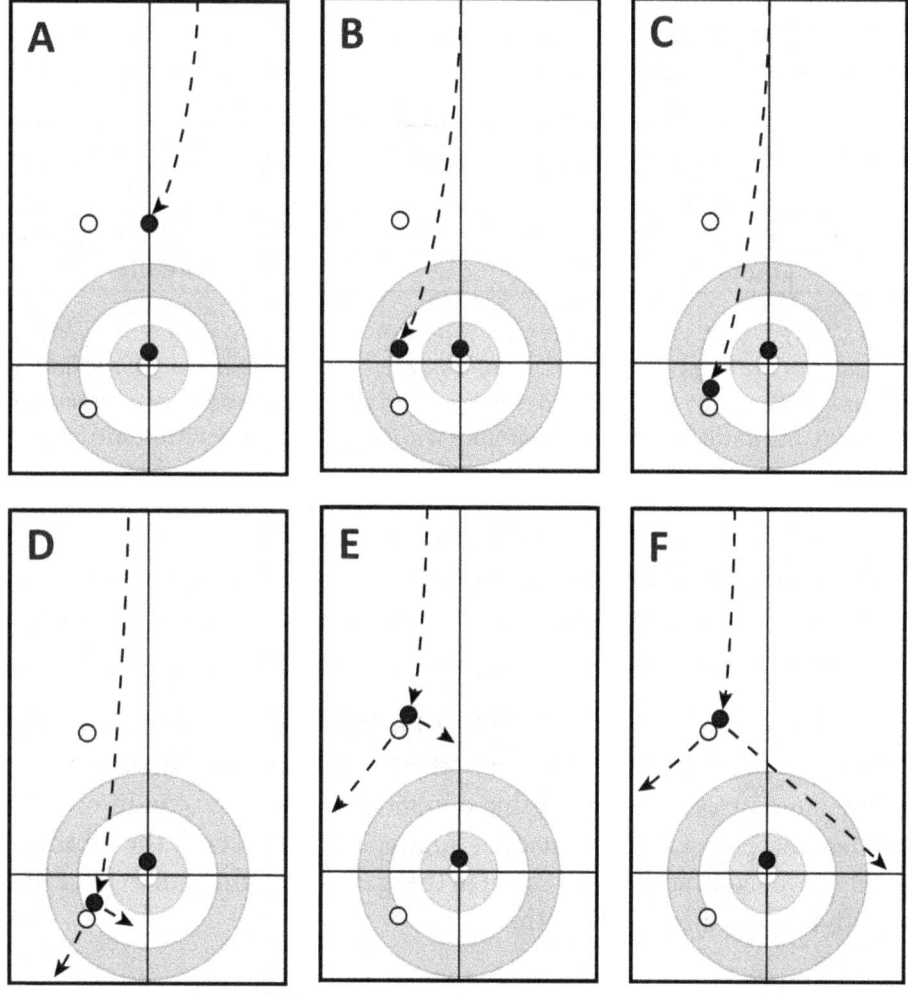

Discussion

Non-Hammer Team

Situation 1: 9th of 10 ends, non-hammer team leads by 1, non-hammer team's 5th stone

The non-hammer team leads by one point in this second-to-last end. Before the end started, the non-hammer team should have set end goals for both this end and the final end. For example: Does the non-hammer team want to force the hammer team to score one point in the ninth so it can have the hammer tied in the tenth? Does the non-hammer team want to steal one and play the tenth up two without the hammer? Or, is the non-hammer team's only goal for this end to prevent the hammer team from scoring more than two points? (Even if the hammer team scored two points, the non-hammer team would only be down by one and it would have the hammer in the tenth end—not a bad position.) Whatever happens, the non-hammer team should avoid giving up three or more points.

	9th End Primary Goal	**10th End Primary Goal**
Example End Plan 1	Force 1	Score 1
Example End Plan 2	Steal 1	Prevent hammer team from scoring more than 1*
Example End Plan 3	Prevent hammer team from scoring more than 1*	Score 1/Steal 1/Force 1 (depending on what happens in the 9th)
Example End Plan 4	Prevent hammer team from scoring more than 2	Score 1 (to tie and play extra end), Score 2 (to win)

As a reminder, the goal "Prevent the hammer team from scoring more than 1" is different from "Force 1," because in the "Prevent..." goal, the non-hammer team doesn't care if the hammer team scores 1 or blanks. There are many situations in which that difference matters a lot. For example, if the game is tied in the ninth end, the non-hammer team usually does not want the hammer team to blank and keep the hammer in the tenth.

Again the question arises—why would a non-hammer team ever prefer to force one when it could steal? In Intermediate Mid-End Strategy Scenario 6, we talked about tactical reasons a team might choose to force instead of steal. Here, we'll talk about the strategic reasons.

In this scenario, the non-hammer team would decide how it wants to play the ninth end based on how it wants to play the tenth end. And, in both of those decisions, it will choose the tactics it thinks will be the most successful against this opponent on these ice conditions. For example, if it's had success stealing against this opponent, it might plan to steal both the ninth and tenth ends. Alternatively, if it has failed to successfully steal in this game, it might plan to force one in the ninth and score one with the hammer in the tenth.

Let's look at how teams might pick tactics based on these two end goals:

Steal 1

Aggressive

Here is an example of what the non-hammer team's goal chart might look like if it planned to steal aggressively:

<u>Non-Hammer Team's Goal Chart</u>
  Strongly Want: Steal
  Accept: Force 1
  Avoid: Hammer team scores 2, or Blank
  Can't Allow: Hammer team scores 3 or more

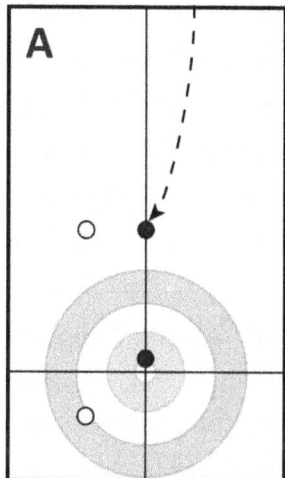

If the non-hammer team wants to steal, it would set up a center guard (Option A).

This shot gives the non-hammer team a good steal configuration. Unfortunately, it also leaves the hammer team with a rock behind a corner guard that it could use as a second point, if it can foil the steal attempt. This is a classic example of aggressive tactics. As we talked about earlier in the book, the more aggressive a team is, the more it increases its chances of having a very good outcome and a very bad outcome at the same time.

Conservative

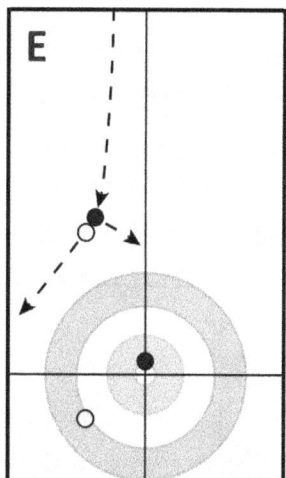

It's possible for the non-hammer team to attempt a relatively conservative steal by hitting the corner guard and rolling for a center guard (Option E). However, not many teams trying to steal would do that at this point. This is a very fussy shot—the roll needs to be perfect or the non-hammer team will either create a new corner guard for the hammer team, or roll out and allow the hammer team to set up for an easy deuce.

Force 1

Highly Aggressive

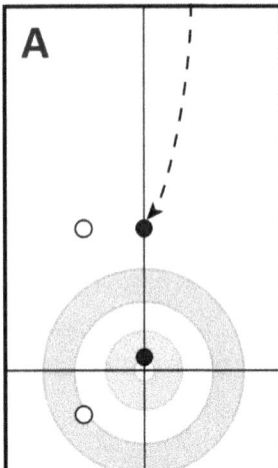

If the non-hammer team were highly committed to forcing and ensuring the hammer team can't blank, it could put up a center guard (Option A). In this case, it would be playing for a closed-center force.

Its goal chart might look like this:

Non-Hammer Team's Goal Chart
Strongly Want: Force 1
Accept: Steal
Avoid: Hammer team scores 2, or Blank
Can't allow: Hammer team scores 3 or more

This is a risky way to force, since the hammer team could potentially accumulate several rocks on the sides of the rings, and the non-hammer team could lose the game if it gives up more than two in this end.

Moderately Aggressive

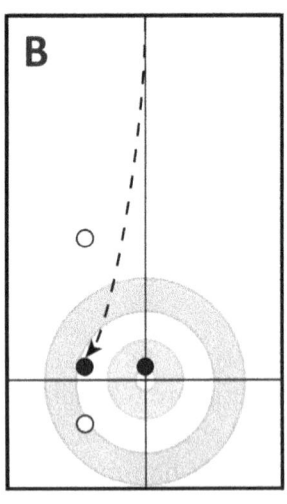 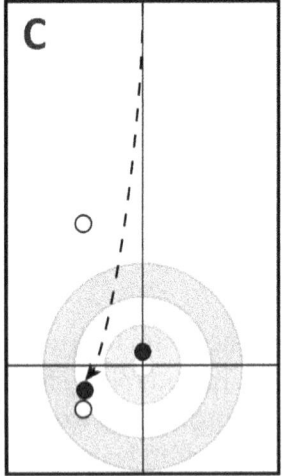

If the non-hammer team were playing moderately aggressively to force, it could draw behind the corner guard (Option B) or freeze to the hammer team's stone in the back of the rings (Option C).

These are more conservative choices than the center guard (Option A) because they give the non-hammer team first and second shot, which lowers its chances of giving up multiple points. (There's an expression, "Sometimes the best defense is having first and second shot.") The non-hammer team is playing for an open-center force.

The upside of the draw to the tee line (Option B) is that it would out-count any other stones the hammer team could draw behind that corner guard. The downside is that it could be easily tapped away.

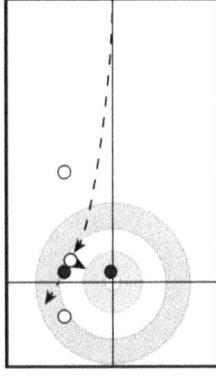

Be aware, the hammer team might choose to hit and roll towards the non-hammer team's rock on the wing. This move gets rid of the shot rock, and, by focusing the play to one area, the hammer team may have an easier time getting rid of multiple opponent stones in a single turn.

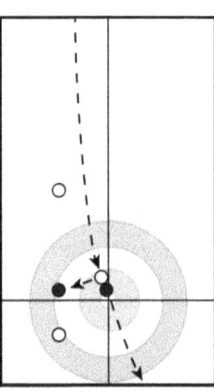

264

The upside of the freeze to the back rock (Option C) is that the non-hammer team's stone would be very difficult to move and would do a good job of neutralizing the hammer team's stone in the back. The downsides are that the hammer team could freeze to both stones, or...

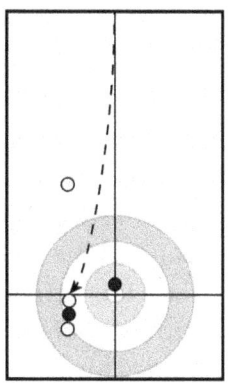

...it could hit the non-hammer team's shot rock and roll behind the corner guard to reestablish that potential second point behind cover.

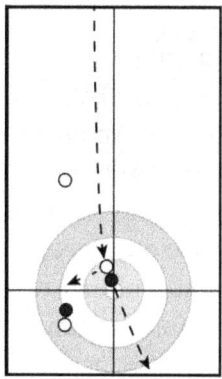

Conservative

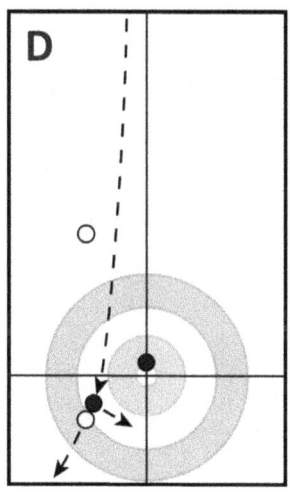

A very conservative non-hammer team might force one by taking out the hammer team's stone in the back of the rings and sticking somewhere on the rings (Option D).

This choice is considered conservative because it removes the hammer team's stone (and a team can't count two points if it can't keep two rocks in play!) However, because the non-hammer team is reducing the number of rocks in the rings, it makes it easier for the hammer team to blank. (For example, if the non-hammer team hits and accidentally rolls out, the hammer team has a great chance to blank.) Again, conservative play reduces the odds of a really bad outcome, but also reduces the odds of a really good outcome. The very conservative non-hammer team's goal chart might look like this:

Non-Hammer Team's Goal Chart
Want: Force 1
Accept: Blank or Steal 1
Strongly avoid: Hammer team scores 2
Can't Allow: Hammer team scores 3 or more

If the non-hammer team misses the hit on the back rock and takes out the corner guard instead (Option F), that isn't a bad pro-side result.

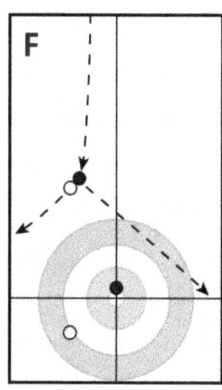

The corner guard is a dangerous rock. It could allow the hammer team to hide multiple stones in the rings. (See the "Using a Corner Guard to Score 3" section in the "Tips for Using Corner Guards" chapter.) By removing the corner guard, the non-hammer team makes it difficult for the hammer team to score more than two points. For example, if the non-hammer team did remove the corner guard and roll out, the hammer team would likely use its next stone to hit the non-hammer team's rock and roll to the right to split the house and set up a deuce. The non-hammer team would now have open access to hit either one of the hammer team's stone. With some good hits and rolls, the non-hammer team could get rid of both (See Beginner Scenario 4). Even if the non-hammer team simply exchanges hits and holds the hammer team to two points, that's not a bad result. The non-hammer team would get to play the last end down one with the hammer, which is better than the situation it would face if it accidentally gave up three!

Intermediate Scenario 7—Three Variations

How might the non-hammer team's plans to "Force 1" or "Prevent the hammer team from scoring more than 1 or 2" change if the rocks were in a slightly different position?

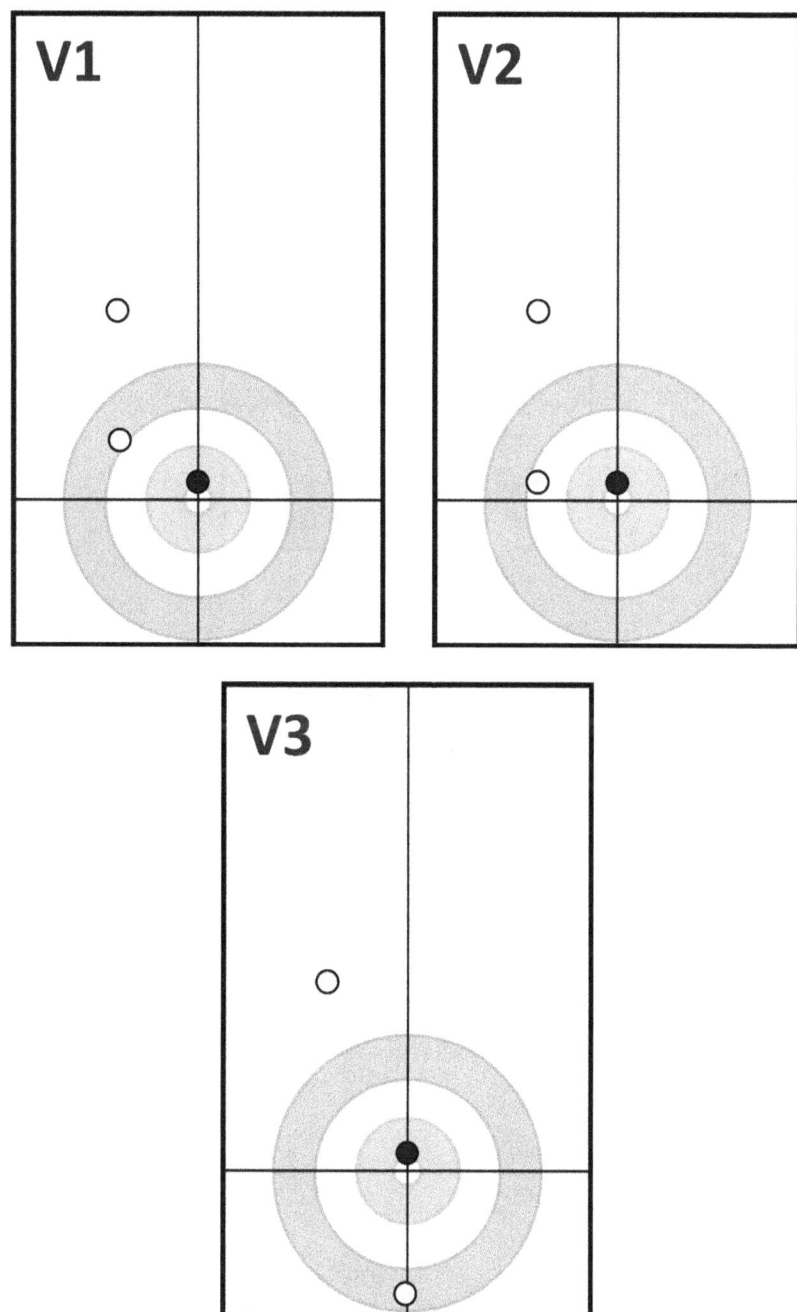

Intermediate Scenario 7—Variation 1

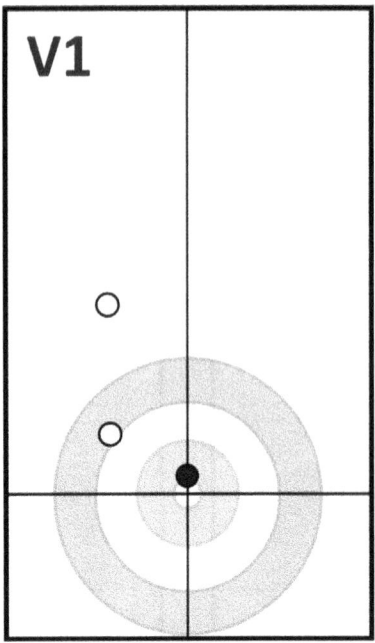

Discussion

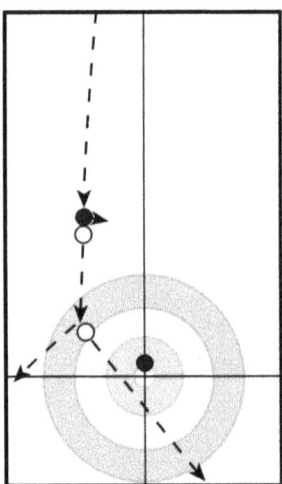

In this variation, the non-hammer team may not be able to hit the hammer team's rock in the rings directly, but it can play a double takeout on that rock and the corner guard.

Intermediate Scenario 7—Variation 2

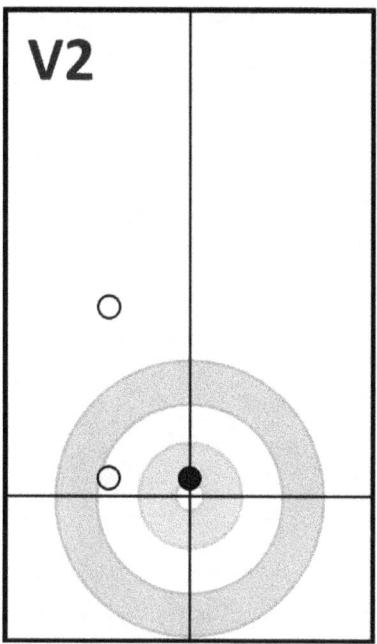

Discussion

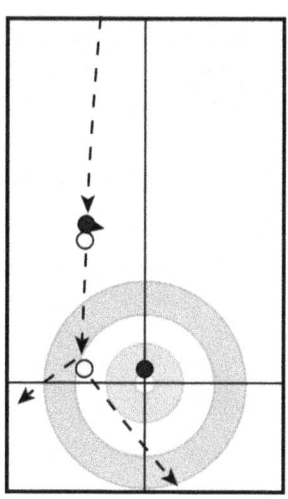

Depending on the position of the corner guard, the non-hammer team could attempt a double takeout.

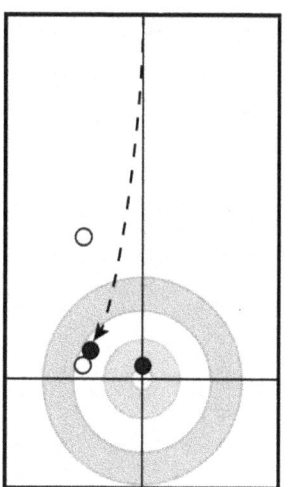

Alternatively, the non-hammer team could freeze to the hammer team's stone in the rings to out-count it.

Intermediate Scenario 7—Variation 3

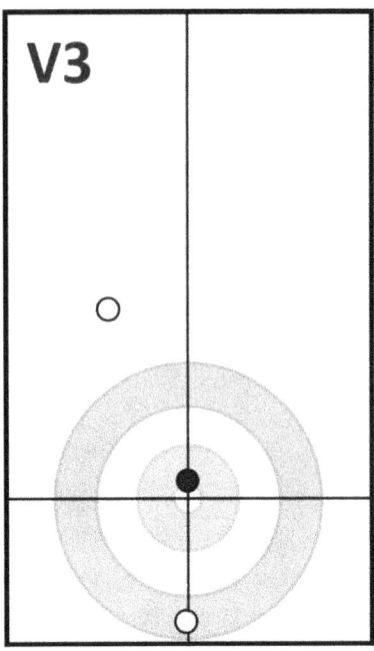

Discussion

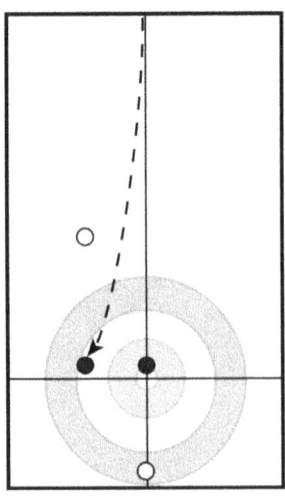

There's no easy shot on the hammer team's rock, but the non-hammer team can still draw behind the corner guard to take away the spot the hammer team wants to use and out-count the hammer team's stone in the back.

In all of these cases, the non-hammer team could still use a center guard (Option A) to play for an aggressive force or steal.

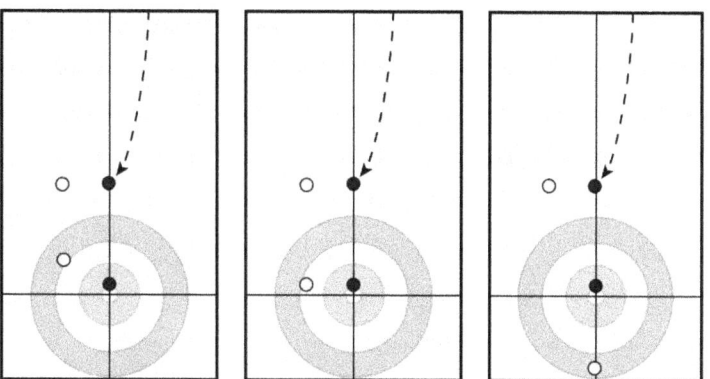

Intermediate Scenario 8

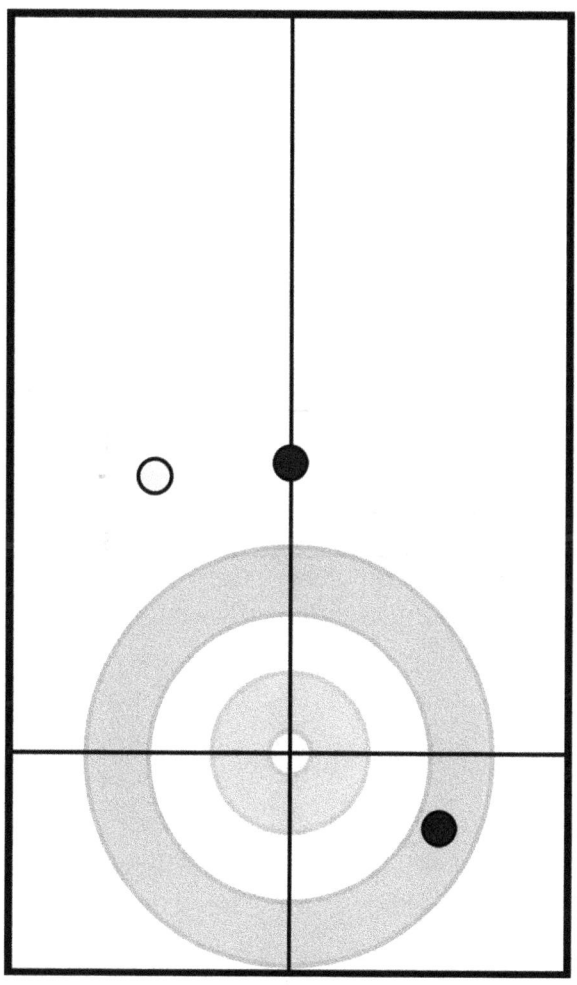

Intermediate Scenario 8

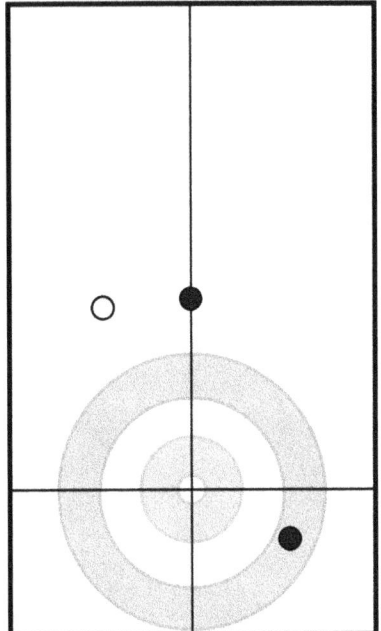

Questions

Hammer Team

What end goal and shot would you choose:
- **Situation 1:** 4th end of 10-end game, hammer team down by 1, hammer team's 4th stone
- **Situation 2:** 8th end of 10-end game, hammer team up by 2, hammer team's 4th stone

Hammer Team's Shot Choices
  (A) Remove the center guard
  (B) Draw behind the center guard
  (C) Draw behind the corner guard
  (D) Hit the non-hammer team's stone in the rings
  (E) Freeze to the non-hammer team's stone in the back of the rings

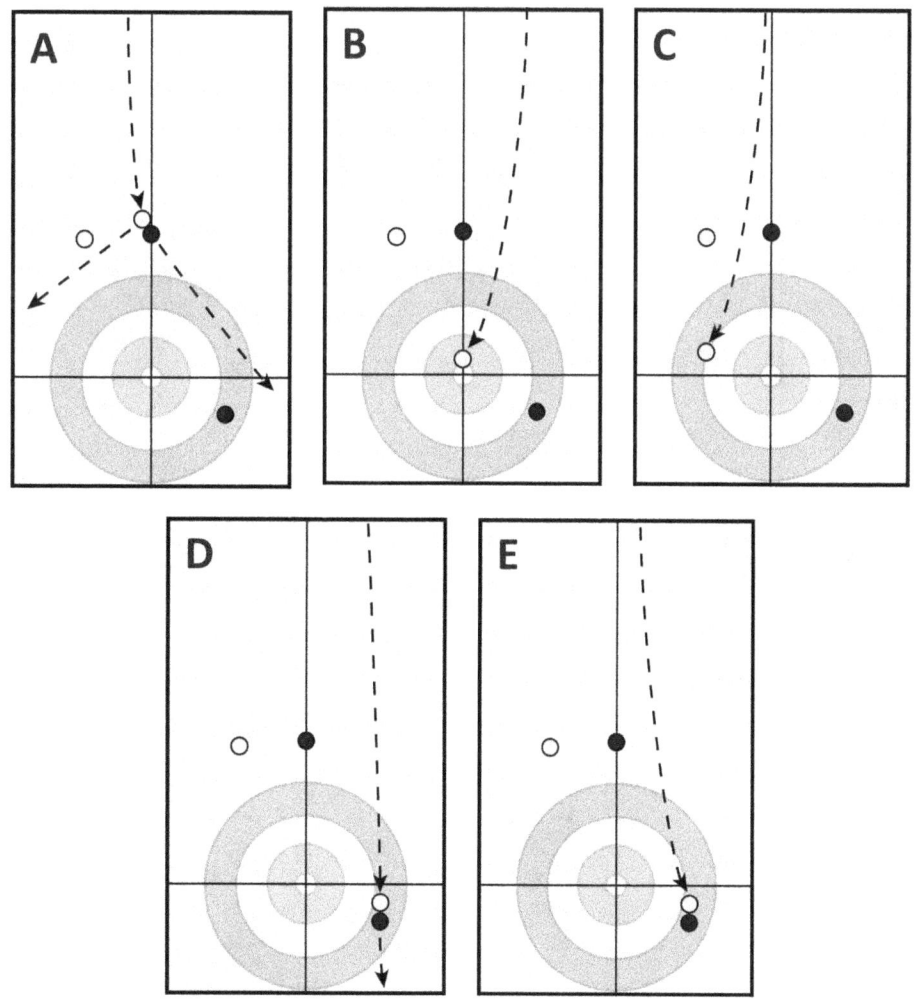

Discussion

Hammer Team

Situation 1: 4th end of 10-end game, hammer team down by 1, hammer team's 4th stone

This is a perfect opportunity for the hammer team to go for a deuce. It can do it in a variety of ways.

Score 2

Aggressive

An aggressive hammer team's goal chart might look like this:

Hammer Team's Goal Chart
  Strongly Want: Score 2
  Accept: Score 1 or Blank
  Avoid: Steal 1

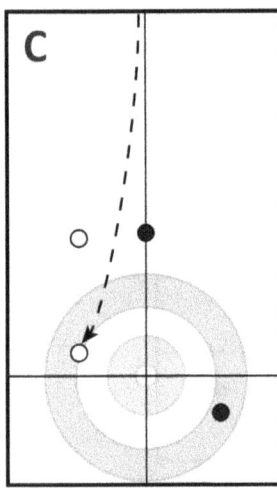

This aggressive team is very committed to scoring two, and, although it would prefer to avoid a steal, it's willing to take that risk to get a deuce. As a result, this team would likely draw behind its own corner guard (Option C). With this shot choice, the aggressive hammer team is ignoring the non-hammer team's threats for now and developing its offense by getting a "second point" in place. Once it has that second point established, then it will worry about foiling the non-hammer team's steal or force plans.

Conservative

A conservative hammer team would be very interested in getting two, but would want to simultaneously work to reduce the chance of a steal. A conservative hammer team's goal chart might look like this:

Hammer Team's Goal Chart
  Want: Score 2 or Blank
  Accept: Score 1
  Avoid: Steal

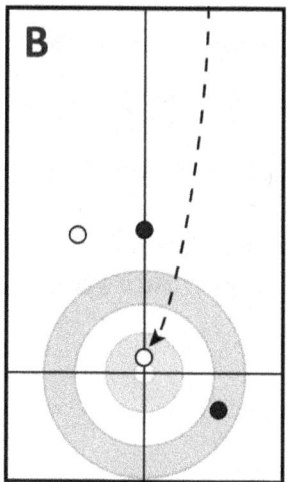

In this case, the hammer team might choose to draw behind the center guard (Option B). This allows it to get a rock in play behind cover, while making it more difficult for the non-hammer team to steal by occupying that crucial location. A conservative hammer team would worry about getting the second point later. (This is somewhat similar to a "Center Pile Deuce.")

So why wouldn't the hammer team hit (Option D) or freeze (Option E)? It could, but these shots aren't as helpful to getting a deuce as the draw behind the corner guard (Option C), or the draw behind the center guard (Option B). The hit and the freeze leave the hammer team's stone open behind the tee line, and they leave the button available for a non-hammer team draw. And more important, the non-hammer team's stone in the back corner of the rings isn't a scoring threat. It's behind the tee line and a long way from the button, so the hammer team could easily out-draw it with its last rock.

The hit does make sense if the hammer team is playing ultra conservatively and might want to blank later (like the "Deuce or Blank" example in the "Deuces" chapter). It's unlikely, though, that the hammer team would choose the freeze over the draw behind the corner guard as a way to generate two.

Situation 2: 8th end of 10-end game, hammer team up by 2, hammer team's 4th stone

The hammer team is in an excellent position to win this game. Obviously it would be great if the hammer team could score two points here—that would virtually guarantee victory. However, the hammer team would still be in good shape if it could blank or score one. The only outcome it really needs to avoid is allowing the non-hammer team to steal. (The non-hammer team's plan at this point would probably be to steal in all three of the remaining ends to win the game.)

With that in mind, here's what the hammer team's end goal chart might look like:

Hammer Team's Goal Chart
Want: Score 2
Accept: Score 1 or Blank
Strongly Avoid: Steal

Very Conservative (Prevent a steal)

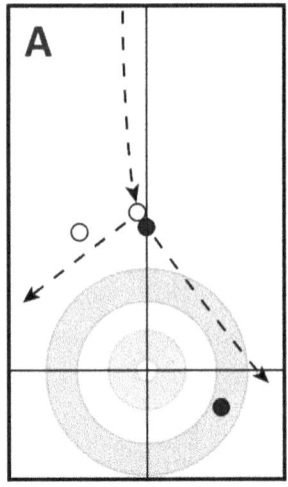

The "threat rock" is the non-hammer team's center guard, because the non-hammer team needs it to steal. Since the hammer team's most urgent end goal is to avoid a steal, the hammer team would probably take out that guard and roll its shooter out, too. (Option A) The hammer team does not want to give the non-hammer team any place to hide. (Again, the non-hammer team's rock is not a significant scoring threat because it's behind the tee line far from the button.)

Moderately Aggressive

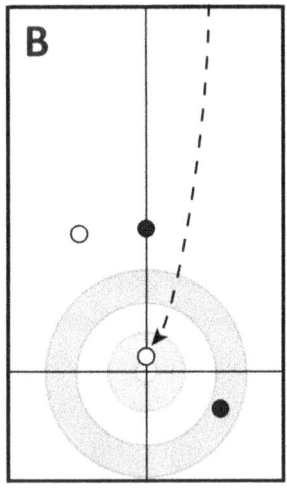

The hammer team could take a moderately aggressive approach and draw behind the center guard (Option B). By doing this, it virtually rules out a blank possibility (because it is adding a rock into play behind cover where it will be difficult to remove). However, it does make the steal more difficult by occupying the button position. And, it makes a deuce more likely because it puts more rocks in play.

Intermediate Scenario 9

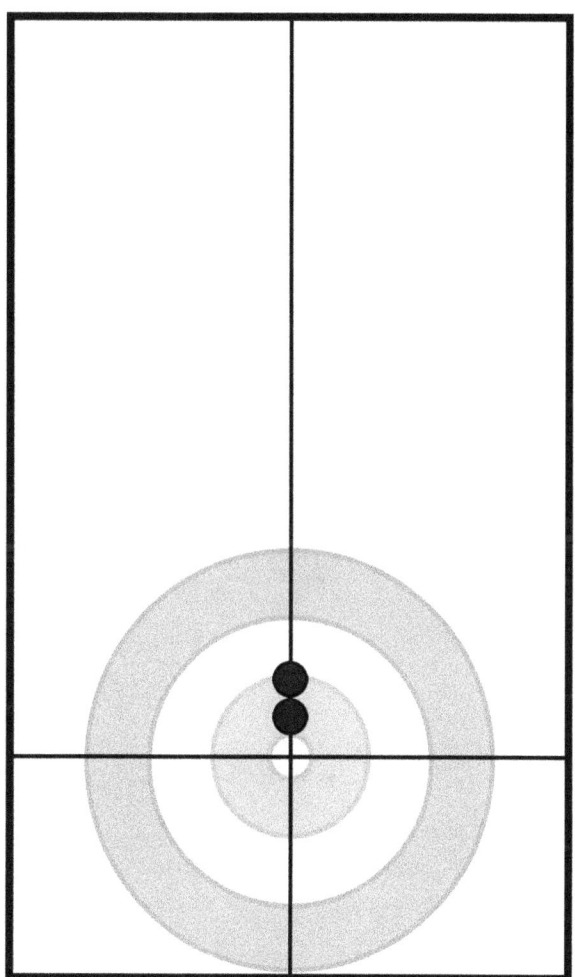

Intermediate Scenario 9

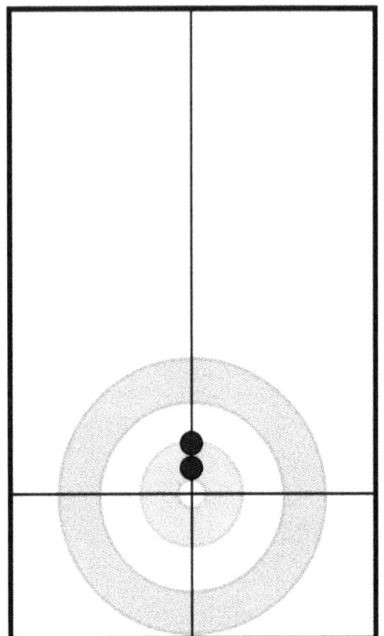

Questions

Hammer Team

What end goal and shot would you choose:
- ▸ **Situation 1: Last end, tied score, hammer team's 4th stone**
- ▸ **Situation 2: Last end, hammer team down by 2, hammer team's 4th stone**
- ▸ **Situation 2: Last end, hammer team down by 2, hammer team's 6th stone**

Hammer Team's Shot Choices
(A) Hit the frozen stones
(B) Corner guard
(C) Tap the frozen stone

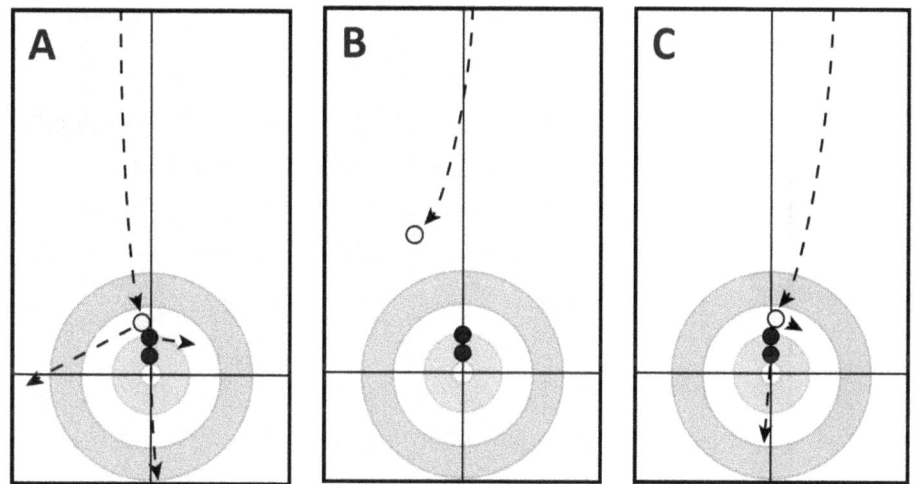

Discussion

Hammer Team

Situation 1: Last end, tied score, hammer team's 4th stone

The game is tied and this is the last end, so all the hammer team needs to do to win is score one point. A blank would be okay, since the hammer team would keep the hammer for the extra end. The only thing the hammer team can't allow is a steal. The hammer team's goal chart for this end might look like this:

Hammer Team's Goal Chart
Want: Score 1
Accept: Blank
Can't Allow: Steal

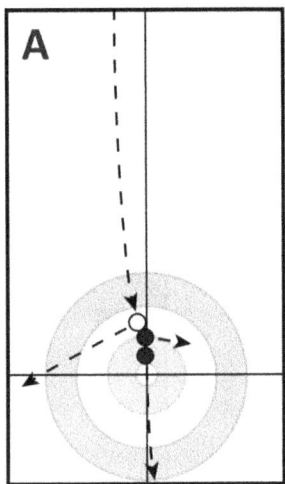

Since the hammer team's most urgent issue is to avoid a steal, it needs to hit the non-hammer team's stones (Option A). It may take more than one hit to move them both off behind the button. The hammer team's tactical goal for this end is to keep the center clear so it can make an open hit or draw to the button with its last rock to win the game.

Situation 2: Last end, hammer team down by 2, hammer team's 4th stone

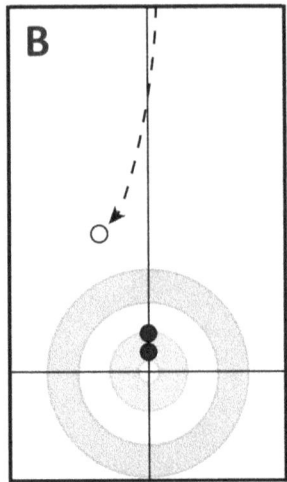

The hammer team needs to score two to stay alive and three to win. The hammer team's goal chart might look like this:

Hammer Team's Goal Chart
Want: Score 3
Need: Score 2
Can't Allow: Any other outcome

The non-hammer team's rocks in the middle of the rings are obviously a problem for the hammer team. However, the bigger problem for the hammer team is finding a way to keep at least two rocks in play. The best way to protect rocks in the rings is to use guards, and since it is still early in the end, the hammer team has time to try to get a corner guard in play (Option B).

Because the Free Guard Zone time is over, the non-hammer team can peel the guard. The hammer team must hope the non-hammer team has a partial miss—either a flash, a hit-and-stay (to leave a guard), or a jam—for it to win.

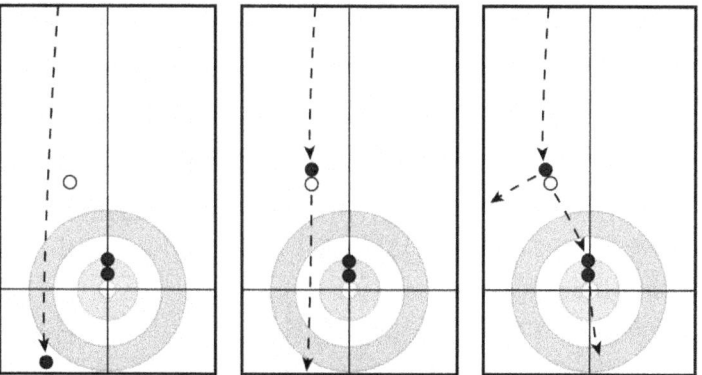

The hammer team will likely need the non-hammer team to miss (as above) to get three points.

Situation 3: Last end, hammer team down by 2, hammer team's 6th stone

This is the same situation as Scenario 2 above, but now the hammer team has only three stones remaining. Here, again, is the hammer team's goal chart:

Hammer Team's Goal Chart
    Want: Score 3
    Need: Score 2
    Can't Allow: Any other outcome

The hammer team could put up a corner guard (Option B), then use its final two stones to hit the rocks in the middle, but that plan will only work if the non-hammer team misses both of its remaining shots, which is not too likely.

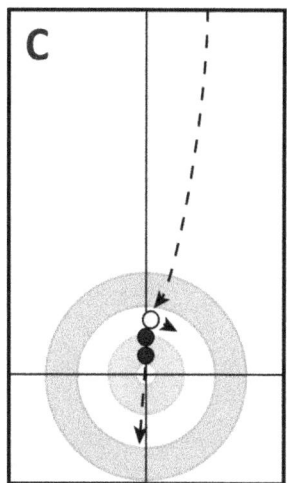

Fortunately, guards aren't the only way to keep rocks in play. The hammer team can tap the rocks in the center and use them as backing (Option C). Let's look at an example of how this could play out….

283

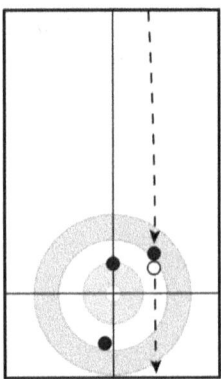 After the hammer team taps the frozen stones slightly off-center (Option C), the non-hammer team hits the hammer team's open stone. Now the hammer team cannot score three to win.

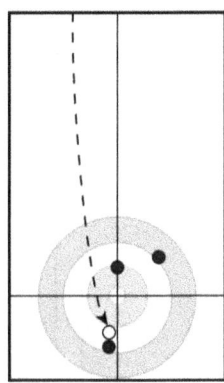 The hammer team makes a perfect freeze to the back stone and sits second shot.

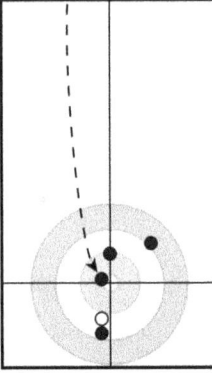 The non-hammer team does not have an easy hit to remove that stone, so it tries to freeze, but is slightly short.

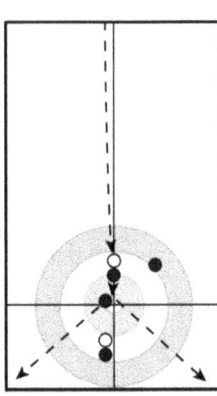 The hammer makes a double take out and stays to tie.

Note that even in this scenario, the hammer team needs to shoot perfectly and needs at least a partial miss from the non-hammer team just to tie the game.

Plan B and Pro-Side Error

All teams and all players—no matter how experienced and talented—miss shots. Smart teams pick shots that can have a good outcome ("Plan B"), even if the shooter misses a little. Smart team members know how to throw (with "pro-side error") so that if they do miss, they'll get a good Plan B outcome. Let's look at a few examples....

Plan B and Pro-Side Error Scenario 1

First End, Non-Hammer Team's First Rock

Here's a very simple starter example. Imagine it's the first end of the game. The non-hammer team's end goal is a "conservative steal." That means: The non-hammer team would like to steal. It's willing to accept having the hammer team blank or score one. However, it wants to avoid allowing the hammer team to score two or more. Its goal chart looks like this:

<u>Non-Hammer Team's Goal Chart</u>
    Want: Steal 1
    Accept: Blank or Hammer team scores 1
    Avoid: Hammer team scores 2 or more

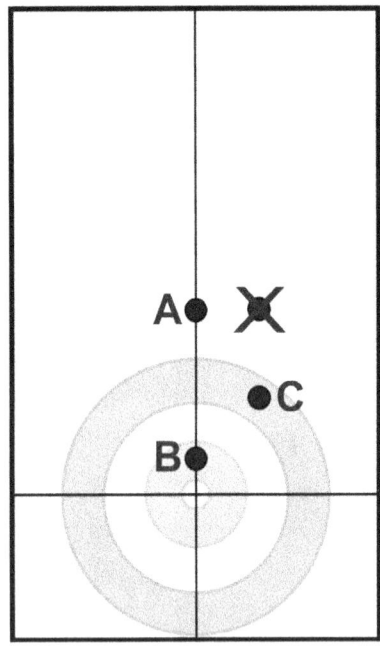

Because the non-hammer team's primary goal is to steal, its skip calls for a tight center guard. That shot is Plan A, because it's the one most likely to help the team reach its end goal—a conservative steal.

The non-hammer team's acceptable outcomes are "Blank" or "Allow the hammer team to score one and only one point." The best starting shot to get to those end goals is to draw in front of button. Therefore, the draw is the Plan B.

Finally, the outcome the non-hammer team absolutely wants to avoid is allowing the hammer team to score two or more points. Since hammer teams usually need corner guards to score multiple points, the non-hammer team must absolutely avoid accidentally putting up a corner guard. The non-hammer team would be better off drawing anywhere in the house (Plan C) than putting up a corner guard.

The non-hammer team's skip communicates this to the rest of the team. The lead now knows it is okay to be a little heavy, but it's very important to get the line right—that's the pro-side way to shoot. The sweepers know if the rock is off-line and heading towards a corner guard position, they should sweep it into the house (Plan C). That's the pro-side way to sweep.

Plan B and Pro-Side Error Scenario 2

Last End, Non-Hammer Team's First Rock

Now let's look at the first shot of the last end under two different score situations—first, when the non-hammer team is down by one, then when the non-hammer team is up by two.

Non-Hammer Team Down by 1

The non-hammer team is down by one and absolutely, positively needs to steal at least one point to stay alive. Here's what the non-hammer team's goal chart might look like:

<u>**Non-Hammer Team's Goal Chart**</u>
Want: Steal 2
Need: Steal 1
Can't Allow: Any other outcome

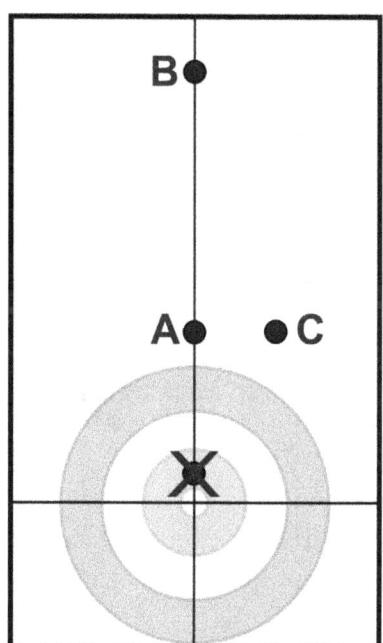

The non-hammer team needs to steal, so it needs at least one center guard. The team's skip calls for a tight center guard with the first rock. That's the team's Plan A. If the team is planning to use two center guards, the skip could equally well have called for a high center guard with the first rock, so that is the team's Plan B.

If that first rock goes into the rings, the hammer team will hit it, so it's better for the rock to be anywhere in the Free Guard Zone—including a corner guard—than on the rings. Therefore, a corner guard is the team's Plan C. (Normally, corner guards help the hammer team. However, when the non-hammer team is going to lose if it can't keep rocks in play, any kind of guard will help in some way. In this case, a corner guard might help the non-hammer team by blocking the hammer team's hit and draw paths to the button.)

Since the non-hammer team's lead understands that any kind of guard is good, he knows the shooting pro-side is to be light. (It would be better for the rock to just barely get over the hog line than to be one inch into the rings.) The sweepers also understand this, so they know their sweeping pro-side is to leave the rock high, even if it's going to be a corner guard.

Non-Hammer Team Up by 2

In this situation, the non-hammer team is up by two points. If the non-hammer team can prevent the hammer team from scoring more than one, it wins. If the non-hammer team can prevent the hammer team from scoring more than two, the non-hammer team will get the hammer in an extra end, and thus have a good chance of winning. Here's what the non-hammer team's goal chart might look like:

Non-Hammer Team's Goal Chart
Want: Prevent the hammer team from scoring more than 1
Need: Prevent the hammer team from scoring more than 2
Can't Allow: Hammer team scores 3 or more

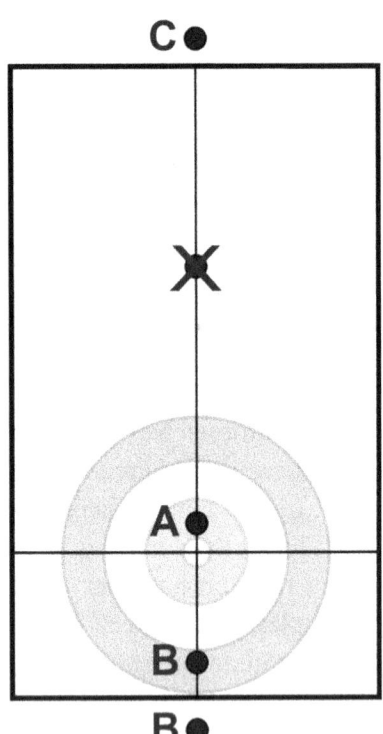

There are several different end plans the non-hammer team could use in this situation, ranging from a "steal at all costs" to a "conservative force." Because the only outcome the non-hammer team must absolutely avoid is allowing the hammer team to score three points, the non-hammer team would likely chose a conservative plan, like a "conservative force."

If the non-hammer team chooses a "conservative force," the skip will call for a draw in front of the button with the team's first rock. That's Plan A.

Because the non-hammer team does not want to give the hammer team any guards to hide behind, it would be better for the non-hammer team's lead to throw the rock to the back of the house—or even completely through the rings—than to leave a guard. So, throwing deep or through is Plan B.

The non-hammer team's lead understands this, so he knows the pro-side error on the shot is to be heavy. The sweepers understand this, too, so they know to err on the side of sweeping more.

However, if the rock were very light and would stop on its own just short of the hog line, the sweepers pro-side would be to stop sweeping and let it "hog," rather than sweep it over for a guard. Again, it's better for the non-hammer team to have no rocks in play, than to have a guard.

ADVANCED TIP One topic I don't discuss much in the book is: When should the non-hammer team throw one or both of its first rocks through the house? A non-hammer team might do this late in the game if it is up by a significant number of points (e.g., 3 or more in the final end, or 4 or more in the second to last end, etc.) The reason is—the non-hammer team doesn't want to give the hammer team anything it could use to help it keep rocks in play. Most non-hammer teams don't start throwing rocks through until they have at least a three-point lead. This is because throwing through gives the hammer team a free turn to set up a guard. If the non-hammer team has only a two-point lead and throws both of its rocks through, the hammer team can set up two corner guards. Now the hammer team has a great chance of scoring at least two points. If the non-hammer team draws at least one stone near the button, the hammer team will eventually have to spend a turn moving that rock, and while it does that, the non-hammer team can attack the hammer team's guards or rocks in the rings.

That being said, in this example, it would be much better for the non-hammer team to throw through than put up a center guard. This is because, if the non-hammer team did accidentally put up a guard, not only would it give the hammer team a free turn, it would also give the hammer team offensive help by creating an additional place for it to hide rocks.

Plan B and Pro-Side Error Scenario 3

Hammer Team's First Rock

Now we'll look at two examples of pro-side errors for the hammer team's first rocks. Both examples are of tied games—one is a first end, and the other is a final end. Notice how differences in the hammer team's end goals change the Plan Bs and pro-side errors.

First End
In the first end, the hammer team could choose from a wide range of end goals and tactical plans, from an "Aggressive Deuce" to a "Conservative Deuce or Blank."

In this situation, let's imagine the non-hammer team begins with an aggressive move by putting up a center guard. Let's also imagine that the hammer team has decided that, while it would like to score two, it doesn't want to take big risks in the first end. Thus, it has chosen the somewhat conservative "Center Pile Deuce" tactical plan.

The hammer team's goal chart might look like this:

Hammer Team's Goal Chart:
Want: Score 2 or Blank
Accept: Score 1
Avoid: Steal 1

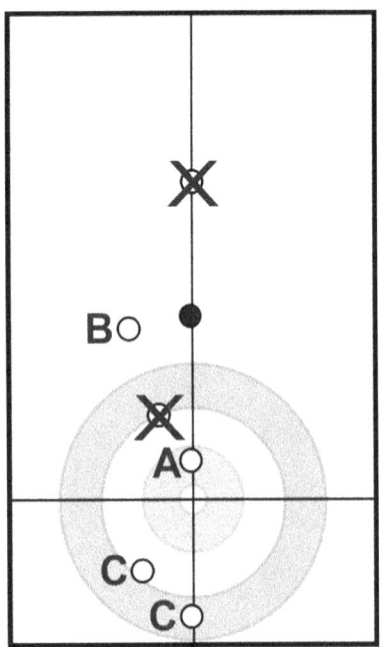

The hammer team's skip will call for the lead to throw a draw to the front four-foot behind the center guard. That's Plan A.

Since it would be good for the hammer team to score two, and because this is a time in the game when the hammer team can afford to take risks, now would also be an appropriate time for the hammer team to put up a corner guard. Therefore, a corner guard would be the team's Plan B.

The lead understands this, so he knows he can err a little light and a little wide and still make a valuable shot. The sweepers also know that if the rock looks like it won't bury behind the center guard, it's better to leave it short as a corner guard than to sweep it to the front half of the rings where the non-hammer team can hit and roll off it behind cover.

If the rock is heavy and looks like it will go behind the tee line on its own, the sweepers will take it to the back of the house, where it's less useful for a non-hammer team freeze. That's the team's Plan C.

The only shot the hammer team must absolutely avoid is adding another center guard. That would help the non-hammer team steal. If the rock looks light and tight, then the team should sweep it for a tick—or any other alternative it can find!

Last End, Tied Score

Now imagine this is the last end of the game. Again, the score is tied, but this is a completely different situation. The hammer team would like to score one point, but its primary objective is to prevent the non-hammer team from stealing and winning the game.

The hammer team's goal chart might look like this:

Hammer Team's Goal Chart
Want: Score 1
Accept: Blank
Can't Allow: Steal

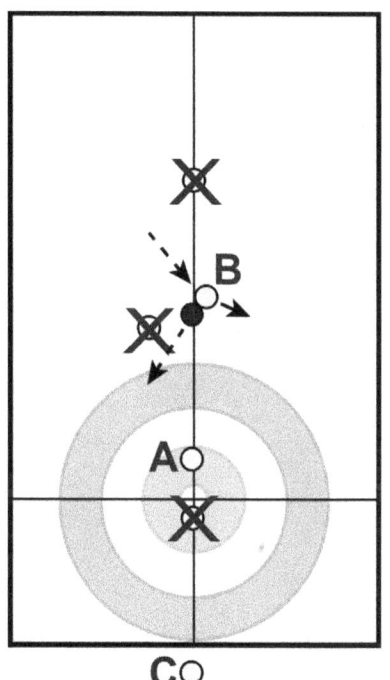

The hammer team's skip decides that the best way for his team to prevent a steal is to draw in first. Therefore, he calls for a draw to the front button. That is Plan A.

Moving the center guard would also help the hammer team, so the tick is the hammer team's Plan B.

The three shots the hammer team must absolutely avoid are: (1) Putting up any kind of guard, since that would give the non-hammer team a place to hide, (2) Tapping the center guard straight back to the button, and (3) Drawing just behind the button where the non-hammer team can freeze to sit shot behind cover.

The hammer team's lead understands this, so he knows he can err a little narrow and heavy and still make an effective shot. He absolutely must not come up short and leave a guard. The sweepers also understand this, so they would let a very light shot hog, or sweep a guard-weight shot into the house. The sweepers and the skip know that if the shot is narrow, they will need to make sure the shot ticks the center guard at an angle instead of tapping it straight back. Finally, the sweepers know it would be bad to put a rock behind the button where the non-hammer team can freeze to it, so if they think that's where the rock is going, they will sweep it to the back of the house—or even through the house. Those are the hammer team's many pro-side options.

Plan B and Pro-Side Error Scenario 4

Don't Make Things Worse!

Sometimes pro-side error is about not making things worse. In fact, sometimes it's better to have a total miss, than to make a half-shot that helps your opponent. Here's an example from my real life:

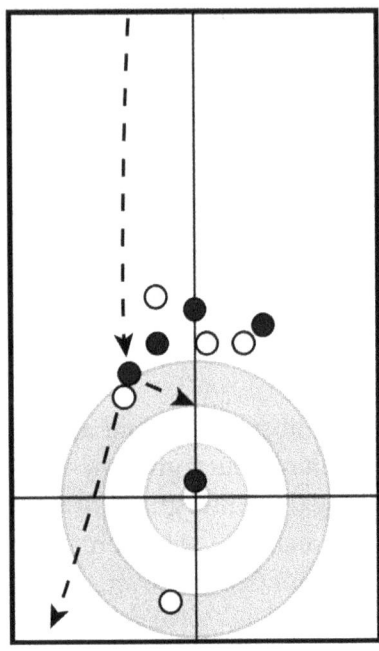

Attempted shot

In a middle end of a close game, my team was set up well to steal. We had a rock on the button behind a mess of cover. We attempted to take out an opponent stone in the left front eight-foot and roll to the center to give ourselves even more cover.

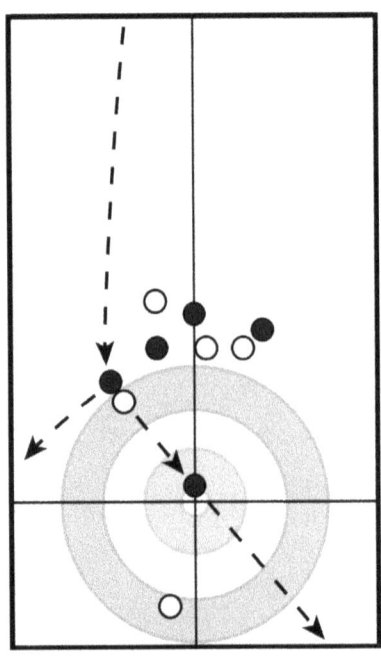

Actual shot

It was a good plan. Unfortunately, the shooter came out a little wide. We should have swept like crazy to keep our rock from touching the opponent stone. Alas, we did nothing. Our rock curled and raised the opponent stone back onto our shot rock. It took out our rock and sat on the pin in its place. Sometimes a total miss is better than making things worse!

Pro-Side Error Game

Here's a simple game we invented at the San Francisco Bay Area Curling Club to get students thinking about "what ifs?" Here's how we organized it for a class. (Of course, you can also play on your own!)

Set up a curling strategy board and eight cards or tokens with the following messages written on them:

- Wide and Heavy
- Wide and Good Weight
- Wide and Light
- On Line and Heavy
- On Line and Light
- Narrow and Heavy
- Narrow and Good Weight
- Narrow and Light

Divide the students into two teams and give a scenario. (For example: It's the last end of the game and the hammer team is down by two.) Then ask the students to call shots for their team. Once they've picked a shot—including which turn they should take—ask them what would be the best way(s) for the shooter to miss. (In this example, the non-hammer team would want to put its first rock in the front four-foot. A good miss would be to put the rock anywhere in the center-front of the house or to throw through. A bad miss would be to put up a center guard.)

Then draw one of the cards or tokens and find out how the shooter actually missed. Ask the players how they should call the sweep to make the most of this errant shot or to minimize the damage.

Game pieces made from poker chips

PART 5

PUTTING IT ALL TOGETHER AND PLAYING IN THE REAL WORLD

Real-Life Game Sequences

The next section is a great example of strategy in real life. Here are the final three ends (7, 8, and an extra end) from the 2013 US Men's Arena National Championship gold-medal game. The skips are experienced and call a disciplined, thoughtful game. The players are good, but human, so (1) this is an achievable level of play for committed club curlers from both arena and dedicated ice clubs, and (2) the shots called are realistic for club curlers.

One challenge with learning strategy from watching the Olympics is that the players can consistently make spectacularly difficult shots, so they call strategy that is not applicable to club curling. If you are interested in seeing a wider variety of play, from the US Olympic Trials to regular league play, check out the web-based "12th End Sports Network" at www.tesn.us. They broadcast the game I am about to present, and (at the time I'm writing this in 2013) it is in their game archives.

In this game, the team from Dallas/Fort Worth, Texas, faced off against the team from Kalamazoo, Michigan. Both teams had a mix of experienced, high-level competitive curlers and new, all-arena curlers:

Dallas/Fort Worth
 Skip: Nick Myers
 Third/Vice: Jeffrey Knott
 Second: Stephen Kleppe
 Lead: John Lambert

Kalamazoo
 Skip: Garnet Eckstrand
 Third/Vice: Kent Elliott
 Second: Marcus Gleaton
 Lead: Chris Gleaton

The shots that were called are shown with a fine dotted line. The shots that were actually made are shown with a longer dashed line. Dallas has dark blue stones, and Kalamazoo has light yellow stones. This is an 8-end game.

End 7

Score: Dallas 6, Kalamazoo 4
Kalamazoo has the hammer

Dallas - Rock 1

Call Draw to the front four-foot
Result Tight center guard

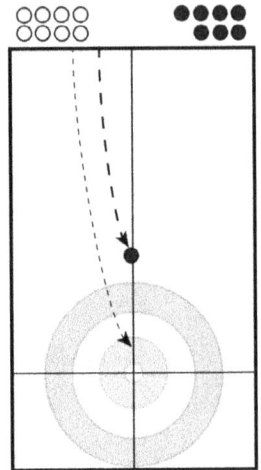

Commentary: By calling for a draw into the house, Dallas' skip shows he wants to play conservatively and likely intends to force one. This is a good plan, since, if it works, Dallas would get to play the 8th end up one with the hammer—a great position!

Kalamazoo - Rock 1

Call Tight corner guard
Result High corner guard

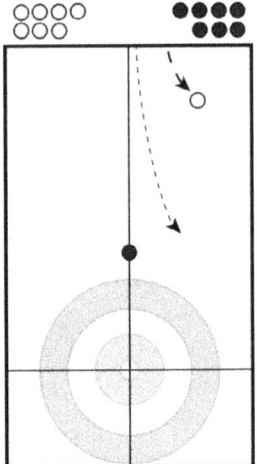

Commentary: By calling for a corner guard, Kalamazoo's skip shows he wants to play aggressively for at least two points.

Dallas - Rock 2

Call Draw behind center guard
Result The team sweeps hard to get by the guard and ends up deep

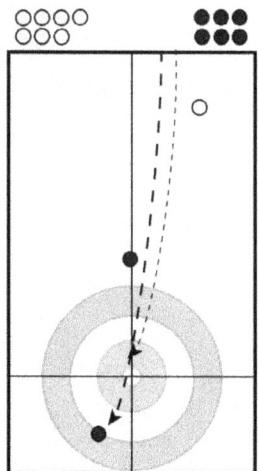

Commentary: This is a good pro-side sweep by Dallas, since ticking the guard would have given Kalamazoo at least one more corner guard—which would help them score multiple points.

Dallas - Rock 3

Call Take out at least one corner guard
Result Double takeout of both corner guards and the shooter rolls out

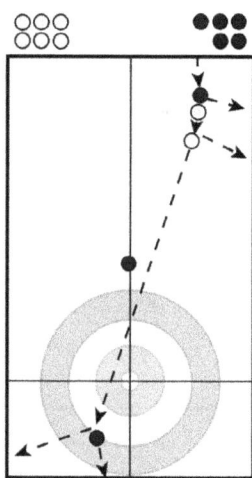

Commentary: Dallas got a very helpful pro-side error!

Kalamazoo - Rock 2

Call Draw behind the corner guard high in the house
Result Corner guard

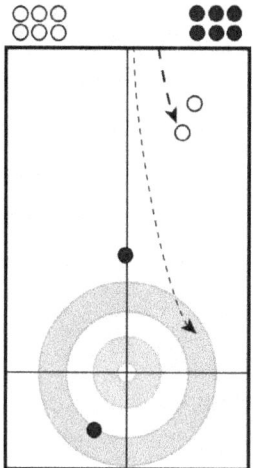

Commentary: This is not a bad pro-side error, since Kalamazoo will need guards to keep rocks in play. The shot would have been a little better if it were closer to the rings, or if the rocks were separated slightly more.

Kalamazoo - Rock 3

Call Draw behind the center guard to the front four-foot
Result Draw behind the center guard to the top eight-foot

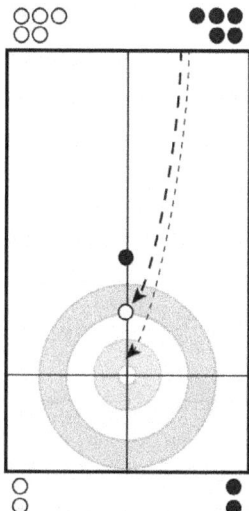

Commentary: Dallas' slight miss on its first shot comes back to haunt it. Since Kalamazoo wasn't able to keep its own guards in play and the Free Guard Zone time is over, it uses Dallas' unintended guard as it works to get two counting stones into play. (All guards can help the team that needs to score!)

Dallas - Rock 4

Call Run back the center guard onto Kalamazoo's stone

Result Take out the center guard and roll to the right side as a corner guard

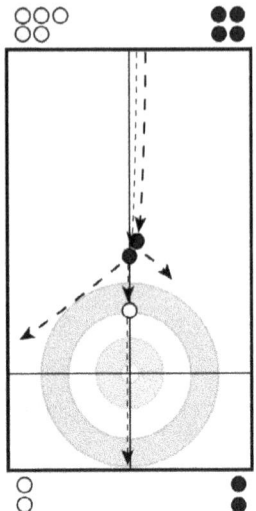

Commentary: Removing the center guard to uncover the Kalamazoo stone is a good pro-side result. Creating the corner guard is not as helpful.

Kalamazoo - Rock 4

Call Draw behind the corner guard to the tee line

Result Draw behind the corner guard to the back twelve-foot

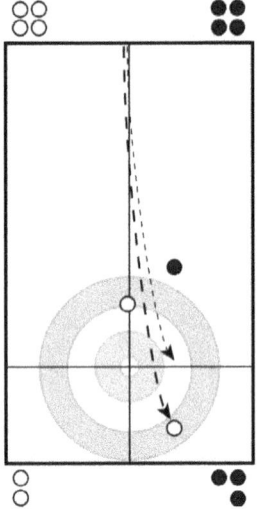

Commentary: The Kalamazoo team attempts to capitalize on Dallas' partial miss by drawing behind the corner guard. It's not ideal to be behind the tee line, but at least Kalamazoo now has two rocks in the rings!

Dallas - Rock 5

Call Double takeout

Result Single takeout of top rock and the shooter rolls out

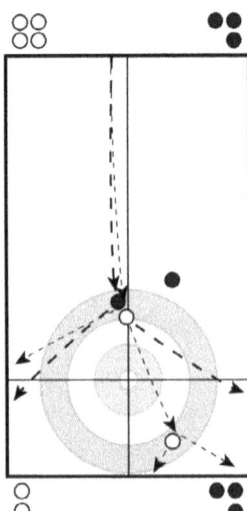

Commentary: The Dallas team makes the smart move and hits the top rock first. If it gets the double, great! If not, at least it has eliminated one stone and stays in position to hold the Kalamazoo team to two points. (The Dallas team would still be in good shape if the Kalamazoo team scored two in this end, because then the Dallas team would get the hammer tied in the 8th.)

Kalamazoo - Rock 5

Call Draw behind the corner guard to the tee line

Result Corner guard

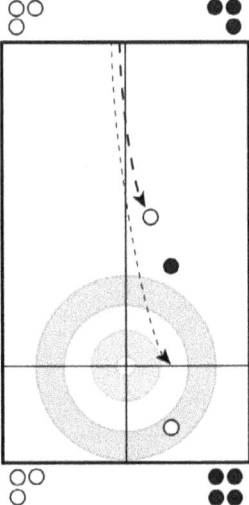

Commentary: This is a good miss in that it adds more cover for Kalamazoo to draw behind on the wing. It's a tough miss in that the Kalamazoo team needs rocks in play, and the Dallas team might be able to take out the rock in the back twelve-foot with its next stone. Also, if Kalamazoo had been able to draw a second rock behind the corner guard, it may have been able to get three points in the end.

Dallas - Rock 6

Call Take out the guard and roll the shooter out

Result Take out the guard and roll the shooter out

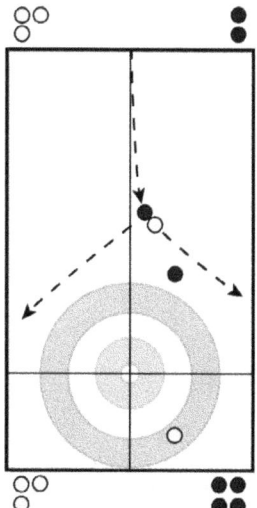

Commentary: Rather than worry about Kalamazoo's one rock in the rings, the Dallas team clears a guard to try to prevent Kalamazoo from scoring a big end. (Dallas sees that three-point threat!)

Kalamazoo - Rock 6

Call Draw behind the corner guard on the tee line

Result Draw to the back eight-foot

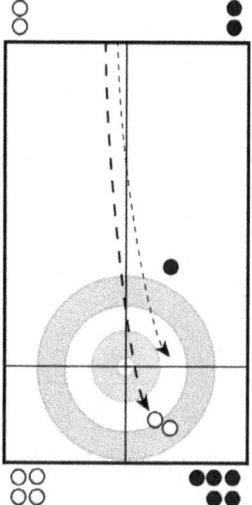

Commentary: Again, Kalamazoo tries to get two rocks into scoring position in the rings and possibly set up a three-point end. On the plus side, it succeeds in getting a second rock into the rings. On the minus side, the two rocks are very close together in the back of the rings, where they can both be hit.

Dallas - Rock 7

Call Double takeout

Result Double takeout

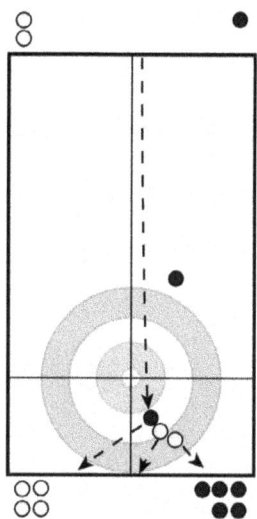

Commentary: Dallas capitalizes on Kalamazoo's slight miss and makes a double takeout. This significantly reduces Dallas' risk of giving up a big end.

Kalamazoo - Rock 7

Call Draw behind the corner guard on the tee line

Result Draw to the back eight-foot in the open

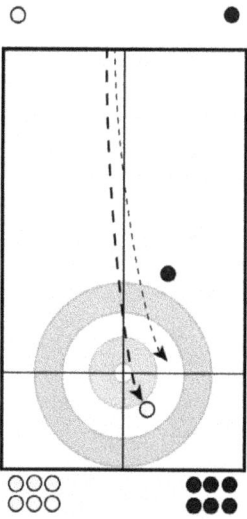

Commentary: Kalamazoo had two rocks left and a corner guard, so even at this late stage of the end, it still had a chance to get a deuce. Unfortunately, this rock didn't quite curl enough.

Dallas - Rock 8

Call Hit and stay on the rings
Result Hit and stay on the rings

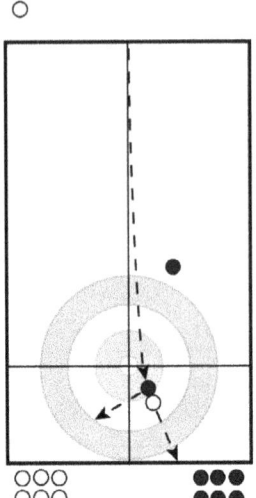

Commentary: Dallas hits Kalamazoo's open rock and ends its deuce chance. Dallas keeps its own stone on the rings in a last-ditch effort to force Kalamazoo to score one. (An even better result would have been to roll behind the corner guard to make it more difficult for Kalamazoo to remove the stone to blank.)

Kalamazoo - Rock 8

Call Hit and roll out to blank the end
Result Hit and roll out to blank the end

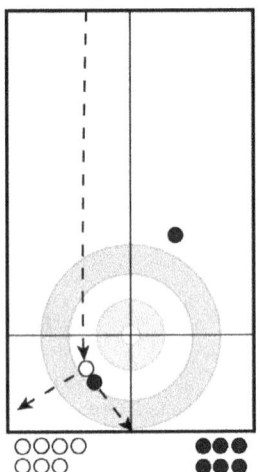

Commentary: For this shot, the Kalamazoo team had to decide whether it would rather play the eighth end down two with the hammer, or down one without. It chose to keep the hammer.

Result: Kalamazoo blanks the end.

End 8

Score: Dallas 6, Kalamazoo 4
Kalamazoo has the hammer. This is the last end of regulation play.

Dallas - Rock 1

Call Draw to the front four-foot
Result Draw to the back eight-foot

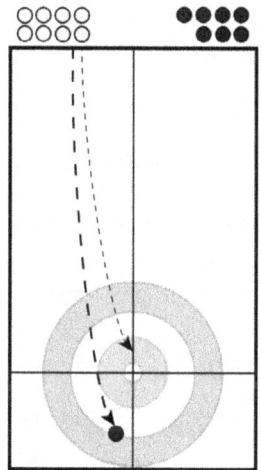

Commentary: Dallas begins again with the same approach—it puts a rock in the rings and tries to "prevent the hammer team from scoring more than one or two." It is up by two, so if it can hold Kalamazoo to one, it will win the game.

Kalamazoo - Rock 1

Call Corner guard
Result Takeout

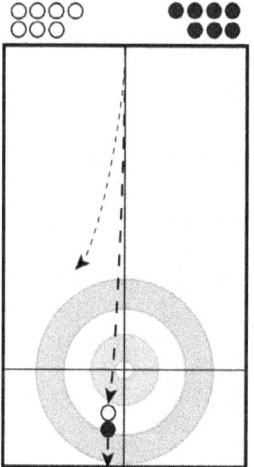

Commentary: Kalamazoo again chooses an aggressive style of play to try to score two or more. It would much rather have had a guard than a hit so it could take advantage of the Free Guard Zone to get rocks in play, but as misses go, this isn't bad!

Dallas - Rock 2

Call Takeout
Result Takeout

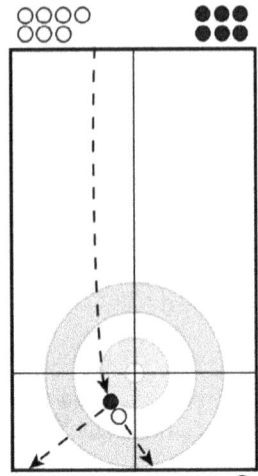

Commentary: Dallas continues on its plan to prevent Kalamazoo from scoring more than one or two. It's a reasonable choice to roll out here, since leaving a rock in the back could give Kalamazoo a place to freeze.

Kalamazoo - Rock 2

Call Corner guard
Result Corner guard

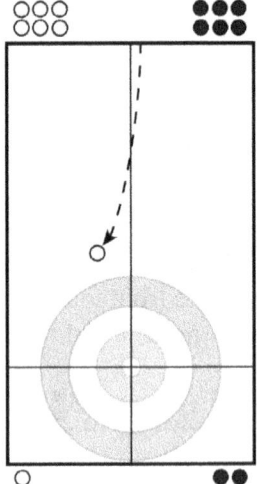

Commentary: Kalamazoo puts up a great corner guard. Unfortunately, the Free Guard Zone time is now over. Kalamazoo will now need Dallas to have some partial misses to be able to keep rocks in play.

Dallas - Rock 3

Call Take out the corner guard and roll the shooter out
Result Hit and stay

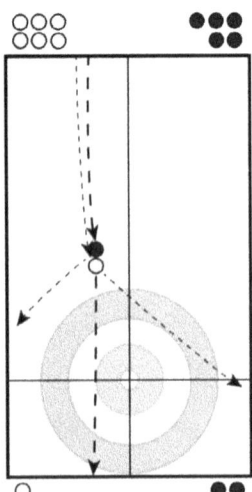

Commentary: This half-made shot by the Dallas team is, unfortunately, just the kind of break the Kalamazoo team needs to help it create guards. It does, at least, somewhat improve things for Dallas because having its own stone up front means it could run or tap it back later to score.

Kalamazoo - Rock 3

Call Corner guard on the right side
Result Corner guard on the right side

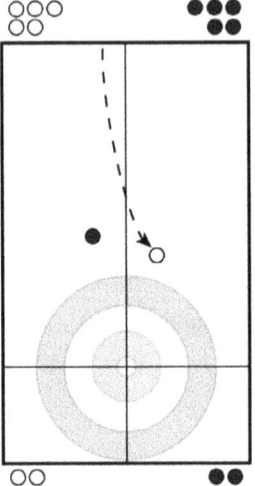

Commentary: Instead of drawing in right away, Kalamazoo puts up a second corner guard. (This is like the "Aggressive Two-Corner Deuce" open.)

Dallas - Rock 4

Call Take out the right corner guard and roll the shooter out

Result Take out the right corner guard and roll the shooter out

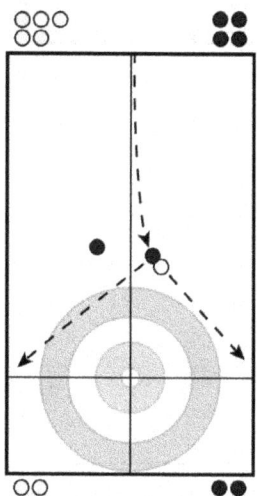

Commentary: Dallas shows discipline and sticks with its plan to prevent Kalamazoo from having places to hide rocks.

Kalamazoo - Rock 4

Call Corner guard on the right side

Result Draw to the top twelve-foot on the right side

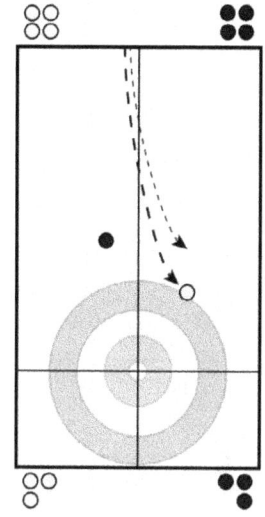

Commentary: Kalamazoo also shows great discipline as it sticks to its plan to establish good cover.

Dallas - Rock 5

Call Take out the rock in the top twelve-foot and roll out

Result Take out the rock in the top twelve-foot and roll out

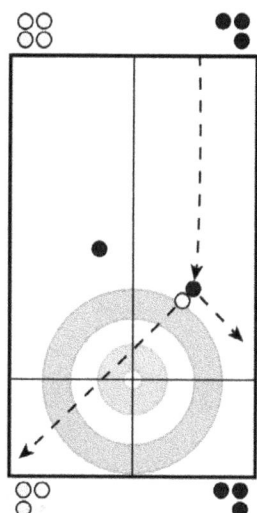

Commentary: Again, Dallas sticks with its plan to keep the front clear.

Kalamazoo - Rock 5

Call Corner guard on right side

Result Corner guard on right side

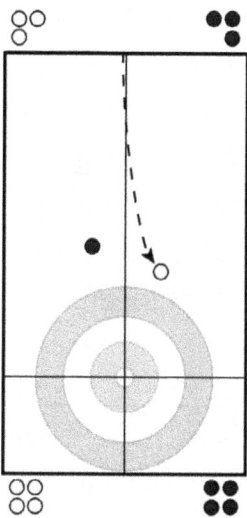

Commentary: Curling is a game of persistence!

Dallas - Rock 6

Call Take out the right corner guard and roll out

Result Take out the right corner guard and roll slightly towards the center

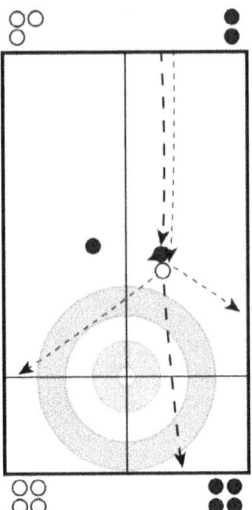

Commentary: Again, Dallas has only a slight miss, but gives a big break to Kalamazoo.

Dallas - Rock 7

Call Double takeout on the guard and counting stone on the right.

Result Take out the corner guard and roll the shooter out

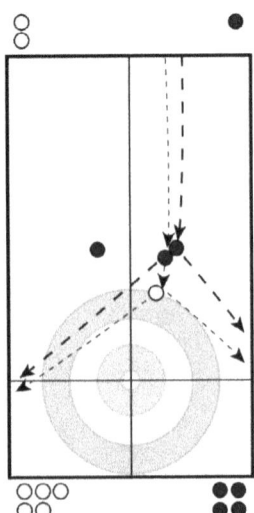

Commentary: This is a half shot, but a good half shot, because it takes away a guard that Kalamazoo could have used to hide multiple rocks. It also opens the front so Dallas can have a clear hit on the rock in the rings with its next turn. Remember, Dallas' number one goal in this end is to not give up more than two. In all likelihood, it has accomplished that goal on this turn.

Kalamazoo - Rock 6

Call Draw behind the right corner guard to the tee line

Result Partial draw behind the right corner guard to the top twelve-foot

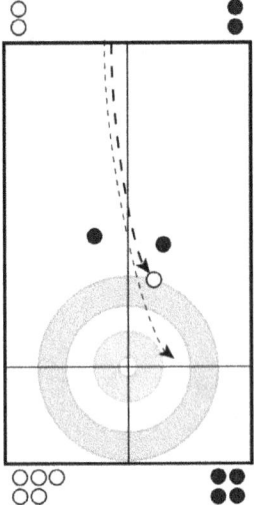

Commentary: The Kalamazoo team is running low on rocks—it only has three left and it needs two points to stay alive. With a heroic sweep, the Kalamazoo team gets a rock in the rings partly behind cover. However, the rock is dangerously close to the corner guard, so both could be removed with one shot.

Kalamazoo - Rock 7

Call Draw behind the left corner guard to the tee line

Result Draw behind the left corner guard to the back eight-foot

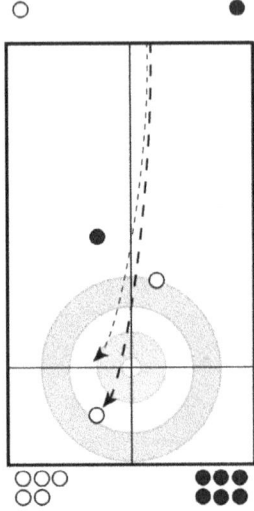

Commentary: Even though this rock isn't perfectly positioned, it's still a terrific shot for the Kalamazoo team. Kalamazoo now has two rocks in play—exactly what it needs to stay alive.

Dallas - Rock 8

Call Double takeout
Result Single takeout and roll out

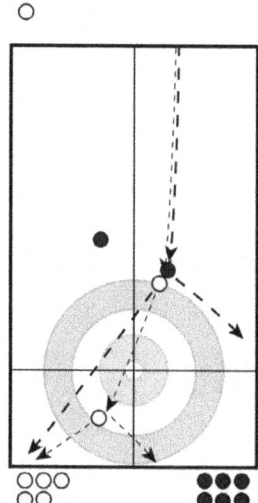

Commentary: Dallas must take out one rock to tie the game, and it does this. The double would have won the game, but it wasn't absolutely necessary.

Kalamazoo - Rock 8

Call Draw anywhere in the house for a second point
Result Draw to the back eight-foot for a second point

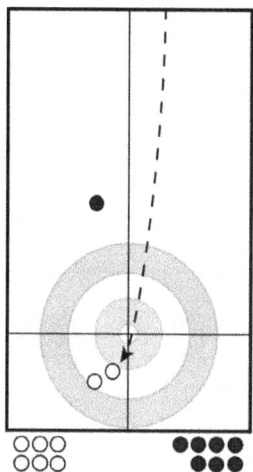

Commentary: With persistence, near-perfect execution, and help from a couple of very slight misses, the Kalamazoo team gets its deuce. The game is tied and will go to an extra end.

Result: Kalamazoo scores two, ties the game, and forces an extra end.

End 9 - Extra End

Score: Dallas 6, Kalamazoo 6
Dallas has the hammer.

Note: In this end, the team with the hammer (Dallas) has blue rocks. This is the only time in the book when the hammer team has blue rocks!

Kalamazoo - Rock 1

    Call Tight center guard
    Result Mid-to-high center guard

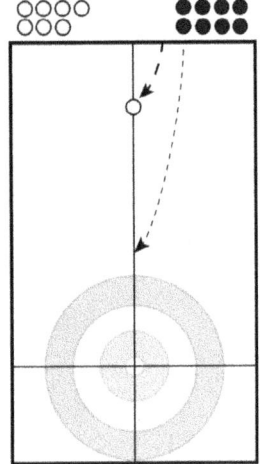

Commentary: The Kalamazoo team absolutely must steal in this end and successfully puts up a center guard to do so. The call was for a tight guard, but a higher guard will also work. (This is like "Pro-Side Error Scenario 2.")

Dallas - Rock 1

    Call Draw to the right side of the tee line
    Result Throw through the house

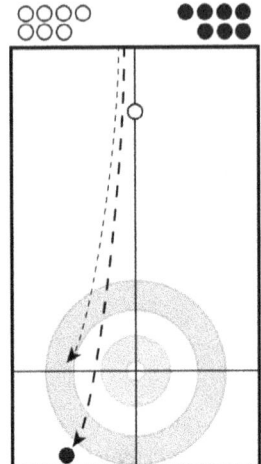

Commentary: This is like the "Open Wing Deuce" setup. This miss is not a big deal, since this end will be played for control of the center. However, a rock sitting second-shot on the side might have been helpful late in the game if Dallas hit and rolled out with its final rock. Dallas could have chosen to draw to the center, but is likely planning to hit the center guards later and doesn't want to accidentally jam.

Kalamazoo - Rock 2

Call Tight center guard
Result Tight center guard

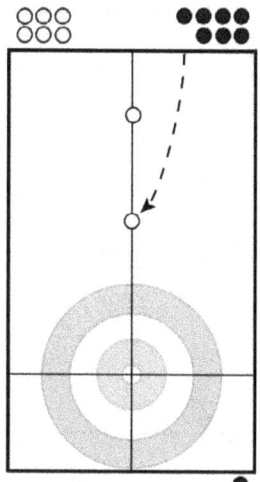

Commentary: This is a very good shot as the Kalamazoo team sets up an aggressive steal. (See the "Aggressive Steal" open.)

Dallas - Rock 2

Call Draw behind the guards to the top four-foot
Result Draw slightly exposed, slightly deep

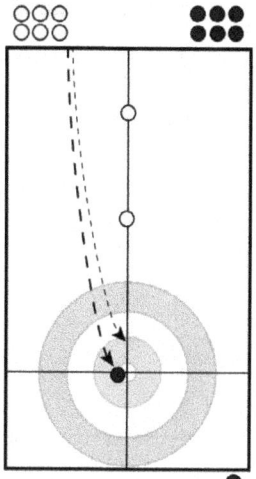

Commentary: Kalamazoo established two great center guards that will be difficult to remove, so Dallas has now changed its plan and is attempting to prevent the steal by drawing in first. Even though this shot is nearly perfect, because it is slightly exposed and slightly deep, Kalamazoo may be able to use it to get a rock nearly frozen for shot behind cover.

Kalamazoo - Rock 3

Call Freeze to Dallas' stone near the button
Result Tick the close guard and roll to create a tight corner guard

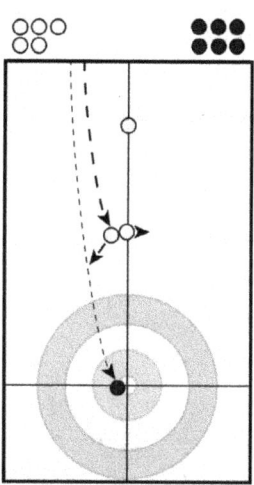

Commentary: With this shot, Kalamazoo tried to take advantage of the slight miss by Dallas.

Dallas - Rock 3

Call Double takeout and roll to the side
Result Double takeout and roll to the side

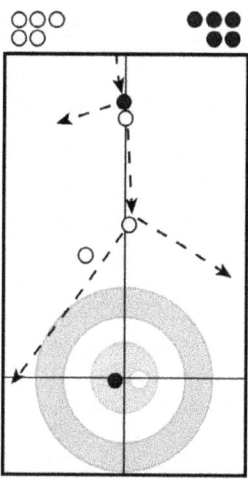

Commentary: Now that the center guards are slightly angled, the Dallas team has a chance to take them both out and roll its shooter out—and it does. This shot helps Dallas with its primary objective—keep the front clear and the button accessible for the skip's final shot.

Kalamazoo - Rock 4

Call Draw to the front twelve-foot
Result Draw to the front eight-foot

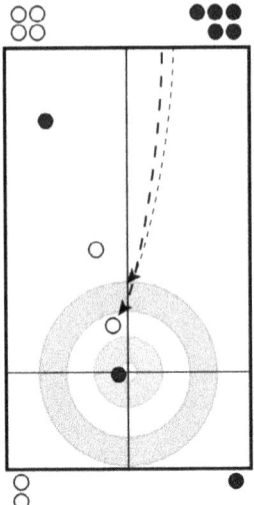

Commentary: Kalamazoo is in a bit of trouble. It needs to get a center guard and shot rock near the button to steal—and it doesn't have either. In fact, Dallas has a rock on the button that Kalamazoo will need to move slightly in order to score. For this shot, Kalamazoo's skip called for a rock at the top of the rings. This would have served as a very tight center guard, but could also be run back, if necessary. This miss isn't bad, but it isn't in a great position because it won't be easy to tap back.

Kalamazoo - Rock 5

Call Freeze to Dallas' stone near the button
Result Tick own stone in the front eight-foot

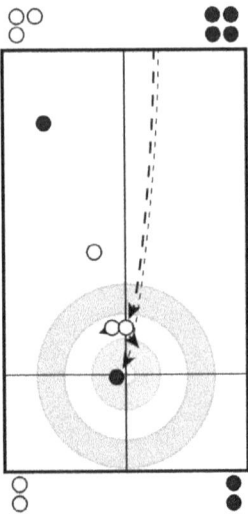

Commentary: Since the Kalamazoo team has some protection from its corner guard and rock on the rings, it's attempting to get shot rock now, and will worry about fully guarding later.

Dallas - Rock 4

Call Double takeout
Result Flash

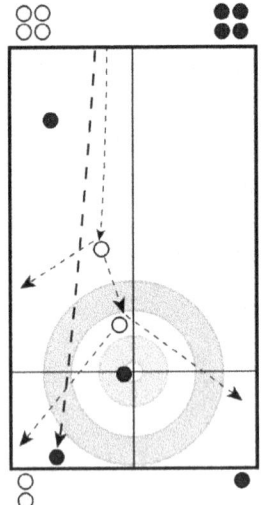

Commentary: The Dallas team again is focused on clearing the front, starting with the top trouble stone.

Dallas - Rock 5

Call Hit and roll in
Result Hit on outside and jam. The shooter and struck rock roll out, and the rock near the button rolls to the back left corner of the house

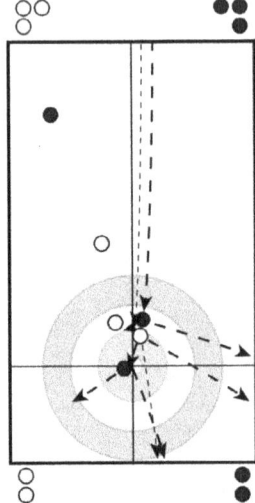

Commentary: Although this is a miss, it does clear some potentially dangerous junk out of the middle—including the Dallas team's stone that Kalamazoo had been trying to freeze against in order to get a protected shot stone.

Kalamazoo - Rock 6

Call Close center guard
Result High center guard

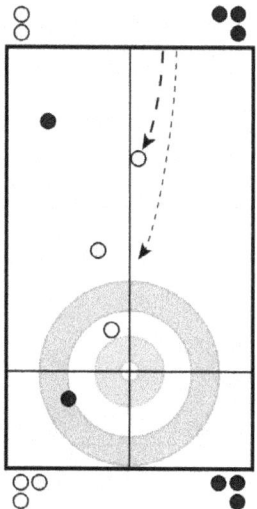

Commentary: Kalamazoo resumes guarding. Again it needs a rock on the button behind a center guard to steal.

Dallas - Rock 6

Call Double takeout
Result Single takeout

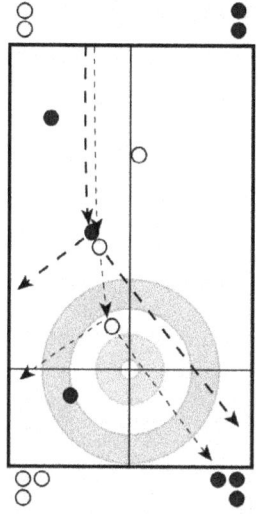

Commentary: Often, teams with the hammer will try to keep two paths to the button clear so if the non-hammer team manages to block one, the hammer team will still have access for its last shot. Dallas is attempting to do that, and to remove Kalamazoo's shot stone.

Kalamazoo - Rock 7

Call Draw behind the center guard
Result Tap the rock sitting in the front eight-foot

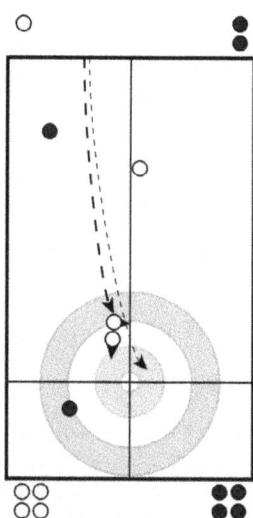

Commentary: Even though this is a slight miss, it is still a valuable shot, because Kalamazoo now has first and second shot.

Dallas - Rock 7

Call Double takeout
Result Double takeout

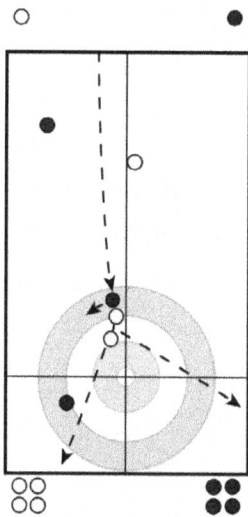

Commentary: Dallas succeeds in clearing a second path to the button.

Kalamazoo - Rock 8

Call Draw behind the center guard to the tee line

Result Draw behind the center guard to the back four-foot

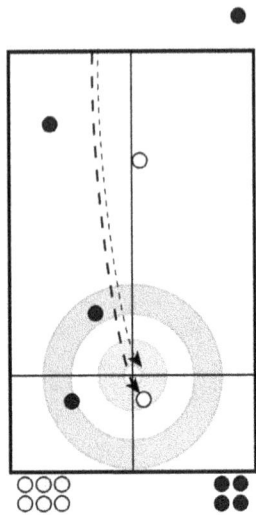

Commentary: This is the Kalamazoo team's last rock. Again, in order to steal it needs a center guard and a rock behind cover. It has the center guard, so now it needs to draw. The rock is a little deep, which leaves a possible shot for the Dallas team to win.

Dallas - Rock 8

Call Draw for shot rock to win

Result Ticked the rock in the front twelve-foot and rolled too far

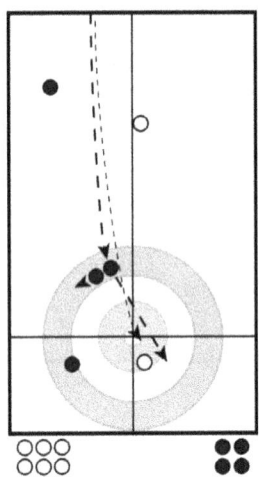

Commentary: The Dallas team's rock is slightly heavy and doesn't curl enough to use the Kalamazoo team's rock for backing. This small miss means victory for Kalamazoo.

Result: Kalamazoo steals and wins!

Congratulations to both Kalamazoo and Dallas on a terrific game and on their success at the first US Arena National Championships! And many thanks, again, to the USCA, both teams and the 12th End Sports Network for letting me use this game as a great example of strategy principles and disciplined play!

New Curler Tactics

There are two philosophies for how to skip a team of new curlers: (1) Call what you would normally call and don't "dumb-down" the game, so they will learn to make shots. (2) Adapt your strategy to use shots that new curlers are more likely to make.

If you are in the first group, skip this section! If you are in the second group, read on! Here are some tricks for increasing your teammates' shooting percentages:

Tip 1: Communicate clearly

A lot of shots get missed by newbies (or are not thrown with a good "pro-side error") because they simply don't understand the purpose of the shot. For example, if you need to steal and call for a tight guard, the newbie may not understand that it's better to be 10 feet light with a high guard than to be one foot heavy and on the rings. One communication technique you can use during games is to point to one shot and say "Plan A," then point to a second shot and say "Plan B." It can, however, be time consuming to explain everything to newbies during a game, so get together off-ice and go through a few simple scenarios and communication signals. You can also debrief about a few situations from each game afterwards.

Tip 2: Pick shots your team members can make—and if they aren't making any consistently, pick one shot and play that over and over again until they learn to make it.

If your team seems to be struggling with everything, pick one shot (for example, an in-turn draw) and call that every time. Use an in-turn draw to put some tight guards up front with your first rocks, then use in-turn draws to tap them back. If opponent stones are in the rings, use in-turn draws to freeze to them or tap them. If opponent guards are blocking your path, use in-turn draws to tick or tap them out of the way. Get the idea? As the game and league progress, your teammates will learn the ice speed, and they will make more and more shots. (I won a league with a newbie team using this tactic.) Sometimes the best shot is the one you can make!

Tip 3: Don't hit

A missed hit gets you nothing, but a missed draw usually leaves a rock in play somewhere. If your opponents put rocks near the button, try freezing to them or tapping them back. You are more likely to have some kind of useable result.

If you absolutely have to hit, use a light hit weight, like hack, so the range of weights the newbies are throwing is smaller. (Alternating between big hits and delicate draws can throw off even an experienced curler's draw weight.)

Here's an example of how to play with taps instead of hits. (In this example, the hammer team members are the new players who don't hit consistently.)

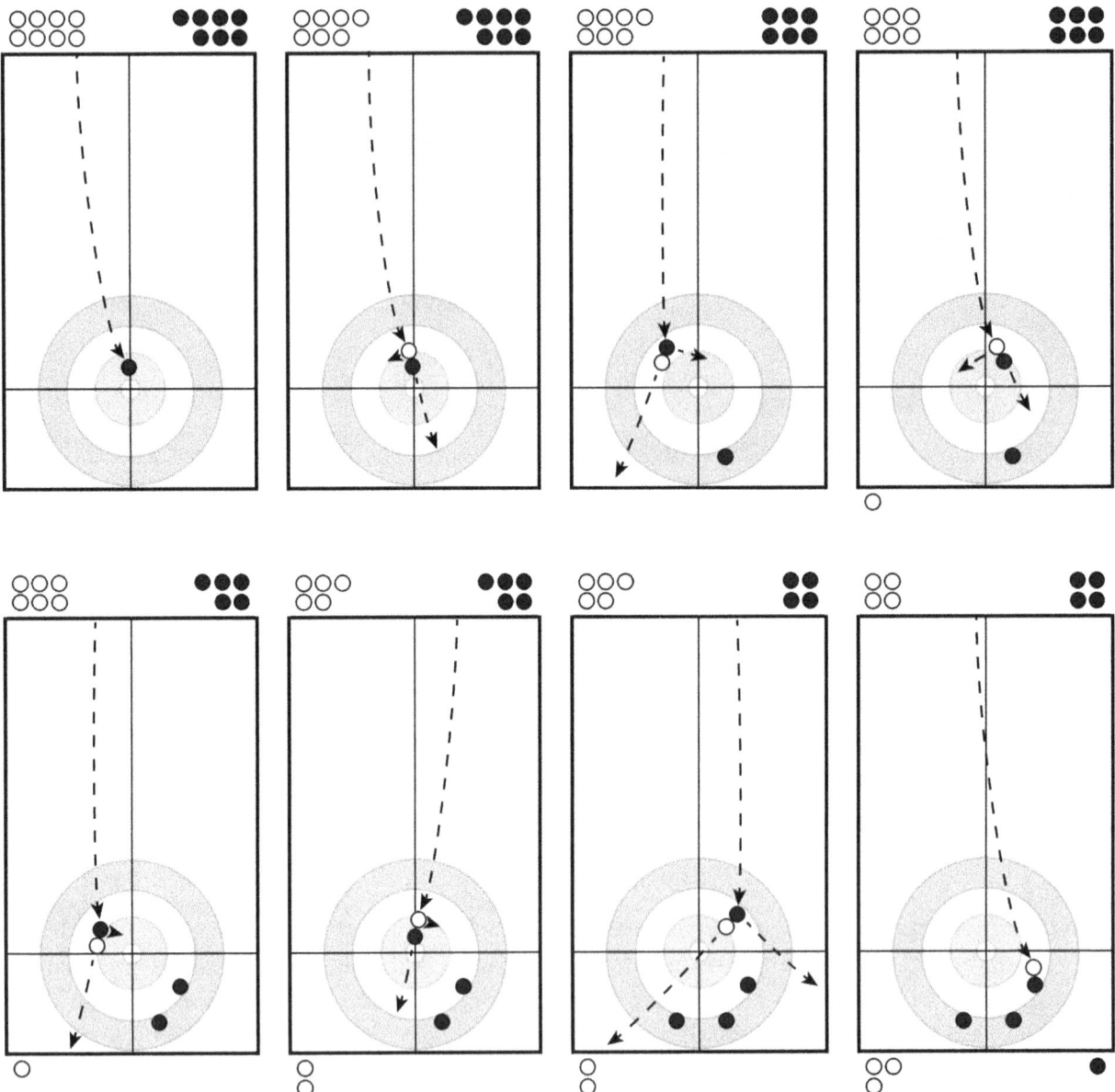

In this sequence of diagrams, the hammer team taps the non-hammer team's stones to the back of the rings, while the non-hammer team hits the hammer team's stones out. Eventually, the non-hammer team hits and rolls out (or at least away from the four-foot), and the hammer team can freeze for shot. Now it will be difficult for the non-hammer team to remove the hammer team's stone without jamming. Canadian curling great and former US head coach, Ed Lukowich, calls this tactic, "The Great Wall," because the hammer team can build a wall of opponent stones in the back of the rings to help it keep rocks in play

Tip 4: "Push the pile."

I used this tactic a lot when I first started curling. Often, my team would miss a number of shots early in an end, and our opponents would build a wall of junk out front with a rock or two hidden near the button. Instead of continuing to hit (and miss), we'd freeze to the pile, then tap to push all of the rocks back. Our opponents' junk would even prevent them from being able to hit to remove our stones!

Here is an example of how this might play out:

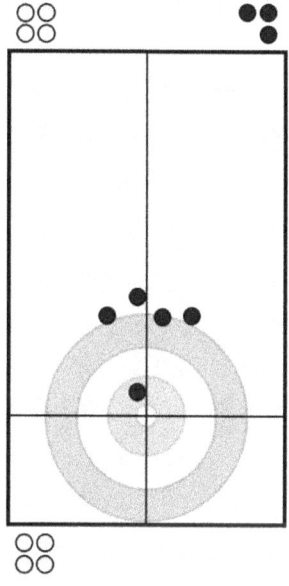

Aaaahhh!!! Sometimes the hammer team misses a lot of shots and trouble piles up.

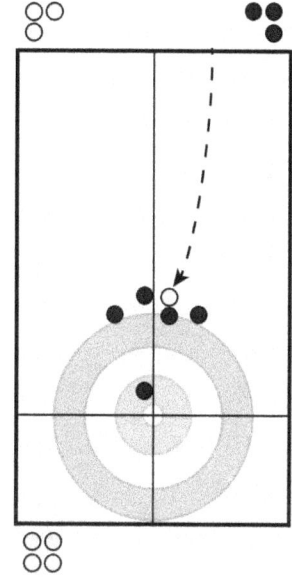

Since the hammer team isn't hitting well, it decides to freeze to the pile, instead.

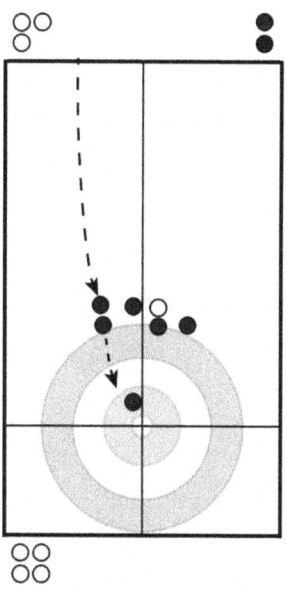

The non-hammer team doesn't have an easy hit on the hammer team's stone. It has two choices to continue its steal effort—it can guard the hammer team's stone to make it more difficult to use, or it can raise another one of its stones. In this example, the non-hammer team chooses to raise a stone. This will give it a better second shot rock and sets up a possible steal of two.

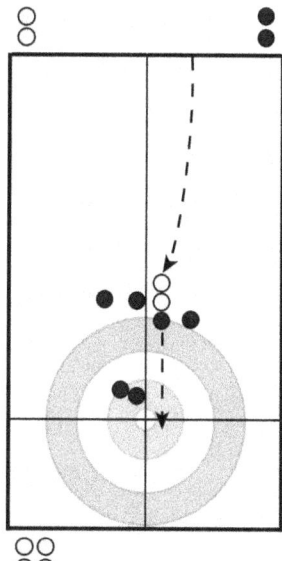

The hammer team taps its frozen stone, raising its opponent's stone into the back four-foot. This might seem bad, but at least now the hammer team has access to the button—and the non-hammer team's stones near the button will make it difficult for the non-hammer team to hit the hammer team's stones without jamming.

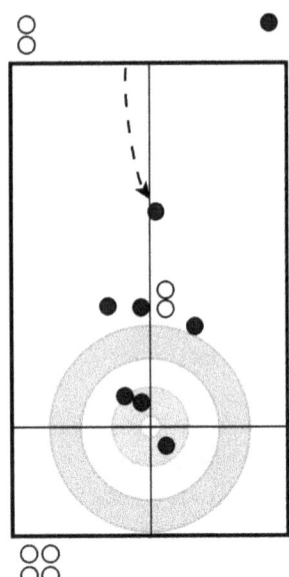

The non-hammer team decides not to try a risky hit and guards instead—but only half covers the hammer team's stones.

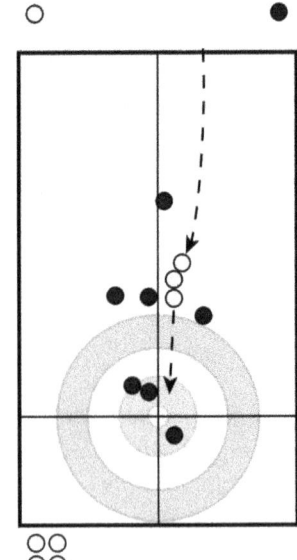

The hammer team can now tap to get shot rock, or at least out-count some of the non-hammer team's stones.

Arena Ice Tactics

When I talk about arena ice, I mean hockey ice, not an arena that has been flooded and converted to championship ice. Arena ice has skate marks on it. It's been scraped by a Zamboni. It's usually sloped and uneven. And, the rocks are often in poor condition from being frozen in snow and carried out of storage every week.

There's not much I can do to help you with the rock problem, other than warn you to be observant. As for the ice, here are a few tips and tricks that can make it easier to manage.

Tip 1: Be observant and believe what you see.

This is good advice for curlers on all ice surfaces. Here are a few common arena ice features to look for:

Latitudinal Features

Perfect Ice

In a perfect world, a curling sheet would be level and rocks thrown with tee-line weight would curl four feet on every line with both clockwise and counter-clockwise rotation. (That's the assumption we've made throughout this book.) Conditions like that do exist in many dedicated curling facilities and in high-level competitions.

Cross-section of perfect ice

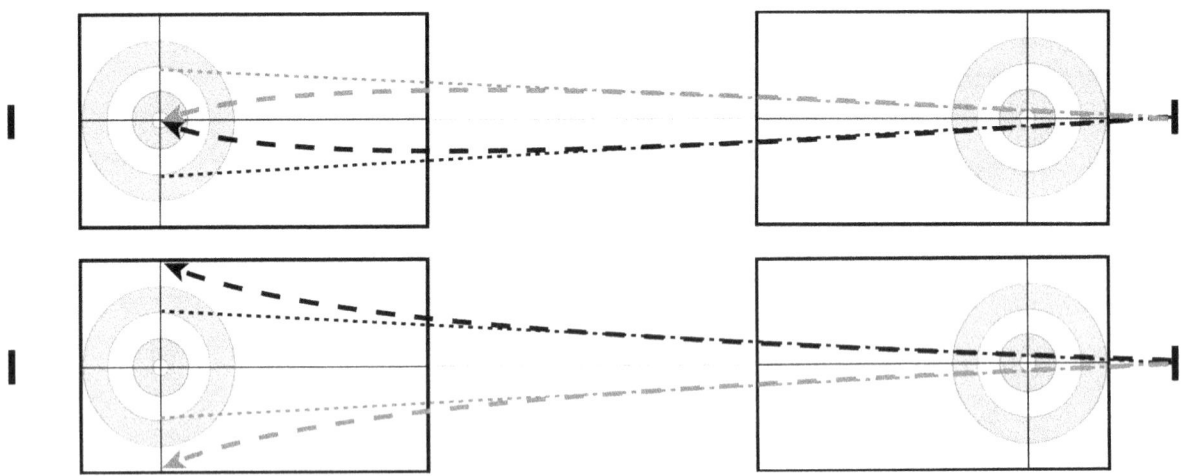

*Perfect ice is level and curls four feet in both directions. In this and in all of the following illustrations, **clockwise turns are shown in black**, and counter-clockwise turns are shown in grey. The fine dotted line shows the aiming point.*

Negative Ice

Negative ice is so sloped, the rock slides back down the hill more than it curls. Instead of curling in the "positive" or "natural" direction, it moves in the "negative" direction. Sometimes ice has a slight slope, so it appears to curl a lot in the downhill direction and curl a little or run straight in the uphill direction. That ice might be called "sloped" but it is not truly "negative." With negative ice, the rocks all move in the same direction—downhill. (Some ice surfaces are a mix of normal areas and negative areas. For example, an area near a wall might be very low or very high, and this could cause negative behavior.) The only way to get a rock to some parts of the house on a negative sheet may be to hit and roll up the hill.

There is some disagreement among curlers as to whether sweeping on negative ice makes rocks fall more. I believe this is true, because I believe sweeping reduces the rock's grip on the ice, which normally causes it to curl.

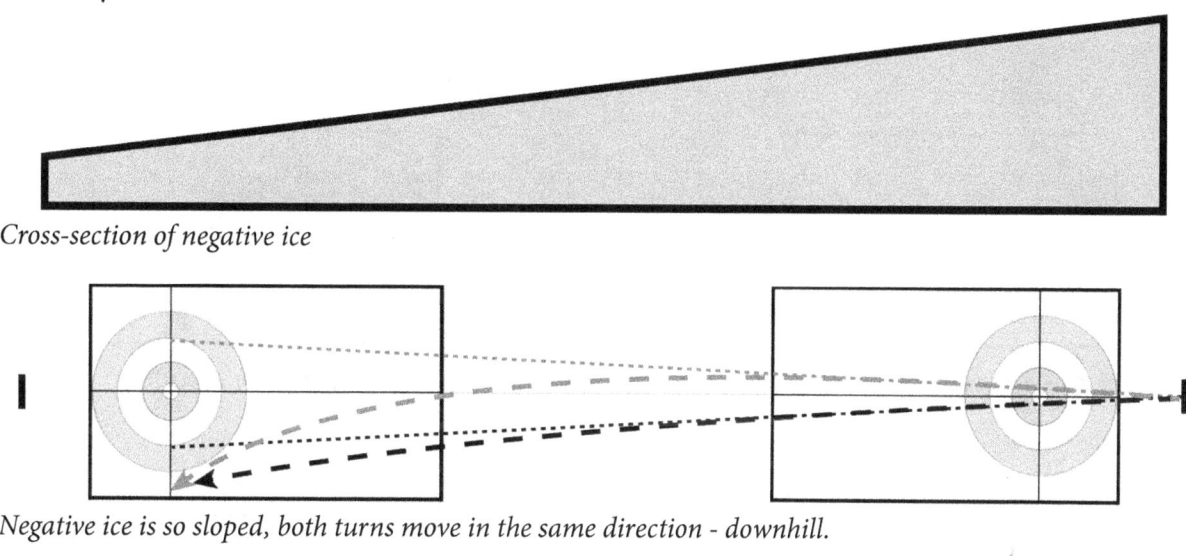

Cross-section of negative ice

Negative ice is so sloped, both turns move in the same direction - downhill.

On a perfect sheet of ice, there would be two paths to the button—one on each side of the center line—and center guards would be positioned on the center line.

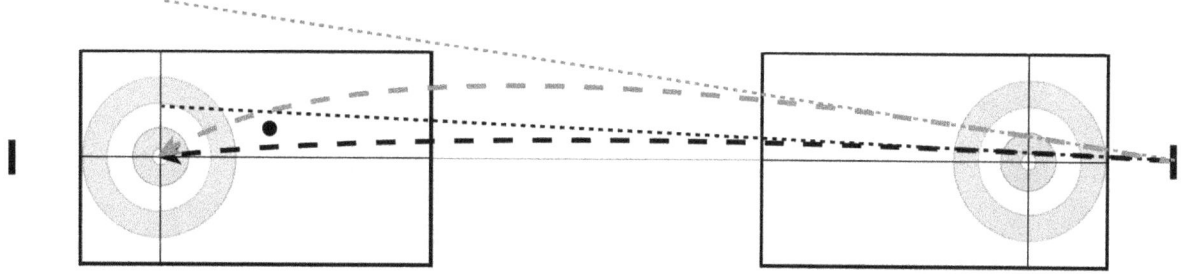

On a negative sheet of ice, there would be still be two paths to the button, but they might both be on the same side of the sheet. The center guard would also shift and appear to be a corner guard.

Banked Ice

Banked ice has at least one area with an upward curving bank. On banked ice, the further out you throw, the more the rock will seem to curl back down. In fact, a rock thrown towards the high part of the bank may curl past a rock thrown near the bottom of the bank. Again, a hit and roll may be the only way to get rocks to some parts of the house on a severely banked sheet.

Cross-section of banked ice

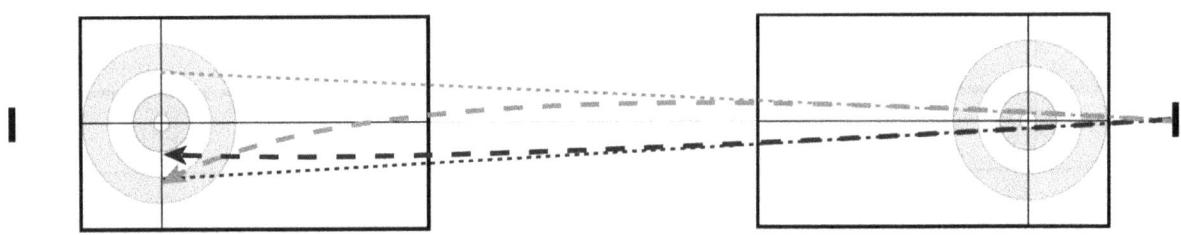

On banked ice, one turn will curl dramatically, while the other will be nearly straight or negative.

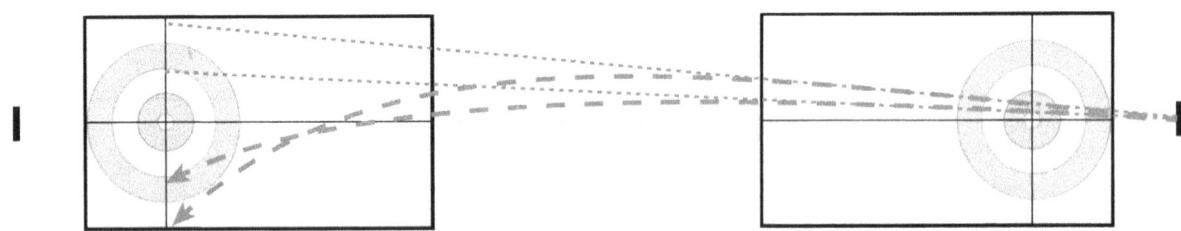

On banked ice, rocks thrown up on the steeper part of the bank will curl more than rocks thrown on the flatter part. That means a rock thrown at a wider angle could curl past a rock thrown at a narrower angle.

Dished Ice

Dished ice is banked on both sides. In arenas, dished ice is usually caused by bad Zamboni cut patterns that have allowed the sides of the ice rink to get higher than the center. However, sometimes dished ice is created purposefully—even in dedicated facilities—to create more curl. For example, if a club is having difficulty getting its ice to curl, the ice makers may build up the pebble on the outside of the sheets to make the rocks move towards center. This makes it easier to draw to the middle. However, it can also create a weird phenomenon in which rocks thrown at any angle all curl back to the center line. Also, on dished, ice sweepers do not need to wait for the rocks to "take the curl" to start sweeping—rocks will curl approximately the same amount regardless of when the sweepers begin.

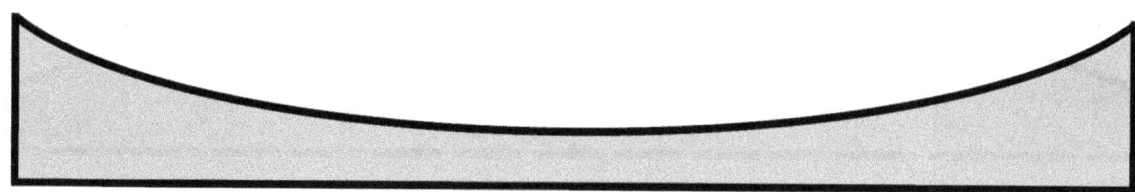

Cross-section of dished ice

On dished ice, rocks thrown outside in at many different aim points may all go to the button.

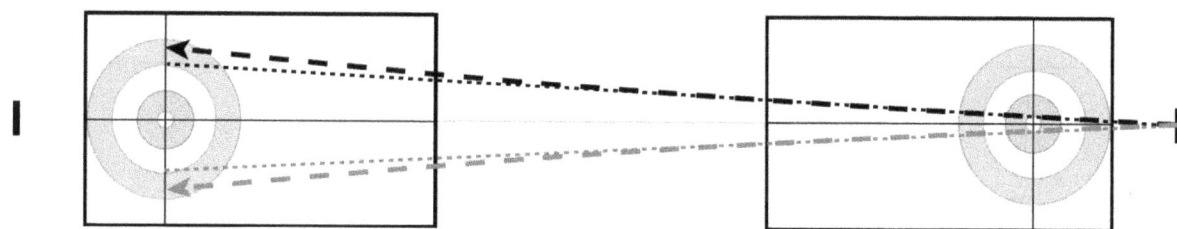

On dished ice, rocks thrown inside out may not curl much, if at all.

Peaked Ice and Ridges

Peaked ice is high in the middle. This can happen if the entire arena is high in the middle and low on the sides. It can also happen if a Zamboni blade is tilted. Some peaked ice is rounded, and some has a severe ridge at the top. Some ice is peaked down the length of the sheet, but some is peaked only in areas near the house where the Zamboni turned or cross-cut in an odd way. It may be possible to draw rocks up to the top of the ridge, where, due to the slope, they may be difficult to take out. (Slow moving rocks grip the ice more and have an easier time going uphill than fast rocks.)

It can be very difficult to steal on peaked ice, because it is difficult to draw behind center guards.

Cross-section of peaked ice caused by uneven amounts of flooding, scraping, or pebbling

Cross-section of ridge caused by an uneven ice scraping blade

On peaked ice, rocks thrown outside in don't curl much.

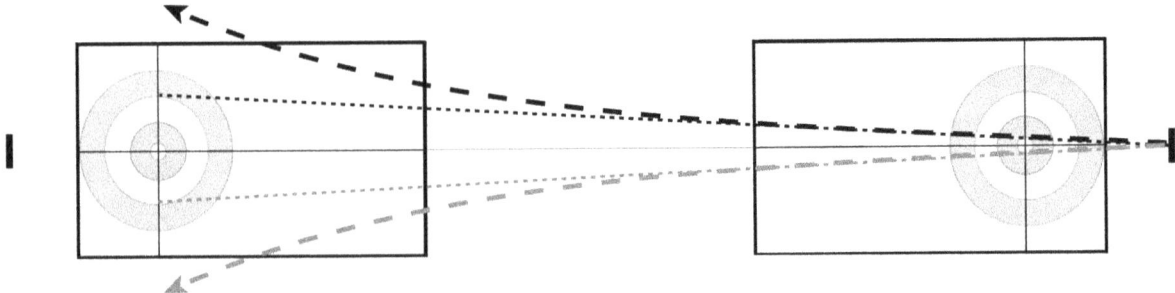

On peaked ice, rocks thrown inside out curl a lot.

In this picture, the ridge is represented by the fine dotted line. Be careful throwing rocks near the edge of a ridge. If they cross over, they will suddenly curl dramatically.

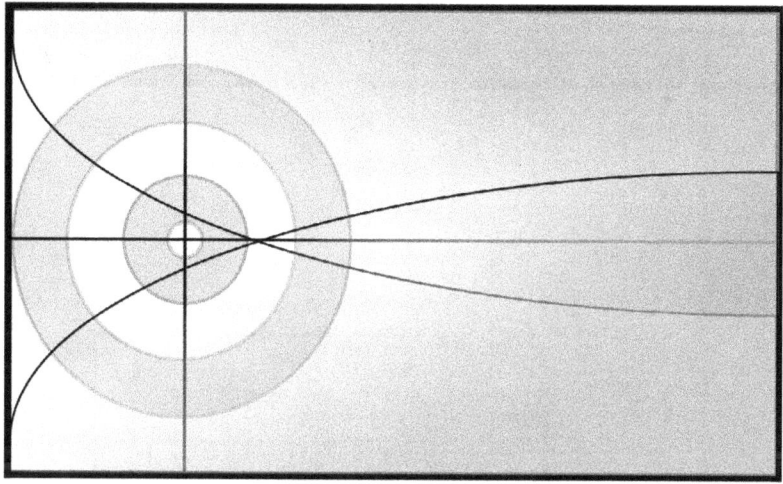

Here's a funky scrape problem I used to see regularly in an arena club I visited. As shown in this picture, the Zamboni scrape would miss a section of ice in the back of the house. (The arcs represent the edge of the Zamboni scrape. The darker areas represent deeper scrapes and lower parts of the ice. The light wedge shape in the back of the house is a high plateau.) On days when this happened, it was possible to draw up onto the plateau (because draws gripped the ice), but not hit (because hits deflected off the banked sides of the Zamboni cut). This made it difficult or impossible to move rocks off the button.

Shelves

Some ice has a sloped area and a high plateau-like shelf. Rocks released up on the level shelf will, of course, take a very different path than ones released on the slope below. Watch out for this if you have some team members who release close to the back line and others who release close to the hog line. Long-sliders may release their rocks up on the shelf, while short-sliders may release on the slope.

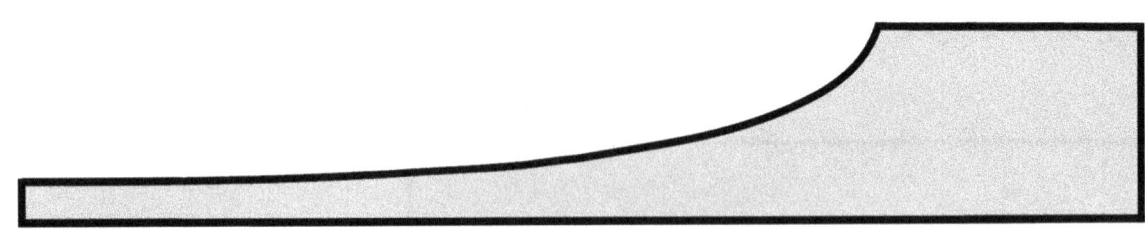

Cross-section of ice with a shelf and bank

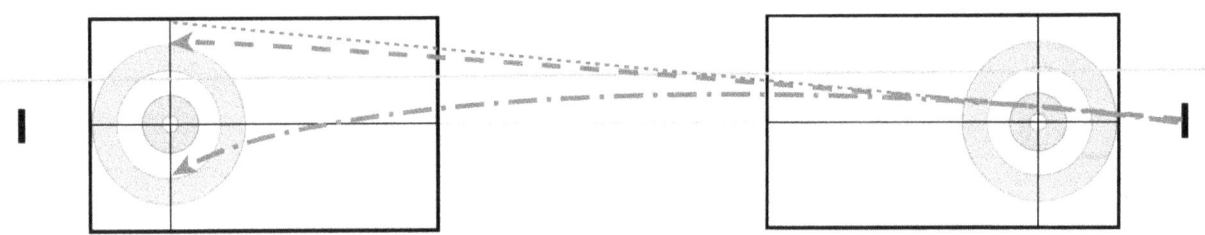

In this diagram, the solid pale blue line represents the edge of the shelf. The area above the line is a high plateau, and the area below it is banked. If two teammates throw at the same target, but release at different places, their rocks may behave very differently. For example, if one teammate releases very early (dot and dashed line), his rock won't ever get up on the shelf and will curl a lot because of the bank below. However, the rock of another teammate who releases late (dashed line), will go up on the bank then run straighter on the level ice. Thus, the two rocks will end up in very different spots, even though both people hit the broom.

Channels

A channel is a low path in the ice—like a half-pipe. You may notice rocks move in an S-curve as they travel down a channel. Sometimes rocks that go into channels all pop out moving in the same direction, but sometimes they pop out in different directions, depending on where they entered the channel. Again, watch out for this if you have both long-sliding and short-sliding teammates.

Cross-section of ice with channels

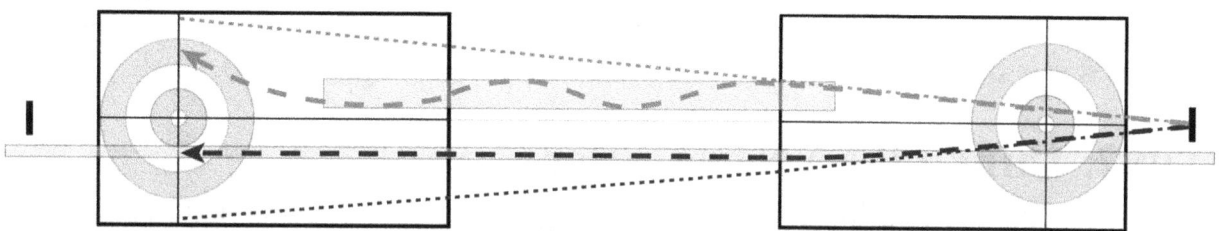

Rocks sometimes bounce around in an S-shaped curve as they travel down wide channels. Rocks travel in a straight line down narrow channels. Some channels run down the full length of the sheet, and others are short and may only last for a few feet.

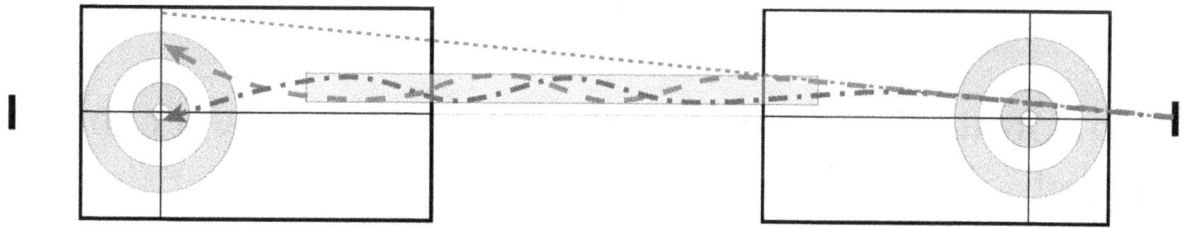

If team members release at different distances, their rocks will enter the channel in different places and can exit in different directions.

Snow, Skate Marks, and Bumps

Use these to your advantage! If you can draw a rock up onto a snow bank, it will be very difficult for your opponent to take it out. If you can draw a rock behind some big bumps created by water dripping from the ceiling, you can use those bumps as guards.

Longitudinal Features

Low-End Ice

Some ice rinks have a high end and a low end in the long direction. This means the ice may be a fast 24 seconds hog-to-tee in one direction and a slow 21 seconds in the other.

Low-Middle Ice

Sometimes ice sheets are low in the middle (near the hockey red line) and banked upwards near the rings and hacks. The nice thing about this is you can throw nearly any weight you want and your rock will stop in the house!

Tip 2: Think Like a New Curler

If the ice is really bad, sometimes the best strategy is to play like a newbie and throw mostly tight guards and draws. It can be very difficult to hit on oddly-sloped ice. Try to place your rocks on tricky spots and sucker your opponent into trying to take them out. (And if you're on the receiving end of this tactic, respond with freezes and taps. Don't waste a bunch of shots on a hit that can't be made!)

Tip 3: Control the paths to the button... wherever they may be!

If you find yourself on severely sloped ice, the paths to the button will shift. A rock that looks like a corner guard might really be a center guard.

For example, on normal ice, the two draw paths to the button might look like this:

On level ice with normal curl, there are two draw paths to the button, one on either side of the center line. A center guard would be on the center line.

On tilted ice, the two draw paths to the button might look like this:

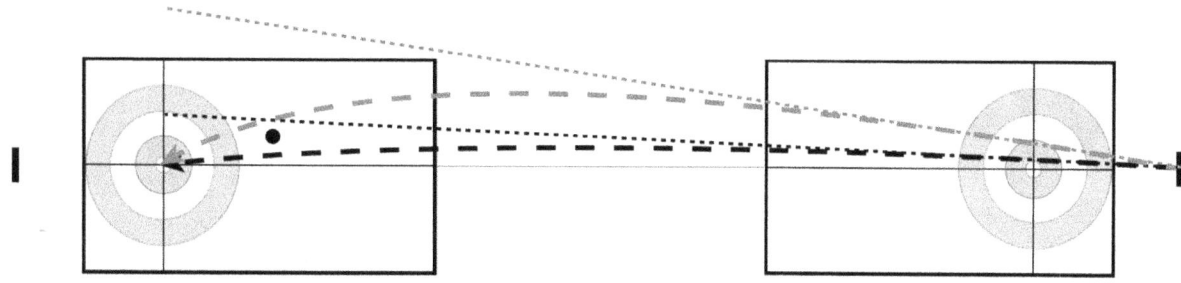

On tilted or negative ice, there would still be two paths to the button, but they would shift to compensate for the slope of the ice. The center guard would also shift to the side and be in a position normally occupied by a corner guard.

Curling Folk Wisdom

These bits of curling folk wisdom aren't right for every situation, but there is truth to them. Always use your game and end plans first when planning tactics, but if you feel stuck, perhaps one of these sayings can spark an idea!

"Hit when you're up, draw when you're down."
Teams that need points need rocks in play—even opponent stones. If you're down and your opponent puts rocks near the pin, try tapping them back instead of removing them from play. They can become backing to keep your rocks in play. (For more on this, see the "The Great Wall" tactic in the "Tips for New Curlers" chapter, and "Intermediate Strategy Scenario 9.")

"All guards help the team that needs points."
All guards help the team that needs points—even opponent guards. Guards keep rocks in play. Draw around them, tap them back, but don't remove them unless you absolutely must to get access to the pin. (For more on this, see End 7 of the "Real-Life Game Sequence" chapter.)

"Hit for show, draw for dough."
Long runbacks look cool, but humble draws win games. Don't get suckered into trying fancy shots by fans shouting, "Chicks dig the double!" Chicks dig winners more.

"A skip should have four-foot weight in his or her back pocket."
The draw to the four-foot ring is the skip's bread and butter shot. A skip doesn't need to be the best shooter on the team, but he or she must feel comfortable making this shot at any time to save an end.

"Only chicks hit rocks behind the tee line with the hammer."
Yeah, this one's insulting, but it is memorable! Here's the point: If you have the hammer and your opponent leaves a rock behind the tee line, most of the time, you should see that rock as a tool to be used, not a problem to be removed. This is especially true if you follow the previous tip and your skip has four-foot weigh in her back pocket. For example:

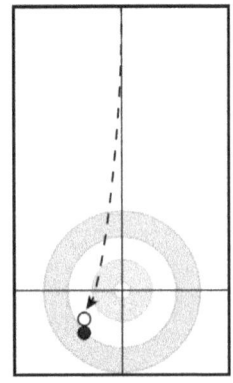

If the hammer team's goal is to score multiple points, it's usually better off freezing to opponent stones behind the tee line than hitting them.

The two major exceptions are (1) if you have a big lead and your goal is to keep your opponent from scoring, or (2) if you have a chance for a big end. (For more on this, see "Beginner Strategy Scenario 3.")

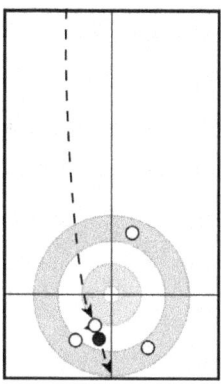

"If you have the hammer, play to the wings. If not, play to the center."
This is one of the principles we covered in "Simple End 1" in the "Three Types of Strategy" chapter. The hammer team wants to keep the center open so it can hit or draw with its last rock to be sure it scores. The non-hammer team wants to control the center so it can either score or out-count any rocks the hammer team might get on the wings.

"You can't win a game in the first end, but you can lose it."
Scoring four in the first end doesn't guarantee you'll win the game, but giving up four (especially against a good team) can make it extremely difficult to come back. (For more on this, see "Beginner Strategy Scenario 3.")

"Don't give up big ends."
As Allison Pottinger, the skip of the 2012 US Women's Worlds Team, said about three-point ends, "It's nice to get 'em, but it's not so nice to give 'em away!" Sometimes you need to take big risks if you're down by a lot (or even down by a little at the end of a game), but be thoughtful and judicious about risk at other times. It's tough to dig out of a hole.

"You don't need to win every end to win the game."
Often, new teams feel the need to score in every end. Remember, the only "W" that matters is the one at the end of the scoreboard. Sometimes, it's better to force one and get the hammer than try a risky steal to score. (Remember the "Don't give up big ends" principle!)

"Play the scoreboard."
Be smart! As with the rule above, always keep your eye on the big picture—the final score. If you are up by three points in the second-to-last end, it's okay to give up two points. You'll still be up one with the hammer in the final end—a very strong position!

"Keep doing what works."
The general tactical rule of thumb is to hit when you're up and draw when you're down. However, some teams are only successful with one style of play. If that's you, honor that. For example, if you built a lead by throwing lots of draw shots to steal repeatedly, consider continuing with that, especially if your team doesn't hit as well as it draws. While it's true there is a risk you could give up a big end and lose your lead, choosing shots your team doesn't make consistently is a sure way to leak points.

"The best defense is a good offense," or *"The best defense is first and second shot."*

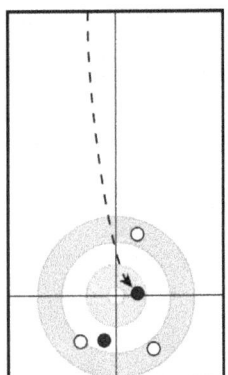

When you find yourself with a lone shot rock in a sea of opponent stones, sometimes the best way to prevent disaster is not to guard your rock or hit opponent stones, but rather to draw for second shot. You might not score, but you might avoid giving up four. (Again, see "Beginner Scenario 3" for more on this concept.)

"Don't let your opponents play the same shot twice."
Teams do learn from experience, so if you give your opponents the opportunity to throw the same shot twice, chances are, they will make it.

"Stop your opponents from doing what they want to do."
If you're not sure what your best shot is, think about the problem in reverse. Try to guess what shot your opponent would like to make and block that, or try to guess what shot your opponent would least like you to make.

"Make your opponent play on new ice first."
This rule is especially true for arena curlers who play on uneven, unpredictable ice. If you can force an opponent to take a turn no one's seen, or play a critical draw on a line that hasn't been used in a long time, a lot of the shot will be guess work, and the odds of success go down. On the flip side, if you can follow a path your opponent has just used, then you've got extra information and a better chance of making your shot.

"It's better to make the second-best shot than to miss the best one."
There are times when you absolutely have to make a "TV shot" to get your team out of trouble. The rest of the time, choose shots your team has a high probability of making and that have more helpful "Plan B" outcomes in case you do miss.

FINALLY...

Beyond studying goals and tactics, there are three more things you can do to help yourself and your team play smarter and win more games:

Be Observant

Be observant. Watch the ice. Is it changing? Is it curling more or less? Is the ice getting faster on paths where people have thrown more often? Is the pebble getting flatter and slower in areas where people have swept more often? Pay attention to the weather and temperature. Does the ice getting frostier as the sun goes down, or as games around yours end?

Watch your opponents. Stand behind the opposing skip when he or she is in the house so you can see if the shooter slid to the broom and had a clean release. (That will tell you if you can take the same ice for the same shot later.) Do your opponents have a turn or shot they particularly like to throw—or one they struggle with? Do your opponents prefer a certain style of play?

Be Flexible and Resilient

Curling is a long game. Be patient and maintain your focus and energy level throughout the game. You will do well if you can adapt to the tactics your opponents are using—and force them to change their tactics and plans. You will do well if you are able to stay positive when you have setbacks. As one of my coaches, Leslie Frosch, once said, "No one tries to miss."

Give Yourself an Opportunity to Win

Finally, give yourself an opportunity to win. Losing by one point is the no better than losing by five. If you need to play conservatively to keep the score close for a while, that's okay, but when the time comes, be aggressive and take the risks necessary to win. As another one of my coaches, Barry Ivy, often says, "Don't be so focused on not losing that you forget to play to win!"

Glossary

Aggressive Teams that use an aggressive style of play are willing to risk giving up a large number of points to get points. A team using aggressive tactics will use draws and guards to get lots of rocks in play.

Biter A rock that is partially on the rings

Brick Slang for the rock (e.g., "That guy can really throw the brick," meaning, he's a really good shooter)

Burn A moving rock is said to be "burned" if someone or something (other than another rock) touches it after it crosses the near hog line. There are intricate rules for how to deal with these situation in the "USCA Championships Rules and Procedures" booklet online.

Button The one-foot diameter circle at the center of the rings

Can Slang for the button (e.g., "Put it on the can," meaning, draw to the button)

CCA Canadian Curling Association

"Christmas tree" formation Rocks arranged in a diagonal line so that it is difficult or impossible to hit the shot rock and stay for shot

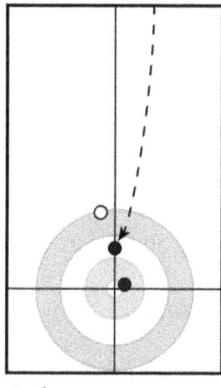
A draw to create a Christmas tree formation

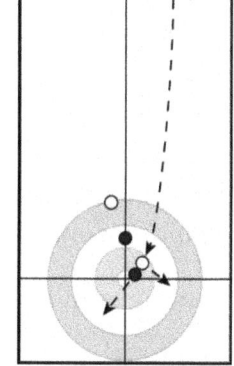
It's difficult to move the shot rock and stay for shot

Conservative Teams that use a conservative style of play are willing to give up the opportunity to score a lot of points in order to minimize their opponent's chance to score. A team using conservative tactics will hit often to remove rocks from play.

Control	A light-to-medium hit weight whose path can be controlled well with sweeping
Deuce	Slang for scoring two points with the hammer
Drive by	Slang for a hit that misses completely and "drives by" the target rock without making contact
Firm	A heavy hit weight, good for removing multiple stones and for situations in which you don't want the rock to curl much
Flash	Slang for a hit that misses completely and goes by the target rock without making contact
Fudgy ice	Ice is called "fudgy" when the pebble has worn down and the rocks move in unpredictable ways. For example, on fudgy ice, rocks might slide sideways instead of curling, slow down by significant or unpredictable amounts, or appear to pick.
Hack	(1) The rubber "starting block" at each end of the ice sheet that the shooter stands on to push out. (2) A light hit weight that would stop at the hack if it didn't hit anything.
Hammer	Curling term for the last rock of the end
High	A "high" guard is close to the hog line and far away from the rings
Hit the broom	Slang for sliding out directly on-line. (The skip holds his or her broom as an aiming point for the shooter.)
Hog	The "hog line" marks the inside edge of the in-play zone. The shooter must release the rock before it begins to cross the near hog line for it to count as a legal throw, and rocks must fully cross the far hog line to be in play. A "hog line violation" occurs when the shooter releases the rock past the near hog line, and the rock must be removed from play. A "hogged rock" is too slow to make it over the far hog line and must be pulled from play.
House	Curling term for the rings
In-turn	Curling term for a right-hander's clockwise turn and a lefty's counter-clockwise turn. These turns are called "in-turns" because the shooter's hand and elbow sometimes move inward when applying this turn.
Jam	A jam occurs when a team is trying to take out an opponent stone, but hits it at the wrong angle and accidentally drives it onto one if its own stones, removing its own stone and leaving the opponent's stone in its place.
Narrow	A shot is said to be "narrow" if it is thrown inside the intended aiming point. It may over-curl past the target.

Normal A medium hit weight that teams often use as their default hit weight. (Alternatively, some skips use this term to mean the hit weight each individual shooter normally throws.)

Out-turn Curling term for a right-hander's counter-clockwise turn and a lefty's clockwise turn. These turns are called "out-turns" because the shooter's hand and elbow sometimes move outward when applying this turn.

Pair of pants Slang for two rocks from one team sitting side-by-side separated by a small gap. If you hit them in the "crotch," you can take them both out.

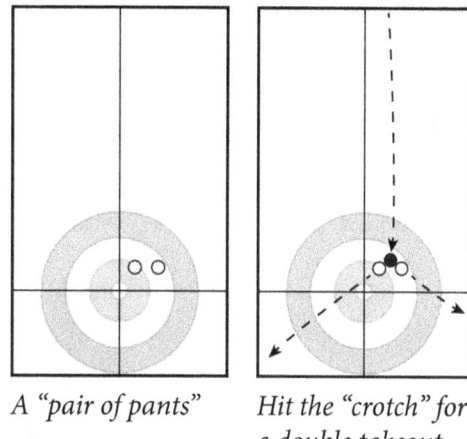

A "pair of pants"   *Hit the "crotch" for a double takeout*

Peel A very fast hit weight

Pick A rock is said to "pick" when a speck of debris gets caught underneath it, and causes it to veer off line or change rotation

Pin Slang for the "tee," the small hole or dot at the center of the rings. During a measurement, the tip or pin on the end of the measuring device is anchored to that spot.

Playdown "Playdown" is the curling term for a qualifying competition before a championship. For example, if you want to compete at the Club National Championships, you must first win your regional playdown.

Pot Slang for the button

Quality shot rock A rock very close to the pin that would be difficult for the opponent to out-draw

Rock/Stone The words "rock" and "stone" are used equally and interchangeably in curling

Shooter (1) The person who is throwing the rock. (2) The rock being thrown.

Shot (adj.)	The rock on the rings closest to the center of the target is the "shot rock." The next closest rock on the rings is the "second shot," and so forth.
Stick (n.)	Slang for the skip's broom
Takeout	Curling term for a hit
Tight	(1) A shot is said to be "tight" if the rock is thrown inside the intended aiming point. It may over-curl past the target. (2) A guard is said to be "tight" if it is close to the rings.
Tee	The mark or hole at the exact center of the rings
Wick	When a rock "wicks" off another stone, it just barely hits the stone's edge and deflects off of it.
Wide	A shot is said to be "wide" if it is thrown outside the intended aiming point. It may not curl enough to get to the intended spot.
Wings	The sides of the sheet and rings. Usually, any rocks farther than two feet from the center line are considered to be on the wings.
USA Curling/ USCA	The United States Curling Association—the national governing body for curling, which selects athletes to represent the US at World and Olympic competitions
USOC	The US Olympic Committee
USWCA	The US Women's Curling Association
WCF	The World Curling Federation

www.ingramcontent.com/pod-product-compliance
Lightning Source LLC
Chambersburg PA
CBHW080331170426
43194CB00014B/2524